INTERPRETING RELIGION

Interpretive Lenses in Sociology series

Series editors: **Thomas DeGloma**, Hunter College, City University of New York, and **Julie B. Wiest**, West Chester University of Pennsylvania

---

The *Interpretive Lenses in Sociology* series provides a unique forum for scholars using a wide range of interpretive perspectives to explore their approaches to uncovering the deep meanings underlying human actions, events, and experiences.

Forthcoming in the series:

Interpreting the Body
Between Meaning and Materiality
Edited by **Anne Marie Champagne** and **Asia Friedman**

Interpretive Sociology and the Semiotic Imagination
Edited by **Andrea Cossu** and **Jorge Fontdevila**

Interpreting Subcultures
Sense-Making From Insider and Outsider Perspectives
Edited by **J. Patrick Williams**

Interpreting Contentious Memory
Countermemories and Conflicts over the Past
Edited by **Janet L. Jacobs** and **Thomas DeGloma**

Positive Politics
Interpreting Right and Left Authoritarianism
Edited by **Lynn S. Chancer** and **Neil McLaughlin**

Find out more at
bristoluniversitypress.co.uk/
interpretive-lenses-in-sociology

Interpretive Lenses in Sociology series

Series editors: **Thomas DeGloma**, Hunter College, City University of New York, and **Julie B. Wiest**, West Chester University of Pennsylvania

Find out more at

bristoluniversitypress.co.uk/interpretive-lenses-in-sociology

INTERPRETING RELIGION

Making Sense of Religious Lives

Edited by
Erin F. Johnston and
Vikash Singh

BRISTOL
UNIVERSITY
PRESS

First published in Great Britain in 2024 by

Bristol University Press
University of Bristol
1-9 Old Park Hill
Bristol
BS2 8BB
UK
t: +44 (0)117 374 6645
e: bup-info@bristol.ac.uk

Details of international sales and distribution partners are available at bristoluniversitypress.co.uk

© Bristol University Press 2024

British Library Cataloguing in Publication Data
A catalogue record for this book is available from the British Library

ISBN 978-1-5292-1161-0 hardcover
ISBN 978-1-5292-1162-7 paperback
ISBN 978-1-5292-1164-1 ePub
ISBN 978-1-5292-1163-4 ePdf

The right of Erin F. Johnston and Vikash Singh to be identified as editors of this work has
been asserted by them in accordance with the Copyright, Designs and Patents Act 1988.

Cover design: blu inc, Bristol
Front cover image: pixabay - Comfreak - fire-1783922

Contents

List of Figures and Tables

Figures

Tables

Notes on Contributors

Jessica Marie Falcone is Professor of Anthropology at Kansas State University. She has published widely in the area of transnational Asian religious practices, including Buddhism as practiced in person and in virtual worlds. Dr. Falcone's first book, *Battling the Buddha of Love: A Cultural Biography of the Greatest Statue Never Built*, about a proposed mega-statue project in India, was published by Cornell University Press in 2018. Her current ethnographic work examines religious practice and social change at a century-old Soto Zen temple in Hawai'i.

Rebecca Kneale Gould is Associate Professor of Environmental Studies at Middlebury College where she co-directs the Religion, Philosophy and Environment focus. She is the author of *At Home in Nature: Modern Homesteading and Spiritual Practice in America* (2005) and the co-creator, with Phil Walker, of the 2012 documentary film, *The Fire Inside: Place, Passion and the Primacy of Nature* (fireinsidefilm.com). Gould writes and teaches broadly within the religion and ecology field, focusing on contemporary religiously based environmental advocacy. She also writes regularly about Thoreau, most recently authoring "The Whiteness of Walden: Reading Thoreau with Attention to Black Lives," in H. Otterberg et al, *Thoreau in an Age of Crisis: Uses and Abuses of an American Icon* (Brill, 2021).

Aseem Hasnain is Associate Professor of Sociology at Bridgewater State University. He completed his PhD from UNC Chapel Hill and has a Post Graduate Diploma in Natural Resource Management from IIFM, India. His areas of interest are political sociology, cultural sociology, race and ethnicity, and African American studies. His current research projects engage with: modernity; capitalism; development; environment; race/caste; and ideology. His research on majoritarian politics and indigenous social movements, comparative human rights, and the Israeli–Palestinian conflict have been published in peer-reviewed journals such as *Social Movement Studies*, *Sociologists Without Borders*, and *Sociological Sciences*. His engaged scholarship is published in popular publications such as *Scroll.in, Countercurrents.com*, and

The Bridgewater Review. He has extensive work experience in community organizing, natural resources management, and development.

Titus Hjelm is Professor in the Study of Religion at the University of Helsinki. Previously he was Reader in Sociology at University College London. His publications include *Peter Berger and the Sociology of Religion: 50 Years after The Sacred Canopy* (ed, Bloomsbury Academic, 2018), in addition to several other books and many journal articles on the sociology of religion. He is the co-editor of the *Journal of Religion in Europe* and the founding chair of the American Academy of Religion's Sociology of Religion Group.

Janet Jacobs is Professor of Distinction of Women and Gender Studies and Sociology at the University of Colorado. Her research focuses on ethnic and religious violence, gender, mass trauma, and collective memory. She is author of five books, including: *Hidden Heritage: The Legacy of the Crypto-Jews,* for which she received the Outstanding Book Award from the Society for the Scientific Study of Religion (2003); and *The Holocaust Across Generations: Trauma and Its Inheritance Among Descendants of Survivors*, which was awarded the Outstanding Book Award by the American Sociological Association section on War and Peace (2017). She is also author of *Memorializing the Holocaust: Gender, Genocide and Mass Trauma*, and of numerous articles and book chapters.

Erin F. Johnston is Senior Research Associate in the Department of Sociology at Duke University, where she leads qualitative data collection and analysis for the Seminary-to-Early Ministry Study. Before coming to Duke, Erin was a Postdoctoral Research Fellow in the Graduate School of Education at Stanford University. Her research focuses on periods of personal change and transformation in an effort to better understand the dynamic intersections between the cultural and the individual. Her work has appeared in journals such as *Sociological Forum, Qualitative Sociology, Symbolic Interaction*, and *Review of Religious Research*, among other outlets. She holds a PhD in sociology from Princeton University.

George Lundskow earned his PhD in sociology at the University of Kansas. He currently serves as Professor and Chair of Sociology at Grand Valley State University in Michigan. His research brings together social psychological theory with historical-comparative methods to study religion, Right-wing extremism, and social change. In other words, he studies the intersection of god, money, power, and violence and how these forces shaped the rise of and present-day conflict in the United States.

Jodi O'Brien is Professor of Sociology at Seattle University and Director of SU ADVANCE, a National Science Foundation-funded program for the advancement of women and faculty of color. Her work focuses on everyday discrimination, and transgressive identities and communities. Her books include *The Production of Reality*; *Social Prisms: Reflections on Everyday Myths and Paradoxes*; and *Everyday Inequalities*. Her recent articles include "Stained-Glass Ceilings: Religion, Leadership, and the Cultural Politics of Belonging," and "Seeing Agnes: Notes on a Transgender Bicultural Ethnomethodology." She is the editor of the *SAGE Encyclopedia of Gender and Society*, and was until recently editor of the public sociology journal, *Contexts*. She also serves on the Board of Directors for the Puget Sound Ignatian Spiritual Exercises in Everyday Life.

Vikash Singh is Associate Professor of Sociology at Montclair State University. He studies religion, social and psychoanalytic theory, and issues of race, caste and neoliberal governance. Singh is the author of *Uprising of the Fools: Pilgrimage as Moral Protest in Contemporary India* (Stanford University Press, 2017). He has published in *Ethnic and Racial Studies*, *Sociological Forum*, *Ethnography*, and *Subjectivity*, among other places.

Evan Stewart is Assistant Professor of Sociology at the University of Massachusetts Boston. His research focuses on how people gain and lose trust in institutions, including religious disengagement, religious authority in public life, and controversial issues in the public sphere. This work has appeared in *Social Forces*, *Sociological Theory*, and *The Sociological Quarterly*, among other outlets. He holds a PhD in sociology from the University of Minnesota.

Yong Wang is Associate Professor of Sociology at Montclair State University. His research interests are largely driven by an obsessive concern with the rise and possible return of totalitarianism.

Daniel Winchester is Associate Professor of Sociology at Purdue University. His research examines how cultural practices shape human experience, identity, and action, with a particular focus on the study of religion. He has conducted ethnographic studies of conversions to Islam and to Eastern Orthodox Christianity, and is currently working on a project analyzing how Evangelical missionary organizations work to shape contemporary Christians' understandings and experiences of "the global." His research has appeared in journals such as *Social Forces*, *Sociological Theory*, and *Sociology of Religion* and received awards from the Culture and Theory Sections of the American Sociological Association.

Series Editors' Preface: Interpretive Lenses in Sociology – On the Multidimensional Foundations of Meaning in Social Life

Sociology is an interpretive endeavor. Whatever the approach taken to study and explain an aspect of social life – qualitative or quantitative, micro or macro – sociologists work to interpret their data to reveal previously unseen, or to clarify previously misunderstood, social forces. However, within the broad field of sociology, and under the purview of its kindred disciplines, there are many scholars who work to unpack the deep structures and processes that underlie the *meanings* of social life. These interpretive scholars focus on the ways that social meanings constitute the core structures of self and identity, the ways that individuals negotiate meanings to define their shared situations, and the collective meanings that bind people together into communities while also setting any given group or context apart from others. From this perspective, meaning underscores social mindsets and personal orientations in the world, as well as the solidarities and divisions that define the dynamics and mark the boundaries of our social standpoints and relationships. Furthermore, such scholars are concerned not only with how the individuals and groups they study actively make and remake the definitions that are central to their lives, as well as how those understandings influence their behaviors, but also how they seek to impact the world with their meaning-making processes. In this regard, meaning is of paramount significance to both the extraordinary moments and the routine circumstances of our lives.[1]

In their efforts to illuminate the deep social foundations of meaning, and to detail the very real social, political, and moral consequences that stem from the ways people define and know the world around them, interpretive scholars explore the semiotic significance of social actions and interactions,

An extended series introduction is available for open access download at: bristoluniversitypress.co.uk/interpretive-lenses-in-sociology.

narratives and discourses, experiences and events. In contrast to those who take a positivist or realist perspective and see the world – or, more precisely, argue that the world can be known – in a more direct or literal light,[2] they use various approaches and draw on different interpretive traditions to decipher their cases in order to better understand the deep social, cultural, and psychic foundations of the phenomena they study. From such interpretive perspectives, a fundamental part of any social phenomenon is not directly evident or visible. Rather, the core foundations of meaning underlying the cases scholars study need to be unpacked, analyzed, and interpreted – and then rearticulated – to comprehend their deeper essences.[3] And they do this work of interpretation from various angles and perspectives, using different "lenses." It is with such interpretive lenses, in sociology and beyond, that we concern ourselves here. How do the people we study make sense of the world? How do they cooperate with others to construct shared understandings, and how do such actors define their situations for various audiences? Furthermore, how do scholars understand their sense-making processes and interpret their actions and experiences? How do they get at the deep social forces, culture structures, and relationships underlying the topics and themes they study?[4] Finally, how do their interpretations allow scholars to construct new and powerful explanations of social phenomena? How do they "possess explanatory torque" with regard to various topics of widespread significance (Reed, 2011: p. 11; see also: Garland, 2006: pp. 437–8)?

This is the perspective from which we organized a unique conference, *The Roots and Branches of Interpretive Sociology: Cultural, Pragmatist, and Psychosocial Approaches*, in Philadelphia, Pennsylvania, in August 2018. From this endeavor, we learned that many scholars were excited by our call to bring them to the table to discuss their interpretive lenses with one another. Many almost intuitively grasped the distinctions we made among traditions and camps in the field (the cultural, the pragmatist/interactionist, the psychosocial, and others) that could be gathered under the umbrella of a broader "interpretive" agenda in sociology. And why not? We make such distinctions between different camps, with their various theoretical and methodological traditions, when we teach. This is how we organize many of our journals, our professional societies and their sections, and other scholarly institutions. We also often use such categories to explain our scholarly identities. In line with these distinctions, qualitative interpretation has developed simultaneously along different paths and among a field of factional communities, and the proponents of these different camps make various claims to distinguish their respective approaches from others.

However, despite the fact that we use such distinctions to delineate our disciplinary field, they rarely sync neatly with the work scholars actually do when they interpret the cases, communities, and issues they study. Rather, in their practices of social research and in their acts of interpretation, scholars combine and integrate elements of different traditions and programs in various ways that help them to focus on and make sense of their experiences as scholars. In other words, the process of interpretation comes alive in the practice of research and, more particularly, in research situations that demand a range of theoretical and methodological tools to illuminate and articulate the social foundations of meaning central to the case at hand.[5] Thus, over the course of their work, scholars develop interpretive lenses that help them find answers to the questions that drive them. While this may not come as a surprise to many readers, we rarely interrogate or compare the nuances of these lenses explicitly.

The purpose of this series is to interrogate, explore, and demonstrate the various interpretive lenses that scholars use when they engage their areas of interest, their cases, and their research situations. Each volume is centered on a substantive topic (for example, religion, the body, or contentious memories) or a particular interpretive-analytic method (for example, semiotics or narrative analysis). The editors of each volume feature the work of scholars who approach their central topic using different interpretive lenses that are particularly relevant to that area of focus. They have asked each author to explicitly illustrate and reflect on two dimensions of interpretation in their work, and to explore the connections between them. First, they asked authors to address how the individuals and communities they study assign meanings and achieve shared understandings with regard to the core topic of their volume. In doing so, authors address the social and cultural forces at play in shaping how people understand their identities, experiences, and situations, as well as how they frame their accounts, motivations, and purposes while acting and performing in the world. Second, volume editors asked contributing authors to explicitly reflect on their interpretive processes and approaches to unpacking the meanings of the social phenomena they study. Some authors present new material while others provide a reflexive overview of their research to date, but all illustrate and discuss the work of interpretation and the central significance of meaning. Such conscious reflection on our interpretive traditions and lenses – on how they shape our analytic foci (in terms of what cases we explore, at what levels of analysis, and with regard to which social actors) and the ways we find meaning in our cases – can illuminate under-recognized or unspoken choices we make in our work. Further, it can expose blind spots and suggest new frameworks for dialogue among scholars. This reflexive dimension, along with the diversity of lenses featured together in each volume, is what makes this series unique. In this vein, and to these ends, we hope the volumes of this series will present arrays of interpretive lenses that readers can use while working to make sense of their own cases and to develop new perspectives of their own. In the process, we also hope to advance the dialogue about interpretation and meaning in the social sciences.

In this inaugural volume, Erin F. Johnston and Vikash Singh present a collection of essays that features different interpretive lenses that scholars use to elucidate the meanings of religion in social life. As the collection makes evident, those who study religion might focus on deeply engrained culture structures (as manifest in collective stories of good and evil or in rituals separating the sacred and the profane) that bind adherents together into a collective unit, or they might view religious meaning as emergent in smaller groups, such as families or local parishes, or as fundamentally arising from lived and embodied practices that give significance to religious lives and religious selves. They might highlight the nuances of daily religious life or the significance of religious meaning across generations. They might also variously see religion as primarily an ideological system that powerful actors use to dominate others and enforce social exclusion, or alternatively as a vital means of resistance to power and domination, depending on the angles from which they approach their cases. Above all, however, contributors to this volume show how they combine various tools in creative ways to reveal the meanings of religion in their cases. Exploring a range of substantive topics and applying various methods, each contributor provides their own valuable insights into the social foundations of religious meaning, and the insights of each differ from the insights of the others. The sheer diversity of the interpretive lenses illustrated in these pages highlights the profound breadth and multifaceted character of the field. Thus, this volume also uncovers new and rich frameworks for dialogue around the themes that emerge from the ways these various authors reflect on their scholarship, as well as the ways that Johnston and Singh tie the collection together with their keen commentary. Scholars and students of religion working from any perspective will find this book to be an important and refreshing statement on the ways that we can explore and interpret the meanings of religion and understand religious lives. We are thrilled to feature this important book as part of our *Interpretive Lenses in Sociology* series.

Thomas DeGloma
Hunter College and the Graduate Center, CUNY

Julie B. Wiest
West Chester University of Pennsylvania

Notes

[1]   On the centrality of meaning in interpretive social analysis, see Reed's (2011) important work on interpretation and knowledge, especially his discussions of the "interpretive epistemic mode" (pp. 89–121) and the "normative epistemic mode" (pp. 67–88).

[2]   See Reed (2011), especially on the "realist semiotic and the illusion of noninterpretation" (p. 52).

[3]   Indeed, this is what Clifford Geertz (1973) meant when he called for "thick description" in ethnographic analysis.

⁴ Alfred Schütz ([1932] 1967, pp. 205–6; 1970, p. 273) recognized the layers of interpretation we point to here when he argued, "The thought objects constructed by the social scientist … have to be founded upon the thought objects constructed by the common-sense thinking of [people], living their daily life within their social world. Thus, the constructs of the social sciences are, so to speak, constructs of the second degree, namely constructs of the constructs made by the actors on the social scene." Geertz (1973, p. 9) made a similar distinction when he argued "that what we call our data are really our own constructions of other people's constructions." See also: Reed (2017, pp. 29–31) on "interpreting interpretations." Such a distinction also informs the fundamental premises of psychoanalysis, as the analyst is always in the business of interpreting interpretations and unpacking layers of symbolism.

⁵ See also: Tavory and Timmermans (2014), who advocate engaging the process of research and interpretation armed with "multiple theoretical perspectives" (p. 35).

References

Garland, D. (2006) "Concepts of Culture in the Sociology of Punishment," *Theoretical Criminology* 10(4): 419–47.

Geertz, C. (1973) "Thick description: Toward an Interpretive Theory of Culture," in *The Interpretation of Cultures*, New York: Basic Books, pp. 3–30.

Reed, I.A. (2011) *Interpretation and Social Knowledge: On the Use of Theory in the Human Sciences*, Chicago: University of Chicago Press.

Reed, I.A. (2017) "On the Very Idea of Cultural Sociology," in C.E. Benzecry, M. Krause, and I.A. Reed (eds) *Social Theory Now*, Chicago: University of Chicago Press, pp. 18–41.

Schütz, A. (1967 [1932]) *The Phenomenology of the Social World*, Evanston, IL: Northwestern University Press.

Schütz, A. (1970) *On Phenomenology and Social Relations*, Chicago: University of Chicago Press.

Tavory, I. and Timmermans. S. (2014) *Abductive Analysis: Theorizing Qualitative Research*, Chicago: University of Chicago Press.

Introduction: Interpretive Approaches in the Study of Religion

Erin F. Johnston

The chapters in this volume cover a lot of ground. The authors draw from different theoretical and methodological approaches and apply these varied lenses to a range of empirical and substantive topics, from totalitarianism in China to the religious beliefs and practices of descendants of Holocaust survivors. However, what unites these studies is their *interpretive* approach to the study of religion (see: Schwartz-Shea and Yanow, 2013; Yanow and Schwartz-Shea, 2014 for useful overviews). Interpretive approaches are centrally concerned with meaning and meaning-making; "Humans making meanings out of the meaning-making of other humans ... this is the heart of what it means to be an interpretivist" (Pachirat, 2014). Interpretive scholars document and analyze the meanings people give to objects, experiences, events, actions, practices, and people (including themselves) as well as the *process* of meaning-making – how meanings are constructed, established, transmitted, debated, contested, and changed. Interpretive scholars also examine the *implications* of meaning, documenting how and in what ways meanings matter. Meaning, from this perspective, whether expressed via discourse, ritual, or emotion, not only reflects but constitutes social realities and social action. Finally, interpretive approaches share core assumptions about meaning-making, analyzing meaning as intersubjective, relational, and *situated* in particular communities and contexts. As a result, interpretively inclined researchers emphasize the importance of scholarly reflexivity – a commitment rooted in the acknowledgement that scholarly work is itself an act of world-construction, one that intersects in myriad ways with the interpretive work of the people and groups we study.

Beyond these commonalities, however, we find many ways to enter into the interpretive study of religion. Interpretive work spans disciplines – from sociology to anthropology, history to the field of religious studies – and can fall under a range of theoretical and substantive umbrellas, including cultural sociology (Edgell, 2012), symbolic interaction (Collins, 2011; Tavory, 2016), pragmatism (Smilde, 2007), or the study of "lived religion" (McGuire, 2008; Ammerman, 2016; Hall, 2020). Interpretive studies also span levels of analysis. Meaning and meaning-making can be examined at the individual level or the macro level, from individual narratives and the micro-situational dynamics of constructing shared meanings to the discursive construction of religion as codified in federal laws or religious texts. Interpretive scholars, as a result, make use of a wide range of methodological approaches. We see examples of this breadth of disciplinary backgrounds, levels of analysis, and methods in the chapters that make up this volume – with research based on in-depth interviews, ethnographic fieldwork, historical methods and survey data from scholars trained in sociology, anthropology, and history.

Interpretive scholars also understand and study meaning in different ways – as Robert Wuthnow has argued, "Meaning has many meanings" (Wuthnow, 1989) – and often, with different goals.[1] Some interpretive scholars foreground individual-level meanings and meaning-making; in other words, they examine how people give meaning to themselves and to the world around them. This focus is most commonly associated with work in cultural sociology, symbolic interaction, and studies of lived religion (Collins, 2011; Edgell, 2012; Ammerman, 2016) and tends to utilize interview and/or ethnographic approaches. While such scholars foreground the individual (and sometimes individuals in interaction), they simultaneously strive to situate deeply held and seemingly personal meanings in social and historical contexts, tracing the complex dynamics between individual meaning-making and available cultural templates – including how actors use individual narratives and practices to challenge and sometimes change dominant cultural scripts.

Jodi O'Brien's chapter (Chapter 1) on queer Christians, for example, asks: How do queer Christians make sense of themselves? And more pressingly: How does someone who has been cast as "sinner," or "afflicted," and/or "inherently disordered" rewrite their place in this script? O'Brien argues that "embracing contradiction" is the "conceptual pivot that enabled both individuals and congregations to rewrite the prevailing script." The idea of "living the contradiction," at both the individual and collective level, opened up a new role for queer Christians – not as outcast or sinner but as martyr who possesses a special mission (or quest) to move the Church and their fellow Christians toward compassion and reconciliation. This new interpretive framework draws from existing values and discourses within the Christian community – including a logic of radical inclusivity – and brings them to bear on the lives of queer Christians. In doing so, it opens up new possibilities for action at the individual and collective level, becoming an important basis for the affirmation of queer Christians as full-fledged members of the religious community. O'Brien's analysis of the shifting narrative options available to queer Christians vividly demonstrates the "recursive relationship between the availability or source of scripts, self-understanding, and self-presentation."

Janet Jacobs's chapter (Chapter 2) examines "spiritual worldviews and ritual innovation" among descendants of Holocaust survivors. In doing so, Jacobs positions religion not just as a vehicle for the memorialization of the past or a mechanism in the transmission of trauma – but also as a means through which the present and future are creatively reimagined. Drawing on rich life history data, Jacobs explores how religion shapes and is shaped by the realities of genocide and its associated trauma. Her research foregrounds the family as a site of religious formation and the role of history, memory, and trauma in shaping the dynamics of religious socialization. Jacobs shows how religious traditions and historical events are refracted through familial practices, relationships, and histories. Her work also, however, highlights "the adaptive and creative religious responses" of descendants who not only draw from but also modify the traditions and practices that marked their religious upbringings. The ritual innovations she documents seek to both preserve religious heritage and "move beyond a familial legacy of pain and suffering." In doing so, Jacobs' chapter deftly captures the dynamic interplay between stability and change, institutions and individuals, history and the present.

Interpretive approaches are sometimes pigeon-holed and straw-manned as only interested in the (relatively inconsequential, so it is argued) realm of the discursive – meanings that are conscious, explicit, and deliberative. However, implicit, automatic, and "embodied" cognitions are themselves acts of meaning-making, as much of interest to the interpretive scholar as texts, narratives, and discourses. Automatic and habitual responses – such as emotions and moral judgments – reflect deeply ingrained cultural schema (Vaisey, 2009) and can be interpreted as evidence of meaning-in-action. Moreover, the experiential/embodied and the conceptual/discursive are not wholly separate but deeply intertwined. Interpretive scholars are well-positioned to attend to the dynamic relationships between the explicit and implicit, as Daniel Winchester's chapter on *enactive ethnography* demonstrates (Chapter 3; see also: Pagis, 2010; Winchester and Green, 2019).

Winchester argues that "doing it" – taking on the religious practices and activities of those we seek to understand – can help researchers elucidate the visceral nature and experience of religious practices for practitioners. Religious people, after all, not only inhabit symbolic worlds but embodied and sensual ones, as well (see also: Neitz and Spickard, 1990). And religious practices not only reflect symbolic worlds – as texts to be read (Geertz, 1966) – but also shape meaning-making "below the level of explicit symbolization and discourse," through the cultivation of certain (shared) forms of awareness, perception, sensation, and memory. Winchester's chapter illustrates the power of the enactive approach for "tracing the intimate connections between the somatic and symbolic registers of religious action." As his examples convincingly demonstrate, embodied experiences in practice often become the grounds for more explicit (religious) meaning-making. These experiences, Winchester finds, "call out" for interpretation and become "interpretive vectors" – the building blocks of embodied metaphors and analogical windows for the community's symbolic world. It is through practice then, Winchester argues, that "moral discourse and religious symbolism become more deeply integrated into converts' phenomenological realities, making new religious interpretations of self and world ... more experientially persuasive." From this perspective, the taken-for-grantedness often associated with religion can be traced to an interplay between the embodied and discursive, the experiential and symbolic.

Rebecca Kneale Gould's chapter (Chapter 4) on "ethnographic silences" also draws us beyond the explicit world of talk, pushing us, instead, to consider the importance and varied meanings of the spaces *between* words. Silences, Gould reminds us, convey meaning, too. Gould's chapter opens up new questions for interpretive scholars of religion: What do silences *indicate* – comfort or tension, awe or avoidance, a breakdown of communication or space for deeper engagement? How are silences *experienced* – as capacious or strained, welcomed or awkward? Where, when, and how do silences *construct* religious meaning (as in, for example, the silence of a monk or a religious chapel)? And how do we, as scholars, make sense of the silences we encounter? While interpretive scholars often "traffic in words," Gould's chapter reminds us of the power, salience, and varied *meanings* of silence.

Gould's chapter also draws our attention to subjective meanings *in interaction* – to what happens when people with divergent conceptions of the same reality, like the secular and religious environmentalists she studied, come into contact. Gould argues that the occasions of silence she describes reveal "the silencing effect that religion can have when it enters into certain nonreligious (or 'not necessarily religious') places and spaces" as well as "the ways in which explicitly secular spaces may have a silencing effect on religiously identified people." These silences make "history come alive," reflecting the mutual suspicion with which the secular and religious environmental activists have "long viewed each other." They also draw attention to the limits and boundaries of "cooperation, collaboration and shared purpose" between groups of activists with different interpretive frameworks for the work they do. While there is ample room for collaboration, these efforts, Gould argues, are likely to be successful only "to the extent that conversations about 'real presence' remain muted or disguised."

Each of these four chapters foregrounds deeply held and seemingly personal meanings, highlighting their construction, contextualization, evolution, and interaction. The analytical lenses these authors bring to bear, however, lead them to foreground different aspects of the religious lives they seek to understand – identity and self-understanding (O'Brien), socialization, memory and trauma (Jacobs), embodied practices like fasting and prayer (Winchester), and interactional silences (Gould). Each enhances our understanding of the situated nature of religion and religious lives while providing useful tools and insights for understanding religion across different communities and contexts.

Other interpretive scholars, however, foreground meaning and meaning-making at the collective level while backgrounding more individual or personal meanings. This empirical focus leads to different questions: How do societies and/or social groups assign meaning/s to objects, events, people, or groups? In what ways are these meanings constructed, contested, and/or changed? What role does power play in shaping which meanings – and *whose* meanings – become dominant and/or taken for granted? Here, too, scholars seek to contextualize the meanings and processes of meaning-making they uncover, situating them in particular times and places, and tracing how meanings evolve and change over time.

Aseem Hasnain's chapter (Chapter 5), for example, traces the discursive strategies used by religious elites to shape public perception of the Shia religious minority in India across three distinct historical moments. He finds that the "shifting content" of their collective identity claims corresponds with changes in the primary audience and dominant discourses that mark the public sphere in each historical period. More specifically, changes in the nature of "the public" – of who and what defines the "perceived default majority" – shapes the ways in which Shia present themselves and the discursive strategies they deploy. Common across these periods, however, is the discursive positioning of the Shia minority in opposition to Sunni Muslims. Hasnain's analysis demonstrates the dynamic interplay between the discursive strategies used by social groups and the structural realities and socio-political contexts within which those groups are situated – their relative size and status, dominant political attitudes and concerns, and the broader political and religious fields. His analysis balances a focus on stability and fluidity in the study of collective identities by "focusing on moments of congealed identity within a longer period of shifts and changes." Hasnain's chapter demonstrates that how we fashion ourselves, not only individually but collectively, is relational and both constrained and enabled by situational dynamics (including the perceived audience) and societal structures, which themselves shift and change over time.

Titus Hjelm's chapter, likewise, draws our attention to the processes and implications of meaning-making at the collective level (Chapter 6). Hjelm, however, foregrounds how "religion" itself is constructed and defined, as well as when, where, and how the meanings and boundaries of religion are contested and debated in public discourse. In doing so, he advocates for a critical discursive approach, which asks: What "counts" as religion in a given social and cultural context, and "what is being *done* when religion is talked about in a particular way?" What are the "action orientations" dominant discourses of religion imply, and what or who do they serve? By way of example, Hjelm analyzes the framing of Finland's Evangelical Lutheran Church (ELCF) as a "folk church." He traces the historical roots of this terminology and examines how this conceptual frame is deployed in two separate contexts –the self-presentation of the ELCF and parliamentary debates about the ELCF and its privileged status. In both cases, the "folk church" is used to link the ELCF to Finnish national identity, history, and culture in ways that suggest efforts to undermine one would undermine the others. Hjelm argues that this discourse works "ideologically by downplaying the church-state connection and in doing so, reproduces the privileged position of the ELCF." Hjelm's analysis points to both what is said and what is *not* said – like Gould, Hjelm argues that "silences matter" and that "absences are as important as presences" – in order to demonstrate how the ELCF's "perpetual privileged status" remains unchallenged. Hjelm's chapter makes clear that collective meanings are not just of intellectual interest. The way societies give meaning to people, groups, and events have real consequences – they shape action orientations that significantly impact social, cultural, and political realities.

While Hasnain and Hjelm focus on the (contested and evolving) meanings of a particular religious group – Shia Muslims – or category – "folk religion" – two other chapters in the volume analyze the content and consequences of much broader and more comprehensive ideologies: totalitarianism (Yong Wang) and white supremacy (George Lundskow). While focused on very different cases and cultural contexts (China and the USA, respectively), both chapters demonstrate the utility of interpreting seemingly "secular" ideologies through the lens of religion, tracing "homologies" between "the religious proper" and "the secular ideological." George Lundskow's chapter (Chapter 7), for example, identifies the essential doctrines – namely, belief in "a divine hierarchy of superior and inferior races that mandates strict social and cognitive boundaries" (that is, white supremacy) – and essential rites (namely, regenerative violence against those perceived as the Evil Other) of what he argues is the "true religion of the United States": white male ethnonationalism. While not an established religion, Lundskow argues that this ideology "evokes both the emotional passion and life and death commitment of religious faith, which shapes perception of social issues as well as worldview." Ultimately, Lundskow argues, "If a set of beliefs and practices feature divine imagery, explain the order of existence, supersede material reality, call people to fulfill moral obligations and require acceptance based on faith, then it's a religion, consciously or not." This chapter, like Wang's, convincingly demonstrates that the conceptual and interpretive "tools in the repertoire of sociological inquiry of religion" (Wang) – such as the sacred/profane, rituals and rites, and the transcendent – can help us better understand seemingly secular ideological formations.

Beyond merely documenting homologies between religion and white male ethnonationalism, Lundskow's chapter also illustrates the very real consequences of this ideology. Focusing on two key historical moments – US reconstruction after its civil war, and the 20th century labor movement – Lundskow examines how this "faith" has "thwarted racial reconciliation and material social progress," over and often against material interests. At both historical moments, "many whites chose a violent white supremacy and a majority chose to at least tolerate it, even if it meant lower income and quality of life for themselves as well." White male ethnonationalism, Lundskow argues, "played the role of religion" by providing "religious validation" for wealthy, white Americans to pursue "ever more wealth and power." For Lundskow, whiteness, like religion, provides "consolation," a consolation strong enough to justify "racist discrimination and violence" and preclude the development "common human identity and socioeconomic progress for a broad multitude." Lundskow's analysis positions white supremacy *as religion* – an ideology that constructs the world and shapes action, in both explicit (in discourse and narrative) and implicit (in emotion and experience) ways.

Wang's chapter (Chapter 8) stakes out a different position regarding the relationship between religion and secular ideologies. He argues that we should discard the boundary between the religious and pseudo-religious entirely and instead acknowledge that not only is "the religious social" but "the social is religious." His analysis of totalitarianism in China shows that the modern state does not merely demonstrate homologies with religion but is founded on secular theological concepts, a "miraculous founding gesture" and worship of a charismatic leader. On the one hand, the new state is built on the "traditional imaginary" of the Emperor and his minions. Yet, there was also something new – the treatment of Mao as a god to be worshipped. The Evil Others in this ideological formation are the small business people and landowners who must be "purged" in the process of social change. Ultimately, Wang argues that, "[m]odernity, despite its insistent rejection of religion in the names of reason and science, has populated the world with its own deities and created its own sphere of the sacred and the profane." His chapter traces the lingering vestiges of religion in the seemingly secular.

Regardless of their very distinctive differences in substantive focus, theoretical frameworks, and/or methods deployed, each of the chapters in this volume illustrates the core commitments that mark the interpretive approach. The authors foreground meaning and meaning-making, and acknowledge (and assume) their indeterminacy. This view of meaning-making is reflected in the authors' commitment to *contextualizing* and *situating* meaning and meaning-making in particular places and times, articulating how meanings are informed by history and contested in the present, but also how they project forward into the future. Each of these chapters also demonstrates the power of interpretive approach for moving us toward expanded notions of causality – explanations that take seriously mutually constituting and contingent relationships between meanings, their foundations and evolutions, and their consequences for social action and social structure.

Scholarship as interpretation

We also see in this volume the importance and centrality of reflexivity in interpretive research. Each chapter reminds us of the need for close attention to how we, as scholars, make sense of the people, events, and processes we study. Scholarly work is itself an act of interpretation. Our data does not "speak for itself": We must make sense of our observations and then convey the meanings we find there to our often-varied audiences. And ultimately, as Winchester argues in his chapter on enactive ethnography, no matter how close we come to capturing the reality of religious lives, we are always "translating religious actions, beliefs, and experiences into the secular vernacular of our social science." We are, as Winchester notes, "playing a different kind of language game" than those whose lives we study.

The scholarly interpretive process often requires that we categorize and classify what we observe, creating labels, names, and typologies out of the people, events, objects, stories, and lives we study. Categories and concepts are important foundations for understanding and knowledge, scholarly or otherwise. Without shared categories (and shared definitions of them), we can end up talking past one another and struggle to generate cumulative knowledge. However, as several chapters in this volume show, acts of classification are always fraught: categories are debated and contested among scholars themselves, between scholars and those they seek to understand, and within and between the communities they study. The disaggregation of existing categories can move us toward greater accuracy and nuance in our classifications, but questions will always arise about which dimensions matter most and where and how to draw the boundaries between sub-groups. The categories scholars use are not just matters of semantics. They have real impact. Categories can easily mask or obscure reality as much as they reveal it, changing the way we understand and see the world around us.

Evan Stewart's chapter on nonreligion, for example, (Chapter 10) asks: What does it *mean* to be "nonreligious"? In asking this question, Stewart acknowledges the *interpretive* challenge faced by scholars: "nonreligious" means different things to different people. The meaning of nonreligion varies at the individual level (What do people mean when they claim "nonreligious" as an identity?) and the collective level (How are the nonreligious or nonreligiosity understood in different communities and societies?), as well as among scholars (How do scholars define the boundaries and content of "nonreligion"? How do different definitions shape what we think we know about this group?). Stewart shows, for example, that claiming a nonreligious identity sometimes reflects an active rejection of religion but in other cases it reflects a general indifference toward religion. This distinction is substantively meaningful and important. Lumping these two groups together may obscure important differences in their beliefs, attitudes, and/or behaviors. The most common solution to this problem has been disaggregation, as Stewart says: "splitting the broad category of 'none' or 'nothing in particular' into more finely grained categories of nonreligious experiences and attitudes." This strategy has generated a proliferation of categories: "unchurched believers," the "spiritual but nonreligious," and committed versus passive seculars.

As Stewart points out, however, the creation of new and ever more specific categories always fails to capture some degree of complexity, generates the possibility of mis-categorization and oversight, and can cause discordance and confusion across studies and disciplines which use different systems of classification. Stewart, however, proposes a way out: rather than measuring differences in *kind*, he suggests that researchers measure differences in *magnitude* along core dimensions of religion such as belief, behavior, and belonging. The value of this proposal – to better "map the complexity" – is demonstrated in Stewart's empirical examples, which show the varied combinations and degrees of secularity and nonreligion among those who fall under the broad umbrella of the nonreligious (as well as those who identify themselves as religious). He identifies different repertoires of attitudes toward personal and public religion and maps those patterns across categorical groupings. In doing so, Stewart finds that some people who identify as "nonreligious" are more similar to the religiously affiliated than to other religious "nones" (such as atheists and agnostics). The same is true in reverse: Some respondents who identify as religious more closely resemble the unaffiliated in their cultural repertoires.

Jessica Marie Falcone, like Stewart, begins from a place of dissatisfaction with available scholarly categories; in this case, for identifying and studying contemporary Buddhists and Buddhisms (Chapter 9). Falcone argues that existing categories – such as ethnic versus elite, convert versus cradle, Eastern versus Western – tend to conflate nationality with ethnicity and/ or ethnicity with religious heritage, and as a result, mask a good deal of variation (and similarity) among practitioners within and across these groups. They also, Falcone argues, write some people out of the story entirely. For example, these categories fail to capture people of Asian heritage who were not enculturated as Buddhists but embrace the tradition later in life, as well as white, US-born practitioners raised by Buddhist parents. Falcone proposes a similar solution for overcoming this challenge as the one taken by Stewart; she proposes a "heritage spectrum," based on relative degrees of enculturation (not ethnicity) and along which both practitioners and traditions can be arrayed. The heritage spectrum, Falcone argues, is "a more accurate, complex, and inclusive typology" that allows us to capture more of the nuance and diversity in the life stories and trajectories of Buddhist practitioners. Both Falcone and Stewart point us toward new approaches to categorization and classification –approaches which strive to capture and allow for complexity while also aiming to reduce the complexity enough in order to communicate *meaningful* patterns of variations in ways that are legible to others.

"Getting it right," however, is not the only issue to consider when reflecting on the scholarly categories we create. Hjelm's chapter also reminds us that acts of definition, classification, and categorization are bound up with power and social stratification, an important consideration for scholars whose work often requires creating categories and frameworks of interpretation that necessarily constrain meaning. Here then, we must also consider how scholarly and "lay" classifications intersect and interpenetrate in other ways. Falcone, drawing on the writing of Ian Hacking (Hacking, 1986), acknowledges the potentially constructive (rather than merely denotative) implications of scholarly categories. In creating categories, we sometimes participate in the very act of "making people up" (Hacking, 1986). Stewart, for example, relates that when sharing his work on nonreligion, he often gets a similar response – "That's me!" Similarly, previous scholarly work on religious "nones" and the "spiritual but not religious" have had the effect of popularizing these categories, making them available and accessible to individuals who adopt them as means of self-identification and self-understanding. Our work does not merely document the world but actively participates in constructing it.

The dialogical relationship between scholar and subject or object of study is a two-way street. We, too, as scholars and as people, are shaped by our exposure to and immersion in other social worlds. Jodi O'Brien's piece on queer Christian lives vividly illustrates this dynamic interplay. O'Brien's chapter traces how her own self-understanding and interpretive frames have been shaped and transformed by her scholarly work: in hearing the stories of others, she "has been troubled into an immensely expanded awareness," encountering new possibilities for giving meaning to herself and others. O'Brien's chapter also acknowledges the ways in which her pre-existing interpretive frameworks shaped what she chose to study, how she studied it, and what she found. This constraining effect begins quite early in the research process: what we find interesting and worthy of research is often rooted in what piques our curiosity, what we find "puzzling." For O'Brien, this was the lives and identities of those who identified as *both* queer and Christian, a combination that she "personally couldn't make sense of." O'Brien's scholarly frameworks also shaped the questions she asked, leading to early "failures" as her frameworks of meaning collided with those of the people she sought to understand. O'Brien, drawing on symbolic interactionist theories of identity and stigma, assumed that queer Christians were tasked with "managing" the "double stigma" of being gay and Christian. Her interviewees, however, pushed back against this framing, arguing that their identity was instead *defined* by contradiction. This conflict of interpretive frameworks ultimately enhanced O'Brien's understanding of queer Christian lives. It also led her to (re)consider her own relationship to religion and "the narrowness of [her] coming out story." Here, we see a scholar whose work models the kind of self-consciously subjective stance that Weber saw as foundational to social scientific research (Weber, 2017).

For others, like Winchester, being affected and transformed by the research process is a self-conscious and deliberate strategy, a method and means for understanding. Winchester argues that "doing it" – doing the things the people we study do – can "unearth layers of religious meaning that would otherwise remain hidden from view." Winchester's goal is to understand and to explicate the religious worlds of those he practices alongside "from within": to better understand how participants experience these practices, the meanings they give to practice, and the ways in which the corporal experience and conceptual meanings are deeply intertwined. By enacting key religious practices, Winchester learns something about what it *feels* like to perform the *salat* (Islamic ritual prayer) or to fast in the Eastern Orthodox tradition. Doing so provides Winchester important insights into how those practices help constitute religious meanings and identities. As one of his interlocutors informed him, the practice of salat does not *mean* you are submitting to God, it *is* submission to God. By taking on this practice, Winchester seeks to lessen "the interpretive, experiential, and epistemic space between" himself and those he seeks to understand. In committing to feeling the pangs of hunger or striving to reorganize his life around the schedule of salat, Winchester shows how the researcher's body becomes an instrument of understanding and knowledge. If meaning is evident in and intertwined with bodily experience, taking on practices that foster these experiences can enhance our understanding. This methodological approach, perhaps more than any other, brings the interpenetration of researcher and researched into sharp relief. Of course, as Winchester acknowledges, the lessening of this gap always remains incomplete.

Janet Jacobs, on the other hand, positions herself as both scholar and witness – an empathetic listener and a "blank slate" on which memories of the Holocaust and its traumas "are inscribed." As a witness, Jacobs listens, empathizes, and *validates* the stories of research participants. As a scholar, she aims to capture and convey the meanings and experiences of those she spoke with, in ways that resonate with those whose stories she tells. Providing space for these stories to be told and ensuring that those stories are heard (through presentation and publication) provide witness to the trauma and challenges these individuals have faced. Yet, just as the religious lives of her respondents are refracted through familial relationships and histories, so too are her respondents' stories refracted through the interpretive lenses of the author. As scholars, we, too, build symbolic worlds from the varied bits and pieces we inherit.

Jacobs, Winchester, O'Brien, and Falcone primarily seek to understand religious worlds "from within" – from the vantage point of the individuals who inhabit them. They aim to build on and generate *experience-near* (Geertz, 1974) interpretive frameworks. Jessica Marie Falcone's chapter, for example, takes seriously the importance of accurately capturing and portraying the diversity of experiences, identities, and forms of practice among modern Buddhist practitioners. She strives to generate an interpretive framework that "fits" with the self-understandings and varied life trajectories of those she studies. She argues that as scholars, "it is our duty to critique ourselves toward more perfect categories." Her goal is to generate interpretive frameworks that are not only "scholastically useful" but also culturally contextualized and which "would not be deemed exclusionary by those we hope to fairly represent in our writing." Ultimately, Falcone argues for a nuanced relationship between "emic" and "etic" perspectives: "The etic vantage point of an anthropology of Buddhism must take into consideration the emic realities of our interlocutors to ensure that our external, 'expert' terminologies are cohesive and true, as well as inoffensive and inclusive." Doing so reflects Falcone's commitment to scholarship as critique: "Because reframing toward inclusivity is part of a precise, careful scholarship." Scholarship acknowledges and bears witness, drawing attention to social groups and experiences that may otherwise be overlooked.

Other interpretive scholars, however, generate more *experience-distant* (Geertz, 1974) interpretations of social life – conceptualizations that do not necessarily align and may even be actively contested by those who are the object of study. This does not, however, negate the value (nor the accuracy and/or usefulness) of the proffered interpretations. George Lundskow, for example, argues that the actions of white individuals at key moments in history are best understood as rooted in "the faith of white male ethnonationalism." The people whose actions he strives to understand may (likely would?) disagree with his analysis. Yet, the job of the scholar is not only to capture meanings from within but to document how actions and events are shaped by forces and ideas that are not always available to conscious reflection. From this perspective, "fit" with the experience and meanings of those being studied is less important than the pragmatic *usefulness* of the scholar's interpretive framework for "making sense" of the events and social realities in question. As Hjelm argues, for some scholars, "The question then is not about truthfulness [or resonance, as the case may be] but usefulness."

The world constructing power of scholarship is no less evident in studies that offer more experience-distant conceptualizations – such as those of Hasnain, Wang, and Lundskow – even as reflexivity is less clearly foregrounded. In each of these chapters, the authors select particular historical moments for analysis. These moments are then made understandable in relation to one another and, perhaps more importantly, in and through the interpretive work of the authors, who foreground some aspects of these moments and background others, placing these moments in conversation with conceptual and theoretical frameworks in an attempt to "make sense" of these events. Here, as in the other chapters, scholarship itself is clearly an act of interpretation, one that can have effects beyond academic understanding.

Regardless of the author's primary goals – whether it is to provide a detailed description of the life worlds of those being studied *from within* or a more experience-distant account of how ideologies shape history – scholarly work is always rooted in acts of interpretation. The interpretive frameworks scholars deploy and those which they develop can enable new forms of understanding, but they also foreclose and constrain interpretive horizons. Scholarly work implies or lends itself to particular "action orientations" (as Titus Hjelm's chapter defines it), whether intentionally or not. Interpretive scholars, focused on the contextualization of meaning-making, are well-positioned to acknowledge and analyze their own interpretive processes as well as the dynamic interplay between scholarly and "lay" interpretations. Ultimately, as the chapters in this volume show, the research process mirrors, in many ways, our object of study: interpreting religion is itself an unfolding, dynamic, and constitutive process which is generated through both deliberative reflection and embodied understanding.

Interpreting religion and beyond

Many of the founding thinkers in the social scientific study of religion advocated for interpretive approaches – most notably, Max Weber (Weber, 1981; 2017 [1949]) and Émile Durkheim (Durkheim, 2001 [1912]). More recently, influential thinkers such as Clifford Geertz (1966, 1974), Mary Douglas (2003 [1966]), Peter Berger (1969), and Robert Bellah (1967) have continued and expanded this interpretive tradition. Geertz famously described religion as a "model of and model for" reality, advocating that scholars "read" religious rituals like texts – these practices, he argued, rooted in the local cultural context, reflect the broader symbolic worlds within which they were situated. For Berger, religion was defined as a cultural system – a system of meaning made plausible by social relationships and interaction with others (Berger and Luckmann, 1966). As a result, Berger questioned whether religious meaning systems, as comprehensive and overarching, could survive under modern conditions of globalization and fragmentation (Berger, 1969). Throughout her various works, Mary Douglas highlights the interplay between social structure and symbolic representations (Douglas, 2013 [1963]) and foregrounds the importance of social classification, drawing attention to how objects, events, and situations are organized in and through shared schemas (Douglas, 2003 [1966]). We see the foundational insights of these works running through all the chapters in this volume.

More recent trends and "turns" in the social scientific study of religion – such as the turn toward "lived religion" (McGuire, 2008; Ammerman, 2016; Hall, 2020) and/or "practice" (Ammerman, 2020; Wuthnow, 2020) – tend to be defined by their empirical foci. Scholars of lived religion have focused attention on religious life outside of traditionally religious spaces: religion as lived and practiced by the laity rather than formal religious rituals, theologies, institutions, and/or authorities. This work offers rich and detailed descriptions of the particularities of religious lives in different times and places. The more recent "practice approach," part of the broader "practice turn" in the social sciences, focuses scholarly attention on what people do and what people say (as talk, too, is a social practice (Wuthnow, 2011)). Interpretive approaches also share an empirical focus – on meaning and meaning-making – as well as a set of core commitments and assumptions such as the indeterminacy of meaning and corresponding need for contextualization and reflexivity.

As Titus Hjelm argues in his chapter on the critical discursive approach in the study of religion, interpretive approaches move us beyond questions about what religion *is* (substantive approaches), what religion *does* (functionalist approaches), and whether religion is growing or declining, important as those questions may be, and toward a focus on *how religion works* – on the world-constructing power of religion and religious discourse for individuals, groups, and societies. Interpretive approaches in the study of religion tend to be marked by a focus on *processes* – sacralization, socialization, public claims-making, religious change. Interpretive scholars focused on religious practice, for example, are less interested in the number of people who pray, the frequency of prayer, or in whether and in what ways prayer "works," but rather in what religious practices *mean* (Douglas, 2003; Geertz, 1966) and in "how practices construct particular forms of religious subjectivity and experience" (Winchester in this volume). Religious practices, as Winchester argues, "generate meaning, form subjects, and create the 'aura of factuality' that often surrounds religious symbols." In other words, they help *constitute* religious worlds and selves. Interpretive scholars focused on identity and self-understanding, such as O'Brien and Hasnain, are less interested in how many people identify with a given category or in the varied outcomes associated with these identities; they are more interested in how those identities are constituted – how people make sense of themselves and when, whether, and how possibilities for self-understanding change or evolve over time. Religion, from the interpretive perspective, is neither dependent variable nor independent variable (Yamane, 2000; Smilde and May, 2015) but rather a process and a context – an array of practices, objects, places, institutions, interpretive frameworks and cognitive schema, that are both constructed by and construct religious lives.

The chapters in this volume demonstrate the breadth of interpretive research on religion and make clear that interpretive studies continue to enhance and enrich our understanding of religion and religious lives. They show us that religious meanings are sometimes explicit, evident in discourses, texts, and narratives as well as in rituals and practices (which can themselves be 'read' as texts), and other times implicit, situated in the pre-reflective realms of ideology, cultural schema, bodily habits, emotions, and sensations. The contributing authors consider the religious meanings of individuals (and how those meanings come to be "experientially persuasive" [see Winchester]) as well as the varied meanings people, including scholars, give to religious groups and to religion itself (see Hasnain, and Hjelm). They variously foreground the importance of practice, discourse, and/or categories in making sense of religion's role in social life. These different starting points lead the authors to ask different questions, use different methods, and ultimately, come to different conclusions. The relative strengths (and weaknesses) of these different approaches emerge in relation to the particular cases and questions being asked. Each starting point, however, reminds us that meaning and meaning-making are central to religious life and to our (scholarly) understanding of it. This volume provides an orienting toolkit for interpretive scholars who seek to make sense of religious life.

While the chapters in this volume demonstrate the continued value of interpretive approaches in the study of religion, specifically, they also demonstrate the impossibility of separating the religious from the nonreligious, of attempting to silo social scientific work on religion as something separate from the study of culture and society writ large. The meanings of religion and religious identities are formed and reformed on the public stage and the claims-making that occurs there is "eminently political," blurring the boundaries between religion and politics, identity and interest (Hasnain). Religious meanings move beyond the boundaries of formal religious spaces and institutions (Gould). Sacralization, it seems, can occur anywhere – in soup kitchens (Bender, 2003), hospitals (Cadge, 2012), at home, and in the workplace (Ammerman, 2013). Likewise, the forms of meaning and practice that are often thought to mark "the religious" – transcendence, charisma, ritual, calling, the sacred and profane – can be fruitfully applied to help us better understand and make sense of events, groups, people, and processes that at first glance seem decidedly secular (see Lundskow, and Wang). The "religious" itself is a category that creates and serves as a symbolic foil to the secular and the nonreligious (Stewart). The way in which those boundaries are constructed and enacted and the ways in which they are transgressed (and to what effects) – including for example, the silences evoked by religious presences as Gould so aptly shows us – are all matters of import for interpretive scholars not only within but beyond the study of religion (see Hjelm).

Ultimately, the chapters of this volume enrich our understanding of social life in spaces far beyond religious institutions, and the insights generated from them have much broader utility (see also: Guhin, 2014; Winchester, 2016 on exporting findings from the sociology of religion). O'Brien's analysis of how queer Christians make sense of themselves reveals broader patterns and insights into how individual and collective meaning-making intersect and intertwine. Winchester's study of religious practice illuminates how shared meanings, religious or otherwise, become "experientially persuasive" (see Winchester). The study of how "religion" and the "religious" are constructed and deployed as categories, shaped by power and generating both meaning and exclusion, can help inform our understanding of how discourse constructs and reflects power, inequality, and status in other social fields (see Hjelm in this volume; see also: Taves and Bender, 2012). Interpretive approaches, united by their focus on meaning and committed to documenting its indeterminacy, contextualization, and relationship to social structure and power, lend themselves to nuanced explanations and expanded notions of causality – ones that are complex, contextualized, and constitutive. Often asking "how" rather than what or why, interpretive approaches enable us to see the dynamic and complicated interplay between stability and fluidity, tradition and innovation, history and the present, as well as between structure and agency, individual and collective, explicit and implicit, both within and beyond "the religious proper."

Note

[1] The different approaches outlined are not mutually exclusive, as the chapters in this volume demonstrate. They are separated here for the purposes of illustration.

References

Ammerman, N.T. (2013) *Sacred Stories, Spiritual Tribes: Finding Religion in Everyday Life*, Oxford: Oxford University Press.

Ammerman, N.T. (2016) "Lived Religion as an Emerging Field: An Assessment of its Contours and Frontiers," *Nordic Journal of Religion and Society*, 29(02): 83–99.

Ammerman, N.T. (2020) "Rethinking Religion: Toward a Practice Approach," *American Journal of Sociology*, 126(1): 6–51.

Bellah, R.N. (1967) "Civil Religion in America," *Daedalus*, 96: 1–21.

Bender, C. (2003) *Heaven's Kitchen: Living Religion at God's Love We Deliver*, Chicago: University of Chicago Press.

Berger, P.L. (1969) *The Sacred Canopy: Elements of a Sociological Theory of Religion*, New York: Anchor Books.

Berger, P.L., and Luckmann, T. (1966) *The Social Construction of Reality: A Treatise in the Sociology of Knowledge*, New York: Doubleday.

Cadge, W. (2012) *Paging God: Religion in the Halls of Medicine*, Chicago: University of Chicago Press.

Collins, R. (2011) "The Micro-Sociology of Religion: Religious Practices, Collective and Individual," Philadelphia, PA: Association of Religion Data Archives.

Douglas, M. (2003 [1966]) *Purity and Danger: An Analysis of Concepts of Pollution and Taboo*, New York: Routledge.

Douglas, M. (2013 [1963]) *The Lele of the Kasai*, New York: Routledge.

Durkheim, É. (2001 [1912]) *The Elementary Forms of Religious Life*, Oxford: Oxford University Press.

Edgell, P. (2012) "A Cultural Sociology of Religion: New Directions," *Annual Review of Sociology*, 38: 247–65.

Geertz, C. (1974) "'From the Native's Point of View': On the Nature of Anthropological Understanding," *Bulletin of the American Academy of Arts and Sciences*, 28(1): 26–45.

Geertz, C. (1966) "Religion as a Cultural System," in Michael Banton (ed.), *Anthropological Approaches to the Study of Religion*, London: Travistock, pp. 1–46.

Guhin, J. (2014) "Religion as Site Rather Than Religion as Category: On the Sociology of Religion's Export Problem," *Sociology of Religion*, 75(4): 579–93.

Hacking, I. (1986) "Making People Up," in *Reconstructing Individualism: Autonomy, Individuality, and the Self in Western Thought*, Stanford: Stanford University Press, pp. 161–71.

Hall, D.D. (2020) *Lived Religion in America: Toward a History of Practice*, Princeton, NJ: Princeton University Press.

McGuire, M.B. (2008) *Lived Religion: Faith and Practice in Everyday Life*, Oxford: Oxford University Press.

Neitz, M.J., and Spickard, J.V. (1990) "Steps Toward a Sociology of Religious Experience: The Theories of Mihaly Csikszentmihalyi and Alfred Schutz," *Sociology of Religion* 51(1): 15–33.

Pachirat, T. (2014) "We Call It a Grain of Sand: The Interpretive Orientation and a Human Social Science," in Yanow, D. and Schwartz-Shea, P. (eds) *Interpretation and Methods: Empirical Research Methods and the Interpretive Turn*, New York: Routledge.

Pagis, M. (2010) "From Abstract Concepts to Experiential Knowledge: Embodying Enlightenment in a Meditation Center," *Qualitative Sociology* 4(33): 469–89.

Schwartz-Shea, P., and Yanow, D. (2013) *Interpretive Research Design: Concepts and Processes*, New York: Routledge.

Smilde, D. (2007) *Reason to Believe: Cultural Agency in Latin American Evangelicalism*, Oakland, CA: University of California Press.

Smilde, D., and May, M. (2015) "Causality, Normativity, and Diversity in 40 Years of US Sociology of Religion: Contributions to Paradigmatic Reflection," *Sociology of Religion*, 76(4): 369–88.

Taves, A., and Bender, C. (2012) "Introduction: Things of Value," in *What Matters? Ethnographies of Value in a Not So Secular Age*. New York: Columbia University Press.

Tavory, I. (2016) *Summoned: Identification and Religious Life in a Jewish Neighborhood*, Chicago: University of Chicago Press.

Vaisey, S. (2009) "Motivation and Justification: A Dual-Process Model of Culture in Action," *American Journal of Sociology*, 114(6): 1675–1715.

Weber, M. (1981) "Some Categories of Interpretive Sociology," *The Sociological Quarterly*, 22(2): 151–80.

Weber, M. (2017 [1949]) *Methodology of Social Sciences*, New York: Routledge.

Winchester, D. (2016) "Religion as Theoretical Case, Lens, and Resource for Critique: Three Ways Social Theory Can Learn from the Study of Religion," *Sociology of Religion*, 77(3): 241–60.

Winchester, D., and Green, K.D. (2019) "Talking Your Self into It: How and When Accounts Shape Motivation for Action," *Sociological Theory*, 37(3): 257–81.

Wuthnow, R. (1989) *Meaning and Moral Order: Explorations in Cultural Analysis*, Oakland, CA: University of California Press.

Wuthnow, R.J. (2011) "Taking Talk Seriously: Religious Discourse as Social Practice," *Journal for the Scientific Study of Religion*, 1(50): 1–21.

Wuthnow, R. (2020) *What Happens When We Practice Religion? Textures of Devotion in Everyday Life*, Princeton, NJ: Princeton University Press.

Yamane, D. (2000) "Narrative and Religious Experience," *Sociology of Religion*, 61(2): 171–89. doi: 10.2307/3712284.

Yanow, D., and Schwartz-Shea, P. (2014) *Interpretation and Method: Empirical Research Methods and the Interpretive Turn*, New York: Routledge.

1

Making Sense of Queer Christian Lives

Jodi O'Brien

> Queer Christians wrestle with dominant narratives, deviate from social scripts, and resist condemnation to a life without hope for loving partnerships. (King, 2021)

Religion is a living, dynamic sociocultural entity through which people make sense of themselves and the worlds they inhabit. Religiosity is a lived experience subject always to interpretation, one's own, as well as the outside observer. An interpretivist lens onto the lives and experiences of queer Christians highlights the significance of situated cultural contexts in understanding collective social change as well as individual sense-making. An interpretive framework also reveals the complexities of supposedly dominant or hegemonic institutions, such as religion, as sources of both inclusion and exclusion, of meaningful self-understanding and simultaneous oppression. Interpretive analyses explore the sources of the scripts or narrative frameworks that queer Christians draw from in constructing an oppositional self, the variation among the self-stories that emerge from grappling with these tensions, and the subsequent transformation in dominant narratives and social relations. In this chapter, I explore the vastly expanding repertoire of narratives through which LGBTQ Christians make sense of themselves and their lives. I also reflect here on how one queer sociologist, me, has been troubled into an immensely expanded awareness through engaging with queer Christians who are (re)naming their place in scriptures, families, congregations, and politics.[1]

This story begins in the mid-1990s when I happened into the nascent "open and affirming" movement taking shape in several mainline Protestant congregations. My curiosity had been piqued by gay and lesbian Catholics and Mormons marching in Pride parades in major urban cities. At the time, onlookers didn't really know what to make of these folk marching with pride for both their queerness and their religiosity. Some viewers even booed. Who were these people, I wondered? Politically, this was a moment of extreme antipathy between Christians and queers: Christian charismatics such as Anita Bryant and Jerry Falwell had ascended to national prominence in their demonization of homosexuality and their claims that AIDS was God's revenge for lives lived in perversion. Meanwhile, queer activists were publicly outing closeted religious leaders, loudly denouncing organized religion as synonymous with oppression and repression, and labeling religious practices as deluded. Who were these self-described queer Christians trying to straddle this divide, seemingly stigmatized on both sides?

Sensing a potential research opportunity, I applied for and was granted a seed "fund for the advancement of the discipline" by the American Sociological Association. I didn't have much to go on at the time. The "homosexuality" question had been in active play in Protestant congregations since the 1960s, but with little attention from sociologists. The literature was scant and consisted mostly of first-person accounts of struggling with same-sex attraction while trying to maintain a faith tradition (Bouldrey, 1995); calls for reconciliation with the "exile" (Fortunato, 1982; McNeill, 1988), and some academic forays into "queering" religion (Bernstein, 1997; Comstock, 1997). In religious studies, there was a smattering of case studies of congregations grappling with the question of homosexuality (for example, Hartmann, 1996; Gill, 1998). Psychology had a slightly more robust literature, but the focus was on shame, mental health, and self-esteem, with the general conclusion being that gay and lesbian Christians suffered lower self-esteem and more mental health issues as a result of being cast off from their religious communities (see: Rodriquez, 2001).

Unbeknownst to me when I began my own research in 1995, a massive wave of both academic and activist interest in "queering Christianity" was just beginning to form. Pulled by the tides of a rising Christian Right "moral majority" movement, this wave began to crest in the late 1990s and came crashing down to create new shores of awareness and affirmation that have significantly reshaped the political and cultural landscape in the two decades since. As sociologist Tina Fetner observes, the 1990s union of the religious Right and the Republican Party and its pronounced anti-gay agenda charted the subsequent course of LGBTQ activism, including the focus on marriage equality (Fetner, 2008). This turning tide has flooded scholarship, politics, and lives with richly nuanced ways of understanding the experience of being queer and Christian. LGBTQ-supportive faith-based political movements, the articulation of queer theologies, the proliferation of multiple ways of being queer and Christian, and the rise of formal affirmative statements by mainline Protestant churches are some of the notable streams that have emerged in the past 20 years. Internet technology has also been a significant driver in generating new directions and opening new possibilities for queer Christians. But when I embarked on my original research journey, all this was yet to come.

In this chapter, I describe some of the shifting narratives of self-understanding that have emerged among queer Christians in the past two decades, specifically, apologist and mosaic/radical inclusion scripts. These narratives of reconciliation reflect sociohistorical contexts and are enacted through individual engagement with specific reference groups that serve to authorize or legitimate different ways to be queer and Christian. I also explore briefly the recursive relationship between the availability or source of scripts, self-understanding, and self-presentation. A central thread woven into this chapter is a consideration of how my own self-understanding, and my subsequent scholarship, have been shaped by this journey of self-articulation through tension and contradiction.

Shifting narratives

Writing in the early 1980s about his patients and his own experiences, psychotherapist John Fortunato observed that Christianity is a total meaning system; it provides a complete ontology for understanding the world and one's place in it. According to this system, there is no place for the homosexual. We are exiles who are "spun off" with no hope of redemption (Fortunato, 1982; and see: O'Brien, 2004). Fortunato describes this exile as the "gay predicament." One cannot be a good Christian and also be openly, actively queer. Until recently, for those of us who came into self-understanding through the script of Christianity, the realization that we might be sexually or gender nonconforming presented an irreconcilable quandary – how are we to know ourselves if our central system of meaning rejects us? When I began my research in 1995, I was interested in how active, LGBTQ Christians made sense of themselves and their place within a story in which they were, according to the dominant narrative, utterly "spun off" from the possibility of salvation (Fortunato, 1982).

My own interest was in understanding a self-conflict that I personally couldn't make sense of. The options for the young Christian coming out at the time, as I was aware of them, included re-narrating religion as oppressive and fleeing its binding chains, or remaining closeted and accepting the cloak of shame imposed by the Christian narrative of homosexual acts as sin. In *Telling Sexual Stories* sociologist Ken Plummer (1995) observes that coming out stories are a discursive experience that provide camaraderie among people whose queer lives often place them at odds with family and community. Stories about the anguish of leaving religion and being abandoned by family were a common part of my own coming out experience and served as an entrée into a new gay flock. Derisive, judgmental talk about those who stayed in the church and remained closeted was common in cultivating new gay friendships and served to establish a situated identity that acknowledged these conflicting narrative boundaries. Within these "out" circles, there was a subset of folk whose self-understanding remained deeply tied up with the anger and pain of being ejected from their childhood galaxy of meaning. They became the "anti-religion" activists, keeping the church firmly within their hearts and minds, but as a symbol of fierce resistance. I was part of another subset who wanted mostly just to move on and put religion behind us, to not let it take up any more space in our self-story. Thus, when I encountered these doubly proud queer Christians, I really had no idea how to make sense of them; there was no place for them in my story.

In addition to my limited personal experience, my initial foray into the field of queer Christianity was marked by illiteracy in the scholarship of religion. The sociology of religion that I encountered in the early 1990s focused on macro-level sociopolitical aspects of religion. Religiosity, or individual-level experiences in faith-based communities was, like the sociology of sexualities, marginal to mainstream sociology. I wrote an entire dissertation on the Mormon "spirit of cooperation" without any formal training in religiosity. I also neglected to note anywhere in that dissertation my own cultural background as someone raised in Mormonism. This omission of subject position would be unthinkable now, but at the time reflected the stalwart discourse of researcher objectivity in which I had been trained (O'Brien, 2009). Although it's embarrassing to look back on now, I carried two assumptions into my initial fieldwork that reflected this illiteracy: the normative belief that religiosity is the equivalent of being conservative, and the notion that my own religious background had no bearing on my scholarly work.

My hubris and lack of insight rendered me ill-prepared to talk with the first openly gay, actively Christian folks who agreed to be interviewed. Using a narrative culled from the interpretive social psychological framework I was using at the time, I asked subjects to explain how they "managed" the "double stigma" of being gay and Christian (for example, Goffman, 1963). The first three interviewees each expressed bewilderment at the question, one even remarking, "I'm not sure what you mean by double stigma, but if you mean this contradiction in my life, well, it defines me." I knew after those first interviews that I was missing something, that I wasn't getting it. Troubled, I backed away to grapple with my own sense that I was imposing a narrative on these folks that simply didn't make sense to them. These reflections led me to consider, perhaps for the first time in my academic life, my own relationship to religion and the narrowness of my own coming-out story. From this inside-out place of reflection, I began to hear something I'd been missing in my conversations with these gay Christians: I *am* the contradiction; I *live* the contradiction; this contradiction *defines* me. This realization reoriented me and enabled me to enter more fully into what I eventually came to understand as the characteristic discourse of the queer Christians I encountered.

Energized by this new insight, I returned to interviewing, this time asking simply, "How do you experience the contradiction of being Christian and gay?" I was amazed to find that people could talk for hours about this without additional prompting. Contradiction (and its companions, tension and complexity) was the core of the narrative through which the gay Christians I encountered made sense of themselves and guided their lives. As I wrote about subsequently in "Wrestling the Angel of Contradiction" (O'Brien, 2004), a narrative of embracing contradiction as a *raison d'être* shaped not only self-understanding, but served as a discursive orientation for interpersonal relationships within congregations and, eventually, as an organizing basis for congregational shifts toward an open and affirming position (O'Brien, 2005; see also: Thumma and Gray, 2004).

Rewriting the script

In a story centered on procreative, binary "gender complementary" as *the* path to salvation, there is no place for the aberrant homosexual.[2] Taking a page from the American Psychiatric Association, by the early 1980s many mainline Christian denominations had shifted the role of the homosexual from "sinner" to "afflicted," but the homosexual remained irrevocably "disordered" and the call was still to celibacy and denouncement of one's feelings (Conrad and Schneider, 1980). How does someone who has been cast as "sinner," or "afflicted," and/or "inherently disordered" rewrite their place in this script, without actually jettisoning the entire script (which is what I and many like me had done)? Through 60 in-depth interviews followed by three years of ethnographic immersion in congregations, I learned that "embracing contradiction" was a conceptual pivot that enabled both individuals and congregations to rewrite the prevailing script.

Many queer Christians report simultaneous feelings in late adolescence of intense spiritual longing or awakening and same gender attraction. They describe this time in their lives as one of deep anguish, an experience of "wrestling with the angels" that represent their contradictory selves. Steps along the path to embracing this contradiction include an initial phase of pleading with God to "cure" the homosexuality, followed by some kind of realization in line with Christian logic that if God is perfect, and God is love, then there must be a place of acceptance for the homosexual. From here, several possibilities open up for (re)writing oneself: one organizing logic is to embrace a life of celibacy by recognizing oneself as "afflicted" with a cross to carry that requires discipline and self-sacrifice in order to receive special love and acceptance. The queer Christians I met came to a different realization, that of being called to live fully into their contradiction as a kind of martyr or Christian soldier sent to force fellow Christians to practice radical acceptance (O'Brien, 2004).

Although it wasn't available to me at the time, sociologists Tom DeGloma and Erin Johnston (2019) posit a process of "cognitive migration" that usefully describes the journey undertaken by queer Christians, a journey that includes an "awakening," "self-actualization," and a "quest." The logic of radical inclusivity is deeply embedded in Christian biblical (New Testament) stories of Christ's life among the margins of society. Interpreted this way, queers are in company with lepers, and the poor, and mistreated as those most deserving of Christ's love and most emblematic of the gospels' message. Centering on this truth and recasting oneself as walking in the margins with Jesus is a powerful awakening that serves as the basis for a cognitive migration which is then actualized through confrontations with family and church community members demanding that they recognize and affirm you as God's intended creation. This new self-understanding becomes increasingly more articulated, and often more political, as individuals speak out against their "exile" and develop a logic of radical inclusion grounded in principles of Christian love and acceptance.

Queer Christians who remain in church communities that aren't fully welcoming describe a "calling" or quest to educate and move fellow Christians toward compassion and reconciliation. Collectively, for congregations to embrace this narrative of acceptance and affirmation requires grappling with a long-standing tension that is a distinguishing characteristic of different denominations: beliefs and practices centered in an unchanging biblical authority (as interpreted by clergy), or a "living" theology that is moved by the mysteries of God and centered in the practice of unconditional love. The active presence of queer Christians claiming the position of God's gift or sign has forced congregations to wrestle with this tension directly. The result has been an "open and affirming" movement whereby congregations have explicitly rewritten their charters around a living, dynamic theology centered in unconditional love. This movement has been driven by awakened queer Christians whose self-actualization revolves around ongoing reconciliation within their own church community and who see this "labor" of "troubling" exclusionary Christian beliefs and practices as their quest (O'Brien, 2005).

Reconciliation scripts

The proliferation of the internet in the early 2000s ushered in a new day for queer Christianity and coalesced a myriad of emergent reconciliation stories into recognizable narrative fields. The seeds sown by early questioners-turned-activists grew into a full-fledged social movement with the availability of online communications. The communicative density of internet networks has provided questioning Christians with an abundance of accessible alternative stories and critical theologies by which to make sense of their own experiences. Books, online chat groups, listserves, and even online dating sites now cater to queer Christians. An "army" of academic scholarship has arisen in tandem with this outpouring of queer Christian experience. One especially significant offshoot is queer theology, of which there are several branches. Queer theologian Linn Tonstad provides a compelling review of the many contemporary iterations of queer theology (Tonstad, 2018). Despite such a plethora of possibilities within theological scholarship, most queer-identified Christians pick up only snippets of these new theologies as they make their way through the numerous blogs and books now available. These snippets are then woven into broad narrative arcs, each with distinctive scripts for how to be a queer Christian.

Although there are many variations on these scripts, I find it heuristically useful to divide them into two broad arcs: apologetics and mosaic expansionists/radical inclusionists. My criteria of distinction between these two arcs is authorizing audience or reference group, and narrative source of legitimation or truth.[3] "Apologetics" refers to a reasoned argument justifying the existence of homosexuality within Christian cosmology (typically using the Bible as authority). In other words, queer apologetics is the use of biblical texts to justify and argue for queer inclusion. It seeks to reconcile being LGBTQ and being Christian as noncontradictory, while still subject to biblical interpretations of morality.

As the term implies, "mosaic expansionists" believe truth exists in multiple forms and reject the established church as the ultimate source of authority. Truth is to be found in the *practice* of Christian values as expressed in lived experience and radical inclusion. These distinct orientations offer differing logics for self-understanding, behavior, and communal engagement, and have ushered in distinct social movement paths. In other words, the migratory path of self-awakening, actualization, and quest leads in different directions with distinct implications for individual life course, relationships, communities, and theologies.

Apologetics

Apologetic strategies argue that queer identity is not inherently sinful and make the case for the inherent compatibility of LGBTQ people and Christianity. The intended audience is fellow Christians who require a biblically authorized identity as the basis for reconciliation. In other words, this is an insider-focused logic of appeals whereby inclusion and belonging are bestowed through the legitimating discourses of the dominant group. Among congregations that accept the logic of a biblically legitimate queer

identity, there is a significant division regarding the question of sexual activity –
celibacy or not. This division has coalesced into two camps, each with its own
derivative narrative on how to be queer and Christian. The terms "Side A"
and "Side B" have become popular parlance in online spaces for denoting this
division and are commonly referenced, including among clergy with websites
seeking to understand and support their homosexual flock. Side B follows
a traditional Christian logic whereby it is not a sin to be gay, but there is no
biblical authorization for same gender sexual relationships, therefore celibacy
is the only acceptable reconciliation of one's queer sexual orientation and
faith. The Side A approach emphasizes God's love and desire for all people
to be happy and fulfilled. Accordingly, these folks see same-gender sexual
relationships, especially as expressed through committed attachments similar
to marriage, as permissible and a reflection of God's grace.

Historically, gender complementarity and the gift of procreation undertaken
through the sacramental union of marriage are the pivotal logic of inclusion
or exclusion among congregations grappling with the question of what to do
with LGBTQ members. Several of the people I interviewed initially would
now be considered Side A queer Christians. Queer Christians finding voice
in the 1980s and 1990s were focused on acceptance of the homosexual person
as whole and wholesome, neither sinner nor afflicted. While this approach,
a precursor to Side A Christians, didn't advocate celibacy, it did downplay
sexuality. The subsequent push for same-gender marriage grew out of this
narrative logic and was intended to demonstrate the sameness of LGBTQ
couples as loving, family-oriented, Christian citizens. The slogan at the time
might have been: "We're here, we're queer, let's all go to church."

Another set of congregations wrestling with the same questions, concluded
that there is no biblical authority permitting same-gender sexual activity,
but that they too are called to love the homosexuals in their midst. This
variation has been codified in the current Side B narrative and is manifest
in churches that call themselves "welcoming" but not "affirming." These
congregations would strongly distinguish themselves from the far religious
Right, but politically have tended to join the movement to block or
overturn marriage equality. A simple Google search produces a multitude of
resources for living a celibate life. A sampling of titles conveys the dominant
themes: *Spiritual Friendship: Finding Love in the Church as a Celibate Gay*;
Washing and Waiting: Reflections on Christian Faithfulness and Homosexuality;
Single, Gay, Christian: A Personal Journey of Faith and Sexual Identity; and *Costly
Obedience: What We Can Learn from the Celibate Gay Christian Community*. The
central narrative in this logic of organizing Christianity and nonconforming
sexual attraction is that this is one's personal cross to bear and, through
patience and obedience, the heavenly rewards will be rich.

From a secular perspective, this conditional welcoming may seem little
different from earlier narratives; however, this turn has done much to remove

the stigma of queerness and opened up new possibilities for inclusion in queer cosmology. Academics and activists tend to render Side B Christians or celibate queer Christians as deluded or unaware of their oppression in being set apart by their faith communities. A common orienting hypothesis in papers I have been asked to review is that Side B Christians suffer lower self-esteem. Researchers whose findings suggest otherwise sometimes seem suspicious or doubtful of their participants' self-reporting. But from the perspective of many of these individuals, a biblically sanctioned homosexual identity has removed many layers of anguish and exclusion. This authorized identity releases them from the grip of an irreconcilable contradiction and allows them to leave the closet and throw off the cloak of shame that had, previously, defined their faith existence. The logic of celibacy makes room for active engagement in their faith community. Mental health professionals have begun to tout the benefits of a narrative that provides for an existence beyond sin, a pathway to "embracing the exile" (Fortunato, 1982). Notably, many Christian churches open to celibate homosexuality also now actively denounce gay conversion therapies as harmful and ineffective. The logic of an authorized gay celibacy has made it possible for them to reject these conversion therapies and, instead, to provide training workshops for clergy on how best to acknowledge and support queer congregants.

In "How Big is Your God?" (O'Brien, 2005) I described the drawn-out process congregations undertook in the early days of the open and affirming movement in determining whether and how to be LGBTQ-inclusive. This process, sometimes as long as three years, revolved almost entirely around the question of sexuality, specifically whether same-gender sexuality, expressed through a committed union, was in any way permitted in the canon of Christianity. Those congregations that eventually authored open and affirming charters pieced together a narrative that holds that the Bible really says nothing definitive about homosexuality but is very clear about the sacrament of marriage. Further, God's love is beyond our full knowing, but we are called to practice it to the best of our ability through full inclusion of all types of people. Accordingly, queer folks, especially those living in committed unions, must somehow fall within God's grace (O'Brien, 2005). As several scholars of social movements have observed, the enthusiastic participation of these open and affirming congregations was a tipping point for the eventual passage of marriage equality laws (Moon, 2004; Fetner, 2008).

Mosaic expansion/radical inclusion

In contrast to apologetic strategies which look for legitimizing authority within existing church doctrine, another approach centers on the mystery or unknowingness of God. Ontologically, this approach emphasizes that the desires we experience reflect the vast potential of an emergent mosaic theology of relationships that transcends gender and sexual binaries and is not necessarily limited to monogamous attachments.[4] In this narrative arc, authority is anchored in embodied, lived experience actualized through ecclesiastical, community and (chosen) family structures. Truth is forged through wrestling the tensions of desire and faith. In this reconciliation we come to know God's love and intentions for us. The truth that *emerges* through lived religious experience may or may not be reflected in formal systems of beliefs and practices anchored in sacred texts, maintained by trained elites, and conducted in official houses of structured worship (Talvacchia et al, 2019).

The mosaic aspect of this approach reflects not only a "welcoming and affirming" stance, but is also a reference to being in step with science and real embodied lives. As one nonbinary, queer Christian I interviewed, who locates themselves in this camp puts it: "God wrote the book of nature before the Bible, and we need to learn to read these other signs – bodies and nature." In this logic, sexuality, and especially gender, are not only nonbinary, but the lived reality of experiences, especially expressed through queer and transgender lives, suggests that God's creation of bodies may be more of a mosaic. For Tonstad, "God's love radically transgresses every boundary ... Christianity is at its heart a radical, boundary-transgressing message of God's love, which includes all without distinction." Echoing common logics in queer theology, Tonstad's rationale for this is that the nature of Christ " 'transgresses' the boundary between divine and human" and that "Christ's body is symbolically multigendered" (Tonstad, 2018: pp. 32–3).

The idea of queer Christians as especially spiritual, holy, magical, or sacred and holding the power to transform religion is a prolific narrative that has launched numerous queer ministries in the past decade. A core belief among this emerging group of pastors and practitioners is that queer Christians are more bodily aware, communitarian, connected and relational in healthy ways that reflect early Christian communities and teachings. The idea of nonbinary bodies as divinely created and endowed with a specialness of spirit and insight is especially compelling for many transgender and gender nonbinary Christians. Transpirituality is an emerging branch of queer Christianity rooted in the idea of "transbilliance" which posits transgender and gender nonconforming people as magical, sacred, creative beings with the potential to transform the world.

Within this story, the queer Christian features as a modern-day mystic with a special holiness and insight that will transform and revitalize Christianity. The way forward in this quest is radical inclusivity, which requires a capacity to dance with difference, uncertainty, and contradiction. Gender and sexual nonbinary Christians present others in their faith communities with the opportunity to practice this dance, with its ultimate promise of transcendent grace. This narrative re-posits the common contemporary refrain of tolerance predicated on "We're not sinners, we're born this way," into a challenge of: Born what way? What is God showing you with our presence? How are you being invited to stretch your own binary ideas and to practice radical love for all God's creation? Instead of, how can the church find a way to legitimate and accept us, these questions coalesce into a focus on what the church can learn from us. Current book titles – such as *Queer Virtue: What LGBTQ People Know About Life and Love and How it Can Revitalize Christianity*; *Outside the Lines: How Embracing Queerness Will Transform Your Faith*; and *Queer Christianities: Lived Religion in Transgressive Forms* – reflect this orientation and actively reposition the queer Christian as teacher, guide, or shepherd.

In their introduction to *Queer Christianities: Lived Religion in Transgressive Forms*, the editors posit three similar arcs to those I outline here and which they describe as a "trinity of states of queer Christian life: celibacies, matrimonies, promiscuities" (Talvacchia et al, 2014, p. 3). They note that these "states of lived religion" reflect the three common relationship trajectories in Christian form: entering into a sacramentally blessed union, maintaining celibacy, or embarking beyond these known and accepted relational forms into "promiscuities." Their opening statement is suggestive of their place in the "promiscuities" or what I am calling the mosaic camp: " 'Queering' Christianity may be necessary today not because Christianity is unqueer but because it has forgotten its own radical queerness. The sexual nonconformists' experience is the one that forces all Christians to acknowledge the parlous gift that is sexuality itself" (Talvacchia et al, 2014, p. 3).

This narrative revision of a church that has strayed from its original orientation was a common theme in my 1995 interviews. This earlier wave of queer Christian activists recast themselves as saviors sent to "force" all Christians to reckon with their intolerances and to help them find their way back to the fullness, the bigness of God's love. The notable variation in this contemporary narrative is the emphasis on sexuality. Talvacchia and her colleagues continue:

Many queer religious people find their bodily and their spiritual experiences to be the twin lodestars of their lives. The non-normative character of their desires and relationships makes them unusually aware of their own agency as religious people … it is in the crucible of actual lives that religious practices and ideas thrive or wither, it is also in this crucible that religion is recast and reinvented. (Talvacchia et al, 2014, p. 7)

This logic of practicing radical inclusivity as a living manifestation of Christ's ministry is accompanied by an identity narrative that holds that queer

Christians' souls, because they are forged in the margins, are creatively divine and intended as guides. The underlying logic of the sacredness of liminality can be found in much Christian discourse: God dwells in the in-between or liminal spaces. Precisely because of their experiences navigating marginality and oppression, queer people emerge from this crucible as divine spirit guides, uniquely sighted with the way forward for a revitalized church. A companion theme to this is community (rather than doctrine) as the source of legitimizing authority.

Reconciliation scripts in context

When I teach "Wrestling the Angel of Contradiction" (O'Brien, 2004) in my interpretive social psychology course, I remind students that when I was conducting this research, the internet was sparsely networked and not widely available. In other words, a young Christian anguishing over their feelings of same gender attraction could not just Google "gay Christian." For most of my students, it's incomprehensible that Google didn't always exist (let alone serve as a verb). Similarly, queer characters were not notably available in the media (Netflix didn't exist, and Ellen Degeneres hadn't come out!). When we were represented, it was as stock stereotypes played for a laugh, or as creepy villain, or, very occasionally as the object of pity. Politically, we were tropes cast either as morally defective beings from which others deserved protection (especially children) or flamboyant characters (drag queens) and militant strategists (man-hating dykes) with an agenda that threatened to topple the empire. Where in these narratives could the queer Christian find a place for themselves as the emblem of God's love and grace that they aspired to be?

An enduring question from my early research is the sources of cognitive awakening and (re)scripting that these queer Christians articulated for themselves in order to find an identity other than the cast-off sinner. At the time I was conducting this research, it was very unlikely, especially in suburban or rural areas, that these folks had access to others like them, especially as guides or sources for reinterpreting the shame/sinner narratives they were brought up with. For me, one of the most fascinating aspects of this early research is the way in which a critical mass of queer Christians *individually* rewrote themselves into their Christian narrative as divine hero-activists rather than damned perverts. They did so in isolation from others like them, but drawing from the same source material, which they similarly re-visioned in new directions using the same narrative logic and resulting in a collectively new identity for themselves. It is a fool's task to try to ascertain the determining factors between those who, at the time and given the available scripts, chose a narrative of shame/affliction and consigned themselves to a closet versus those who paved the way for the affirmation and reconciliation movement. Nonetheless, I continue to be fascinated by this distinction and especially the process of personal cognitive migration.

Retrospectively, the folk I interviewed and those I talk with today who came of age and came out in those earlier decades all recall at least one significant other who made them feel something beyond shame; someone in a position of authority who modelled for them Christianity as unconditional love and mirrored back acceptance and affirmation. Some people also recalled having come across a book or hearing a sermon that raised compelling issues about their original beliefs and prompted them to begin questioning. For instance, one interviewee recalled being introduced to a womanist theological interpretation of the book of Genesis that led her to wonder just how much other "patriarchal misinformation" she had ingested. A question for the interpretive sociologist is the sources that inspire revised narratives and subsequent cognitive migrations. The development of an oppositional consciousness requires more than simply realizing, "I've had enough;" it requires re-writing one's place in the script. The queer Christians I engaged with manifest what might be called a "post-oppositional consciousness" – a sense of self-understanding that not only reflects rewriting their role as sinner/afflicted, but that moves beyond hating and othering the oppressor to a discourse that enables them to embrace their "oppressors" and to see themselves as "liberating" agents for all. It is worth considering the extent to which this liberatory, inclusive self-understanding is intrinsic to the logics of a (re-oriented) religious discourse.

Beyond contradiction?

Another direction for deeper inquiry is the degree of struggle or self-conflict experienced by contemporary queer Christians in a supposedly more accepting environment. Recently, several sociologists engaged in research with Christians who identify as queer have observed that their interviewees report minimal to no conflict or self-contradiction. Sociology of religion scholar, Todd Fuist writes that he was surprised by stories he was hearing among friends and interview subjects in which they claimed to be wholly included in their religious communities (Fuist, 2016). He suggests that the scholarship on queer Christianity would benefit from a stronger focus on the "sociotemporal context" in which queer Christians are situated. Fuist's observations are a useful corrective to research that assumes trans-contextual antagonism between religiosity and queerness. Indeed, the proliferation of open and affirming churches, the strong faith-based activism for marriage equality, and the expanding presence of healthy LGBTQ people featured in popular media reflect significant inroads into mainstream culture among queer folk in general and some queer Christians in particular. Accordingly, it makes sense that many current LGBTQ folk practicing Christianity are finding a welcoming spiritual home in their congregational communities. As religion scholar Melissa Wilcox (2020) has noted, "open and affirming" has become a sort of brand signifying general liberal attitudes with regard to a host of wedge issues such as abortion and women clergy. In the marketplace of religion, people are choosing congregations that bear this brand as a reflection of their own sociopolitical self-understanding. Interrelationally, expressing active allyship with LGBTQ people reinforces this self-understanding and animates the church "brand."

While I agree with these observations, I am concerned that in the rush to assume that acceptability and inclusion have become the new normal, we risk eclipsing groups who continue to be extremely vulnerable to Christian-based exclusionary practices that inflict considerable spiritual, psychological, and often material damage. My own ongoing research and experience indicate that queer-identified Christian youth as well as people whose significant family and community ties have been forged in conservative Christian environments continue to be extremely conflicted. The salience of significant others and reference groups is especially pronounced in understanding the very different experiences among these people and those interviewed by Fuist (who himself is hinting at the same with his concept of "sociotemporal" context).

Regarding the observation among some scholars that many contemporary queer Christians report experiencing very little self and interpersonal contradiction in their families and faith communities, my working hypothesis is that involvement in specific congregations with robust reconciliation scripts provide family and community members with narratives for inclusion and affirmation. Conversely, members of more conservative congregations cling to narratives of sin, affliction, and damnation; this is the referential context in which queer Christians, especially youth, are struggling to find a place for themselves. I also hypothesize that parents and family members who may not be particularly religious, but whose only moral basis of understanding gender and sexuality is generalized cultural Christian narratives, are also highly likely to interpret same gender attraction or nonconforming gender behavior through the trope of queer = sin/afflicted. In the absence of alternative affirming narratives and positive encounters with LGBTQ people, this trope pits the supposed excesses of modern, urban cultures against "better days" and serves as a basis for a generalized rejection of those who are unfamiliar and feared (see: Stein, 2002). This line of analysis emphasizes the significance of reference groups and available scripts which serve as the interpretive basis for making sense of difference, even among family members. Sociotemporal context is an important aspect in understanding the varying experiences of inclusion/exclusion among queer Christians, but it can result in explanations framed in terms of class, race, and geographical differences that simply don't hold up empirically. Intersecting sociotemporal context with an interpretive/narrative analysis provides a more granular, robust, and accurate understanding of the different ways in which LGBTQ Christians and their families make sense of themselves. These scripts may be nuanced and complex, but they have considerable influence on how queer Christians cultivate self-understanding and move through the world.

The significance of affirmative communities

As an illustration of this intersectional analysis, consider LGBTQ youth. As a group, LGBTQ youth living in religious communities continue to be at significant risk for suicide, and these alarming rates are only the tip of the iceberg. Suicidal ideation is a surface expression of a submerged glacier of extreme fear, distress, anxiety, isolation, and low self-worth (O'Brien, 2018). Especially vulnerable are LGBTQ youth whose primary relationships are in religious communities. Psychologists use the term "minority stress syndrome" to refer to everyday interactional circumstances in which a person is not only made to feel different, but must relentlessly gauge and navigate safety, the right to expression, and making others comfortable in their presence. This emotional labor is most exhausting in situations in which the minoritized person is isolated from others who share their perspectives and experiences (for example, persons of color in predominantly white spaces). In such situations, the healthy person calibrates a resilient self by anchoring their sense of belonging in the groups with which they identify. In other words, despite exclusion from dominant groups, they experience a sense of interior home and belonging through family and community.

Parents and religious leaders are often the most significant source of self and social understanding for queer Christian youth. The message that there is no place for them in this constellation of family and community – other than self-erasure and/or a cloak of shame – is devastating. Cast adrift, they flay about in a sea of confusion trying to make sense of themselves. The anguish of this struggle for self-understanding may be exacerbated by heightened visibility in popular culture and media. In the search for self-meaning beyond a narrative of sin and shame, the gulf between the family and church that are rejecting you and the lifestyle portrayed in commercially driven media may seem impossible to cross for a young person whose only understanding of that alternative world is a narrative of damnation as expressed by significant others. The contradiction of not being acceptable to those you are most closely connected to, while a larger world seems increasingly accepting but beyond your grasp, leaves these youth wondering: "What's so wrong with me?" Consequently, LGBTQ youth trying to come out in religious communities are at considerable risk of drowning in this sea of exclusion.

The good news, and an area worthy of consideration for interpretive sociologists interested in reconciliation narratives, is that faith-based community and educational environments that are welcoming and affirming often serve as a life raft for these youth. In recent years, I've had the opportunity to participate in a European Union Research Council-funded project launched by British interpretive sociologists, Yvette Taylor and Ria Snowden (Taylor and Snowden, 2014). Focused explicitly on queer-identified Christian youth, this project operates from the premise that recovery from the trauma of family and faith community stigma and rejection is most effective when youth are presented with alternative narratives for understanding themselves *within* their Christian context. In other words, when these youth experience the possibility of belonging with regard to reference groups that are salient for them and have the opportunity to engage with significant others who offer positive reflected appraisals – in this case, Christian-identified project leaders and peers – they are able to reimagine a more redeeming place for themselves within their existing cosmology.

Sociotemporal context and the articulated/actualized self

Listening to stories of queer Christians as they describe their experiences in grappling with the contradiction that defined their lives is profoundly moving for me. As I have learned more about these experiences, I've been compelled to revisit my Meadian approach to the "self as conversation" (Meltzer, 1966) and begin thinking in terms of the self as a conversation managing tensions and contradictions. Who we are, how we see and experience and express ourselves, reflects our *process* of wrestling contradictions and conflict. We are this *process*. Our internal dialogues and interpersonal engagements are manifestations of the scripts wherein we find self-meaning and our navigation of multiple, shifting, often contradictory reference groups and significant others. This exploration has opened me to the work of Gloria Anzaldúa (1987) who posits that those occupying multiple, marginal social positions, the ones who traverse social borderlands, have a "mestiza consciousness." This mixed or multiple consciousness is characterized by greater flexibility and a capacity for holding and engaging with contradiction. The result is a greater self-reflexivity (those in subordinated subject positions can't take much for granted) and a more "articulated" self-understanding (O'Brien, 2022), which is then actualized through the quest of bringing awareness to others.

In a dissertation on leadership formation, my colleague Eddy Salazar (2008) found that in Jesuit universities with strong reconciliation narratives integrated into the curriculum, LGBTQ students were significantly more likely than their peers to self-identify as leaders and to be involved in leadership activities on campus and in their communities. Ironically, the Jesuit emphasis on social justice becomes part of the quest narrative of these students as they come into their own self-accepting awareness and actualize it through campus involvement. As I described earlier in the chapter, this sense of a special calling to lead others in radical inclusion is a common aspect of the cognitive migration of nascent queer Christians. Many of the queer Christians I have come to know since I first began my inquiries in the 1990s describe a process not only of self and community reconciliation through shifting narratives, but a sense of being more self-aware and compassionate. They attribute this heightened consciousness to continuous navigation of many different and contradictory relational fields. Echoing Anzaldúa, linguist Kim Young Yun describes a similar "heightened existential alertness" among bilingual people who are constantly crossing cultural and linguistic boundaries (Yun, 2000: p. 5). This continuous code-switching requires an attentiveness not typically required of those whose monocultural or hegemonic position enables them to take interactional narratives and routines for granted. A consequence of this code-switching for self-understanding and interaction is a more articulated awareness of the rules of engagement and one's place in them. While this awareness does not alleviate the very real oppression of religious-based gender and sexuality regimes, it does give the self-actualized queer Christian a sense of liberation (and the resulting felt calling or quest to liberate others).

Self-actualization quests and social movements

A full inventory of the scope and diversity of "welcoming and affirming" social movements that have arisen in the past two decades is beyond the scope of this chapter, but a unifying theme is the recursivity between self-articulation through reconciliation, and subsequent actualization through congregational social action. Although apologist and radical inclusionist narratives offer divergent reconciliation logics and locate legitimating authority differently, both involve a quest for self-actualization that is realized through communal education. Whether advocating for inclusion within doctrinal interpretations that accept all God's children (celibate or in committed unions), or pressing for radical theological change as fomented by those who have been traditionally excluded, both narrative arcs call the queer Christian into action for congregational change. As I've noted throughout the chapter, the social movements that emerged as a result of these engagements have vastly expanded access to and awareness of reconciliation scripts for individual LGBTQ Christians. The emergent action is also having considerable effect on churches and theologies. By way of conclusion, I offer some observations on the collective "cognitive migrations" transpiring among contemporary US Christian churches. These are broad-stroke insights intended to inform more in-depth research by including a focus on narratives of reconciliation and the different migratory pathways their logic points to.

One of the most notable recent examples is the marriage equality movement, the success of which ultimately came through significant support from multifaith church coalitions across the US. The architecture for marriage equality was erected in the 1990s by self-described "log cabin Republicans" seeking to overturn various anti-gay agendas by highlighting the citizen-oriented Christian family values and lifestyles of "good" gays. Advocates such as gay Christian writer Andrew Sullivan wrote prolifically on the affinities between "upstanding, family-oriented" gay Christians and the church. Zeroing in on the logic of a committed loving couple as central to both religious and civic wellbeing, Sullivan and others like him sought to combat and overturn the notion of the promiscuous, flamboyant urban gay. Congregations wrestling with their own affirmation tensions understood this as an opportunity to extend inclusion to lesbian and gay members by allowing them to participate in God's plan of committed unions.

Many radical queer Christians have expressed tension around the idea of marriage equality. As a basis for state-conferred rights and benefits, they appreciate the necessity of the movement, but as a basis for inclusion, marriage – gay or straight – is deemed an exclusionary practice for parsing out belonging along traditional lines of sexuality, companionate love, and nuclear family values (O'Brien, 2007). Similar to general apologist or radical inclusionist logic, the dividing line is between inclusion within existing traditions and institutions or a call to dismantle these in favor of more wide-reaching inclusion. My own observation is that some of the most noteworthy current shifts are occurring within supposed Side B (or celibacy) churches as a result of the more broadly inclusive sociotemporal context unfolding around them. Despite the logic of marriage equality as reflecting an apologist stance, and perhaps because one consequence of this has been increased visibility, association, and acceptance, many churches are feeling a pressure to pivot toward more inclusion.

Recently, even theologically top-down religions such as Catholicism and Latter-day Saints (LDS, Mormons) have indicated a more welcoming stance. Premised in the 1970s revisionist logic as articulated in the Vatican II Catechism, homosexuality is no longer a sin, but an "affliction" that one is born with. Accordingly, fellow Catholics (in this case) are called to exercise tolerance and support, and the "afflicted" homosexual is called to a life of celibacy. For many years, this logic provided lesbian- and gay-identified Catholics with some measure of self-assurance that they were still part of God's plan and gave them the particular quest of redemption forged in the crucible of celibacy. More recently, amid the rise of marriage equality and against the backdrop of the clergy sex scandals, a new generation of Catholics are clamoring for wider acceptance and recognition. A handful of nuns and priests are overtly acknowledging their queerness: taking up discourses and practices intended to mark them as queer, while still maintaining their vows, including celibacy. For this group, celibacy is a sacred instrument of the priesthood, not a punishment or redemptive condition for nonconforming sexuality. Accordingly, they favor same gender marriage and families. Pope Francis recently garnered international attention with an utterance that monogamous, same-gender families deserve state recognition through domestic partnerships. Stopping short of "marriage" as blessed with the sacred sacraments, the Pope seems to be suggesting that queer couples should not be exiled to lives alone and that they deserve intimate relationships. Whether sex acts within these state-sanctioned relationships is to be condemned or condoned (or most likely ignored) will likely become a much- debated theological conundrum in Catholicism.

In 2018, the Latter-day Saints faced extreme criticism from within and extensive negative public denouncement following a decision of church authorities to exile same gender couples who legally married. Many church members were especially appalled that this decision included denying recognition to children of queer couples. Operating from a Side B logic, Mormon leaders faced the dilemma of acknowledging lesbians and gays in relationships, something that couldn't be conveniently ignored once the couples married. This harsh stance, which the church has subsequently backed away from officially, reflects an unfolding tension in apologist scripts: how much inclusion of the sexual deviant can be authorized? Not surprisingly, given that authority in these scripts resides with official doctrinal sources and those authorized to interpret the sources, the tension is played out as a division between increasingly restless congregants and church leaders and has become a wedge issue for these churches.

Within this field of conflict, many queer Catholics and Mormons and their supporters are amplifying the narrative of unconditional love and acceptance, and drawing on Christ's example of radical inclusion as a foundational principle. For these Christians, authority is still in church teachings; the battleground of truth is in who or what has the authority of interpretation. For Christians whose denominational legitimacy is premised on a divinely appointed living prophet or spokesperson (for example, the Pope or the LDS President) this presents a significant conundrum. The most vocal queer Catholics and Mormons use the logic of "conscience" and rely on the relational goodwill of local authorities (parish priests and lay ministers respectively) to push for emergent change. Still, these queer Christians are forging a self, albeit a resistant self, *within* the restrictive narrative as authorized by their official church. Their quest is to change the minds and hearts of those in charge. The logic that drives this narrative is that the edifice of the church and its leaders can be wrong about God's truth, but that there is an ultimate truth. For Mormons in particular, the recent history of denying full membership to persons of African descent serves as a profound example of a violent doctrinal wrong rooted in human prejudice, not spiritual truth.[5] Just as it took a few courageous leaders questioning the legitimacy of the LDS Church's limitations for its Black members, so now Church leaders must be persuaded to act with courage and to right these wrongs. This logic is a call for full inclusion within the existing LDS Church, not a call for theological change per se.[6]

One of the driving forces within these Side B churches is pressure from congregants who, themselves, are increasingly likely to have LGBTQ friends and/or family members. Taking a cue from contemporary social scripts that are now widely available, these members want their church to be more affirming. A recent report of sociopolitical tensions among Catholics in the Western US finds that members are increasingly disaffiliated with the Church as being "out of touch" with contemporary issues around gender and sexuality. Conversely, they are likely to feel more affiliation if their parish is involved in social justice activities around these issues. The resulting trend is increasing tension between church authorities and congregations, including parish priests, that are practicing inclusivity that may not be strictly in line with doctrinal teachings. This tension is playing out up the chain of Catholic hierarchy and revealing clear divisions at all levels of the Church.

My own sense is that among those churches inclined toward any version of being welcoming and affirming there is a migration toward increasingly radical inclusion rooted in a neo-liberation theology. Congregants who remain in these churches, regardless of gender and/or sexual expression, are increasingly aware of cultural shifts around inclusivity generally and find themselves caught up in a zeitgeist of critical self-examination. Consistent with narratives of Christian reconciliation, this self-examination is actualized through congregational reckonings. Similar to the forging crucible of contradiction wherein individual queer Christians find their divinity, when congregations grapple with the tensions of practicing inclusivity, they must hash out truth through tension and debate. It is this process itself, going deeper into fears and scapegoating, through which the community comes to practice a living, dynamic, radical inclusionary, always expanding path. It is in this dancing with tension and contradiction that individuals and congregations spin deeper into the mysteries of God. God is big, God is change. Within this recursive dynamic, members absorb narratives of inclusion, increase their own awareness and actualize it through congregational pressure to manifest greater inclusivity. Literal migration between churches – either to a church practicing an inclusivity that reflects the parishioner's own awakening, or to one that does not make these demands for self-reckoning, is one of the defining dynamics of contemporary membership in Christian churches.

In 2016, I participated in a working group of scholars and activists convened by Fordham University's School of Theology to address the theme, "Beyond Obergefell: LGBTQ People, Religious Communities, and the Possibilities of Reconciliation." In this gathering I saw evidence for an emerging hybrid of apologist/radical inclusive narratives fermenting in the collective acknowledgment of voices from the margins. Over three days of close engagement, our conversation ricocheted between testimonies of ongoing discrimination and the potential of queer theologies and ministries to transform these harmfully exclusionary beliefs and practices. Several participants were part of ministries and activist groups directly combating the psychological, material, and spiritual violence that many churches subject queer folk in their communities to, especially youth. As the gathering concluded, we collectively articulated the emergent conference theme as: "Colonialist Christian mythology no longer works and queer folk are inhabiting a new narrative that is ushering in epistemological change characterized by embodied, experiential knowing, and lived religious experience resulting in a pastoral rather than legalistic sexual ethics." Bishop Yvette Flunder, founder of the City of Refuge Church and known for her bold talking back and public shaming of other Black ministers whom she deems discriminatory, addressed the group in a closing keynote in which she repeatedly emphasized, "The time is *now.*" The time is now to throw over the "fragile patriarchy" and "rigid hierarchy" that, in her assessment, characterize many African American churches. "How can we have a healthy Christianity when it was taught to us through slavery?" she continued. In her analysis, the most discriminatory "iron fist" churches are trapped in an "oppression sickness" whereby oppressing others (specifically LGBTQ folk) supposedly props up an otherwise shaky patriarchal hierarchy. For Bishop Flunder, the daughter and a granddaughter of southern Baptist ministers, the only way out of this twisted legacy of white supremacy, the only way to fully embrace the culture of Christ without the oppressiveness of the church, is to celebrate and lead from the margins.[7]

In the conclusion to "How Big is Your God?" (O'Brien, 2005), I speculated that as individuals and congregations grappled with the challenges of inclusion for queer Christians, there would be a significant theological turn toward lived experience and unconditional love as a source of legitimating authority. While by no means a dominant Christian narrative (yet), the vast proliferation of open and affirming congregations that have arrived at their stance using this theological approach suggests that the narrative has troubled existing lines of authority considerably. Looking to the future, I note that an emerging and deeply resonant queer Christian narrative is rooted in the logic of liberation theology. In its original conception, liberation theology holds that God and scripture can only be known through the experiences and voices of the poor. Radical inclusion queer Christians are articulating what I see as a neo-liberation theology: the future is with those whose perspectives and voices are forged in the liminality of exclusion, erasure, and the struggle for gender and sexual sovereignty. These struggles generate a

39

politics of creativity outside the status quo and provide insight and wisdom in how to grapple with the "beautiful messiness" of human experience.[8]

Notes

[1]   Throughout this chapter I use the generally inclusive "queer" and "LGBTQ" interchangeably except in cases where religious groups do not acknowledge bisexual and/or transgender folk, or when the groups or individuals self-reference explicitly as gay or lesbian.

[2]   There is a robust critical feminist literature on "gender complementarism" as a persistent ideal in Christianity that purports the essential "complementary" differences between men and women as a basis for healthy family and social relations and institutions. See, for example, Marie Griffith, Kristen du Mez, and Sally Gallagher and Christian Smith.

[3]   For further discussion of "reference groups" see: Shibutani, T. (1955) "Reference Groups as Perspectives," *American Journal of Sociology*, 60(6): 562–9.

[4]   Queer Christians who hold this logic are sometimes referred to as "Side O" but the designation is not typically self-referential and is used more by self-referencing Side A and B queer Christians as a distinction.

[5]   For reasons not officially documented, the LDS Church prohibited men of Black African descent from holding the priesthood for more than a century. In 1978, notably as the civil rights movement became increasingly institutionalized, a prophetic revelation removed the restriction. No account was given at the time, but in 2003 the Church posted an essay stating that the earlier practice was rooted in racist human fallacy, not spiritual truth.

[6]   Jesuit priest, James Martin, provides a similar narrative for Catholics. The *New York Times* best-selling author and corporate businessman turned priest has a national reputation for tackling sticky issues in Catholicism with wit and grace. In his 2017 book, *Building a Bridge: How the Catholic Church and the LGBT Community Can Enter into a Relationship of Respect, Compassion, and Sensitivity*, he uses the image of a two-way bridge to invite Catholics and LGBT (his initials) folk to find common ground. Without actually upending official doctrine, but emphasizing the unassailable dignity of all persons, Martin's book has become a much-used tool among Catholic communities seeking reconciliation.

[7]   I'm grateful to one of the editors of this volume who noted the similarities in "Christianity as a template for the Hegelian dialectic of contradiction and reconciliation, for Marx's notion of the revolutionary class, and to a large extent for the revolution that is modernity itself."

[8]   Although more secular, a similar narrative is fomenting among BIPOC activists calling for racial equity and accountability: those whose lives are forged in the margins are not in need of saving; rather, they are the harbingers of liberation.

References

Anzaldúa, G. (1987) *Borderlands/La Frontera: The New Mestiza*, San Francisco: Aunt Lute.

Bernstein, M. (1997) "Celebration and Suppression: The Strategic Uses of Identity by the Lesbian and Gay Movement," *American Journal of Sociology*, 103(3): 531–65.

Bouldrey, B. (ed) (1995) *Wrestling with the Angel: Faith and Religion in the Lives of Gay Men*, New York: Riverhead Books.

Comstock, G.D., and Henking, S.E. (eds) (1997) *Que(e)rying Religion: A Critical Anthology*, New York: Continuum.

Conrad, P., and Schneider, J. (1980) "Homosexuality: From Sin to Sickness to Lifestyle," in *Deviance and Medicalization: From Badness to Sickness*, Philadelphia, PA: Temple University Press.

DeGloma, T., and Johnston, E.F. (2019) "Cognitive Migrations: A Cultural and Cognitive Sociology of Personal Transformation," in W. Brekhus, and G. Ignatow (eds) *The Oxford Handbook of Cognitive Sociology*, Oxford: Oxford University Press.

Fetner, T. (2008) *How the Religious Right Shaped Lesbian and Gay Activism*, Minneapolis: University of Minnesota Press.

Fortunato, J. (1982) *Embracing the Exile: Healing Journeys of Gay Christians*, San Francisco: Harper Collins.

Fuist, T. (2016) "It Just Always Seemed Like It Wasn't a Big Deal: LGBT Religious Identities in Context," *Journal for the Scientific Study of Religion*, 55(4):770–86.

Gill, S. (ed) (1998) *The Lesbian and Gay Christian Movement: Campaigning for Justice, Truth, and Love*, London: Cassell.

Goffman, E. (1963) *Stigma: Notes on Management of a Spoiled Identity*, New York: Simon and Schuster.

Hartman, K. (1996) *Congregations in Conflict: The Battle over Homosexuality*, New Brunswick, NJ: Rutgers University Press.

King, W.E. (2021) "A Match Made in Heaven: Queer Christians and Dating Apps," Unpublished Dissertation, Seattle: University of Washington.

Martin, J. (2017) *Building a Bridge: How the Catholic Church and the LGBT Community Can Enter into a Relationship of Respect, Compassion, and Sensitivity*, San Francisco: HarperOne.

McNeill, J. (1988) *The Church and the Homosexual*, Boston: Beacon Press.

Meltzer, B. (1966) *The Social Psychology of George Herbert Mead*, Michigan: Western Michigan University.

Moon, D. (2004) *God, Sex, and Politics: Homosexuality and Everyday Theologies*, Chicago: University of Chicago Press.

O'Brien, J. (2004) "Wrestling the Angel of Contradiction: Queer Christian Identities," *Culture and Religion*, 5(2): 179–202.

O'Brien, J. (2005) "How Big is Your God? Queer Christian Social Movements," in *Genealogies of Identity: Interdisciplinary Readings on Sex and Sexuality*, Amsterdam: Rodopi, pp. 237–61.

O'Brien, J. (2007) "Queer Tensions: The Cultural Politics of Belonging and Exclusion in Same Gender Marriage Debates," in *Interdisciplinary Readings on Sex and Sexuality*, Amsterdam: Rodopi, pp. 125–49.

O'Brien, J. (2009) "Sociology as an Epistemology of Contradiction," *Sociological Perspectives*, 52(1): 5–22.

O'Brien, J. (2018) "LGBTQ Mental Health," *Conversations*, 54(1): 37–9.

O'Brien, J. (2022) *The Production of Reality*, 7th edition, Thousand Oaks, CA: Sage.

Plummer, K. (1995) *Telling Sexual Stories: Power, Change, and Social Worlds*, London: Routledge.

Salazar, E. (2008) "Leadership Development: Perceptions of Gay and Lesbian Student Leaders in Jesuit Universities," Unpublished Dissertation, Seattle: Seattle University.

Stein, A. (2002) *The Stranger Next Door: The Story of a Small Community's Battle Over Sex, Faith, and Civil Rights,* Boston: Beacon Press.

Taylor, Y. and Snowden, R. (eds) (2014) *Queering Religion, Religious Queers,* New York: Routledge.

Talvacchia, K.T., Larrimore, M. and Pettinger, M.E. (eds) (2019) *Queer Christianities: Lived Religion in Transgressive Forms*, New York: NYU Press.

Thumma, S. and Gray, E. (eds) (2004) *Gay Religion*, Lanham, MD: AltaMira Press.

Tonstad, L. (2018) *Queer Theology: Beyond Apologetics*, Eugene, OR: Cascade Books.

Wilcox, M. (2020) *Queer Religiosities: An Introduction to Queer Studies in Religion*, Lanham, MD: Rowman and Littlefield.

Yun, K.Y. (2000) *Becoming Intercultural: An Integrative Theory of Communication and Cross-Cultural Adaptation*, Thousand Oaks, CA: Sage.

2

The Intergenerational Transmission of Trauma: Religion, Spirituality, and Ritual among Children and Grandchildren of Holocaust Survivors

Janet Jacobs

The study of the intergenerational transmission of Holocaust trauma is a wide-ranging field of research that primarily focuses on the transference of traumatic feelings and behaviors to succeeding generations. Within this vast field of inquiry, the preponderance of research suggests that the psychosocial transference of tragedy and loss within survivor families leads to the inheritance of fear, anxiety, and sadness among children as well as grandchildren of survivors (Bar-On, 1995; Kellerman, 2001). While the psychiatric literature in the field is extensive and far-reaching, the importance of religious culture to the intergenerational transmission of trauma has received far less attention, an oversight that is particularly significant given the role that descendants assume as carriers of both genocidal trauma and a threatened religious heritage. The goal of this chapter, therefore, is to investigate the relationship between inherited trauma and religious beliefs and practices among children and grandchildren of survivors. In particular, the chapter will examine the construction of spiritual worldviews and ritual innovation among descendant generations. In general, the chapter shows that we need both a broad cultural lens and sensitivity to the nuances of local culture and ritual interaction among family members if we are to more effectively and fully interpret what we mean by *trauma*, how we understand its social transmission to individuals not directly exposed to the traumatic event, and how we can understand the impact of trauma across generations.

The specific contributions that this work makes to the study of religion and traumatic inheritance lies in a number of important areas of research.

First, the chapter provides an investigation into the relationship between genocide, religion and traumatic inheritance, as religious culture becomes a vehicle for both the memorialization of the past and the means by which a religious/spiritual future is reimagined. Second, the chapter makes use of an interpretive framework that, in its departure from the prevailing psychological approach to traumatic transference, focuses on the social structures of family and culture – religious beliefs systems and ritual practices – through which a history of genocidal trauma is passed on from one generation to the next. Third, the chapter offers an exploration into the adaptive and creative religious responses that children and grandchildren of Holocaust survivors employ as they negotiate the responsibility of culture-bearing for future generations among an historically threatened religio-ethnic population. Finally, the methodological approach that is applied to this study of religious culture and inherited trauma incorporates the notion of the researcher as both witness and scholar, a qualitative sociological approach that illuminates the multiple roles that researchers of trauma assume in exploring and interpreting the lived experience of those who have inherited and shared a traumatic past.

Methodology and the researcher as witness

The sample population for this research is comprised of 50 children and grandchildren of Holocaust survivors of Nazi death and labor camps. Participants were obtained through contacts with Children of Holocaust Survivor organizations, university student groups, and snowball sampling that provided referrals to other participants. Although the religious upbringing of the respondents varied, nearly half of the respondents were raised within the Jewish Conservative movement, while the remainder were raised in Orthodox, Reform or nonaffiliated homes. At the time of the interview, two-thirds of the respondents, while culturally identifying as Jews, reported no institutional affiliation. Among those who were affiliated, their affiliations ranged from modern Orthodox to more nontraditional movements such as Jewish Renewal.

The primary data-gathering mode for the research involved in-depth interviews and the recording of life history narratives. Following a semi-structured interview format, the interview schedule included open-ended questions that focused on the family's Holocaust history, the transmission of knowledge about the Holocaust within the family, the religious beliefs and rituals of survivor family members and the religious beliefs, practices and ritual observance of the participants. All of the interviews were conducted in confidence, taped, and then transcribed for analysis. The majority of the interviews took place in the homes of the participants. Because of the familial location of the interview sites, the respondents frequently shared photographs, family documents and family artifacts that had survived the Second World War. In some instances, the process of sharing led to tours through the participant's home, as he or she pointed out framed photographs of their parents or grandparents before and after the war, and of other family members who did not survive. At other times, respondents produced surviving Nazi documents, such as identity cards, or carefully assembled scrapbooks that chronicled their family's ordeal and survival. Thus, the settings of the interviews were, in many cases, field sites in and of themselves – spaces of memory and family culture where recollections of the past and narratives of childhood were enhanced by familial surroundings that enriched and recalled the respondent's ties to loss, survival and catastrophe. As a result, the interviews were often deeply emotional both for the respondents and for myself, as each of us negotiated the feelings engendered by the persistence of traumatic memories and the recounting of a life personally informed by the Jewish genocide of the Second World War.

In listening to the stories of the children and grandchildren of survivors, I was often the first person with whom they shared their memoires, their fears, and their religious and spiritual worldviews. As the listener, I thus became "the blank screen" on which their memories were "inscribed for the first time," a role that placed me in the position of those who bear witness to a terrible past (Laub, 1992: p. 57). The knowledge that is derived through this mode of data collection interweaves structures of memory with deep feelings that are exchanged between the researcher/listener and trauma narrator. Accordingly, the interpretive framework that I bring to this analysis of the intergenerational transmission of trauma incorporates my dual role as researcher and witness –as scholar and empathic listener. In bringing together these two interrelated and dynamically connected aspects of qualitative methodology, my discussion of the findings begins with an exploration into genocide and constructions of God.

Survivorship and the intergenerational transmission of religious beliefs

The research on religious beliefs among survivors of the Holocaust offers a wide variety of theological responses to the trauma of suffering and genocide. While the post-Holocaust debates among Jewish theologians and clergy tend to address the larger metaphysical questions of the existence and nature of God (Cohn-Sherbok, 1996; Jacobs, 1993; Goldberg, 1995), survivors of the Holocaust bring their own worldviews to the experience of survivorship that inform the meaning systems out of which their children and grandchildren develop a spiritual sense of self. Previous studies suggest that while survivors of the Holocaust hold varied and often conflicting sets of beliefs, three responses to survival tend to be most prevalent: a continued and unchanged belief in the patriarchal God of biblical Judaism; a strengthened belief in God; and a loss of belief in God (Marcus and Rosenberg, 1988; Carmil and Breznitz, 1991; Blumenthal, 1993; Waxman, 2000). Further, the research reveals that within these varying religious responses, survivors express a broad range of emotions surrounding their feelings about God, including rage, a sense of abandonment, and gratitude for survival (Marcus and Rosenberg, 1988).

In turning to the narratives of descendants, respondents report that among their parents and grandparents, and especially their fathers and grandfathers, rage toward and fear of God were among the most predominant emotions that were conveyed in the post-Holocaust family. Typically, rage was expressed over questions of God's existence. In the following account, a daughter who was raised in a nonreligious home describes the anger with which her father addressed questions surrounding God:

"I would talk about God and my father would talk about science. I think science for him was like a religion. He doesn't really talk about God a lot and when he does it is in a mocking way that sometimes lead to anger in a way that he really relished. I mean, you could just tell he was just like reveling in his anger when the topic of God came up."

In more religiously traditional homes, respondents reported the confusion they experienced over a parent's or grandparent's rejection of God, even as he or she insisted upon strict adherence to religious law within the family. A son explains:

"It was weird mixed messages. He [my father] was so non-religious and pissed off at God and he couldn't believe any of it, yet he felt like he had to keep me in the yeshiva and be a member of the synagogue. And I always felt like, What are you talking about? You are saying this, and you are forcing us to do that."

This participant referred to his father's beliefs as a kind of "religious schizophrenia" in which God was simultaneously denied and feared. In this case, the responses of the survivor parent vacillated between a belief in the nonexistence of God and fear of God's punitive powers. As reported by the respondents, fear of God was particularly strong among those survivors who believed that, in return for survival, God demanded a strict adherence to religious law. A granddaughter of an Auschwitz survivor describes the culture of fear that permeated her religious upbringing thus:

"My grandfather, who was one of the older people to survive, lived very close to us. And my mother was always afraid because he would go into a rage if we were not keeping all the laws and customs. So he would come over on Saturday and touch the TV to see if it was hot and if we had been watching television. He was a fanatic and his strong beliefs and fear of God overshadowed everything else – even his relationships with his siblings and his children."

The strict religiosity to which other survivors adhered was sometimes framed by the strong conviction that those who survived did so because they had remained observant even under the harshest of conditions. Thus, strict adherence to tradition often emerged out of gratitude and fear of God. A woman in her mid-fifties offered this perspective on her mother's religious observance and her mother's belief that God had personally saved her from perishing in the camps:

"She believed in God and therefore she was spared. She thought that people in the camps weren't religious, weren't kosher and that they might not have believed as well as she did. She was stringent and rigid in terms of kosher. She had this personal relationship to God and that meant, for example, that she would often expound about God. She was very much convinced that her views were right and therefore God had recognized that in this personal relationship that she had with God, that he had spared her."

As these and other narratives illustrate, the religious undertones of traumatic transference created a cultural environment in which intense and sometimes conflicting feelings around God resulted in the creation of an emotionally charged spiritual atmosphere out of which succeeding generations shaped their own understandings of God and/or the meaning of the divine. In response to their parents' and grandparents' fear, anger and confusion surrounding God, descendants often reject the religious ideas of their family, developing instead a diversity of belief systems in which notions of the divine are reimagined and reconceptualized. The varied spiritual worldviews that the descendants have embraced include both transcendent and immanent meaning systems that reflect a desire to create a more personalized and adaptive approach to an understanding of the sacred. As such, the nontraditional worldviews of the descendants generally follow two trends in modern religious thought in which spirituality is distinguished from religiosity in contemporary society. These trends are the belief in a personalized rather than institutionalized notion of a higher power and the search for meaning through immanence and personal forms of transcendence (Roof, 1993; Spilka and McIntosh, 1996: Zinnbauer et al, 1997).

Belief in a higher power

Within the social scientific study of religion, the concept of a higher power is associated with traditional forms of religiousness that highlight a belief in and relationship to an externalized and transcendent god figure or divine being (Zinnbauer et al, 1997). Within a Judeo-Christian worldview, the notion of a higher power is typically gendered and male-centered. It is thus significant to note that, although over half the respondents expressed belief in a higher power, their conceptualizations of the divine frequently challenged the patriarchal context through which the sacred is construed. In this regard, the participants tended to be cautious in their use of the term "God" precisely because of its gendered meaning, preferring terms like "higher power" that acknowledge the existence of a transcendent being without reinstating the problematic biblical God of survivor culture. A number of examples will help to illuminate this point. In the first example, a woman whose mother survived Auschwitz refused to raise her children as Jews, creating in her daughter a deep spiritual longing:

> "For me, I went through various phases in what I think about God. This is all stuff that I came up with. First, when I was a child, I decided there was no God. I asked my mother, 'How come you didn't raise me Jewish?' I think she said, 'How could a Jewish God do this to me?' That suggested to me there was no God. So, I went around saying there was no God. Then I started thinking about the universe and how did things start, and I couldn't come up with a scientific answer. So, I thought maybe that is where the God piece comes in. God created the spark that started it all. That's what I thought for a long time, but it was never good enough. It wasn't enough. I walked around with this kind of emptiness. A lot of people have this void we are trying to fill. What I finally learned is that you have to fill it with a relationship to something bigger than yourself, a higher power. That is where I draw my comfort."

As this account reveals, the participant's belief in a higher power serves a number of important socio-emotional functions. The most significant provides a personal connection to a divine being that offers comfort and satisfies a longing for spiritual meaning in the daughter's life. Another case, that of a son of survivors, offers a somewhat different perspective on the individual's relationship to a higher power:

> "I consider myself an agonistic Jew. I have a very, very hard time believing in God due to what my family went through in the war. It kind of raises the question: If there is a God, why did this continue

to happen, the persecution, all the way up to the killing, the mass killing? Where was God? But then my mother was only 11 years old, running and hiding. One of the many nights that they slept outside, my mother woke up in the morning and about a foot from her head was a big piece of shrapnel. I guess, if there is a God, that is why it didn't hit her in the head and kill her. So, I think probably there must be something, some higher power that looked out for her – her parents did not survive but she did. She escaped twice. How was that possible for such a young girl?"

This account emphasizes the significance of the divine as a source of survival. Within this theological paradigm, belief in a higher power is tied to a belief in a spiritual protector who is responsible for saving the lives of survivors, as another respondent explained:

"The strongest spiritual feelings I have actually center on my parents' survival of the Holocaust. Do I believe that it was a random thing? I don't. My mother didn't either. My mother was an incredibly spiritual person. My mother always said, 'I didn't survive for me, and it wasn't for you. It was for the grandchildren, that is why I was chosen to live.' I think there is some sort of a master plan. And I struggle all the time with the idea of something being predestined or not. Where does individual choice come in and where does the master plan, the higher power change our destiny?"

Another descendant whose parents survived numerous death camps and raised their children within the Conservative tradition, offered this insight into his relationship to the divine:

"I believe there's a higher power. And part of it is, I want to believe. Because it is a crutch to help when things happen and you don't feel like you're alone. And of course, I am not totally convinced. But I want to believe. I find comfort in that mindset and that, with this higher power, there is also an afterlife, some utopia where you don't have any worries and that it is a better place."

Finally, a granddaughter of survivors also expressed a belief in a higher power. Here, she describes her spiritual evolution:

"As I pulled away from the *mitzvot* [commandments] and the day-to day interaction with the Jewish community, I simultaneously started searching for other interpretations of spiritual beliefs. What I found is a core belief – a higher power that has an influence in our daily lives.

Nothing is coincidence. There's a purpose for every aspect of what you experience, day in and day out. And I do believe that."

As the narratives of higher power strongly suggest, children and grandchildren of Holocaust survivors have a deep-seated need to believe in a spiritual power that gives purpose to life. Because their worldviews have been shaped by the knowledge of their parents' suffering, descendants express a belief in a spiritual presence or entity which offered the possibility of survival and thus the affirmation of the existence of a life-giving force to whom the descendants turn for comfort and solace. This spiritual response to traumatic transference, while rejecting traditional beliefs in a patriarchal god, nonetheless preserves a belief in an externalized divinity through which hope for the future and for humankind is sustained.

Descendant spirituality and the turn toward immanence

The turn toward immanence and personal constructions of transcendence comprise the second set of findings on spirituality among descendants. In contemporary Western thought, the concept of immanence has taken on a variety of forms and expressions with the development and proliferation of nontraditional religious movements, including those that are associated with Eastern religious ideologies and feminist spirituality (Christ, 1979; Adler, 1998). Within the broad spectrum that defines an immanent world view, God or the divine is typically understood as emanating from within the individual, fostering a belief in an internalized rather than externalized notion of spiritual or creative power. Immanent belief systems are therefore based on notions of interconnectedness and belief in a unifying spiritual force. Among the descendants in this study, close to half of the respondents adhered to an immanent worldview that emerged out of their disenchantment with and rejection of traditional Judaism.

These findings are closely tied to Roof's (1993) study of new generations of spiritual seekers who, in rejecting organized religion and traditional definitions of God, turn to a more individualized understanding of the divine. While Roof's work focused primarily on the 'baby-boomer generation' – those born between 1946 and 1964, and so the age cohort of children of survivors – the research here suggests that spiritual seekership is also characteristic of the grandchildren of survivors, a post baby-boomer generation who, like their parents, have had access and exposure to alternative and non-Western spiritual traditions. Thus, the turn toward individualized immanence among succeeding generations of survivors is in part a reflection of the shifts in Western religious culture that have led to a greater knowledge of and interest in diverse spiritual practices and beliefs.

Of particular importance to this spiritual trend among descendants is the adoption of an immanent worldview that eliminates the boundaries between the self and the divine. The poet and Jewish theologian Marcia Falk refers to this unifying principle as the "indwelling" nature of the divine:

> ... the new *Sh'ma: The Declaration of Faith* states that the presence of divinity in the world is experienced as indwelling – that is, felt immanently – in all of creation ... The world we know – a world we may learn, through awareness, to love more deeply – is a multifaceted manifestation of a unified creation with a unified source; the many are One. (Falk, 1996: p. 433)

With respect to post-Holocaust theology in particular, the writings of Richard Rubenstein resonate with Falk's perspective. A somewhat controversial theologian, Rubenstein in the 1960s proclaimed the death of God after Auschwitz. Many years later, having been influenced by Eastern teachings on spirituality, he reframed his belief in the divine through an immanent worldview:

> In place of a biblical image of a transcendent creator God, an understanding of God which gives priority to the indwelling immanence of the Divine may be more credible in our era. Where God is thought of as a predominantly immanent cosmos, the cosmos in all of its temporal and spatial multiplicity is understood as the manifestation of the single unified and unifying, self-unfolding, self-realizing Divine Source, Ground, Spirit, or Absolute. (Rubinstein, 1992: pp. 245–96)

Rubenstein's turn toward a nonhierarchical unitive spirituality is evident in the accounts of first-generation descendants who, like Falk, incorporate diverse metaphors to describe the divine as a unifying principle. Among grandchildren of survivors, the path toward spiritual awareness reflects similar themes, as a granddaughter's narrative suggests:

> "I try to avoid the concept of the old man in the sky kind of looking down and just observing. It's harder to define but I tend to visualize energy, you know that is within as well as without – sort of like wavelengths, and that can be anything surrounding us if we're attuned to them and aware of it."

Within the tradition of immanence, a number of respondents have looked to Jewish mysticism and Kabbalistic worldviews to invoke the divine within.

Here a granddaughter of survivors, following her mother's spiritual path, turned to Kabbalistic teachings to find the indwelling "spark":

"My grandparents came from very distinguished Orthodox families in Poland. My grandfather's father was a *rebbe* [rabbi]. And he had devoted students who came from many miles away to study with him. So, my mother and I, we are on this journey together. It is gorgeous, very mystical. I have been studying the Kabbalah as much as I can. But it's still very surface level. The deep, dark secrets of the Kabbalah don't really get revealed unless you are studying all the time. But every bit I've learned, I really love. Each of the spirits [sparks] have their own different aspect and energy surrounding them where you can experience the divine, interacting with them."

Menachem Rosensaft, the founder of the International Network of Children of Survivors, similarly draws on Kabbalistic teachings, reimagining the inner spirit as maternal and feminine:

But what if God was not with the killers, with the forces that inflicted the Holocaust on humanity ... Think of the divine power, the spiritual strength of a mother comforting a child on the way to the gas chamber. If God was present at Auschwitz, it was in the mother, in her words, in her emotions, in the instinct that kept her from abandoning her child ... God permeated every Jew who held a dying parent, or a brother or sister, or a friend, or even a stranger. The mystical divine spark that characterizes true Jewish faith, the *Shekina* [the feminine manifestation of the divine] was in every Jew who remained human to another fellow human being, and in every Jew who defied the forces of evil by risking his or her life to save a Jew. (Rosensaft, 2001: pp. 190–1)

In Rosensaft's construction of the divine he calls upon the maternalism of divinity – the power of life over death and the source of human connectivity – to affirm God's existence during the Holocaust. A similar theme is articulated in the narrative of a daughter of survivors who adopted the term "inner *bubba*" to explain what she described as the "sacred feminine" within:

"The inner *bubba* is the inner grandmother who tends to people and makes sure they have food and passes on what people need to know and make sure everybody's comfortable. It is this total nurturing inner goddess type. It's an archetype."

In comparison with a feminized construction of an inner life force, other respondents turned toward Eastern-based traditions to find a meaningful way in which to understand the divine and to experience the divine within themselves. The account of a child of survivors who was raised within Conservative Judaism illustrates this phenomenon:

"I practice yoga meditation. I've had some deep realizations and experiences. It's not easy but it is very powerful. I feel a universal omnipresence that I am part of, and that God is part of me and I'm the little bubble in the ocean of God, ocean of love, ocean of supraconsciousness, so definitely, when I go in deep meditation that is my goal. Once you are in that deep ocean – that's what I call it because there is no body or mind awareness – it's just a split second of one with the universe. It cannot be described."

Experiencing the divine as an altered state of unified consciousness is found in numerous other accounts, many of which reflect a longing to escape from the suffering of the human condition as it relates specifically to genocide. In the following narrative, a daughter recalled, with great emotion, the moment she experienced her connection to the divine through the memories of terror that her mother had conveyed:

"I was in my early 30s. I must have been searching for something. I went into this community – there were other Jews there too, but I was an atheist. Then I started doing workshops and different forms of meditation. There was a teacher and they were teaching me how to do yoga exercises. I was chanting and trying to let go. I worked really hard at letting go of myself. One day, it all came together and what came up for me was the Holocaust experience. I was seeing dead bodies piled up. I was going through what my mother had gone through. That's when I knew I was directly connected to it. I was screaming. I was in a lot of pain going through it, but the pain was traveling through my body. I wasn't attached to it. At last I got out of my body. So I got to experience what it was like to feel pain but not suffer with it … I looked around and I remember noticing that there was no separation between anything. It was all energy and it was all connected. That's when I knew that we were all connected. It was one of the gifts of my life that totally transformed my whole spiritual outlook."

The desire to transcend the torment of the Holocaust survivor is also evident in the account of a granddaughter who, raised as a secular Jew in Israel, turned toward Buddhism to find a way out of the consciousness of suffering:

"I became an official Buddhist last December. I've been studying Buddhism for five years now. As far as my beliefs on the world, the transpersonal realm, they're derived from Buddhism, not from Judaism. It's just a very different interpretation. It's not related to God – do this, don't do that, punishment and all that stuff doesn't exist. The notion of God from a Judeo-Christian perspective seems slightly childish to me, to be honest. I started doing yoga when I was 19. It's a Hindu practice, but just a different consciousness, a way of exploring myself. Then I picked up my first Buddhism book, *The Tibetan Book of Living and Dying* by Sogyal Rinpoche. So many of the things he talked about, I just felt like I knew them. Like there's a concept called the Four Noble Truths. The first noble truth is that the world is suffering. Suffering is an inherent part of human existence. It's something that I've always felt, fairly young, growing up with my family. It was like everything I knew was in that book, so I started to pursue my studies in the Buddhist community and then it all began to make sense. There is a notion of a creative life force, but it's something that is on a much larger scheme. On the most basic level, inherent in every one of us is the potential of awakening and finding that place – beyond the self, beyond human suffering."

Through unification and connection to the realm beyond the materiality of life's pain, loss and tragedy, children and grandchildren of survivors sustain a belief in the divine through a mystical path that is life-affirming and through which the despair of traumatic transference is diminished. The belief in an immanent divine thus offers the descendants a way out of the consciousness of suffering that is the inheritance of their family's trauma.

The need and desire for a spiritual worldview among children and grandchildren of survivors, whether articulated as a belief in a higher power or the experience of divine immanence, highlights the importance of alternative forms of spirituality across a multi-generational culture of descendants. In comparing these findings with research on post-war Jewry more generally in the US, a number of significant observations can be made. Since the 1980s, research on Jews, God imagery, and belief has suggested that Jews overall do not interpret the Bible literally or believe strongly in the notion of a judgmental God (Roof and Roof, 1984). Especially among younger Jews and those of the post-war generation, God imagery tends to be more personalized and more open to an acceptance of maternal or feminine imagery (Roof, 1999). Thus, when comparing the research on the descendants to studies on Jews more broadly, the findings are consistent with a rejection of biblical literalism and a coinciding greater acceptance, particularly among younger generations, of demasculinized conceptualizations of God that are in keeping with the cultural innovations of the late 20th century.

At the same time, however, the meanings that the descendants bring to new constructions of the divine are deeply embedded in the traumatic legacies of survivor culture and therefore broaden an understanding of the process of spiritual creativity. Among the most prominent studies of post-war religion and spirituality are the well-referenced works of Roof and Robert Wuthnow (Roof, 1999; Wuthnow, 1998). Each of these scholars interpret the changing landscape of religious belief and practice through a lens of tragedy and disillusionment that marked the post-war culture in which the baby boomers (primarily white and middle-class) came to adulthood. Referencing the cultural and political upheavals that impacted the notion of God as a "personal, purposive being, perfect in goodness and supreme in power," (Roof, 1999: p. 74), Roof identified the Holocaust as a catalyst for shifting notions of the divine:

> Contemporary religious pluralism and trends in science, rationality, and secularity have helped to shape, often out of a defensive posture, a generic theism … In the modern era, however, growing numbers have come to find this generic view of God rather bland and uninspiring. With so much death and destruction, tragedy and evil in the world, some find it difficult to maintain a notion of an all-good, omnipotent deity. Although hardly the first to press the question, the boomers have grown up hearing about the Holocaust and have experienced much in their time … . (Roof, 1999: p. 74).

Taking Roof's observations one step further, the descendants of the Holocaust, whose knowledge of this cataclysmic tragedy is both personally and religiously informed, demonstrate perhaps a deeper need to challenge the "generic theism" of modern society. As a unique population of children and grandchildren of survivors, the interpretive frameworks that the descendants bring to the reconceptualization of spirituality reveals how the transmission of trauma transforms beliefs and spiritual ideologies within a descendant group that has been directly impacted by the destruction of the past. Similarly, in addition to the need for spiritual innovation, descendants also turn toward religious ritual as a means to cope with inherited trauma while sustaining their role as culture bearers in the aftermath of genocidal loss.

Ritual: emotion and innovation among descendants of survivors

The study of ritual and emotion is a vast area of research within the field of religious ritual. In this regard, scholars such as Thomas Scheff (1979) and Victor Turner (1969) discuss the emotional aspect of ritual performance that allows participants to express and externalize repressed feeling states. Following Scheff and Turner, Frederick Bird (1995) explored the ways in which religious ritual functions particularly in the family, providing a social mechanism for the cathartic release of feelings that are frequently silenced or hidden. In keeping with the scholarship on ritual and emotion, descendants of Holocaust survivors report that ritual observance in the family provided the space and context for the expression of pain and loss that silently permeated the post-genocide household. According to the accounts of the participants, it was during religious rituals that their parents and grandparents relived and gave expression to the emotions of their traumatic past. In particular, the participants reported that the observance of Yom Kippur (the Day of Atonement), the holiest day of the Jewish year, was especially significant for the evocation of traumatic memory during the period of reflection and repentance that characterizes Yom Kippur observance. In the following account, a 52-year-old son who was raised in an Orthodox home describes how his father's anger toward God became intertwined with the family's adherence to religious tradition:

"My Dad was raised by a very, the word he uses is, 'pious' man. His father was extremely religious. He came from a large family. It was a very rigid reality. This is what life is about, studying Talmud and the Torah. It was really jammed down his throat. Then his dad, my grandfather, was taken away and murdered and the rest of the family was killed. My father and his brother were the only survivors. When he started to raise his own family, he was still coming from this place of guilt and anger ... I had to be bar mitzvahed – there was no choice – we had to keep kosher, keep the Sabbath, fast, light candles, and if my mother showed up at things without her wig, that was like heresy. But Yom Kippur? That was always the hardest, when the anger and bitterness was the strongest. It was just a kind of jammed-down-your-throat – this is the way it is – kind of thing, without any depth; the only feelings were [those] of rage and bitterness."

In addition to expressions of rage, a second and equally powerful set of emotions that were triggered by the observance of the Day of Atonement were those feelings associated with survivor guilt. Because Yom Kippur is a day of atonement, the liturgy for this religious holiday involves the recitation of sins for which the supplicant asks God for forgiveness and mercy. As research on survivors has poignantly shown, the memory of survivorship is often accompanied by feelings of self-blame and guilt that, in the aftermath of catastrophe, contribute to the post-traumatic symptoms of the surviving generations (Langer, 1991; Herman, 1992). It is thus not surprising that Yom Kippur, with its emphasis on sin and self-recrimination, was a difficult and angst-ridden holiday in the survivor family.

The narrative of a daughter will help to illustrate this dimension of the high holiday observance. Piecing together her mother's wartime experiences from stories that she was told as a young child, the respondent recounted how her mother was deported to Auschwitz at age 17 where she survived by working in a munitions factory, although the rest of her family were massacred in Poland. The respondent explained that, although her mother spoke with pride of her survival, there was an unspoken subtext to her stories, an undercurrent of silence, regret and guilt that surfaced especially during her observance of Yom Kippur:

"My mother did not want to raise us Jewish. We were Unitarians. I think that being Jewish was too painful. Having said that, she observed all the holidays. We had Passover, and Yom Kippur was very sad for her. She would gorge herself the day before so that she could spend the whole day fasting ... She would just lay in bed all day. My sister and I were scared because it was the one time a year when her feelings of guilt and grief overwhelmed her, and she couldn't eat or move or even talk to us. There was just this silence and her pain."

As this account reveals, even in nonreligious Jewish households, survivors observed the Yom Kippur ritual, maintaining a yearly tradition in which painful emotions were given expression and visibility in the post-catastrophe culture of the survivor family.

Along with fasting and the recalling of sins and wrongdoing, it is also traditional on Yom Kippur to remember family members who have died. At the onset of the holiday, the lighting of memorial (*Yahrzeit*) candles in the home signals the beginning of a period of remembrance. Accordingly, the participants in this study gave vivid and emotional accounts of kitchens and countertops that were lined with ritual candles, small glass containers with Hebrew lettering that, for the descendant of survivors, came to symbolize the Jewish nature of traumatic loss. A woman whose father died when she was 12 recounted an early childhood memory when her father's only connection to Judaism was framed through this act of memorialization:

"My father escaped deportation, jumped the train and came to Italy. It is unclear whether his parents died in Theresienstadt or Auschwitz. My father grew up Jewish. My grandmother, my father's mother was Orthodox and when he married my mother everyone said she was a foreign woman, even though she was a Jew, because she came from Italy. My mother did not keep a kosher home and was not brought up in a religious home. After the war, my father was not religious, but he kept Yom Kippur and Rosh Hashanah and he always lit a *Yahrzeit* candle for his father. That was very important to me – the only time I would see his grief, when his feelings were not hidden. I remember

I talked to him about it and how important it was. And I light a *Yahrzeit* candle for him every day. I feel I owe it to him."

Grandchildren also recalled lighting memorial candles during this high holiday period, remarking that as young children this ritual was often the first recognition and awareness of the solemnity of the day and of the memory of death that permeated the household. As one granddaughter reported, candles were the signifier of her grandparents' loss and deep sadness, "It's strange but my connection to it all is all about the candles. The Yom Kippur candles and the Holocaust."

While Yom Kippur represents what is perhaps the most emotion-laden ritual in post-genocide households, descendants also describe other forms of observance that left a deep impression. Surrounded by sadness, loss, and anger, the ritual life of the family was frequently described as joyless, rigid, and obligatory. A number of respondents remarked on the rigidity with which their families kept kosher, observed the Sabbath, or strictly maintained the dietary rules of Passover, on their parents becoming angry or upset if a rule or law was violated. Others remarked on the compulsive and often depressing observance of holidays that were celebratory and festive for other Jews, but for their families were unhappy and despairing occasions:

"My parents didn't take particular joy in practicing ritual. They felt that this was the way they were brought up and they didn't want us to lose the identity. I remember hating *Sukkoth* [harvest festival] because we never did anything joyful or exciting. My father didn't go to work. We didn't go to school. But there was no warmth, no bringing us together, just the persistent memory of who was not there, who would not be celebrating with us."

Here, as in other accounts, the practice of ritual established a compelling emotional space where descendants were witness to the survivors' suffering and rage and where the feeling states that the rituals invoked became part of the family's emotional landscape. In response to this legacy of ritualized remembrance, the children and grandchildren of survivors sought out ritual adaptations that, while embracing their ancestral traditions, transformed their meaning and observance for future generations.

Culture bearing and the reinvention of Jewish ritual among descendants

Similar to the spiritual creativity discussed earlier, the children and grandchildren of Holocaust survivors engaged in a process of ritual innovation that signaled a departure from the painful practices of survivor culture. Unlike the turn toward alternative spirituality, however, the descendants' creative ritual lives were designed to preserve the traditions of the past, albeit in less agonized and traumatic forms. As one daughter remarked:

> "As a child of survivors, you feel this obligation to make sure Hitler doesn't succeed. At the same time, you don't want to do it the way your parents did – you want holidays to be fun, to bring joy. So I think you have to do more than just observe the rituals – you have to do it differently."

In rejecting the sadness, grief and rage of the ritualistic aspects of survivor practices, the descendants reinvented Jewish customs in a manner that strongly differentiated their observance from that of their parents. Not surprisingly, among the rituals that were of particular importance to the project of creative innovation were those that focused on Yom Kippur. As discussed above, given the significance and emotional power of the Day of Atonement, the majority of respondents sought ways to bring new meaning to a holy day that had deep associations with despair. A son of survivors described the alternative ritual he created specifically for Yom Kippur thus:

> "We don't do the high holidays. I just can't resonate with them. I guess I am somewhat rebellious around Yom Kippur in particular, about fasting on that day. Yet, being the son of somebody who is a Holocaust survivor, it is hard for me to just ignore the traditions. There are times when I go off on my own for two or three days on a kind of vision quest. I'll sit with myself and not eat and I try to think about what Yom Kippur is designed to do – what it is all about – what does it mean to repent when you have this terrible history."

For the children of survivors such alternatives have great appeal, in part because they offer nontraditional modes of spiritual reflection that are far removed from the overwhelming emotional experiences that their parents had conveyed during high holiday observance. In an interesting and important development, similar themes of reflection and spirituality are also found among second generation descendants. Here a granddaughter describes the meaning with which she approaches Yom Kippur each year:

> "I don't go to services on any other occasion than Yom Kippur. And Yom Kippur feels right to do that. It is always something pretty magical about being in synagogue, even though I don't follow the prayers or the rules. It is the notion of being in community and feeling my spirituality in that space."

While new approaches to Yom Kippur were among the most solemn and serious of the ritual innovations, the reinvention of ritual among the respondents also included other customs, most notably those that were associated with the traditions of the Sabbath and Passover. Here a daughter of survivors offers this view of the weekly Sabbath customs that she practices in her home:

"I don't consider myself religiously Jewish at all. But I definitely practice the Jewish rituals. I made a chalice that I use for Friday night when we light the candles and say the blessings over the wine. We always have Friday night dinner. Our daughter thinks challah is the best food substance in the land. But Friday night candles are the most important ones for me. It keeps my relationship with my parents and yet because we do it so differently – with our own prayers and blessings and family time – it is our own."

Similarly, another respondent, also a mother, recast the melancholy Sabbath observance of her childhood through a lens of connection to family and friends:

"The kids wouldn't give up Friday night for anything. It's the only time that we sit down together. It's a very special night for them. When we were kids, it was so different. It was just us with our parents. They were so busy trying to get life together there was no time for us really – not even on the Sabbath. Now we have our kids and our friends, and we all get together and share the week with one another."

In both of these accounts, the Sabbath, especially Friday night dinner, was maintained as a ritual of connectedness through which Jewish identity was reshaped and sustained. The traditional concepts that mark the Sabbath as a liminal space that separates the sacred from the profane were thus replaced with meaning systems that emphasized familial continuity and cultural connection. This phenomenon was especially pronounced among daughters of survivors, who tended to focus on the relational value of ritual rather than the importance of Jewish law for Sabbath observance.

Among grandchildren, alternative Sabbath observance was also reported by the participants, especially those who grew up within an extended family culture where a survivor grandparent rigidly adhered to and enforced Orthodox practices. In the following account, a college-age grandson whose grandmother had survived Auschwitz and Bergen-Belsen, describes his efforts to keep the Sabbath while distancing himself from his grandmother's traditional demands, such as the prohibition on driving on the Sabbath:

"How I lived growing up was kind of hiding out sometimes. We would have Friday night dinner at my grandmother's and I would drive when I got older but I would pull the car around the block, this is how ridiculous I get, I would pull the car around and walk over and I'll walk back. I still do it when I go home. But that is not how I live here when I am away from home. Here I pray a little every day just for myself. I try to have Shabbat dinner with my friends, and we are just hanging out with each, sharing a meal, lighting candles, eating challah and drinking wine."

The celebration of Passover offers yet another ritual context for innovation and creativity. Here, more than in any other ritual observance, the participants linked the remembrance of Jewish catastrophe with a moral imperative to move beyond an explicitly Jewish worldview, as one respondent explained:

"The holiday that we do in our hearts is Passover. We try to be inclusive in those. We try to go beyond the concept of the slavery of Jews. When I was growing up, my family was always about us and them. That's what my family has always been about, us and them. So I try to be inclusive and open the idea up to the concept of slavery that we have in our world, in our hearts, ourselves, the prisons that we create for ourselves. In that way we don't hide that it comes from a Jewish thing, we talk about it. In that way we bring in some Jewish holidays but with a more universal understanding."

Significantly, Passover provided a ritual context for the descendant's shift from the "us and them" mentality that fueled the fears and anxieties of the survivor generation. Because the story of the Jews' enslavement in Egypt can be read as a timeless parable of resistance and empowerment, Passover is a valuable form of ritual observance for many of the respondents. In seeking to resolve the tensions between a longing to remain connected to Jewish heritage and the need to distance themselves from the trauma of their parents and grandparents, the story of the liberation of the Jews from Egypt was reinterpreted through a more contemporary perspective on enslavement and oppression, an approach to the holiday that separated the descendants from a more problematic ritualized past. In expanding the notion of human suffering beyond the boundaries of Jewish experience, the children and grandchildren of survivors found ways to incorporate values of social justice into their ritual lives, an innovation that helped to define an individual and separate descendant identity.

For others, observing Passover also represents a connection to Jewish culture and to a survivor with whom the descendant shared a special relationship. A 32-year-old woman respondent offered this perspective on the meaning of the Passover *Seder* (ritual meal) in her life:

> "One of the things I like to do is a Passover Seder. I make my own. The last few years, I've gotten together with a friend of mine who likes to do that sort of thing. So we've co-hosted, and that's great. I like leading the Seder, it was what my grandfather did, and cooking for it is a huge part of my ritual for the holidays. I make my grandmother's recipe of gefilte fish from scratch. I've been doing that for a while now, and that ritual, in particular, I just love doing."

Through the yearly re-enactment of the Seder meal, this participant integrates the memory of both of her survivor grandparents (now deceased) into her ritual life. As a grandchild leading the Seder, she replaced her grandfather as the culture bearer of religious practice; in the preparation of ritual foods, she assumed her grandmother's traditional role in the preservation of domestic rites. This narrative thus highlights the ways in which second generation descendants transform ritualized gender norms to allow for the inclusion of traditions that are associated with their grandparents' cultural practices and that provide an emotional connection to the deceased.

Conclusion

The findings of this study contribute to a better and more nuanced understanding of the mechanisms by which genocidal trauma is conveyed to future generations. Expanding upon the extensive studies of social-psychological transference within the post-Holocaust family, the work that is presented in this chapter offers an interpretive framework that looks to the religious culture of the family as a source both for traumatic transmission and the redefinition of a spiritual self among children and grandchildren of survivors who recall the anger, pain and longing for God that their parents and grandparents expressed. In response to the often-fraught religious environment of their upbringing, the descendants of Jewish genocide have turned away from the more traditional paternalistic god of biblical Judaism in favor of alternative belief systems that represent an important departure from the more traditional Jewish views of their parents and grandparents. The meanings that the descendants bring to new constructions of the divine are therefore deeply embedded in the traumatic legacies of survivor culture that have acted as a catalyst for spiritual innovation.

Second, the analysis of the ritual aspects of traumatic transference within the post-genocide family helps to illuminate the ways in which ritual functions as a site of emotional connection for succeeding generations. Here the findings further our understanding of how children and grandchildren of survivors engage in the creation of new cultural forms that fulfill their role as culture bearers in the post-Holocaust family. Like spiritual creativity, ritual innovation is one means by which descendants seek to preserve their religious heritage and, at the same time, move beyond a familial legacy of pain and suffering. Further, in examining the social value of ritual among descendant populations, the work makes visible the structural relations of religious ties that are often undervalued within the more psychological explanations of traumatic transference. In this way, the chapter offers a greater understanding of how religion functions as a source of traumatic inheritance more broadly, providing a sociocultural framework in which to consider the reinvention of spirituality and ritual among future generations.

Lastly, and perhaps most importantly, the methodological approach that is taken here highlights the significance of listening and bearing witness in the study of trauma. Through the development of this project, I became increasingly aware of the ways in which acts of listening, empathizing and validating are essential methodological tools for researching and recording traumatic life histories. As my work with descendants of Holocaust survivors has shown, it is incumbent upon scholars who study trauma (especially in the field of religion and genocide) to create an emotionally safe and supportive research environment for the narrators of unspeakable tragedies and to acknowledge the researcher/listener's role as the "blank slate on which these memories are inscribed" (Laub, 1992, p. 57).

References

Adler, R. (1998) *Engendering Judaism: An Inclusive Theory and Ethics*, Philadelphia, PA: The Jewish Publication Society.

Bar-On, D. (1995) *Fear and Hope: Three Generations of the Holocaust*, Cambridge, MA: Harvard University Press.

Bird, F. 1995. "Family Rituals and Religion: A Functional Analysis of Jewish and Christian Family Ritual Practices," in J. N. Light and F. Bird (eds). *Ritual and Ethnic Identity: A Comparative Study of the Social Meaning of Liturgical Ritual in Synogogues*, Ontario, Canada: Wilfrid Laurier University Press.

Blumenthal, D. (1993) *Facing the Abusive God*, Louisville, KY: Westminster John Knox Press.

Carmil, D., and Blemtiz, S. (1991) "Personal Trauma and World View: Are Extremely Stressful Experiences Related to Political Attitudes, Religious Beliefs, and Future Orientation?" *Journal of Traumatic Stress*, 4(3): 393–404.

Christ, C. (1979) "Why Women Need the Goddess: Phenomenological, Psychological and Political Reflections," in C. Christ and J. Plaskow (eds) *Womenspirit Rising: A Feminist Reader*, Berkeley: University of California Press.

Cohn-Sherbok, D. (1996) *God and the Holocaust*, Wiltshire: Cromwell Press.

Falk, M. (1996) *The Book of Blessings: New Jewish Prayers for Daily Life, the Sabbath and the New Moon Festival*, San Francisco: Harper Collins.

Goldberg, M. (1995) *Why Should Jews Survive?*, New York: Oxford University Press.

Herman, J. (1992) *Trauma and Recovery*, New York: Basic Books.

Jacobs, S. (1993) "Judaism and Christianity After Auschwitz," in S. Jacobs (ed) *Contemporary Jewish Religious Responses to the Shoah*, New York: University Press of America.

Kellerman, N. (2001) "Transmission of Holocaust Trauma: An Integrative View," *Psychiatry* 64(3): 256–67.

Langer, L. (1991) *Holocaust Testimonies: The Ruins of Memory*, New Haven, CT: Yale University Press.

Laub, D. (1992) "Bearing Witness or the Vicissitudes of Listening," in S. Felman and D. Laub (eds) *Testimony: Crises of Witnessing in Literature, Psychoanalysis, and History I*, New York: Routledge.

Marcus, P., and Rosenberg, A. (1988) "The Holocaust Survivor's Faith and Religious Behavior and some Implications for Treatment," *Holocaust and Genocide Studies* 3(4): 413–30.

Roof, W. (1993) *A Generation of Spiritual Seekers: The Spiritual Journeys of the Baby Boomers*, San Francisco: Harper Collins.

Roof, W. (1999) *Spiritual Marketplace: Baby Boomers and the Remaking of American Religion*, Princeton, NJ: Princeton University Press.

Roof, W. and Roof, J. (1984) "Review of the Polls: Images of God Among Americans," *Journal for the Scientific Study of Religion*, 23(2): 201–5.

Rosensaft, M. (2001) "I Was Born in Bergen-Belsen," in A. Berger and N. Berger (eds) *Second Generation Voices: Reflections of Children of Holocaust Survivors*, Syracuse, NY: Syracuse University Press.

Rubinstein, R. (1992) *After Auschwitz: History, Theory and Contemporary Judaism*, Baltimore: Johns Hopkins University Press.

Scheff, T. (1979). *Catharsisin Healing, Ritual and Drama*, Berkeley: University of California Press.

Spilka, B., and Mcintosh, D.N. (1996) "Religion and Spirituality: The Known and the Unknown," unpublished paper presented at the American Psychological Association Annual Meeting.

Turner, V. (1969) *The Ritual Process*, Chicago: Aldine.

Waxman, M. (2000) "Traumatic Hand-Me-Downs: The Holocaust, Where Does It End?," *Families in Society*, 81: 59–64.

Wuthnow, R. (1998) *After Heaven: Spirituality in America Since the 1950s*, Berkeley: University of California Press.

Zinnbauer, B., Pargement, K., Cole, B., Rye, M., Butter, E., Belavich, T., Hipp, K., Scott, A., and Kadar, J. (1997) "Religion and Spirituality: Unfuzzying the Fuzzy," *Journal for the Scientific Study of Religion*, 36(4): 549–64.

3

Doing It: Ethnography, Embodiment, and the Interpretation of Religion

Daniel Winchester

This chapter is about doing it.

More specifically, this chapter is about what I, as an interpretive sociologist and ethnographer of religion, have learned from doing some of the things the people I study do – in particular, the practices they perform in, with, and through their bodies. Ultimately, it is an argument for how actively engaging with and performing the embodied practices of those we study can unearth layers of religious meaning that would otherwise remain hidden from view.

Borrowing a term from sociologist Loic Wacquant (2015), who himself adopts the concept from philosophers of embodied cognition and perception (Varela, Thompson and Rosch, 1991; Noe, 2004), I will call this an *enactive approach* to the ethnography of religion. Put simply, *enaction* refers to the process of knowing by doing: that is, generating or 'bringing forth' knowledge about the world in and through acting within it. As Wacquant, (2015, p. 5) puts it, enactive ethnography implies "immersive fieldwork through which the investigator *acts out (elements of) the phenomenon* [under study] in order to peel away the layers of its invisible properties and to test its operative mechanisms" (emphasis in the original).

As a methodological lens, I view enactive ethnography as a particularly useful approach for the sociological interpretation of religious practices, particularly their corporeal dimensions. Within the broader field of the sociology of religion, 'practice' has become a key term, even vying to supplant concepts such as 'belief,' 'doctrine,' 'creeds,' 'texts,' and 'symbols' as *the* central category around which to empirically and theoretically approach religion (see, for example: McGuire, 2008; Riesebrodt, 2010; Smith, 2017;

Ammerman, 2020; Wuthnow, 2020 for recent theoretical treatments). Practices, in simple terms, are a culture's socially organized methods of going about things in the world, what the theorist of practice Theodore Schatzki (2002, p. 87) has called "a temporally-evolving, open-ended set of doings and sayings" or, elsewhere, "embodied, materially mediated arrays of human activity centrally organized around shared practical understanding" (Schatzki, 2001, p. 11). A focus on 'practice' in the study and interpretation of religion means analyzing religion primarily in and through what people do with, for, and around the things they perceive as religious – for example, socially organized "doings and sayings," such as praying, singing, fasting, meditating, pilgrimaging, venerating, reading, storytelling, and so on, that constitute their sense of the transcendent, godly, sacred, holy, or special.

Along with the turn toward practices within the study of religion has been a call for greater sociological attention to the bodies that perform them. And while the body and its actions have long been of interest to interpretive scholars of religion (and especially scholars of religious ritual), this interest has primarily centered on the expressive and symbolic dimensions of the religiously practicing body. Historically, less attention was paid to the effects of religious practices on the more visceral levels of sensation, perception, and affect: the *feel* of the wooden pew, prayer rug, or carpeted floor under one's backside; the *taste* of the bread at communion or the dates at the end of the day's fast; the *sight* of the magnificence of the massive arches and stained glass windows at St. Paul's Cathedral or the simplicity of a prayer circle at a Quaker meeting; the *sounds* of hymnals, scriptural recitations, or ecstatic worship. Attending to these inescapably sensual, aesthetic aspects of religious practice allows us to begin to understand how practices construct particular forms of religious subjectivity and experience (McRoberts, 2004). But interpreting these important corporeal dimensions of religious practice necessitates that we have methods capable of accessing, as interpretable data, something of what it feels like to perform the practices of a particular religious individual, community, and tradition.

The needed method, I propose, is one of enaction. My argument is that an interpretation of the embodied dynamics embedded in religious practices can best be accomplished through "doing and undergoing" (Dewey, 1934) – to the extent practically and ethically responsible – the practices themselves.

In what follows, I use examples from my own research on contemporary Muslim and Eastern Orthodox converts in the United States to demonstrate some of the interpretive benefits of an enactive approach to the study of religious practices. For reasons of space, and also due to the fact that they are two of the practices with which I have the most significant experience, my examples are from my engagements with two very important religious practices in Islamic and Eastern Orthodox traditions, respectively: (1) *salat*, or ritual prayer, among Muslims; and (2) fasting among Eastern Orthodox

Christians. These are of course selective and specific examples, and the focus on converts means that many of my examples about how these practices are experienced attend to the early stages of becoming a religious subject. But I hope that, through a forthright analysis of how I used my own engagement with them to generate empirical data and theoretical insights, the benefits and wider applicability of an enactive methodological lens will become apparent.

I will elaborate two central answers to the question of, "What does engaging in embodied practices teach us about religious meaning-making and interpretation?" The first is that an enactive approach grants analysts of religion imperfect but nonetheless powerful access to data regarding how practices (re)shape bodily habits and cultivate modes of sensory perception below the level of explicit symbolization and discourse, dictating what kinds of experiences become available for religious interpretation at all. The second is that an enactive approach encourages the analyst to interpret the meaning of religious practices 'from within' – that is, from the perspective and experience of the people who are performing them, tracing the intimate connections that are made between the somatic and the symbolic registers of religious action.

Bodies and souls: grasping the corporeal effects of religious praxis

Interpretive sociologists of religion will likely be familiar with – and inspired by – the work of luminary scholars of religious ritual such as Edmund Leach (1966), Mary Douglas (1966), Victor Turner (1967), and Clifford Geertz (1973), all of whom made compelling cases that we should understand ritual and associated religious practices as forms of symbolic action. Going beyond purely functionalist approaches concerned with what rituals do to reproduce the social order, these more cultural perspectives also analyzed rituals in terms of what they *meant* – that is, the symbolic meanings they encoded, expressed, and communicated in and through action. These scholars inspired generations of interpretivists to conceptualize and analyze religious ritual as a kind of linguistic expression or text, communications that could only be properly decoded when linked to the broader universe of religious discourse and symbolism of which they were a part. From this perspective, the analyst of religious practice 'reads' rituals for what they say about the webs of symbolic meaning in which practitioners live and, subsequently, how rituals translate these webs of transcendent meaning into the realm of concrete social action.

Despite the usefulness and many strengths of approaching religious rituals and other practices as texts to be interpreted, one significant thing that can be learned from actually participating in the corporeal practices of a religious group is an appreciation for this perspective's limits. This is not to say that religious practices do not have important expressive and symbolic dimensions (indeed, as Ricoeur (1984) argues, all human social actions have a hermeneutic component). Religious practices are often steeped in symbolism, and they certainly communicate meanings to and about those involved. But it is to say that an approach that only attends to the expressive dimensions of practice will overlook important tacit registers of meaning-making that underlie these more symbolic registers of the religious body and its actions. More than texts to be read, practices are activities to be done and undergone (Dewey, 1934) – "techniques of the body," as Mauss (1979 [1934]) put it. An enactive or participatory approach can reveal how practices powerfully shape corporeal habits and modes of sensory perception, influencing what "shows up" – and does not "show up" – to consciousness for any kind of symbolic interpretation at all (Leder, 1990; Csordas, 1993; Merleau-Ponty, 2012).

To put some flesh on this somewhat abstract argument, let me move to a concrete example from my own experience in the field. For my own part, the realization of the benefits of 'learning by doing' came early in my sociological career, during the beginning stages of my Master's research on Muslim converts in mid-Missouri (see: Winchester, 2008) and while observing Muslims engaged in Islamic ritual prayer (salat) at the local mosque. Performed five times a day, salat is a complex act of worship involving specific movements of the body such as standing, bowing, prostrating, and kneeling coupled with recitations of Qur'anic verse at particular moments in time. At the end of the congregational prayer, Musad,[1] a Muslim convert I had met previously, approached me and asked me what I thought of the practice. Eager to start a conversation, I decided to demonstrate what little knowledge I had (or thought I had) about it.

"It was really interesting," I began. "I mean, I thought it was great. It means you're submitting yourself to God, right?" I asked. Musad paused for a moment, smiled and corrected me, "Well, not exactly. That's not what it *means*. That's what it *is*."

While at that particular moment in time I did not fully appreciate the significance of Musad's point in differentiating between what prayer "means" and what prayer "is," I did realize he was making a point about the interpretive, experiential, and epistemic space between us. I, from my position as a student of sociology and culture already influenced by the more hermeneutic approaches to religious ritual mentioned above, was reading the practice of salat as if it were a text filled with symbolic meaning. It *conveyed a message* about Musad's identity, his religion, and his relationship to a purported supernatural being. But, from Musad's perspective, prayer was not about expressing a message about submission to God to some outside observer, it was about manifesting his submission to Allah in and through the performance of salat itself. It did not just represent something else outside of or underneath the practice that was meaningful – a creed, a doctrine, a symbol, a belief, a text. It was in no small part constitutive of the sacred act of submission itself.

Of course, the mere existence of this kind of interpretive and experiential gap between a committed convert and an agnostic social scientist is nothing surprising. No matter how close we may try to come to religion's "aura of factuality" (Geertz, 1973), ethnographers are – in the last instance – translating religious actions, beliefs, and experiences into the secular vernacular of our social science. We are ultimately invested in playing a different kind of language game (Reed, 2011) and contributing to a different corpus of knowledge than the religious faithful. Nevertheless, even if the final goal is not to completely collapse the differing perspectives of the practitioner and the analyst of religion, ethnographers run the risk of misinterpreting the nature and power of religion if we fail to interrogate the ways religious interpretations of reality become experientially compelling to some people in some places and times (Harding, 1987). Indeed, failing to interrogate the interpretive divide between detached observer and faithful practitioner of religion felt especially problematic for a case study of conversion like mine, where the question of how an initially foreign religious construal of the world becomes an experientially compelling reality seemed a particularly important one to answer.

So, with Musad's correction in mind, I began to explore how to navigate the experiential distance between researcher and researched, agnostic and true believer, critical sociologist and committed convert – in short, how to account for the gap between my "prayer means" and Musad's "prayer is." While the distance was most certainly a function of differences in personal histories and motives, I also came to realize that the subjective distance between Musad, other Muslims, and myself was also about something much more immediate. Specifically, these differences in understanding were also enforced by what we were physically *doing* at critical moments in space and time.

To unpack my own practice of observing prayer, it involved standing in the very back of the prayer room, pen and notepad in hand, jotting down, as quickly as I could, the meticulous movements and verbalizations involved in the practice. My experience of salat was organized and constructed visually, my eyes darting back and forth from the prostrated worshippers to my notepad and back again. In this way, I was not really 'observing prayer,' not in any religious sense, anyway; rather, through the methodological practice of observing (for example, standing in a physical location distant enough from the practice to visually perceive it as an objectified whole; inscribing the practice on paper in a way that encodes it synchronously) *I was making prayer observable.* I spell all this out not because I think ethnographers are ignorant about what observing actually entails, but to unpack the taken-for-granted nature of ethnographic observation as a particular type of embodied perspective in and on the empirical world. Observing is at base an embodied technique utilized by the ethnographer, one that involves the positioning of one's body in a way that allows for the creation of a particular point of view that objectifies the field – that is, makes it observable – and produces particular kinds of data. This point of view is also a subject position. Put simply, the practice of observing sociologically constitutes one as a sociological observer.

Musad, on the other hand, was observing prayer in a rather different way. While I stood in the back of the room with my pen and notepad, Musad stood side-by-side with other worshippers, knelt on the floor, prostrated himself, and placed his hands and forehead flat against the ground. He recited Qur'anic verse with the rest of the group as he prayed, and collectively stated "Ameen" with the rest of the congregation after each cycle of standing, bowing, and prostrating (a cycle of prayer known as a *rakat*). While my perception of the field was organized visually, Musad's was organized kinetically and aurally. This difference in embodied location, body sense and positionality, then, accounted in some significant part for the subjective distance between Musad and myself. While we inhabited the same physical location, our bodies merely meters away from one another, our practical organization and perception of that space was, in fact, worlds apart.

I only fully appreciated these kinds of embodied distinctions, however, when I, with the encouragement and aid of some of my interlocutors, began to engage in the five daily prayers myself. In learning to perform salat, I also learned important lessons about how the practice reorganizes one's embodied relationship to and experience of space and time. In attempting to, like practicing Muslims themselves, "make prayer" at five distinct times during the day – early morning *(fajr)*, midday *(zuhr)*, afternoon, *(asr)*, dusk *(maghrib)*, and evening *(isha)* – I began to enact and perceive qualitative distinctions between those times and others. More specifically, practicing prayer at five distinct times throughout the day carved out – in and through practice – a distinction between the more relative time of everyday life and the "set apart" (Bell, 1992; Durkheim, 1995) times of prayer.

These temporal distinctions between 'prayer time' and 'not prayer time' were conjoined and reinforced by spatial ones. When the time came for salat, my prayers needed to be performed anywhere I happened to be – at home, rising from my bed; on my university campus, having lunch; in my office; typing up fieldnotes or revising a manuscript, and so on. Spatial distinctions also manifested in the prayer movements themselves, particularly during moments when I had to prostrate myself with knees, hands, and forehead pressed firmly to the ground. As I moved from standing, to bowing, and finally to full prostration, I was again enacting practical and perceptual distinctions, juxtaposing the everyday bodily orientation of standing with the more rarified comportment of prostration.

Intimately related to the perceptual reorganization of the spatiotemporal coordinates of everyday life, I found, was also a reconstruction of habituated memory and attention. Both the prescribed movements as well as the timing of salat required my ongoing work and attention. Especially at the beginning stages of my attempts to make prayer, I struggled to remain mindful of when I was supposed to pray and also found myself in places where performing prayer was highly inconvenient, impractical, or even unsafe (for example, commuting in traffic). Successfully making prayer, I found, also required a deliberate and conscious effort on my part to reorganize my daily habits and routines in ways that prioritized the practice. As one convert, Karen, put it when we were discussing the need to be mindful of prayer: "Like it's always on my mind, because when you pray five times a day, every time of the day you're thinking about, okay, I need to pray. I have to remind myself constantly, you know, I need to pray soon, I need to pray soon." The way this reorganization of memory and attention as well as other distinguishing elements of the embodied experience of salat are interpreted through Islamic theological discourse will be addressed in the next section, but what I want to stress here is how actually participating in the practice allowed me to understand how a meaningful domain of practical and perceptual distinctions was enacted in and through its very performance (Bourdieu, 1977). Beyond or below the rich religious symbolization and discursive interpretation surrounding salat was the carving out of distinctions within the perceptual field and the reorganization of embodied movement, attention, and memory. This is the dimension of "being in the world" that Merleau-Ponty (2012) associated with the "pre-objective," the register of experience that begins not with pre-existing, already interpreted objects but in the more indeterminate realm of action, affect, and perception.

The relevance of this pre-objective dimension for religious practice, interpretation, and meaning-making also became clear to me in a later and more in-depth project on contemporary conversions to Eastern Orthodox Christianity (see: Winchester, 2015, 2016, 2017; Winchester and Green, 2019). Based on the important lessons learned in my early fieldwork on conversions to Islam, I continued to experiment with an enactive approach to my inquiries into how religious meaning systems become compelling and persuasive to people. In this project, one of the practices I participated in most extensively was fasting.[2] More specifically, I fasted along with local Orthodox communities during two of the major Orthodox fasting seasons – the 40-day Nativity Fast before Christmas and the seven-week Lenten or 'Great' Fast before Easter (or Pascha, as it is called in the Orthodox tradition). A central practice within many religious traditions and communities, fasting in Eastern Orthodoxy generally involves abstaining from meat, dairy, oil, and wine (usually interpreted as extending to all alcoholic drinks). In addition to restrictions on types of food and drink, the Church states that one should also greatly reduce food intake, usually eating only one or two small meals during the day.

Like salat in Islam, fasting in Orthodoxy is a subject of rich theological symbolism and discourse. But, also like salat, I learned that an exclusive focus on the symbolic-discursive registers of Orthodox fasting would miss how much of what was meaningful about the practice came from the experience of actively doing and undergoing it.

As with prayer, I found that fasting involved a fundamental deconstruction and reorganization of some generally taken-for-granted bodily routines and habits of attention, extending even to the most visceral depths of my corporeality. Especially in the early stages of my fasts, I found myself inadvertently breaking the fasting rules by habitually reaching for and even ingesting food and drink that I was not supposed to. And even when I began to get a handle on some of my habitual impulses to eat first and ask questions later, strong cravings for particular food and drink items that were no longer acceptable – for example, an omelet for breakfast, a guilty-pleasure cheeseburger, a beer to wind down in the evening – began to occupy the forefront of my waking consciousness. So too, did my rumbling stomach, reminding me of my fast even when the rest of me was trying to focus on work, exercise, or even a casual conversation with friends. Feelings of irritability and annoyance from these hunger pangs and cravings also made an appearance in my lived experience of fasting, as well as small but significant feelings of triumph when, later into a fasting season, I became more acclimated to and adept at the practice, and my negative feelings became less intense and my strong cravings dissipated.

Practicing a fast, I learned, involved nothing less than an inversion of the usual structure of corporeal awareness. As phenomenologists such as Merleau-Ponty (2012) and Leder (1990) have argued, even as embodiment provides the very grounds of human experience of and engagement with the world, our bodies paradoxically tend to recede from experience. In most situations of everyday life, humans attend *to* the world around them *from* their bodies, meaning that the corporeal structures and processes of the body that enable our perspectives on the world are precisely those which can be hardest to disclose to conscious awareness, let alone rigorous interpretation. When I, for example, normally reached for a cold beer or took a bite out of a cheeseburger, my arms, hands, mouth, and general body position were not the focus of my conscious experience. They were instead my generally unproblematic modes of embodied access to the food or drink items that were the center of my action and perceptual awareness. Even more hidden away were the deeply visceral and autonomic processes of swallowing, digestion, satiation, and so on, that accompanied my normal eating and drinking habits.

Yet fasting reversed this normal experiential structure of embodied action and awareness, as dimensions of embodiment that usually remained in the deep background of my awareness were suddenly brought to the fore of attention. Catching myself reaching for or absentmindedly eating suddenly forbidden food disclosed how much of my eating was grounded in unthinking habit and routine. Strong cravings made me more keenly aware of how much of my existence was supported by easy access to and reliance on particular food and drink items. My continuously rumbling stomach made me acutely conscious of visceral bodily depths that were usually hidden away, and my irritability disclosed how much of what I would like to think of as an affable personality is buttressed by having my digestive needs met. I began to feel as if I was 90 per cent stomach and 10 per cent miscellaneous parts.

Once again, though I have not even touched on the important religious symbolism attached to any of these experiences, the corporeal dimensions of the practice – what their effects disclose to perceptual awareness and how they cultivate particular modes of bodily attention, response, and action – are clearly significant. Whether one is a committed believer, an agnostic ethnographer, or something in-between, it is impossible to ignore the fact that *you doing the thing does something to you*. More specifically, actively participating in the bodily rituals, techniques, and practices of a religious community makes it abundantly clear that such practices do not just express pre-existing creedal beliefs nor solely represent symbolic meanings; they also cultivate particular forms of sensory awareness, bodily comportment, practical know-how, and dispositions toward thought and action – what some scholars of religion, following Bourdieu (1977), have conceptualized as a 'habitus' (see, for example: Asad, 1993; Mahmood, 2005; Winchester, 2008). Doing and undergoing religious practices provides an "up-close and personal" ethnographic lens through which to grasp the aesthetic and corporeal dimensions of these practices, also giving lie to the increasingly untenable notion that religions are primarily a matter of beliefs in the brain or creeds in a text.

Moreover, it gives us a way to better understand how these embodied registers of religious practice significantly influence and interact with religious actors' interpretations of their more symbolic-discursive meanings.

From the somatic to the symbolic: interpreting practices from within

While the preceding section has stressed that a good deal of what is meaningful about religious practices operates at the nondiscursive level of embodied experience and so "goes without saying" (Bourdieu, 1977), it remains the case that most religious practices are also the subject of a great deal of explicit symbolism and discursive interpretation. Again, practices – including religious ones – are socially organized "doings *and sayings*" (my emphasis: Schatzki, 2002), and an important aspect of most religious practices includes how social actors reflect on, discuss, and interpret the symbolic meanings attached to them. An enactive approach to analyzing religious practices, therefore, does not abandon the insights of classic symbolic perspectives. But it does adapt and deploy them from a different angle of vision. More to the point, an enactive approach encourages the ethnographer to 'read' the meaning of practices from within – that is, not from the perspective of an observer standing outside the practice but from the vantage point of a practitioner doing and undergoing its corporeal effects.

In my own work on conversion, I have found that the somatic registers of religious praxis interact with the discursive-symbolic dimension in several important ways. One is how the bodily effects of a religious practice make what we might call *interpretive demands*. Scholars of religion since Durkheim have noted that one of the most fundamental aspects of religious thought and action involves a process of demarcation: the "setting apart" of some things from others that creates the distinction between sacred and profane. According to ritual scholar Catherine Bell (1992), ritual itself is constituted in actions that distinguish themselves from others in and through their very performance – a process she terms "ritualization." Indeed, one can think of how rituals involve forms of bodily comportment (for example, kneeling, bowing, prostration, abstinence) and linguistic expression (for example, rarely used languages such as Latin, chanting, and so on) that stand out precisely because they are not generally performed elsewhere in everyday life.

What is remarked on less often by interpretive scholars of religion, however, is how these distinctions and inversions play out phenomenologically, at the level of lived experience (but see: Tavory and Winchester, 2012; Surak, 2017; Pagis, 2019). But, as the examples in the previous section highlight, engaging in religious practices creates a number of notable shifts – even ruptures – in the structure of phenomenal consciousness, directing attention to dimensions of experience that would otherwise remain hidden. These attentional shifts, in turn, "call out" for interpretation. Indeed, especially for new religious inquirers or converts, I found that many acts of interpretation started with questions along the lines of, "What is going on here?" or "Why do I feel this way?" And it was precisely in these moments of questioning that others in the community – usually religious leaders and more seasoned practitioners – would offer an appropriate and often creative religious interpretation, connecting the concrete, bodily experience of the practice to the more transcendent field of symbolism and theological discourse of their respective religious tradition. What also came into focus through involving myself in the "doings and sayings" of particular religious practices was that the corporeal experience of the practice did not just create space for moments of religious interpretation. It also significantly structured the form and content of the interpretation, encouraging practitioners to understand the symbolic meanings of the practice through their bodily experiences of it – and vice versa (Winchester, 2016).

One of the benefits of taking a participatory, enactive approach is that it enabled me to become much more actively involved in – and even subject to – these interpretive processes. Many of the most enlightening and important conversations I had about the meaning and significance of religious practices in the lives of Muslim and Eastern Orthodox converts alike started not with abstract theological discussions but rather through commiserating over the concrete particulars of performing and keeping a practice. Take, as just one example, a conversation I had while having a Lenten meal of spaghetti and homemade tomato sauce with married converts Abby and Jacob during the early stages of the fasting season.[3] Lost in good conversation and heartily enjoying the home cooking, none of us realized until it was too late that we had eaten much more than what would be considered a modest portion appropriate for a fast. Looking down, somewhat sheepishly, at the empty pot after our meal, Abby explained to me that she initially planned for enough leftovers for her and Jacob's dinner tomorrow, a situation Jacob quickly labelled a "major fasting fail." Feeling both sympathetic and highly culpable (I certainly had 'seconds,' if not 'thirds' that evening), I confided that I had found myself unwittingly breaking the fasting guidelines as well, not realizing I was eating too much – or the wrong thing entirely – until it was too late. This became an opening to a conversation about the more symbolic and theological aspects of the practice, but one in which the commentary took place decidedly within and not outside of the contours of the fasting experience itself. More specifically, it became an interpretive moment in which the hunger and appetites of our stomachs became revealed as windows into the purported passions of our souls:

Abby: We're finding out this is part of the learning process involved in fasting. The Holy Fathers write about the "hypocrisy of the stomach." Even when you've had plenty, you want more.

Jacob: It's this habit or addiction of always wanting more and more … The Church Fathers, they say it all begins in the stomach and then it spreads from there. And so we've tried to take that lesson to heart, you know, try to cut back, cut down, focus on what's important.

Me: In what ways, specifically …?

Abby: Well, we're still trying to work it out with the food, obviously [laughs as she points to the empty spaghetti pot in the sink]. But we've decided to cut back on entertainment – frivolous magazines and television, you know … And on consumption, in general, because that's a big way I think we're programmed,

	at least here in the United States, to give in to our passions, to be ruled by our passions, I would say.
Jacob:	Yeah, like it's some great virtue to shop your way into debt ... [I]t's ... the same thing as eating more than you really need, eating even when your belly is so full that it's bursting. Buying crap even when you don't have room in your house for all the other stuff you bought last year. That's how the passions work.
Me:	And so you think fasting has helped you understand that in a new way?
Jacob:	Uh-huh. Definitely.
Abby:	It's just such a tangible experience ... [W]hen you have to try to control one of your most basic impulses – to eat – you kind of recognize these things about your condition at a very concrete level.

Within Orthodox theological discourse, the passions are disordered desires of the soul and believed to be at the root of humans' tendencies toward sinful actions. While every human being is thought to have a natural desire for God, humans' separation from God has meant this desire has become disoriented and turned toward worldly instead of heavenly things (Staniloae, 2002). Only by acquiring knowledge of these passions and how they operate can one reorient them toward God, ultimately transforming the soul's desires from worldly passions to godly virtues (Chryssavgis, 2008).

And, while there is an immense amount of theological writing about the passions within the Orthodox tradition, what was most significant in converts' own religious paths was how these interpretations regarding the workings of their otherwise immaterial souls became manifest in and through the experiences of their bodies. By way of a series of embodied metaphors, the compulsive and insatiable nature of the passions were experienced through analogical association with those of the stomach: an experience over-indulging at dinner became an interpretive vector for reflecting on both the nature of the passions and on the tendency to engage in additional worldly indulgences; battling one's cravings for forbidden foods became metaphorical lenses for evaluating one's more general ability to avoid sin and act according to the ethical standards of God; feelings of irritability and anger due to hunger and the withdrawal of usual foods and drinks became analogical windows into the immaturity of one's spiritual condition; the ability to overcome such feelings and work through one's hunger during a fast became interpretive scaffolding for evaluating one's propensity to walk the narrow path of salvation (see Winchester, 2016 for a more wide-ranging analysis). In and through such practice-generated associations between the experience-near body and the more experience-distant soul, Orthodox moral discourse and religious symbolism became more deeply integrated into converts' phenomenological realities, making new religious interpretations of self and world not only possible, but also more experientially persuasive and compelling (see: Pagis, 2019).

A similar kind of somatic-symbolic interaction occurred within the contours of Muslim prayer. As mentioned in the previous section, attempting to perform salat five times a day entails a qualitative reorganization of everyday temporality. The very activity of engaging in the prescribed cycles of standing, bowing, kneeling, recitation, and prostration at specific times throughout the day creates distinctions between those times and others. Among the Muslim converts I studied, these phenomenal structures became ways to experientially ground a more general symbolic distinction between the mundanity of the world's time and the authoritative and transcendent nature of "God's time." As convert Karen explained it:

"[F]or most of your day you're on somebody else's clock, whether it's your own, your boss's, your friends', your family's, whatever. But when you're praying, that's God's time. And that takes precedence over everything else. Whether you're studying, at work, playing around, whatever, prayer takes precedence. Allah takes precedence."

Yet, as I experienced throughout my engagements with salat, successfully responding to God's time on a consistent basis could prove difficult. Especially during the early stages of my prayer routine, I was either late for specific prayers or missed them altogether. A convert named Nina, however, assured me that this was normal:

"When you first start practicing, you almost feel like there's no way to keep up with this, to remember and make time for prayer every single day. I mean, I know I felt guilty at first because I missed so many prayers because I either, one, put them off, or, two, just forgot to do them ... But, over time, it just kind of takes root with you, if that makes sense."

And indeed, over time, I found that prayer did "take root." The longer I practiced, the more mindful and habituated I became to both when it was time to pray and where I needed to be in order to do so successfully. Practice, so it seemed, took practice. And, according to my Muslim interlocutors, practice also made – if not perfect – at least much improved. More to the point, they told me that successfully making prayer was a sign I was developing a sense of mindfulness or remembrance (*dhikr*) for God and, more generally, the virtue of *taqwa*, an Arabic term that translates to 'piety' or, more specifically, 'consciousness or fear of God.' Much like the appetites of the stomach became a way to metaphorically peer into the passions of the soul among the Eastern Orthodox, the ability to make prayer became an experiential analog for evaluating the state of one's spiritual discipline and development among Muslims. Becoming more disposed to the corporeal demands of prayer was interpreted as becoming more inclined to the spiritual demands of godliness.

As someone engaging in salat for research purposes and who remained fundamentally agnostic about the existence of the God to whom I was supposed to be praying, I remained skeptical of the notion that I was in fact developing ethically and spiritually valued capacities such as taqwa. In fact, I said as much during an extended interview with a Muslim convert named Abe with whom I'd developed particularly good rapport, telling him that, while I was perfectly fine with Muslims in the community thinking I was becoming more pious, I myself did not buy it because, as I put it, "I don't really believe in Allah or Islam in the same way you do."

Abe listened politely as I expressed my skepticism, initially nodding in agreement and saying, "Right" and "Sure, sure." But then he grinned a little, shrugged, and said, "But you never know." "Wait, what do you mean?" I asked him. "It's just ... it was the same kind of thing with me," Abe replied, telling me that, when he first converted to Islam and said the *shahada* – a public declaration of faith one says in order to be recognized as a member of the Islamic faith – he had said it on a bit of a dare and with "doubt in my mind that I would be practicing any religion, especially [one] as regimented as Islam is." "The old Abe," he told me, was pretty irreverent, and he liked to party, drink, and smoke a lot of weed.

I was surprised. The Abe that sat before me at the time of our conversation had been a practicing Muslim for seven years, and though I would not describe him as an overly zealous convert, the Abe I had come to know during my research was notably committed, sincere, and thoughtful in his Muslim faith. I saw him at almost every congregational prayer and found him always eager to discuss religion and give helpful advice about books and other resources on the Islamic faith. When I inquired into how "old Abe" had become the "new Abe," a significant part of his answer was prayer. As he explained it to me:

"The main reason was I got serious about making the prayer ... So I couldn't go to the mosque and pray and then come out and consciously get drunk, you know? There was dissonance there ... I couldn't go every day and humble myself before Allah and then just turn around and defy that. It [drinking and drugs] just didn't feel right anymore."

"So prayer is what changed you?" I asked him.

"Yes," he replied. "Prayer and Allah. And those two are related, of course."

Later in our conversation, I discovered that Abe's seriousness about making prayer was very much encouraged and, significantly, co-interpreted by two Muslim friends and confidants in his congregation as well as his older brother, who had converted to the Nation of Islam while serving time in prison and before Abe had expressed his own interest in Islam (which was of the Sunni variety). He told me:

> "They all knew me well enough to know that I wasn't really gonna be doing what I was supposed to be doing at first ... And, while I didn't really say anything about it to them, I think they knew that I was a little not-serious or flighty, if you will ... And so they were like, 'Hey, before you make any more decisions [about the faith], just make prayer. Just make salat.' It was like a challenge they put to me, you know."

Abe accepted the challenge, and regularly interacted with these three men as he became more deeply engaged and committed to meeting it. Indeed, when he started to succeed in making his five daily prayers on a regular basis (and lessened the amount of time he spent partying and doing other "frivolous stuff," as he called it), they told him it was proof that he was becoming more pious, developing taqwa. He said to me:

> "I wasn't sure I really believed them at first. But eventually I did. It was like, yeah, I can live this life. I can be a better man, inshallah ... It's like the *hadith*[4] says, 'Take one step towards Allah and He will take ten steps towards you.'"

Seeing a small grin come across my face, Abe then laughed and interjected, "Look, man, I'm not trying to make you take shahada right here or anything. I'm just sayin', you never know."

Of course, as someone who was busy fitting Abe's and other religious converts' actions, identities, and experiences into the interpretive categories of sociology, I could be neither angry nor shocked that they might fit my activities into the interpretive categories of their faith. Turnabout is fair play. And I *was* praying after all.

Yet what did come as a pleasant surprise – an interpretive epiphany of sorts – was that, by virtue of actively engaging in the practices of the religious group I was studying, I was also gaining some firsthand access to and knowledge of some of the important techniques of persuasion surrounding religious practices and the conversion process. Indeed, I found in my research among converts to both Islam and Eastern Orthodoxy that most religious inquirers and neophytes began their practices in a somewhat experimental mode – more a stance of "Let me try this out" than full-fledged religious commitment. And, as they engaged with and experienced the bodily effects, practical challenges, and successes associated with religious praxis, there were others in the community to interpretively scaffold these experiences toward deeper religious meanings, motivating the individual to continue on, to discover more, to become someone different, better, more authentic, even holier than before (Winchester and Green, 2019; see also: Johnston, 2017). As I learned – in part by becoming subject to it myself not just with Abe but at several other points throughout my research – this dynamic interplay between the embodied experience and symbolic interpretation of religious praxis was at the heart of the conversion process and the "experiential careers" (Tavory and Winchester, 2012) of religious life and commitment, more generally.

And while I did not convert to Islam or Eastern Orthodox Christianity ("yet," many of the individuals in my research would probably add), my participation did enable me to better appreciate the experiential and interpretive allure of engaged religious practice for those who did – the appeal of the possibilities that might lie behind the phrase, "You never know."

Conclusion

As a methodological lens, enactive ethnography allows researchers of religion to garner some intimate knowledge of the corporeal effects of religious practices on those who do and undergo them, as well as the interpretive connections that are forged between the somatic and more symbolic registers of religious action and experience. Along with an analytic eye trained to look for the social relations and interactions that undergird such practices, the enactive approach can productively blur the line between the object of sociological inquiry – that is, the lived experience of religious practice – and the mode of inquiry, generating fresh insight into how religious practices generate meaning, form subjects, and create the "aura of factuality" (Geertz 1973) that often surrounds religious symbols.

But here some words of caution. Participating in the practices of a religious community as a method of inquiry does not mean that we, as researchers, have unproblematically accessed the breadth and depth of the subjectivities of those we study. Doing what they do, in other words, does not translate into becoming who they are.

I say this not to set up some kind of impenetrable divide between the positions of researcher and researched, faithful believer and faithful social scientist. If anything, an honest assessment of fieldwork practice shows that such subject positions – both 'ours' and 'theirs' – are more dynamic, fluid, and relational than sometimes presented in published accounts (Neitz, 2002; Orsi, 2005; Tavory, 2019). Nor do I say this to imply that the lived experience of religious life is inexplicable and completely closed off from scholarly understanding. Indeed, as other contemporary scholars have demonstrated, the idea that 'religious experience' is ineffable and primarily a matter of what happens within individuals' heads has as much to do with historical attempts to shield religious experience from empirical inquiry than an accurate description of its fundamental essence (Proudfoot, 1985; Sharf, 1998; Taves, 2009; Bender, 2010).

I make this point, rather, to encourage humility as opposed to hubris when it comes to engaging in the practices of others in the field. It is important to recognize that the experience of religious practice is dynamic and changes over space and time. Contrary to old tropes about the timelessness and tradition-bound essence of religion, religious life does not stand still. The way that prayer or fasting (or meditation or yoga, and so on) affect a new convert, for example, can be quite different compared to someone who has been practicing for several years, even decades (see: Tavory and Winchester, 2012). As such, it is important to recognize how the fruits and limitations of an enactive approach are shaped by the positionalities of the practitioners involved, including that of the ethnographer. It is likely true, for example, that enaction provides keener insights into the early stages of a religious career, as both the ethnographer and the religious neophyte, despite their different aims, usually share a similar structural position of being novices and 'outsiders' to the religious community. Nevertheless, it is also the case that having some knowledge of the effects of doing and undergoing religious practices, even if at one point in time, can still grant important insights regarding the experiential and social distinctions religious communities make between 'newcomers and old-timers,' 'amateurs and experts,' 'insiders and outsiders,' 'novices and adepts,' as well as what marks the passages between such statuses over time.

This is to say that an enactive approach, while powerful, remains partial. To most readers, this statement will come across as common sense. As we learn early in our training, all methodological perspectives constrain as much as enable what we can observe, experience, and ultimately know about the social world. But I think it is especially important to reiterate here because there can be a temptation to use 'observant participation' as a badge of epistemic authenticity and authority – "I was there, I did these things, so I know."

Instead, inspired by the title of this edited collection, I encourage those who engage in an enactive mode of ethnographic inquiry to think of participating in practices as fashioning a particular methodological lens, one that, if peered through carefully, allows one to better see (and/or feel, hear, smell, taste) religion *through* the perspective of participation and *from* the perspective of experience. As Robert Orsi (2005) argues, building off the insights of anthropologist Michael Jackson (1989), "experience" need not be conceptualized as a shared subjectivity or identity, but, more productively, as an experimental field in which one explores strategies of connection with those one is attempting to understand. While I do not claim that enactive ethnography can allow one to grasp the full complexity of any one religious person's or community's experience, I hope to have demonstrated how it can help create moments of connection, and what those moments can provide in terms of insight on the phenomenon of religious practice.

Notes

1   To protect confidentiality, all names of research subjects are pseudonyms.
2   In my earlier research among Muslims, I had also participated in the Ramadan fast (*sawm*) but only for the last week of the holy month. My later research with Eastern Orthodox Christians allowed me to engage with fasting for lengthier stretches of time.
3   Being invited over to Orthodox Christians' homes for a meal during a long fasting season became a common occurrence once people in the communities I studied learned that I was engaging in the practice along with them. Not only were the meals and company often excellent, but the conversations that took place during them became important data for my own scholarly interpretations.
4   In Islam, hadiths are narrative accounts of the actions, teachings, and sayings of the Prophet Muhammad.

References

Ammerman, N. (2020) "Rethinking Religion: Toward a Practice Approach," *American Journal of Sociology*, 126(1): 1–46.

Asad, T. (1993) "Pain and Truth in Medieval Christian Ritual," in *Geneaologies of Religion*. Baltimore, MD: John Hopkins University Press, pp. 83–124.

Bell, C. (1992) *Ritual Theory, Ritual Practice*, New York: Oxford University Press.

Bender, C. (2010) *The New Metaphysicals: Spirituality and the American Religious Imagination*, Chicago: University of Chicago Press.

Bourdieu, P. (1977) *Outline of a Theory of Practice*, Cambridge: Cambridge University Press.

Chryssavgis, J. (2008) *In the Heart of the Desert: The Spirituality of the Desert Fathers and Mothers*, Bloomington, IN: World Wisdom.

Csordas, T. (1993) "Somatic Modes of Attention," *Cultural Anthropology*, 8(2): 135–56.

Dewey, J. (1934) "Having an Experience," in *Art as Experience*, New York: Penguin, pp. 36–59.

Douglas, M. (1966) *Purity and Danger: An Analysis of Concepts of Pollution and Taboo*, New York: Praeger.

Durkheim, É. (1995) *The Elementary Forms of Religious Life*, New York: The Free Press.

Geertz, C. (1973) "Religion as a Cultural System," in C. Geertz (ed) *The Interpretation of Cultures*, New York: Basic Books, pp. 87–125.

Harding, S.F. (1987) "Convicted by the Holy Spirit: The Rhetoric of Fundamental Baptist Conversion," *American Ethnologist*, 14(1): 167–81.

Jackson, M. (1989) *Paths Toward a Clearing: Radical Empiricism and Ethnographic Inquiry*, Bloomington, IN: Indiana University Press.

Johnston, E.F. (2017) "Failing to Learn, or Learning to Fail? Accounting for Persistence in the Acquisition of Spiritual Disciplines," *Qualitative Sociology*, 40(3): 353–72.

Leach, E. (1966) "Ritualization in Man in Relation to Conceptual and Social Developments," in J. Huxley (ed) *A Discussion on Ritualization of Behavior in Animals and Man*, pp. 403–8.

Leder, D. (1990) *The Absent Body*, Chicago: Chicago University Press.

Mahmood, S. (2005) *Politics of Piety: The Islamic Revival and the Feminist Subject*, Princeton, NJ: Princeton University Press.

Mauss, M. (1979 [1934]) "Body Techniques," in B. Brewster (ed) *Sociology and Psychology: Essays*, London: Routledge and Kegan Paul.

McGuire, M. (2008) *Lived Religion: Faith and Practice in Everyday Life*, New York: Oxford University Press.

McRoberts, O.M. (2004) "Beyond Mysterium Tremendum: Thoughts toward an Aesthetic Study of Religious Experience," *The ANNALS of the American Academy of Political and Social Science*, 595(September): 190–203.

Merleau-Ponty, M. (2012) *Phenomenology of Perception*, New York: Routledge.

Neitz, M.J. (2002) "Walking between the Worlds: Permeable Boundaries, Ambiguous Identities," in J.V. Spickard, J.S. Landres, and M.B. McGuire (eds) *Personal Knowledge and Beyond: Reshaping the Ethnography of Religion*, New York: New York University Press, pp. 33–46.

Noe, A. (2004) *Action in Perception*, Cambridge, MA: MIT Press.

Orsi, R.A. (2005) *Between Heaven and Earth: The Religious Worlds People Make and the Scholars Who Study Them*, Princeton, NJ: Princeton University Press.

Pagis, M. (2019) *Inward: Vipassana Meditation and the Embodiment of the Self*, Chicago: University of Chicago Press.

Proudfoot, W. (1985) *Religious Experience*, Berkeley: University of California Press.

Reed, I.A. (2011) *Interpretation and Social Knowledge: On the Use of Theory in the Human Sciences*, Chicago: University of Chicago Press.

Ricoeur, P. (1984) *Time and Narrative, Vol. 1*, Chicago: Chicago University Press.

Riesebrodt, M. (2010) *The Promise of Salvation: A Theory of Religion*, Chicago: University of Chicago Press.

Schatzki, T.R. (2001) "Introduction," in K.K. Cetina, T.R. Schatzki, and E. von Savigny, (eds) *The Practice Turn in Contemporary Theory*, New York: Routledge, pp. 10–24.

Schatzki, T.R. (2002) *The Site of the Social: A Philosophical Account of the Constitution of Social Life and Change*, University Park, PA: Pennsylvania University Press.

Sharf, R. (1998) "Experience," in M.C. Taylor (ed) *Critical Terms for Religious Studies*, Chicago: University of Chicago Press, pp. 94–116.

Smith, C. (2017) *Religion: What It Is, How It Works, and Why It Matters*, Princeton, NJ: Princeton University Press.

Staniloae, D. (2002) *Orthodox Spirituality: A Practical Guide for the Faithful and a Definitive Manual for the Scholar*, South Canaan, PA: St. Tikhon's Seminary Press.

Surak, K. (2017) "Rupture and Rhythm: A Phenomenology of National Experiences," *Sociological Theory*, 35(4): 312–33.

Taves, A. (2009) *Religious Experience Reconsidered: A Building-Block Approach to the Study of Religion and Other Special Things*, Princeton, NJ: Princeton University Press.

Tavory, I. (2019) "Beyond the Calculus of Power and Position: Relationships and Theorizing in Ethnography," *Sociological Methods and Research*, 48(4): 727–38.

Tavory, I., and Winchester, D. (2012) "Experiential Careers: The Routinization and De-routinization of Religious Life," *Theory and Society*, 41(4): 351–73.

Turner, V. (1967) *The Forest of Symbols: Aspects of Ndembu Ritual*, Ithaca, NY: Cornell University Press.

Varela, F., Thompson, E., and Rosch, E. (1991) *The Embodied Mind: Cognitive Science and Human Experience*. Cambridge, MA: MIT Press.

Wacquant, L. (2015) "For a Sociology of Flesh and Blood," *Qualitative Sociology*, 38(1): 1–11.

Winchester, D. (2008) "Embodying the Faith: Religious Practice and the Making of a Muslim Moral Habitus," *Social Forces*, 86(4): 1753–80.

Winchester, D. (2015) "Converting to Continuity: Temporality and Self in Eastern Orthodox Conversion Narratives," *Journal for the Scientific Study of Religion*, 54(3): 439–60.

Winchester, D. (2016) "A Hunger for God: Embodied Metaphor as Cultural Cognition in Action," *Social Forces*, 95(2): 585–606.

Winchester, D. (2017) " 'A Part of Who I Am': Material Objects as 'Plot Devices' in the Formation of Religious Selves," *Journal for the Scientific Study of Religion*, 56(1): 83–103.

Winchester, D., and Green, K.D. (2019) "Talking Your Self into It: How and When Accounts Shape Motivation for Action," *Sociological Theory*, 37(3): 257–81.

Wuthnow, R. (2020) *What Happens When We Practice Religion?: Textures of Devotion in Everyday Life*, Princeton, NJ: Princeton University Press.

4

Mind the Gap: What Ethnographic Silences Can Teach Us

Rebecca Kneale Gould

In my early years as a qualitative researcher, I was attuned to words and hungry for what they might teach. Whether it is reading poetry or doing 'content analysis,' I have always loved probing the depth of meaning that can be found in a single word or phrase, deployed in a particular way. Of course, some words are more freighted than others. Anyone engaged in the study of religion will eventually wrestle with words that are so over-determined and saturated that we need yet more words to make sense of what is being said: *karma*, grace, *atman, tawid, mitzvot*, God. What I love about fieldwork is that you can always *ask*. You can probe for more words, more nuance, a short tale, a life story, and with each elaboration, more meanings (as well as contradictions and struggles) will emerge. Whether I am studying texts or conversations, I have always understood words to be the key to unlocking both how people make meaning in *their* lives and how *I* might make sense of their meaning-making practices.[1]

Lately, however, my obsession with words has begun to shift. The wisdom of my mentors, coupled with my own contemplative leanings, has led me to pay more careful attention to silences. What does someone's silence have to tell me? In the midst of an interview, does a moment of silence indicate an evolving sense of trust between me and my conversation partner? Or is that silence a sign of awkwardness or lack of connection? And what of the silences between individuals or groups with whom I am spending time in the field? Are these signs of unease, or indicators of unequal power dynamics and intentional acts of silenc*ing*? Or are these silences signs of comfort – of things understood that do not need to be said? Beyond these particular questions, there is also always the meta-question in the back of my mind: can I trust myself to be a faithful interpreter of the gaps between someone's words?

Sociologist Eviatar Zerubavel reminds us that silence is, indeed, a part of speech and a form of social expression that demands our attention. Not surprisingly, he adds, silence is often ignored by scholars, undertheorized and understudied. This inattention exists in large part because "nonoccurrences ... by definition, are rather difficult to observe" (Zerubavel, 2006: pp. 8–13). In this chapter – with Zerubavel's encouragement, as well as his caveats, in mind – I will explore the uses of silence for those of us whose lives and work are dedicated to interpreting religion, asking questions similar to those posed by Titus Hjelm, in this volume, who considers the power dynamics and 'action orientation' of discourse, including the discourse of silence (see Chapter 6). In particular, I want to reflect back on a range of memorable occasions of silence. These occasions have emerged over decades of research in two overlapping, but distinct, realms. The first is research I conducted on the spiritual dimensions of back-to-the-land practices in the United States from Thoreau's iconic two-year experiment of living in Walden Woods (1845–7) to the work of homesteaders carving out largely self-sufficient livelihoods in rural Maine in the 1990s, some of whom continue to do so today (Gould, 2005). The second is ongoing research and writing that attends to various forms of 'religious environmentalism' particularly in its Protestant, Catholic and Jewish forms. Here – often in the company of my friend and collaborator, Laurel Kearns – my interest has been in mapping the complex relationships between religious identity and environmental commitment on both the individual and institutional level. This research has included everything from extended interviews with self-identified 'green' Christian evangelicals and liberal Jews to mapping the history of denominational decisions to support eco-justice initiatives and climate change activism (Gould, 2007; Gould and Kearns, 2018).

Silence at the shared table

Before digging into how various moments of silence have illuminated these research projects (sometimes in the moment and sometimes in retrospect), let me begin with an *imagined* event involving the kinds of silences that indicate when communication and connection is breaking down along religious-secular lines. While this more 'negative' form of silence is but one kind of silence that I will explore in this chapter, it is an important place to begin, for it reveals the extent to which silencing can occur among those who share central values (in this case, ecological ones), but who differ when it comes to matters of religious identity.

This scenario – a hypothetical 'potluck supper,' where each guest or group brings a dish to a communal gathering – is one that I sometimes put before my students and colleagues when I am reflecting on the overlaps and distinctions between my two primary research projects, but it requires some background information to make sense. Let me also state, at the outset, that although this potluck never actually happened, it certainly could have! The sketch that follows draws on a series of events that are absolutely real and that have transpired over the course of my years of research. The only part that is invented is simply the collapse of space, time and projects, such that self-identified 'secular' homesteaders and religiously identified environmentalists find themselves under one 'green' roof.

First, let me offer some context. As I argued in *At Home in Nature*, the homesteaders with whom I lived in the late 1990s were creative, visionary men and women who lived deeply spiritual lives (Gould, 2005). Many of them – for all kinds of valid reasons, including experiences of harm and abuse – had intentionally distanced themselves from institutional religion. As was the case for Henry David Thoreau, the natural world was, for them, the primary site of meaning and authority. Nature was the sacred center, the ultimate reference point for how these homesteaders understood themselves and their work in the world. "Getting close to nature" was a highly motivating force behind homesteaders' conscious decisions to leave more conventional (and often "easier") lives in the cities and the suburbs. Not surprisingly, homesteaders' stories about these life-altering decisions often resembled conversion narratives in structure, content and tone.

While homesteaders varied in the degree to which they pursued lives of relative self-sufficiency and simplicity (lives that, nonetheless, were often quite complex), they were united by engaging in practices that were at once pragmatic and highly symbolic. For instance, some ritualized the felling of trees, honoring the lives taken for the construction of a home. Others articulated 'theologies of compost' invoking the spiritual lessons of death and rebirth that come from a practice that others might see merely as ecologically responsible organic waste management. Many celebrated and affirmed their ways of living with weekly saunas and potlucks, gatherings that some explicitly referred to as "my church" and "my religion."

The religious environmentalists with whom I have spent time – attending wilderness retreats, political trainings, intra- and inter-faith conferences and extended Shabbat celebrations – share much in common with the homesteaders from whom I learned. They too celebrate practices of simplicity and "food sufficiency" as ecological virtues. For instance, many have created gardens on the grounds of their churches and synagogues, often distributing the homegrown produce to local shelters and soup kitchens. They too are focused on expressing gratitude for what the natural world has to give us, particularly in terms of healthy organic food that feeds both body and soul. And they too are apt to invoke theologies of compost (in this case with the *theo* explicitly present), sometimes even blessing compost piles, as a group of Episcopal priests has done during Rogation Sunday processions at Saint Mark's Episcopal Cathedral in Seattle.[2]

At the same time, however, some clergy and congregants are wary of the term 'environmentalist' or concerned about being seen as 'activists.' Many prefer terms such as 'stewardship' and 'creation care' to describe their religious-ecological work (Kearns, 2014). Some, particularly Christian evangelicals, take pains to point out that in all of their ecological work, from protecting endangered species to combatting climate change, "We are worshipping the Creator, not the creation." In more religiously orthodox contexts, concerns about secularism and 'paganism' often bubble up when clergy or congregants are seen as pushing an explicitly environmental agenda.[3] In sum, self-identified 'secular' homesteaders and religiously identified 'creation care' advocates share much common ground in terms of their love of nature and the central role that ecological concerns, particularly the climate crisis, play in their lives. At the same time, however, significant identity differences shape how they interpret and express these concerns, both to themselves and to others.

So, what would happen, I have often wondered, if many of the people from whom I have learned so much were to gather together for a celebratory fall harvest potluck? How would things go, say, if homesteaders sat down for meal with various members of the Coalition on the Environment and Jewish Life (COEJL), the Evangelical Environmental Network (EEN), and a local United Church of Christ (UCC) Creation Justice group?[4]

I have imagined that everything would go swimmingly at first. Cooks and diners would swap favorite kale recipes and share tips for extending the growing season or for nonviolently warding off slugs. But then what? Would Simon (who fled the Lutheran Church of his youth) overhear pastor John saying grace and walk out the door before the meal has even begun? What would happen at the table if the head of the UCC Creation Justice group started advocating for low-carbon lifestyles as a necessary aspect of "cruciform [Christlike] living?" Would the homesteaders quietly chew their chard, then politely sidestep the theology and move on to describe their favorite carbon footprint calculators? Or would Earnest ultimately get more confrontational, asking gruffly "What does Jesus have to do with any of this?" after which an awkward silence would ensue? And if everyone miraculously made it through the meal (perhaps because the food was so tasty) would some homesteaders beat a hasty departure once the COEJL crowd took out their prayer books to chant the traditional *birkat hamazon* (blessing over the food) with joyful abandon, even if at least half of them did not usually *bentsch* (chant the blessings) at home?

When pondering the arc of my various ethnographic ventures, I have played out this scenario in my mind because the imagined silences (from polite avoidance to actual walkouts) simultaneously amuse, disturb and inform me. As a work of imagined theatre, the opportunities for amusement and entertainment are obvious enough. Nevertheless, the occasions of communication breakdown disturb me because they disrupt the narratives of continuities and connection to which I am naturally drawn as researcher and as a person. After all, if I maintain a genuine, grateful fondness for almost everyone whom I have met in the course my research (which is true) and if all of these people are somehow connected up through both what I have learned from them and their shared ecological commitments, should not everyone be able to enjoy each other's company as much as I have enjoyed theirs?

The answer, unfortunately, is no. Or at least, "not necessarily." Once I get past my own wishful thinking and absorb that answer, these imagined communication gaps then go on to inform me in helpful ways. They do so by reminding me of the silencing effect that religion can have when it enters into certain nonreligious (or "not necessarily religious") places and spaces. Not surprisingly, I am equally reminded of the *opposite* dynamic at work in the imagined room: the many ways in which secular spaces can have a silencing effect on religiously identified people, especially those who are not liberal, pluralistic, mainline Protestants, who are better able to "speak the language" of secular American culture (Ammerman, 2005; Baugh, 2017; Orsi, 2018).

Of course, the silencing effect of bringing religion into generally "secularized" spaces could not be more obvious (see Hjelm, Chapter 6: pp. 136–45). We see it in the news and in our neighborhoods every day. I also often experience this kind of silence in the classroom. Whenever I teach a broad environmental humanities course known as "Contested Grounds," for example, even very difficult conversations about race and class never seem quite as sticky as the conversations about religion. For instance, when I have introduced my students to portions of *Laudato Si* (Pope Francis's (2015) Encyclical on climate change), I often have the experience of some students being completely on board with what Pope Francis has to say, especially his critique of consumerism and unchecked capitalism (a critique that many 'secular' homesteaders share). These students' responses change, however, once they encounter what they describe as "an overload" of explicitly Christian language. The reaction is especially strong when Francis argues that responding to the urgency of the climate crisis is right in keeping with the larger meaning of the Catholic Church's traditional "pro-life" stance (Francis, 2015).

While some students are able to identify the logical brilliance of Pope Francis's theological tactics in making this kind of "protect all life" ecological argument, there are always a few who seem to shut down entirely, seeming fervently to wish that the Pope were not Catholic. Such students claim that, because they are not Christian, do not believe in God and are staunchly in favor of a woman's right to make choices about her own body, they just cannot bring themselves to read any further. This is a kind of 'fingers in the ears' version of silence, where shared ecological commitments cannot bridge the secular–religious divide.

It is precisely because I *wish* such students could see beyond their initial discomfort – which thankfully some eventually do – and precisely because I *wish* a secular homesteader and an evangelical "creation care" advocate could put aside their differences that I find my fictive "potluck gone bad" scenario so useful. It helps me to pay attention to my own biases as a researcher – a theme to which I will return at the conclusion of this chapter – biases which include my underlying hope that everyone could "just get along."

Since I consider myself to be more of an historian who does ethnography than a sociologist of religion per se, the tragicomic potluck scenario also serves me to the extent that it makes history come alive. It brings what I already know intellectually into clearer view. For example, when it comes to religious environmentalism, the historian in me knows that secular environmental activists and people who are strongly religiously identified have long viewed each other with mutual suspicion. These tensions were particularly prominent in the 1960s and 1970s, in the early years of Earth Day organizing and eco-warrior activism. Concerns about counter-cultural irreligion, hippie-paganism and 'monkey wrenching' on the one side and disdain for "outmoded" religious institutions on the other side (institutions understood to be inadequately addressing racism, pollution and the Vietnam war) led to a profound failure of potential alliance-making. This culture of mutual suspicion also led to the under-recognition and under-reporting of the alliances and collaborations that actually *were* being made. (Gould and Kearns, 2018).

This early inability to cross 'secular versus religious' divides and unite in common cause is one reason why religious organizations in the United States have come comparatively late to the environmental table. On the other hand, religious groups' long history of social activism has led many religious environmentalist groups to be (comparatively) less implicated in the over-arching "whiteness" and race-based exclusion commonly seen in leading US secular environmental organizations. Indeed, eco-justice (which includes justice for both humans and all other life-forms) was a common theme in much religious-environmental discourse long before 'environmental justice' entered into the broader environmental conversation (Kearns, 2012).[5]

Being aware of the nuances of this early history is crucial for understanding both the victories and the challenges that shape religious environmental initiatives in the 21st century. Nevertheless, it is one thing to know that history and another to *feel* that history. Ethnography – or in the case of the imagined potluck, the ethnographic imagination – gets me to that place of feeling. Once there, I am better able to examine what is at stake (both religiously and environmentally) when religious difference disrupts both the cultivation of shared environmental values and the possibility of collaborative political work.

Sitting with silence

Let me now turn to an *actual* occasion of ethnographic silence, one that similarly has enhanced both my methodological and historical sensibilities. This scenario is also clearly about religious difference, but, in this case, the differences exist *within* a shared framework: an understood agreement about the value of religiously based environmental work. Not surprisingly, the resonance here is considerably more positive.

It is the spring of 2004 and I have joined a small group of 'creation care' Christians on an ecumenical retreat in the hills of North Carolina. Mainline Christians, Catholics and liberal-leaning evangelicals are all a part of the mix. Some of the attendees are people whom I have already met at a conference sponsored by the Eco-Justice Working Group of the National Council of Churches. Others I know through prior research at events sponsored by the National Religious Coalition on Creation Care.[6] They have welcomed me aboard not only as a researcher, but also as a spiritual fellow-traveler. While I am the only non-Christian on the retreat, I appear to have enough spiritual and 'outdoorsy' credentials to fit in among these religious leaders, who are also avid hikers and deeply committed to the protection of the planet. Here in the South, the concerns are about climate change, but also about species extinction and mountain-top removal for the mining of coal.

We are driving from our base camp at a Lutheran retreat center to a trailhead where we will each get a chance to "connect with nature and God" through group hikes and solo walks. On the way, I am deep in conversation with Luke (at the wheel), a father who looks to be in his mid-forties and who identifies as both Presbyterian and evangelical.[7] Luke is deeply involved in his home church in the Midwest where he is busy leading a small, but active, creation care team in his congregation. He came to the retreat to "get a break," "draw closer to God" and get some good, practical ideas that he can bring back to his congregation.

This is carpool ethnography. I did not know that I would get a chance to talk with Luke for an extended period of time and I am planning to make the most of it. I move the conversation in the direction of Luke's creation care group and the work he is doing in that context, hoping at some point to dig more deeply into his own theological self-understanding. As we head toward the mountains beyond Boone, I am following the conversation where Luke wants to take it, but hoping to uncover what I am generally after in more formal interviews: how, where and in what ways does Luke see the connection between being a Christian and caring for the natural world? Moreover, what leads Luke not only to make changes in his daily life to support this work, but also actively to promote creation care in his congregation, sometimes in the face of considerable resistance? Where and when do tensions and difficulties arise for Luke and how do he and his fellow congregants (and the pastor) negotiate tricky terrain?

Knowing that I am a college professor, Luke nudges the conversation in a slightly different direction. He wants to talk about books. And who am I to resist such an invitation? Nevertheless, I use his questions as an occasion to test out how some eco-theological ideas will land with Luke on the receiving end. I start with the work of Calvin DeWitt, wetland ecologist and Professor Emeritus of the Nelson Institute of Environmental Studies at the University of Wisconsin. DeWitt has spent much of his life weaving together his ecological and theological (Reformed) commitments. (Indeed, DeWitt would likely object to my "weaving" metaphor and respond: "What do you mean *weave together*? They *are* together!") I surmise that DeWitt is someone Luke would love to know and I have read enough of DeWitt's work to feel comfortable capturing his stance (DeWitt, 1993).[8] Before too long, however, I shift to what it is like to *be* with Cal DeWitt.

I vividly remember joining a group on a morning nature walk with Cal at a 2002 interfaith conference sponsored by the National Partnership on Religion and the Environment (NPRE) in rural Connecticut.[9] We headed off from the conference center – some of us mistakenly thinking we would get some semblance of exercise – with precise instructions: as soon as someone notices something interesting "in nature" the task is to stop, exclaim "Wow!" and wait for everyone else to gather around the source of a given observer's awe. We walk for less than a minute when someone shouts "Wow!" and we pause to investigate a beech leaf. Cal crouches down to pick up the leaf, then provides some biological rationales behind its structure and function. Ten steps later we are pondering a paper-thin, dried-up snakeskin. After maybe an eighth of a mile, there is another "Wow!" as we observe with admiration how well a dead mouse has been "recycled" by a turkey vulture.

Our walk begins and ends with prayer. While I wonder if the non-Christians among us are discomfited by DeWitt's praise of Jesus as the model steward of the earth – "the One who created, sustains, and reconciles the creation" – I sense (at least in myself, and I *think* in others) an interfaith spirit of generosity, fueled by common environmental commitments not to mention obvious delight in the Wow Walk (DeWitt, 1993: p. 23). This means – in contrast to the fictive potluck – that Cal is not being (discernibly) silenced, nor are participants choosing to walk away.

I relay this story to Luke (*sans* my internal wonderings about non-Christians' potential discomfort) and Luke is all in. He is eager to read DeWitt and even more eager to *meet* DeWitt. Luke responds with nature walk stories of his own, using similar language about Jesus and the glories of God's creation.

With at least 20 minutes of driving yet to go, I decide to take the discussion of "ecological Christians I admire" in a different direction, this time invoking the life and work of Sallie McFague, a Methodist-turned-Episcopalian who taught at the Vanderbilt Divinity School and also served as its Dean.[10] McFague firmly identifies as both a feminist and an environmentalist. She writes compellingly about how her feminism informs her environmentalism and vice versa. I leave out all of this contextual information when describing her work to Luke, but I speak genuinely of what first brought me to McFague's writing, which is her lifelong interest in the theological power of metaphor.

"For instance," I observe, "McFague asks us to consider the ecological potential of imagining our earth as the body of God." Silence.

"Of course, she isn't saying that the earth *is* the body of God." I wait a moment, but no comment is forthcoming from the formerly chatty Luke.

"She's asking us to *consider* how such a metaphor might change our thinking, and then, ideally, our actions." More silence, and I don't know what it means. Luke's general demeanor seems calm, as best I can discern. I decide to keep going, knowing full well that I am about to head out of bounds, but too curious not to see what happens when I do.

"This is part of her broader metaphorical theology," I continue, trying not to sound too professorial as I proceed. "McFague want us to move beyond the problematic metaphors of God as Father and King" (McFague, 1993). Luke continues to be quiet and this time I intentionally step into the silence with him. After a long pause, Luke glances over at me and then back at the road.

"What does she mean by *metaphor*?" Of course, Luke knows what metaphor is. His query is theological. "I just don't get that metaphor part. I mean there's the Father, and the Son and the Holy Spirit. That's it. Why does she want to mess with that?"

We both sit with the question. "I mean, if she thinks the Earth is God's body, that's pantheism." I nod, not in agreement per se, but to indicate that I am following Luke's trajectory. I decide not to get into McFague's careful distinctions between pantheism (which she rejects) and panentheism (which she upholds). My point is not to persuade, but to learn.

Luke's several silences have set a tone and changed the pace. They invite me to follow suit. We drive for a while in quiet, a quiet that is slightly unnerving and yet, oddly enough, somehow simultaneously comforting. Eventually, we get back to talking about his creation care group.

Looking back, what did I learn from Luke's silences? First, what I remember above all else is a capaciousness in this discussion that lingers with me to this day, perhaps now more than ever given the stark absence of cross-cultural dialogue that defines US culture in the 2020s. As with the imagined potluck, the silences in this conversation were primarily indicators of difference, differences between two Christian articulations of ecological commitment and concern. The silences may also have been evoked by the differences between me, a liberal, Jewishly identified researcher (from a religiously pluralistic family tree) and Luke, a liberal evangelical Presbyterian. Nevertheless, the silences – in my experience of them, at least – mostly had the effect of slowing down a delicate conversation and enlarging its capacities. Room was made so that both parties could navigate the territory of difference in respectful, mutually appreciative ways.

From a methodological perspective, it is worth noting that it is unlikely that I would have had this kind of conversation in a more formal, sit-down interview. I suppose I could have planned to inject Sallie McFague's theology into every structured conversation I had with an ecologically concerned Christian, using her work as a kind of theological litmus test. But, for a variety of reasons, that was never something I wanted to do. Within the more organic context of "carpool ethnography," however, a conversation about books became an opportunity for clarification. The occasions of silence were invitations for me to explore where a liberal leaning, creation care oriented, evangelical Presbyterian might draw the line theologically. That Luke drew the line exactly where I thought he would was neither boring nor disappointing. It was, in fact, a quietly exhilarating moment, confirming "in real life" what solitary, intellectual reflection alone could never quite capture.

Just as the imagined potluck between homesteaders and environmentalists helps me to *feel* historical and sociological tensions that I know to be alive, so too did my conversation with Luke help me to *feel* theological distinctions in ways that my own comparative reading of DeWitt and McFague never quite accomplished.[11] On the drive to the trailhead, *the conceptual became embodied*, first through silence, then in words and still later in continued companionship on the trail. For while McFague had gone "too far" for Luke, thankfully, I had not. Our shared commitment to the fate of the earth continued to bind us together in common conversation beneath the trees. I believe that the silences had helped us to get there.

The sounds of difficult silence

The silence of communication breakdown never feels as good as the kind of capacious conversation I have just described. Even so, I remain grateful for what they also have to teach me. Indeed, I have squirmed through difficult ethnographic silences that were not nearly as entertaining as the fictive potluck over which I, obviously, have complete theatrical control. Moreover, while the gaps between secular and religious environmentalists are ones that I always hope can be bridged, it is the spaces that separate religious people from one another that I find to be especially intriguing, and also, often, the most disturbing. My drive with Luke leaned more on the encouraging side. But this has not always been the case.

I remember well a silence that was never truly broken when a group of young alumni, from across the spectrum of American Jewish identity, gathered in the Berkshires for a reunion. The attendees had all been recipients of a highly competitive fellowship, corresponding with their senior year in high school. This fellowship included a summer of study in Israel, as well as multiple gatherings for learning and community-building throughout the year. Now in college, these alumni, from different fellowship years, were gathered for a *Shabbaton* (weekend retreat) of spiritual study, community building, seeing old friends and making new connections. The fellowship is designed to bring together teenagers who value Jewish learning as a creative and dynamic undertaking. Welcoming and negotiating pluralism (from gender identity to the myriad ways one might identify as Jewish) lies at the heart of the program's mission. As various students on the retreat recalled, the first challenge they all faced in Israel was how such a diverse group could observe Shabbat together in ways that were workable for everyone. It was clear from the various stories that were remembered and shared – often accompanied by nervous laughter – that working through such challenges had been no mean feat at the time. Nevertheless, as their retrospective reflections made apparent, communicating and negotiating across difference was a value that these young Jewish leaders clearly appreciated and supported.

The chosen theme for this annual reunion was "Judaism and environmentalism." To a certain degree, this theme was imposed from without by a few leaders within the group who had planned the retreat. This particular retreat, then, was different in tone when compared to the many inter- and intra-faith gatherings I have attended where the deeply felt connection between religious identity and environmental commitment was precisely what had brought people together in one place. While some people present at the fellowship reunion were self-identified "eco-Jews," others had not given much thought to whether and how Judaism was (or even ought to be) connected to environmental work. I suspect this difference played a role in the difficult conversation that unfolded one evening.

When talk turned to environmental practices that could be taken up by Jewish communities and congregations, one young man – I'll call him Jacob – expressed considerable skepticism about whether Orthodox Jews (of various stripes) would be anything but a hindrance to ecological efforts. "I mean look at what they're doing. Leaving lights on all night. Using Styrofoam cups and plastic utensils. I don't see any progress here."

While Jacob avoided the more accusatory option, "Look at what *you're* doing," no doubt, the handful of modern Orthodox youth in the circle experienced these words as explicitly directed toward them. Jacob's comment landed like a thud in the room. At first, there was no response. To me, the thud seemed particularly loud (if silence can be loud), because I had been in that very room many times before. The setting was a retreat center whose longstanding pluralistic mission was not unlike the mission of the fellowship which these college students had received. At this retreat center, pluralism and 'all-stream Judaism' was always highly valued, discussed, debated, renegotiated and bravely, if imperfectly, upheld. That was clearly *not* what was happening in this moment.

There followed a pause that seemed much longer than it probably was. I was tempted (as both scholar and peacemaker) to make everyone aware of the explicitly ecological *and* Orthodox nonprofit organization, *Canfei Nesharim*, but as a guest at this conversation, I held my tongue.[12] Eventually, a few others in the room piped up in response to Jacob's comments. Several self-identified "eco-Jews" observed that Jacob was jumping to conclusions and making unfair characterizations. Jacob, however, was resolute, almost defiant. He rearticulated his previous points, now emphasizing that the environmental crisis was much too urgent for Orthodox Jews not to re-examine their practices and "keep up with the times." More silence followed. The hour was late and after some failed attempts to move on to other topics, several people expressed the desire to call it a night.

While clearly accustomed to working with and across religious difference, none of these fellowship alumni seemed willing to stay in the room to hash things out. Why? Maybe it was because, after all, this gathering was a reunion and a retreat, a weekend away from the stresses of college life with all of its deadlines and intensities. Maybe the collective feeling was that they had all already done the hard work of negotiating religious difference during their fellowship year and that was *not* the work they were going to do that night. Or maybe because many people in the room were not committed environmentalists, they did not have enough skin in the game to want to invest in this particular battle. And, of course, people were tired.

Nevertheless, I suspected then (and perhaps more so now) that the conversation was not entirely over. How I would have liked to have been a peripatetic fly on the walls of the various cabins to which these college students retreated! Did some people simply move on to topics that mattered more to them? Did others say to each other: "What was *that* about?" Did some bemoan the fact that this tense conversation was not processed in the moment, given that they had all presumably learned the very skills to *do* such processing? I will never know, and that is perhaps why this particular occasion of silence has long stuck with me.

Self-silencing

The fourth scenario of silence on which I wish to reflect, comes not from my own ethnographic work on religious environmentalism, but from the work of my colleague, Amanda Baugh. In her book, *God and the Green Divide: Religious Environmentalism in Black and White*, Baugh describes a series of interactions she had with Teresa, a woman who actively participates in a gardening club, "The Purple Radishes" (Baugh, 2017). The club itself is connected to Unity Temple, a Unitarian Universalist congregation that, for many years, has been a 'partner congregation' with the nonprofit Faith in Place, an Illinois-based environmental justice organization that Baugh compellingly probes and interprets throughout her book.[13]

For Baugh, the work of Faith in Place serves as a window into broader themes and tensions within religious environmentalism, many of which I have been addressing throughout this chapter. In particular, Baugh argues that Faith in Place deploys an underlying progressive, theological and "pluralistic" viewpoint that works well in liberal, rationalistic contexts, contexts populated by Unitarians, mainline Protestants and liberal Catholics, Muslims and Jews. Nevertheless, these underlying theological assumptions about science, modernity and human responsibility are not *fully* pluralistic, because little space is made for what we might call more traditional or orthodox views of the human-nature-Divine relationship. Baugh notes that if a Muslim, Christian or Jew suggested that the effects of severe climate disruption (hurricanes, floods and fires) should be interpreted as divine punishment for human sin, this theological assertion would be received uncomfortably, perhaps even actively resisted. Indeed, Baugh's ethnographic work reveals the dynamics of such resistance. "Faith in Place," Baugh writes, "insisted that religious teachings must adapt to be relevant to modern times ... [and] those who did not [share this viewpoint] encountered significant barriers when they encountered the work of Faith in Place" (Baugh, 2017: p. 147).

It is in the context of assessing some of these barriers that Baugh introduces us to Teresa, an Italian Catholic woman in her forties. Baugh tells us that her interest in meeting Teresa began with Teresa's decision to cancel an arranged interview. This decision constituted the first 'ethnographic silence' in their relationship. Teresa was moved to cancel the interview after reading a line on Baugh's consent form that described Baugh's research as "an attempt to understand how environmental concern is influencing the practice of religion in America" (Baugh, 2017: p. 128).

"I'm a practicing Catholic!," Teresa tells Baugh on the phone, "The garden has *nothing* to do with my religion." When Baugh and Teresa finally do meet in person, Teresa elaborates: "Now that's not to say it's not spiritual for me [her work in the garden], because it really is. But as far as my religious background and the garden, no. No. No. I'm a Catholic and my children are Catholic ... And the environment doesn't really fit into Catholicism for me" (Baugh, 2017: p. 128).

It is a testament to both Baugh's persistence and her empathy that Teresa ultimately agrees to meet in person and elaborate on the sharp distinctions between her experience of gardening as a spiritual practice (something many homesteaders would affirm) and her understandings of her Catholic identity, an identity defined by her commitment to traditional doctrine and the fulfillment of Catholic duties, including strict observance of the holy days of obligation, praying the rosary, and regularly attending Mass with her children.

What is notable in her conversation with Baugh, is the extent to which Teresa effectively silences *herself*, first by attempting to cancel the interview and later, in a different way, by uttering three firm "Nos" in an attempt to draw impermeable boundaries between two different forms of spiritual experience, both of which belong to *her*. It seems that, in order for both of these experiences to stay valid, they must be kept strictly bounded and conceptually apart. There is a significant conceptual space between Teresa's embodied understanding that gardening is a kind of spiritual work and her religious understanding (also embodied, but in a different way) of what it means to be a good Catholic, as well as a good Catholic mother. In Teresa's understanding of herself as a religious person, there appears to be no room for these two modes of spiritual experience truly to coexist. To the extent that gardening-as-spiritual practice seems antithetical to Catholicism (as she understands it), Teresa silences the gardening part in favor of her Catholic identity.

Baugh's interview with Teresa took place in 2010 and Baugh wonders aloud in her footnotes whether Pope Francis's 2015 encyclical on climate change might have helped to take down, or at least soften, the barriers Teresa had put up between her Catholic faith and her spiritual experiences of gardening (Baugh, 2017: p. 193, fn. 3). One wonders, also, how Teresa might have responded to the theological perspectives of the many "Green Sisters" – such as Genesis Farm founder, Miriam MacGillis, and Green Mountain Monastery Founders, Bernadette Bostwick and Gail Worcelo – whose work Sarah McFarland Taylor beautifully describes and interprets in her *Green Sisters: A Spiritual Ecology* (Taylor, 2009). In a similar vein, I find myself wondering whether Teresa might have articulated a different perspective had she been familiar with the history of the Catholic Worker farms that were envisioned by Dorothy Day's colleague, Peter Maurin: small-scale farms, scattered across the North American landscape, often providing food for Catholic Worker hospitality houses or to local communities in need. These farms were first established in the 1930s and some of them remain active to this day.

Baugh's portrait of Teresa sticks with me, in part, because of the many unanswered questions that it raises. To what extent were Teresa's acts of self-silencing rooted in her need to differentiate herself from the stances of her five sister gardeners, all Unitarian Universalists, some of whom articulated a sense that "nature *is* spirituality" in ways that echo many homesteaders' views?[14] Would acquiring a richer sense of Catholic history, including its ecological history, have made a difference for Teresa? The questions I have of Teresa and of American Catholic history more broadly, connect with still larger questions I hope to explore, such as the seeming reluctance of American parish priests to use the pulpit to emphasize and further disseminate Pope Francis's urgent plea for immediate global action to mitigate the climate crisis. What do these "pulpit silences" mean?

Conclusion: silence as presence

When we consider the four scenarios of ethnographic silence that I have unfolded throughout this chapter, one way to interpret them collectively is to describe them as silences that all emerge from anxiety around the "real presence" of the divine, anxieties that Robert Orsi evokes and investigates in his exquisitely rendered *History and Presence* (Orsi, 2018). Given Orsi's emphasis on Catholic history and, in particular, the religious experiences of US Catholics (as well as Protestant and secular responses to those experiences), it is easy to see how Teresa's self-silencing might fit into Orsi's analysis. The real presence of God, whether in the Eucharist or in her daily life, is not up for debate for Teresa. At the same time, Teresa senses that all things "environmental" (even the "spiritual" experience of gardening) are coded as secular (or, at least, Unitarian) and do not belong in – indeed, may actually threaten – her Catholic faith and practice. In essence, Teresa must negotiate, within herself, the complicated dynamics of cultural power, dynamics that are shaped by the larger prevailing narratives of religiosity and secularity in the US.

While Teresa's example is particularly vivid, and also quite poignant, the other scenarios I have described resonate similarly. For Orthodox Jews, for instance, keeping all 613 *mitzvot* ('commandments' according to *halakha*, traditional Jewish law) is also not up for debate. Therefore, it is no surprise that, in an Orthodox context, environmental arguments about "getting real" and turning off lights on Shabbat would not only fall upon deaf ears, but also would serve to close mouths and end discussion. At the retreat I attended, a well-meaning, liberal Jew's inability to acknowledge the real presence of God as a living force behind these commandments brought a potentially fruitful conversation to a premature close. My conversation with Luke about the earth "as the body of God" might have ended similarly were it not for our shared desire, first, to acknowledge clearly where we each would draw some theological lines. Our larger unspoken commitment was to remain in connection with each other, out of our common concern for the fate of the earth and our shared conviction that broad interreligious cooperation and activism might help to mitigate the burgeoning climate crisis.

Finally, my imagined potluck that brings together secular homesteaders and religious environmentalists under one roof (but not for long) demonstrates what decades of research have taught me: that assumptions about religion – coupled with individuals' extensive experiences of religion as an oppressive, "superstitious" and even abusive, force – can lead to an unwillingness to reach across the identity gap between self-identified religious and decidedly *not* religious people. Even so, having dwelled quite comfortably as a participant-researcher in both homesteading and religious-environmentalist worlds, my tendency is to focus on all of the ways in which these groups occupy shared spiritual and environmental territory. Opportunities for cooperation, collaboration and shared purpose are ample, but only, it seems, to the extent that conversations about "real presence" remain muted or disguised (Davie, 1994: pp. 129–30).

By paying attention to ethnographic silences and reflecting on their meanings, as I have sought to do here, my awareness of the complexities of interpreting religion have deepened. For those of us who traffic in words, it is tempting to think that words will tell us all that we need to know. We can think of interviews as texts to be analyzed and, more fruitfully, perhaps, we can learn to be attentive to written archives, listening deeply for the ways in which diarists and letter writers of earlier periods might speak to us as complex, 'living' human beings. But if we pay attention only to the words and not to the spaces between them, we are apt to miss some vital information and, in turn, some significant opportunities for insight. The ancient rabbis have spoken of Torah (the first five books of the Hebrew Bible) as consisting of black fire (the scribed Hebrew words) and mystical, ineffable white fire (the spaces between and around those words). Both demand our attention. Every line on the scroll is hot with meaning, but in different ways.

Paying attention to silences has sharpened my awareness of the power of "religious presence" as Orsi (2018) so richly describes it. In each scenario I have recounted, the silences emphasize the depth and valence of that power. Sometimes people choose silence from positions of strength and clarity, or to acknowledge shared understandings that do not have to be explained. At other times, people experience themselves as *being silenced*, whether by other people or by the reigning atmosphere in the room. Such silences reveal who has cultural power and in what contexts. Some people, like Teresa, may even silence *themselves*, seeking a way to live out realities in their lives that they experience as being in conflict. Such silences do not necessarily have to be about the lived religion – or lack thereof – of the people involved. But when interpreting religion, of course, they always do.

Pondering these silences makes me more aware of my own biases and proclivities, my frequent wishes that such silences can be overcome, that bridges can always be built, that people can always unite in common cause. But *should* such bridging of differences always be sought? Or is this desire for mending the rifts and emphasizing "what unites us" *itself* a reflection of a liberal, Protestant-informed, scholarly bias that, Orsi suggests, we ignore at our own peril (Orsi, 2018).[15] As much as my research drives me to look for those places where we might "all get along," I am now more keenly aware of how that pluralistic optimism might, in fact, get in the way of seeing clearly the data that are before me. As a result – and with much gratitude for Orsi's help in this regard – I am more aware of my *own* tendencies to make insufficient room for the disruptive power of presence. This kind of awareness is worth cultivating, for it can make us not only better interpreters of religion, but also, presumably, kinder and more compassionate human beings.

Not all silences, however, need to "teach us" things about our work as interpreters of religion. Throughout my research, some of the most profound silences that I have experienced are not silences that reveal crevasses opening up between different kinds of religiosity or between religious and nonreligious people who seemingly "should" be uniting in the shared undertaking of protecting our fragile earthly home.

Some silences are quite simply – and profoundly – forms of sacred space into which I have been invited to dwell with another person for a time. They are the silences that come when people talk to me about what it means to live a life devoted to God, or a life dedicated to care for the natural world and, in many cases, to live a life that weaves together a commitment to the divine with a commitment to this sacred earth. Within these silences, tears often arise and, with those tears, sometimes apologies or attempts at explanation and then, often, a return to more silence.

What I hear most often through these intertwinings of words and the intentional refraining from words, is a sense of awe, an appreciation of beauty, and a profound feeling of connection: to God, to the quiet lake, to the pine tree in the backyard extending its branches toward the sun. Some speak of their experiences as a felt connection to Christ, or to the Creator or to the Breath of Life.[16] Others consciously avoid God language and praise the scientifically explainable, but still ineffable, miracles of photosynthesis and natural selection. In every case, I have heard some kind of evocation of, and gratitude for, the experience of Real Presence – whether natural or more-than-natural – that animates our world. These are the kinds of silences that make the task of interpreting religion its own kind of sacred work.

Notes

[1] This chapter is dedicated to Nancy Tatom Ammerman who first introduced me to the sociology of religion and assured me that talking to real people "counts" as research (Ammerman, 2016). I have not been the same since! For that and a lifetime of continued mentorship, thank you, Nancy.

[2] I am grateful to the late Jim Mulligan and to Ruth Mulligan, leading forces in the founding of *Earth Ministry* (earthministry.org/) in Seattle, Washington, for providing me with photographs of these events and telling the stories behind them. Rogation Sunday

in the US Episcopal Church occurs on the fifth Sunday after Easter Sunday. Observance usually includes an outdoor procession and prayers for agricultural flourishing. St. Marks' creation care agenda is significant and includes a commitment to have a net-zero carbon footprint by 2030. The Cathedral also currently hosts a "Cathedral Bees" project, having installed several rooftop hives to promote pollination and honey-bee resilience.

3   In this chapter, while being sensitive to the objections that might come from some religious communities, I am primarily using the term 'religious environmentalism' as a broad, scholarly descriptor for a wide range of religiously based, ecologically oriented campaigns and practices.

4   For the Evangelical Environmental Network, see creationcare.org/. For the Coalition on Environment and Jewish Life, see www.coejl.net/. While COEJL was taking a particularly active role in educating the Jewish public (as well as a wider audience) on the connections between Judaism and environmentalism in the late 1990s and early 2000s, more recently Hazon (hazon.org/) has come to the fore of Jewish ecological activism, alongside the longstanding Shalom Center (theshalomcenter.org/) and the more recent Dayenu (dayenu. org/), "a Jewish call for climate action."

5   Many eco-justice advocates fail to note, for instance, that the first analysis of racial injustice in the siting of toxic waste sites, *Toxic Waste and Race in the United States* (1987), was a study conducted under the auspices of the UCC Church (*Toxic Waste and Race in the United States: A National Report on the Racial and Socio-Economic Characteristics of Communities with Hazardous Waste Sites* (United Church of Christ, 1987).

6   For the National Religious Coalition on Creation Care, see www.nrccc.org/. The work of the Eco-Justice Working Group of the National Council of Churches (begun in the mid-1980s) is now being conducted under the auspices of Eco-Justice Ministries at www. eco-justice.org/.

7   This portrait of my conversation with "Luke" is based on my field notes from this research trip. While my notes did not capture every word of the conversation (I did not write up the notes until that evening), the description I am providing here is a faithful portrait of what transpired.

8   See, for instance, Calvin B. DeWitt, *Earth-wise: A Biblical Response to Environmental Issues* (DeWitt, 1993). I wish to extend to Cal a warm thank you for the gift of this book, as well as the gift of time spent together in sacred ecological conversation at a National Religious Partnership for the Environment (NRPE) gathering in 2002.

9   The National Religious Partnership for the Environment (www.nrpe.org/) was founded in 1993 by four key religious environmental organizations: the Environmental Justice Program of the US Conference of Catholic Bishops – and now also the Catholic Climate Covenant: (catholicclimatecovenant.org/) – as well as the aforementioned Evangelical Environmental Network (EEN), the Coalition on the Environment and Jewish Life (COEJL, in alliance with the Jewish Council on Public Affairs [JCPA]) and the Eco-Justice Working Group of the National Council of Churches (now Eco-Justice ministries). As of 2020 (although not necessarily reflecting 2020 data), the NRPE website states: "This alliance represents more than 114 million Christian and Jewish adherents and more than 156,000 parishes across the US." Since the 1990s, a significant number of other religious environmental organizations have been founded, some of them now more active than the four listed here. But, with the exception of some significant "small but mighty" grassroots organizations, NRPE set the stage for most of the religious environmental work that later emerged.

10 At the time of her Vanderbilt appointment, Sallie McFague was the first and only female Dean of any Divinity School in the United States. In the scenario I am describing here, I refer to McFague in the present tense, both because I am speaking about her writing and because she was alive at the time of my conversation with Luke. Sallie McFague died on 15

November 2019. In my own thinking, I am greatly indebted to McFague's work. I am also deeply grateful to have had brief, but memorable, opportunities to spend time with her.

[11] It is worth mentioning that, despite the denominational labels that separate DeWitt and McFague (Reformed evangelical and liberal Episcopalian, respectively), the actual differences between them are likely less distinct than meets the eye, given their shared passion for earth care and their shared commitment to addressing the climate crisis. Having probed their works and interacted with each of them personally, I am quite confident that McFague and DeWitt would have been able to sit down with each other and find places of agreement that were not easy for Luke to imagine.

[12] See canfeinesharim.org. Canfei Nesharim was founded by Evonne Marzouk. Ora Sheinson is the most recent executive director. The work of Canfei Nesharim was profiled in 2017 by *The Times of Israel* (www.timesofisrael.com/the-12-jews-who-are-leading-the-green-movement). Ora Sheinson tells her own story of awakening on the website The Jew in the City, an organization devoted to challenging assumptions about Orthodoxy while encouraging Orthodox observance. See Sheinson, 2016.

[13] "The Purple Radishes" is a pseudonym that Baugh deploys in order to protect the anonymity of both the garden and the members of the club.

Faith in Place was founded in 1999, beginning as a Chicago-based organization and ultimately broadening its range to include other regions in the state. As is the case with a range of other state-based religious environmental organizations, Faith in Place preserved its status as an independent non-profit, while extending its work by becoming (in 2004) a state affiliate of the national organization, Interfaith Power and Light (www.interfaithpowerandlight.org/). While focused on Illinois, Faith in Place seeks to educate and advocate nationally through its website: www.faithinplace.org/. Faith in Place was profiled in the 2007 documentary film, *Renewal*, produced by Marty Ostrow and Terry Kay Rockefeller.

[14] Baugh, who joined The Purple Radishes to do fieldwork in the community garden, is here quoting from comments made by "Andrea," one of the five Unitarian Universalist "Purple Radishes," (Baugh, 2017: p. 77).

[15] Orsi delivers this warning clearly and succinctly when he writes: "It is historically more accurate – and theoretically and historiographically more generative – to say that 'religion' was the creation of the profound rupture between Catholics and the varieties of Protestantism over the question of presence ... and of their mutual denunciations for practicing what in their respective judgments was not really 'religion'" (Orsi, 2018: p. 32). Orsi goes on to make clear the many ways in which "the study of comparative religion as an academic discipline is thoroughly implicated in this history" (Orsi, 2018: p. 34). For a broader understanding of the richness and complexity of Orsi's argument, see the entirety of Chapter 1, "The Obsolescence of the Gods" (Orsi, 2018).

[16] "The Breath of Life" is the term that Rabbi Arthur O. Waskow (and his many students) most often uses to translate the Hebrew letters YHVH, the tetragrammaton that indicates the name of God.

References

Ammerman, N.T. (2005) *Pillars of Faith: American Congregations and Their Partners*, Berkeley: University of California Press.

Ammerman, N.T. (2016) "Lived Religion as an Emerging Field: An Assessment of its Contours and Frontiers," *Nordic Journal of Religion and Society*, 29(2): 83–99.

Baugh, A. (2017) *God and the Green Divide: Religious Environmentalism in Black and White*, Oakland, CA: University of California Press.

Davie, J.S. (1994) *Women in the Presence: Constructing Community and Seeking Spirituality in Mainline Protestantism*, Philadelphia, PA: University of Pennsylvania Press.

DeWitt, C.B. (1993) *Earth-wise: A Biblical Response to Environmental Issues*, Grand Rapids: CRC Publications.

Francis (2015) *Encyclical Letter Laudato Si Of The Holy Father Francis* (1st edn), Vatican City: Vatican Press.

Gould, R.K. (2005) *At Home in Nature: Homesteading and Spiritual Practice in America*, Berkeley: University of California Press.

Gould, R.K. (2007) "Binding Life to Values," in J. Isham, and S. Waage (eds) *Ignition: How a Grassroots Movement Can Stop Global Warming*, Washington, DC: Island Press, pp. 119–33.

Gould, R.K., and Kearns, L. (2018) "Ecology and Religious Environmentalism in the United States," in J. Corrigan (ed) *The Oxford Encyclopedia of Religion and America*, Oxford: Oxford University Press, pp. 604–46.

Kearns, L. (2012) "Ecology and the Environment," in M.D. Palmer, and S.M. Burgess (eds) *Wiley-Blackwell Companion to Religion and Social Justice*, Chichester: Wiley-Blackwell, pp. 591–606.

Kearns, L. (2014) "Green Evangelicals," in B. Steensland, and P. Goff, (eds) *The New Evangelical Social Engagement*, Oxford: Oxford University Press.

McFague, S. (1987) *Models of God: Theology for an Ecological, Nuclear Age*, Philadelphia, PA: Fortress Press.

McFague, S. (1993) *The Body of God: An Ecological Theology*, Minneapolis: Fortress Press.

Orsi, R.A. (2018) *History and Presence*, Cambridge, MA: The Belknap Press of Harvard University Press.

Sheinson, O. (2016) "How I Became an Orthodox Jewish Environmentalist," in The Jew in the City's series: "Profiles, Stories of Return," jewinthecity. com/2016/01/how-i-became-an-orthodox-jewish-environmentalist. [Accessed 14 December 2020.]

Taylor, S.M. (2009) *Green Sisters: A Spiritual Ecology*, Cambridge, MA: Harvard University Press.

United Church of Christ (1987) *Toxic Waste and Race in the United States: A National Report on the Racial and Socio-Economic Characteristics of Communities with Hazardous Waste Sites*, New York: United Church of Christ, Commission on Racial Justice.

Zerubavel, E. (2006) *The Elephant in the Room: Silence and Denial in Everyday Life*, Oxford: Oxford University Press.

5

The Public Sphere and Presentations of the Collective Self: Being Shia in Modern India

*Aseem Hasnain**

This chapter traces the meaning–making attempts of the Shia religious minority within the larger Muslim community in modern India. I use select periods between the early 20th and early 21st centuries to show how elites use discursive strategies to present their collective self as a distinct and remarkable religious minority in need of protection and promotion. These discursive strategies primarily use word–acts such as petitions, speeches, arguments, and counterarguments through which the Shia perform their distinction in public. Shias claim distinction from the larger Muslim community, which was being labeled negatively. Across these periods, the Shia present themselves in positive light by projecting loyalty toward the British Crown prior to the nationalist movement, by claiming a nationalist position in contrast to the Indian Muslim League during the freedom movement, and by fashioning themselves in the image of the desirable citizen, distinct from both orthodox Sunni Muslims, and opposed to terrorism in the context of Islamophobia. The shifting content in their collective identities correspond with the dominant discourse of the public sphere as the terms of debate change with shifting statecraft, national discourse, and local politics.

*This chapter was constructed on foundational comments and criticism provided by Sandria Freitag, David Gilmartin, Charles Kurzman, Abhilasha Srivastava, Ananya Dasgupta, and Zaheer Abbas, who engaged with early versions of this work. Attendees of the Annual Conference on South Asia (2018) at the University of Wisconsin at Madison also helped me think through my arguments. I also thank Vikash Singh and Erin Johnston for their comments, questions, and patience. Fieldwork for this chapter was supported by generous grants from the American Institute of Indian Studies and UNC at Chapel Hill.

Drawing upon archival material, and interviews conducted during 2012–13, I study shifting religious identity by bringing concepts from three lines of enquiry into conversation with each other. These include Erving Goffman's work on stigmatized identity and performance of the self (Goffmann, 1961, 1963), the public sphere, and Michele Lamont's boundary-making framework (Lamont, 2008; Lamont and Molnár, 2002). I demonstrate how the Shia perform their collective self in public while the public works as a neutral arena and as an actor in varying contexts. I extend the boundary-making framework such that it works not only with the binary of the self and the other, but also with a triangular dynamic of the self, the other, and the public. I argue that the public sphere is not simply an arena, but an actor that actively shapes the collective identity of politically insignificant minority groups, which must adjust their particularities under its identity-blind universalizing requirements.

I combine methods and theories for a multipronged approach to make sense of my materials as this interpretive strategy allows me to go beyond the ways in which scholarship on Indian Shias has been done in the past. Existing works on Indian Shias fall into two categories. The first includes historical descriptions of political and religious elites and descriptions of their culture and rituals (Hollister, 1953; Hardy, 1972; Rizvi, 1986; Cole, 1988; Jones, 2012). The second category has ethnographies of Muharram and other Shia rituals focused on a specific cross-section of time when that ethnography was conducted (Moinuddin et al, 1977; Pinault, 1992; Schubel, 1993; D'Souza, 2014). While ethnographic works provide rich details about the local context and meaning-making, historical works help understand the larger cultural and political background within which the community existed. I combine both these approaches to increase the "depth of field," drawing on a strategy from photography, that allows focusing on near and distant objects simultaneously with acceptable clarity. While I focus on performance and discursive strategies of meaning-making in particular moments in time, I also situate these moments within the broader, and often shifting, political context. I have further strengthened this approach with insights from symbolic interactionism and literatures on collective identity, religion, and the public sphere to enable a fuller engagement with my evidence. This synthesis has allowed me to study a community, its salient anxieties, and its discursive responses to shifting sociopolitical factors in ways that help address theoretical problems in the discipline. While past sociologists treated collective identity in essentialist ways – as primordial and enduring – recent constructivist approaches have made it so fluid that studying it becomes challenging. However, my multipronged approach, of studying collective identity in moments when it became solid within a longer period of fluidity, helps capture how collective identities emerge, establish, sustain, and transform over time. This interpretive strategy has also helped see the blurry distinctions between the religious, social, and political dimensions of the collective self, but above all it has also emphasized the flexibility of religious symbols, sacred memories, and spiritual messages that can be deployed in profane matters including the negotiation for social status and political power.

The Shia in India

Twelver Shia Muslims (Shias henceforth) are a minority sect within the Muslim community. Their sectarian division is traced to disputes over succession after the death of Muhammad, the Prophet of Islam, in 632 AD. The Prophet was succeeded by four caliphs who led the community one after the other. While the first three caliphs were Muhammad's early associates, the fourth, Ali, was his cousin. Partisans of Ali, who constituted the emergent Shia sect, maintained that he was Muhammad's closest protégé and spiritual successor, and that the first three caliphs usurped Ali's right to succession. While the Sunni revere all four caliphs – Abu Bakar, Umar, Usman, and Ali – the Shia do not accept the first three caliphs as their leaders. Instead, they treat Ali as their first Imam (leader), followed by twelve others in hereditary order (Hollister, 1953; Rizvi, 1986).

In India, the Shia have been a small community in Lucknow, Hyderabad, Mumbai (historically, Bombay), and Delhi, where they had considerable influence in the past. Historically, the Shia gained disproportionate political clout due to the Mughal Empire's reliance on Safavid Iran, from where Shia nobility immigrated (Cole, 1988). However, in colonial and independent India the Shia have gradually lost political power to become what several community leaders like to describe as "a minority within a minority." The paradox between their small numbers and the legacy of their historical influence has been central to their politics of representation in modern India. While small communities are generally disadvantaged by mainstream political processes, an enterprising Shia leadership has creatively addressed such challenges through public collective claims. While they continued the project around their collective self, their target audience and claims change over time, corresponding to changes in the larger sociopolitical context.

I trace these claims across three periods where Shia elites and organizations present themselves as a desirable community worthy of recognition, protection, and promotion. The first phase covers the early 20th century, up to 1919 and prior to the establishment of the Indian freedom movement, when the British Crown was firmly in control. The second phase spans the freedom movement, 1919–47, which gradually split into two subnationalist movements culminating in the creation of India and Pakistan. This phase witnessed the fracturing of British political authority and the rise of native elites. The third phase spans 1990 and beyond, when a democratic postcolonial India witnessed the electoral rise of Right-wing Hindutva politics and the revival of aspersions cast on Muslim citizens. The period between 1947 and 1990 has been left out for two reasons, the first being widespread, persistent, and well-planned riots between Hindus and Muslims becoming the dominant factor in group relations (Wilkinson, 2006; Brass, 2011), and suppressing sectarian polemics. The second factor is the inaccessibility of archival material from this period, as government agencies continue to protect it behind the facade of public order and peace.

Sociology of religion and collective identity

Sociologists of religion have been studying connections between identity and religion since the classical period. Durkheim's work on religion focused on rituals that helped form social identity (Greil and Davidman, 2007). Weber also saw religion as one of the fundamental sources of group identity (Clark and Lipset, 2001). Later sociologists of religion also treat identity as one of the central functions of religion as it provides a resilient sense of belonging, in fact they go as far as to claim that religion is sacralized identity (Greil and Davidman, 2007). In recent work too, sociologists of religion have reemphasized how religion is used in public to define collective identities (Lichterman, 2008), or how experiences in religious communities help participants create identity goals for an idealized future (Johnston, 2016). Within sociology of religion, symbolic interactionism (SI) has been a key approach for studying identity, as it focuses on the content and processes of its construction (Greil and Davidman, 2007). Goffman holds a critical place in this area as he studied the interfaces of the self with structural factors in interactions (Greil and Davidman, 2007). In *Asylums* (Goffman, 1961), and *Stigma* (Goffman, 1963) Goffman shows how individuals and groups, stigmatized for their belonging to a place or religious grouping, respond to negative judgments by others and use performance to erect a positive edifice of their selves. Though not a typical scholar of religion, Goffman's work is based on Durkheim's ideas about rituals and their undergirding of the self (Birrell, 1981). This chapter builds on these traditions through an analysis of word–acts, such as petitions, speeches, arguments, and debates, that Shias indulge in as they attempt to reconstruct a distinct, positive, sectarian, collective identity contrasted to the negatively labeled Muslim community in modern India. However, instead of analyzing these interactions at the interpersonal or micro level, I study them at the group level.

The study of collective identity in sociology has traversed an essentialist past and moved onto the contemporary phase of constructionism (Cerulo, 1997). The constructionist stance has been criticized for softening the concept beyond comprehension. Critics ask, "If it is fluid, how can we understand how self-understandings may harden, congeal, and crystallize? If it is constructed, how can we understand the sometimes–coercive force of external identification? If it is multiple, how do we understand the terrible singularity that is often striven for?" (Brubaker and Cooper, 2000: p. 19). Recognizing the problems of essentialism, and the analytic perplexity of the constructivist stance, this chapter studies collective identity formation by focusing on key moments in the 20th century when Shia sectarian identity appears congealed and singular. However, I am sensitive to shifting meanings of collective identity over time. This hybrid strategy, of focusing on moments of congealed identity within a longer period of shifts and changes, allows me to capture how collective identities emerge, establish, sustain, and transform over time.

Identity and boundary making in the public

The moments studied in this chapter include claims about the collective self made public. They include word–acts staged: under the gaze of the public as judge; to the public as audience; in an effort to gain recognition publicly; and to become part of the public. Scholarship on the public sphere is instructive in this context. Habermas's work (1992) has been central to the notions of community and nation, as for him ideas are shared, opinions are contested, and discourse emanates from the public sphere. The idealized public sphere was the sphere of reason where rational arguments and debates could take place without regard to the sociopolitical status of participants, unswayed by self-interest or tradition (Mah, 2000). The public sphere symbolized the ideals of enlightenment and modernity, as it presumed individuals to have rational autonomy marked by the negation of social particularity, identity, or interest. This would ensure that agreements arrived at in the public sphere could apply to everyone, universally, to the mass subject (Mah, 2000).

Habermas's idealized public sphere has been criticized from multiple positions. Scholars of South Asia show that local communities responded to colonial control over the public by replacing rational debates with religious processions, public rituals, and devotional performance to make their claims (Freitag, 1990; Masselos, 1991). There are also arguments that the Eurocentric notions of public and private do not work with the historical and cultural features of South Asian societies (Chakrabarty, 1991; Devji, 1991). Freitag (1990) resolved this dilemma by introducing the notion of the public arena instead of the public sphere, as the space for public contestations where claims in, and to, the public are staged.

Critics have also castigated the idealized public sphere as a narrow concept that excludes more actors than it includes, namely women, queer people, and those without education and property. It excludes any group or individual that appears to be the "other," and therefore the public sphere can only explain elite processes (Fraser, 1992). But other scholars show that these "others" ignore these exclusionary conditions and push at the boundaries of the public while performing their particularities (Eley, 1997; Ryan, 1997). Fraser (1992) and Negt and Kugle (1993 [1972]) also conceptualized counter-publics to neutralize the exclusionary features of Habermas's ideal public sphere. Counter-publics are "parallel discursive arenas where members of subordinated social groups invent and circulate counter-discourses to formulate oppositional interpretations of their identities, interests, and needs" (Fraser, 1992: p. 123), or dissenting webs of communication excluded by the dominant public sphere (Koller, 2010). Michael Warner's work (2014) on queer representations goes on to argue that even private and apparently nonpolitical acts constitute counter-publics.

The ideal public sphere was also criticized for excluding religion (Calhoun, 1992), a lacuna which Habermas later rectified (Habermas, 2006). Scholars of religion suggest that the public sphere is a productive framework for studying interactions within and between faith groups in plural societies (McCallum, 2011). This argument is built on Hauser's (2010) notion of scales, where the larger public sphere is a montage constituted of many smaller ones, that exist in a range of sizes, and that include both public interactions as well as private interactions pertaining to public issues. McCallum (2011) argues that micro public spheres provide a legitimate space for airing the social and political concerns of religious groups, and they allow minority groups to speak despite the hegemonic discourse that dominates the meso or macro public sphere. Criticisms and modifications have made the public sphere a bit amorphous. It is seen as a sphere, space, arena, or idea; it is positioned at several levels – micro, meso, and macro; and it is split between an idealized aspiration and a practical reality. Mah (2000) notes that contradictions between the rational, universal requirements of the idealized public sphere, and the socially rooted realities of individuals and groups underline the phantasmic character of the public sphere. Gilmartin (2015) engages with these contested claims and opens up the notion of the public to have three related and sometimes contradictory meanings and usages: it symbolizes state action for gaining legitimacy; denotes a community of self-directed individuals; and describes the arena between the state and society.

While I acknowledge these debates about the public sphere, I suggest that no matter how phantasmic the idealized, universal public sphere, individuals and groups are heavily impacted by it. It shapes the presentation of their selves as they navigate the tensions between the universal and the particular. I also embrace the multiple meanings and levels of the public sphere and contribute to this scholarship by showing that 'the public' denotes not only state action, self-directed individuals, sphere, space, or arena but also a powerful entity on its own – the majority perceived as the default. This conception of the public is analogous to Herbert Mead's notion of the "generalized other" (Mead, 1934), especially the multiple forms of the generalized other that can coexist in modern, diverse societies, and in relation with which or under the gaze of whom the self is shaped. This specific type of public is an independent actor that exerts its own force on individuals, groups, and processes in its vicinity. This is especially true for small groups such as the Shia. In contrast to larger groups who can contest this independent public, smaller groups such as the Shia instead adjust their collective self under the force of this public.

Since I study group level performances in public, I use Goffman's (1963) insights on stigmatized groups working to reconstruct their positive collective identities. Finally, I draw upon the boundary-making framework (Lamont 2008; Lamont and Molner, 2002) that helps interpret group level identity dynamics. As this approach is used in the context of the self and the other, I extend this framework and add public as the third party to this binary. This helps interpret public group performances through a triangular approach where the Shia represent their collective self, against multiple generalized others including Sunni Muslims as the other, and the public, as perceived default majority. The following sections focus on three distinct periods to show how the Shia perform their collective self in, and to, the public as they respond to shifting sociopolitical contexts.

Sectarian controversies and the Piggot Committee: prior to 1919

This phase describes a period in colonial India when the freedom movement had yet not begun in earnest, the Indian National Congress had established as a pan-Indian organization, aiming at increased autonomy for "the natives". Gandhi had yet not "arrived" in Indian politics, and demands for freedom from the British were marginal. In this period the British Crown was firmly in control, and statecraft was shaped by imperial and colonial sovereignty. Although this created moral contradictions at times, these twin drivers succeeded in maintaining the legitimacy of the British Crown as a rational, neutral arbiter of their subjects dispersed across interest, identity, and faith-based factions (Mukherjee, 2009). In effect, the courts of law and administrators symbolized a public invested in rational debates governed by law and the ethics of objectivity and justice. During this phase the Shia elite performed their distinctions through protests and petitioning while treating the British as the public, as well as the custodians of a neutral public arena.

British administrators in various provinces, especially in the United Provinces (UP), were aware of the Shia as a minority within the larger Muslim community. Among other things, this awareness was created by innumerable memorandums and petitions submitted by Shias. Archival records from the 1880s up to the first two decades of the 20th century show frequent petitions and their responses between the Shias of Lucknow and the British administrators, focusing on issues such as: management of Shia trusts; maintenance of religious buildings; improvement of Shia seminaries; and rights to public rituals. Such communications introduced colonial administrators to Shia religious law and customs, and established the Shias as a community distinct from the Sunnis, within the decision-making mechanisms of the provincial British government. The British acknowledged that the Shias had a "plethora of the professional class among them,"[1] and thus they induced a British understanding that Shias were an eminent class in Lucknow.[2]

British awareness of the Shia sect in North India became more acute during 1905 when the famed syncretism of Lucknow's observance of Muharram, the pride of Lucknow's Shia community, suddenly split into two separate sets of rituals. One was the puritan Shia version, focused on sober mourning for Husain, the 7th-century martyr in Islam, and the other evolved into a set of rituals oriented toward the remembrance of the first three caliphs of Islam. Shias and Sunnis parted ways with public acrimony. Public tensions and violent rioting attracted much attention from the colonial state, which eventually solved the problem by formalizing the separation through inquiries, administrative orders, and police arrangements. Deliberations of the Piggot Committee, set up in 1908 to resolve the Muharram dispute between the Shias and the Sunnis, etched Shia claims of distinction further in the imaginary of the colonial state. This committee was set up to investigate and resolve various conflicts between the Shias and Sunnis of Lucknow in which the provincial government played the role of arbitrator. This committee was headed by a British magistrate and had Shia, Sunni, and Hindu members. The committee summoned expert witnesses, gave audience to petitioners, and interrogated rival claims from both sects. It was under the working of this committee in the state of Uttar Pradesh (then the United Provinces, UP) that the boundaries between the two sects were first negotiated formally, albeit only around the public rituals of Muharram being followed by the respective sects.[3] Piggot Committee functioned as the neutral arena where two groups of colonial subjects argued. But, by the fact that the committee was state action aimed at legitimacy, it also symbolized the public (Gilmartin, 2015) toward which the arguments were addressed.

During and after the deliberations of the Piggot Committee, an international event provided further political opportunities for the Shia. This came through the Turko-Egyptian dispute, where British attitudes toward Turkey were triggering debates within Indian Muslim circles. While the Muslim masses had no direct voice on the issue, a substantive number of educated Sunni Muslims revered the Ottoman Sultan as the Caliph. The Home and Foreign department of the Government of India (GOI) closely monitored public opinion among Indian Muslims as they considered various risks – mutiny by Muslim soldiers in the British Army in Egypt, mass rebellion by Indian Muslim subjects, and troubles in the princely states ruled by Muslims. These records show a large number of petitions from various Muslim associations and organizations demanding British commitments against hurting the Ottoman Sultan. Several such petitions included threats of declaring jihad against the British if a war were to breakout.[4] British attitudes about Indian Muslims in general were thus somewhat shaped by this threat of jihad against the crown.

Shia individuals and organizations identified this opportunity to insert claims about their distinction and divergence from the Sunni majority. Petitions from Shias constituted performance or word-acts targeted at British opinion, that symbolized the public. One such petition was from a Shia cleric of Lucknow who was the official tutor of the Maharaja of Patiala, in Punjab. He disputed the general Muslim opinion about the issue:

> All this is the work of educated Sunnis from Lahore and Aligarh and the Shias have got nothing to do with it, as their religion does not recognize any worldly king as their religious leader. The Shias are loyal subjects of the British government and are highly thankful to the government for their manifold blessings. They hold that according to the Kuran and their religious books *Jihad* is not admissible and the government may be pleased to regard these messages solely from Sunni Muhammadans.[5]

British attitudes toward the Ottoman Sultan were being challenged through a series of protests and demonstrations by Sunni Muslims in the UP. While the newly formed All India Muslim League (AIML) and its leaders made speeches and representations opposing war actions on Turkey and the alleged Russian bombing of the Imam Reza shrine in Meshad (a Shia shrine in Persia), Shia leaders, especially from Lucknow, chose to protest only the bombing of Meshad.[6] In May 1912, protests by Shias created the "danger of serious trouble in Lucknow." This involved a series of public meetings and protests in the heart of Lucknow by Advocate Yusuf Husain and Mujtahid Nasir Husain, who planned to burn Russian flags and incite Shia mobs in Lucknow, to pressure Britain to reign in Russia. The Governor of UP, Sir John Hewett, was so alarmed at these events that he instituted a secret inquiry across the province to gauge public sentiment on the issue. During these protest meetings, Shias from Lucknow took elaborate steps to formally dissociate themselves from the Sunni protests and public writing about the war in Turkey. A meeting of Shia leaders of Lucknow and neighboring Kanpur resolved and communicated to the British (among other issues):

> That we Shias have nothing to do with the Turkish government as the Porte himself is a Sunni ruler; That we Shias do not and will not join

the Sunni Muhammadans in their attempt for boycotting European and English goods; That we Shias have nothing to do with the All India Muslim League and the Majlis Moyadul Islam [a Muslim organization] of Lucknow etc. since they are the Sunni political and religious bodies; and That our loyalty to the British government remains undisturbed even after the disturbances in Persia, the only Shia kingdom in the world; That we pray to God for the prosperity of the British empire as the freedom of religion and safety of our souls and property is only ensured under the aegis of the British crown.[7]

Public representations such as these were meant to press upon the government, publicly, the distinction that Shias assumed and cultivated about themselves. Their effects can be seen in British acknowledgements of the same. In government correspondence on the issue even as early as 1912 and 1913, British administrators from UP acknowledged that the hue and cry raised by Muslims of North India about the Ottoman Sultan was an entirely Sunni project and was actively opposed by the Shias of Lucknow, who were openly professing loyalty to the British Crown.[8] This phase shows how Shia claims of distinction from the Sunni majority were made in two specific ways. During the Muharram polemics between 1905 and 1908, the Piggot Committee was the neutral public arena where Shia and Sunni traded arguments and evidence. Simultaneously however, the committee also functioned as the public, as in state action that the British executed for gaining legitimacy of their subjects. Later, during the Turko-Egyptian War, Shias performed through word-acts, as well as protests in the public arena; this was also, however, for the consumption of the colonial state, the powerful actor under whose pressure Shias adjusted their collective self as a loyal group opposed to the stigmatized disloyal Sunni majority threatening the British with jihad.

Between Khilafat and freedom: 1919–47

The second phase is bookended by the Khilafat Movement (1919–24) and the decolonization that created the twin states of India and Pakistan (1947). This period saw the development and climax of the unified freedom movement and its splintering into two subnational projects. In this period, British power was crumbling in favor of nationalist elites dispersed across the Indian National Congress (INC) and All India Muslim League (AIML). While the British still held state power, their overall legitimacy was weak at best. Local and provincial elections had been inaugurated; the population was witnessing the construction of political autonomy through a colonial version of limited democracy; and the idea of separate electorates for various communities had been initiated, even if it was heavily contested. The Shia addressed a new public in this phase, that was more diverse and included

115

the British as well as "native" elites. Its location was now not only in the public arena or bound to the halls of colonial administration, but also in the provincial and federal legislatures where "native" elites served through elections, and where decisions were taken through debates and democratic maneuvers. Shias responded to these changes by adding to their existing repertoire the persuasion of elected representatives and Indian decision makers in the legislatures. They struck a delicate balance between claims of religious distinction from the Sunni Muslims, and commitment to a secular polity where various communities of faith could coexist on the basis of equitable democratic rights and affirmative action.

Before getting into the events of this period, a little backtracking is essential. The AIML was formed in Dacca, Eastern India on 30 December 1906, well before the Indian freedom movement's heyday, with founding members from across Indian provinces. This included several Shia individuals of influence from Lucknow. The inaugural resolutions passed by the AIML included issues such as the protection of political rights and interests of all Indian Muslims, and it also resolved "to prevent the feeling of hostilities among Muslims,"[9] inadvertently confessing to the presence of such animosities. Within a year of this event, in October 1907, several Shia lawyers, members of the landed gentry, and individuals with higher education joined hands to set up an organization that was visualized as an all-India interest group for the Shia community. This new organization, the All India Shia Conference (AISC), with a membership of 450 had most of its members from the UP, but also from Punjab, Bihar, and Hyderabad (Robinson, 1974; Brunner and Ende, 2001). The AISC was a challenger for the AIML's claim of representing Indian Muslims, even though in its initial years it was not anti-AIML. The AISC also took up progressive causes, such as confronting nepotism around Shia endowments and trusts, and went into litigation for freeing up resources for community welfare. These activities frequently created tensions between Shia factions such as the traditional aristocrats and the new educated elites.[10] AISC's other activities included petitioning the central government for revising census schedules to enable separate enumeration of Shias, and later, in 1914, demanding the government induct an AISC member onto the board of the Oudh Bequest, an endowment of the erstwhile Nawabs of Lucknow that financed Shia pilgrims in British-controlled Iraq and Iran.[11] The AISC mastered the art of drafting petitions, preparing legal notices and lawsuits, and lobbying lawmakers for serving their agenda, thus demonstrating the status of the Shia community as a distinct sect within Islam with very particular needs and demands. While the AISC was an organization of elite Shia men, their work, especially around the freeing up of public endowments and trusts from the clutches of corrupt trustees, gained them considerable popularity among the Shia masses of UP, making it one of several Shia organizations with considerable clout.

Although the Shias of UP had successfully claimed a distinct collective identity for themselves through their contentions during the Piggot Committee deliberations, and the earlier British-Ottoman dispute, the onset of the Khilafat Movement (KM) tested their claims for distinction afresh. Gandhi and the INC transformed the KM from a parochial set of grievances into a nationalist movement that pitched Indian 'subjects' against the British Raj (Minault, 1982; Qureshi 1999). This created a dilemma for UP's Shias, who had consistently disassociated from earlier Sunni demands and had pitched their disassociation as loyalty to the British Crown. However, with the strengthening of the INC-led nationalist movement, the public discourse around the Ottoman Caliph had changed, and disassociating from it completely would have shown the Shias as disloyal toward the nationalist movement. Not only had the discourse changed, but also the nature of the public, which was now shaped not only by British sovereignty but also by the nationalist movement. The public, as default majority, was now increasingly nationalist and anticolonial. However, since this was an ongoing transition, the British were not yet completely out of the picture. Corresponding to this transition, the public was also composite, containing both the British and the nationalists.

Lucknow's centrality to the KM can be gauged by the fact that the Indian Muslim Conference, the event that launched the KM across India was held there in September 1919. The conference invited Muslims of all kinds, including Shias, from across Indian provinces (Minault, 1982). The prime reason was the enthusiastic participation of Maulana Abdul Bari of the Firangi Mahal family, the most influential pan-Islamist cleric in British India of the 20th century (Qureshi, 1999). Bari had long been a Turkish sympathizer, especially since 1910 when his Turkish visit had exposed him to visions of Muslim grandeur. In 1913, after meeting the Ali brothers, he partnered with them and founded the key organization, *Anjuman-e-Khuddam-e-Kaba* (Organization of the Servants of Kaaba) with branches all over, including in Lucknow and Hyderabad (Minault, 1982). Congress support for the KM was also forged in Lucknow with the active role of Abdul Bari. Gandhi had approached Abdul Bari in 1919 to mobilize Muslim support for his civil disobedience movement, from which Muslim masses had remained largely aloof. Abdul Bari negotiated a quid pro quo in having the Congress support the KM. With Congress volunteers pitching in, the first Khilafat Day, on 17 October 1919, witnessed an impressive show of unity between Hindus and Muslims across India including in Lucknow.[12] However, Lucknow posed difficulties in projecting a unified Muslim community standing behind the KM. This was due to the presence of a sizeable and autonomous Shia community that was not onboard.

Gaining Shia purchase into the KM was very important: the absence of support from Muslim minorities would have undermined the claim that the

Khilafat issue had support from all Muslims. Therefore, Shia dissociations notwithstanding, the Ali brothers – proponents of the KM – persistently courted them.[13] The position of the Shias toward the KM was never straightforward. While it was true that some Shia clerics and religious-minded Shia leaders had dissociated from the movement, secular and progressive Shia leaders in Lucknow had become part of the KM because of its anticolonial nature (Qureshi, 1999). However, INC's support inextricably linked the KM with Gandhi and his civil disobedience movement. This transformed the meaning of the KM in the larger context and created a new challenge for Shias vying for audience in the evolving national public sphere.

The Khilafat Conference of January 1920, attended by 400 Muslim delegates from various provinces, included leading Shia figures from Lucknow. Advocate Mumtaz Husain, the Raja of Mahmudabad, and Aqa Hasan, one of the main Shia clerics in Lucknow, signed resolutions passed in the conference in favor of the Ottoman Caliph.[14] The Muharram of 1921 in Lucknow saw fervent Shia support for the noncooperation movement and the KM, though tactically framed as a protest against the bombing of Shia shrines in Najaf. Later in April 1921, Shia organizations in Lucknow passed resolutions supporting the protection of the sacred sites in Arabia.[15] This was again tactical public support given to the KM. Public speeches and petitions by Shia leaders and organizations during the KM struggled to balance the projection of a collective identity, distinct from Sunnis on religious grounds, but overlapping with them in the larger political context of nationalism.

By now a combination of factors had pushed the Shias of Lucknow to rethink their position on the KM. These factors included rumors about the aerial bombing of Shia shrines in Iran and Iraq, the general Sunni propaganda that the Shia disassociation was rooted in their lack of faith in the fundamentals of Islam, and the suggestions that the Shia did not support the nationalist struggle because of their vested interests in being loyal to the British. These allegations became more problematic in the contemporary public sphere, which was no longer monopolized by the British, but also had a distinct nationalist nature. On 6 March 1921, the AISC of Lucknow organized a public discussion on the KM, and their role in it. While most speakers were influential Shia individuals of Lucknow, some non-Shias were also present. The meeting took place at the shrine *Imambara Gufran-ma'ab*, the center of Shia opinion making in Lucknow. Syed Agha Hasan, a local lawyer, reminded the audience of the Shia's religious position, "We don't believe in Kings, we only have our Imams," and yet he set the tone for sectarian unity: "But we also need to protect the Islamic egg. Let me explain this concept. Shias are the yolk of the egg while other Muslims form its white and shell. If this egg is shaken, the yolk will also be under threat. For the sake of our future let us protect the whole Islamic egg." He continued, "The honor of Turkey is the honor of all Muslims, and we must unite to protect its interests." Others also made similar pitches, "The Shia community is part of Islam, and we will not remain safe if Islam is harmed."[16] This was a remarkable statement reflecting a shift away from earlier claims of loyalty to the British. It signaled the Shias feeling confident about aligning with the Sunni majority under the pressure of the nationalist public, without the anxiety of upsetting the British.

Another motivation for the Shia lay in challenging popular notions that the community was too small to be a significant player in politics. A speaker reminded the audience, "Of the seven crore [ten million] Muslims in India, two crore are Shias. And yet this large community is being ignored while minuscule groups such as the Sikhs are pushing ahead their political goals."[17] He added, "We are one of the most important communities of the world, and although we are a minority our courage is not wanting. It is now time when we can use the machine gun of noncooperation and show the government our courage."[18] This was another step in acknowledging nationalists as the new public, as default majority, and in the British being demoted from being the public.

The next set of public claims made by Shia leadership came toward the final phase of the Indian freedom movement, in the 1940s, especially after the AIML's demand for Pakistan had gained traction. During this phase, Shia organizations and leaders disrupted the narrative of a homogeneous Muslim community by appealing to the national public sphere, especially targeting the INC elites, and argued that Shias were an important, substantively numbered, and distinct community separate from Sunni Muslims. Such arguments include the All Party Shia Conference's (APSC) petitions, that opposed the designs and plans of the IML, which they alleged to be a purely Sunni political organization. The collection of petitions and legislative council debates from this period make the following arguments:

> The IML's vision of Pakistan involved a religious state governed by Hanafi religious law which was opposed to Jafari law governing the Shias; The proposed constitution of Pakistan did not intend to treat the Shias as a minority thus endangering their rights in future Pakistan; IML does not acknowledge the Shias as an important community and refuses to negotiate with its leaders and organizations; Shia organizations from across India would oppose the IML plan inside the legislative councils, and outside during provincial elections so as to defeat IML candidates in UP and other provinces.[19]

Similarly, the AISC petitioned the government of India, British members of Parliament, and Congress leaders to claim political positions distinct from the IML, and leaning toward the nationalist INC. These petitions include arguments such as:

Shias are a minority within Muslims just as scheduled castes were among the Hindus and protestants were in Ireland, and hence required special protection for their political and cultural rights; Shias are absolutely different from Sunnis as they have separate mosques, religious teachings, and culture, and in fact there is little or no common life between them; Shias and Sunnis treat each other as heretics and there has been a long sequence of communal riots and violence between them; Sunni Ulama preach against Shia practices and are always attempting to establish that we are not Muslims; The Shia Population in British India is 25 million that adds up to one third of the Muslim population. Also, Shias are advanced in education, trade and charity, and have contributed to the nation through their services in various fields thus making them an important and large minority; The census systematically discounts our numbers by under-counting us across provinces. It refuses to count mendicants and Sufi Muslims, who claim a Shia identity, on technical issues and deliberately enumerates us as a small community. We need to be counted separately on the census to deal with this problem; Even the few Shia members in the IML are opposed to the *sharia* clause for Pakistan, but their opinions are marginalized and ignored; The separate electorate scheme has systematically submerged the demands of the Shias as the IML only allows Sunnis to contest provincial elections and use terror tactics to dissuade Shia voters in all constituencies.[20]

These petitions and demands repeated heavily inflated estimates of the Shia population, and these estimates gradually entered official correspondence within Indian government communications, getting legitimized in official correspondence. In one such letter, Vallabh Bhai Patel, leader of the INC and the Home member of the GoI, wrote to the president of the APSC, acknowledging that the 30 million Shia Muslims in India were indeed marginalized by Sunni Muslims and deserved representation in employment. He also shared his views on the Shia demand for a quota in the separate electorate system of elections: "While I am not sure about the relevance of the separate electorate system of elections in future India, if it were to continue, we have to ensure that such a large community should get its due share."[21]

This second phase, in which British power waned in the face of a rising nationalist movement, shows important changes in the dynamic and location of public claims that the Shia made in support of their distinct status. The public, or default majority, was now constituted by the nationalist movement monopolized by the INC. The AIML and Muslims aligned with it, predominantly Sunni, were gradually labeled as unfaithful to the nationalist cause. Additionally, political reforms inaugurated in the 1930s had integrated Indian representatives into provincial and federal legislative bodies and added them to the list of public spaces where group interests could be presented, debated, and contested.

Shia expressions of their self evolved in this period in interesting ways, on one hand continuing the claims for distinction, but also on the other hand adding layers to what it means to be distinct. They claimed distinction from the Sunni majority, reiterating their religious differences but with a new focus on divergent political interests and positions, by refusing to be represented by the AIML and by rejecting the two-nation theory. The Shia endeavor in this phase was to respond to the larger discourse in a way that presented themselves with a positive identity, in contrast to the negatively labeled "unfaithful" Sunni Muslims. They presented themselves as a nationalist community aligned with the idea of a secular, and multifaith India where minorities could demand affirmative action and have the ability for participating politically under a democratic state's protection. Shias performed word-acts and protested to construct, first, a sectarian identity distinct from Sunni Muslims, and then a positive collective self in response to stigma. This stigma was placed first on the larger Muslim community by the British, who perceived them as potentially disloyal. Later the stigma stuck on Shias themselves, as the nationalists saw them as keeping aloof from the KM. As the broader sociopolitical context changed, so did the notion of the public. Across the two periods in colonial India, the public meant a neutral arena, state action, as well as an independent actor that pressured the Shias to adjust their collective identity. We now move toward the last phase, in independent India, to see how the public and Shia collective self shifted under a new sociopolitical context.

Hindutva and Islamophobia in contemporary India: 1990s and beyond

This phase is in independent India, post-selves Partition, where the Shia respond to contemporary discourse describing their collective in new ways that correspond to changing sociopolitical contexts at the national and regional level. In this phase, I will focus on two interconnected periods, the first being the 1990s, right after the Babri-Masjid-Ram-Janmabhoomi controversy culminated in the demolition of the Babri Mosque by affiliates of the Rashtriya Swayam Sewak Sangh (RSS) (Sundar, 2004; Anderson and Damle, 2018). The second period follows the first and corresponds to the electoral rise of the RSS through its political unit, the Bharatiya Janata Party (BJP), their federal government formation in 1998, and continuing into the present. In this phase, the Indian public decidedly turned away from the top-down legacy of secularism and toward cultural nationalism rooted in Hindutva, a political version of upper caste Hindu supremacy. In this shift, individuals and communities are increasingly evaluated according to their stance for or against Hindutva, as well as their position on majoritarianism, secularism, rights of minorities, and the Islamophobic narrative of global jihad. The Shia orient their performance to the elements of this majoritarian, cultural-nationalist public. They transform their self-presentation in the grammar of patriotism, tolerance, and even Islamophobia as they paint their generalized other, the Sunni community, as Islamists, while framing themselves as the model minority.

The controversy involving the Babri Mosque in Ayodhya, Uttar Pradesh, was revived in the 1980s when the Congress-led government at the center unlocked the disputed complex and allowed access to Hindu devotees for worship during specific days. This event was utilized by the RSS, and its affiliates in mobilizing support for their demands of constructing an exclusive temple for Lord Ram in place of the mosque (Udaykumar, 1997). This mobilization peaked in December 1992 with the demolition of the mosque, the first step in the process of constructing the promised temple. The temple movement, among other consequences, stigmatized the figure of the Indian Muslim as a foreigner, invader, and usurper of the rights of the Hindu community. In this trope, Muslims were cast as intolerant oppressors and Hindus were the oppressed but tolerant natives. The emergence of this discourse created the context within which the contemporary Shia community presented new claims in/to the public, as they continued to find ways for acceptance, security, and political significance.

This period witnessed fervent public opposition by Sunni clerics, community leaders, and Muslim interest groups who opposed the temple movement and asserted their legal and religious rights. Unlike them, most Shia leaders, both clerical and lay, were either absent or muted from the voices of opposition. Instead, some of them tactically aligned with the RSS sponsored movement for the temple and disassociated from the larger Muslim protests. During my interviews with several prominent Sunni leaders in Lucknow I gathered that the Shia absence was seen as a deliberate strategy, whereby the Shias chose to disassociate from the Sunni majority in order to project themselves as not only distinct from the Sunni majority, but also as the opposite of the RSS narrative about Indian Muslims in general. Their considered avoidance from opposing the demolition was a careful strategy to project themselves as "better" Muslims who were tolerant of other faiths, and who were eager to pacify the grievances of the Hindu majority. Further, this public silence was complemented by statements made in private such as, "Shias have nothing to do with the Babri mosque. It was under the control of a Sunni endowment, and was used by Sunni Muslims alone. It's not our battle!"[22] These private statements, which eventually became common knowledge in both Shia and Sunni circles, reinforced the overall message that the Shia leadership intended to transmit – "We are not with the Sunni majority."

The second key context against which the Shia have attempted to fashion themselves collectively is that of Islamist terrorism and Islamophobia. The post 9/11 world has witnessed pervasive Islamophobia that centers on the figure of the Muslim as a potential terrorist, and unconcerned with the lives of innocent non-Muslims. While this Islamophobia has been deployed mainly in Europe and the US, it has also creeped into India where the increasingly aggressive security establishment, State Police departments, an uncritical news media, and social media platforms such as Facebook and WhatsApp have contributed to its growth and acceptance in popular imagination. My interviews captured how the Shia in Lucknow have responded to this discourse. A young Hindu police officer in old Lucknow, whom I interviewed, shared the following with me:

"Shias are not at fault in the Shia–Sunni conflict in Lucknow. I have been posted here for 8 years now and I have read a lot of records and spoken with a lot of Shia and Sunni individuals in this area. Look at the Shia, they are just like us Hindus, they wear talismans like us, they worship the *tazia* which looks like our temples, their Muharram rituals are also similar to many rituals among the Hindus."

He explained the basis for this image of the Shia community: "Just compare the Shia and Sunni in Lucknow. The Sunni dress up like jihadis. Have you seen how they shave off their moustaches and keep long beards? Who are they emulating? Their role models are the terrorists in Pakistan."[23] The officer also shared how his views were based on his interactions with many Shia individuals in his beat. In another interview with a young, firebrand Shia cleric, I asked about this comparison of images that the police officer had shared. The cleric smiled, and said:

"What do I say to this? Everyone knows this. Shias cannot be terrorists; we do not follow that ideology. I tell everyone I meet about the fundamental difference between the Shias and the Sunnis, especially the Wahhabis. It is not in our DNA to take part in such stuff. It is our moral duty to educate the public, especially our Hindu brethren about the dangers of Wahhabi and Salafi ideology and how they brainwash kids in their Saudi-funded madrassas."

He impressed upon me further, assuming I still had doubts, "Tell me, have you ever heard of a Shia terrorist? You never will. We are a peaceful, patriotic *Qaum* (community) that has always considered India our homeland. We are not like them."[24]

Such messages, and the image that some Shia leaders have tried to cultivate in public and private, reinforce how Sunni Muslims perceive Shia interests in the political arena, as one Sunni journalist told me:

"They know that they have no chance in electoral politics. They can't even win a municipal ward election in the old city on their own. Very few Sunnis would vote for a Shia candidate. They have no option but to cozy up with the BJP and RSS, that's their best bet."[25]

This notion that the Shias in Lucknow are close to the RSS and BJP is contested only by some Shias. While most prominent Shia individuals whom I interviewed rejected this notion, the younger and not so prominent Shia respondents agreed to this reality, and also justified it. A young male Shia entrepreneur in the old city questioned me during an interview: "Why should we not support the BJP? Have they harmed us ever? Did they ban the Muharram processions in 1977? No. But the BJP did lift the ban in 1999. So, tell me, which party has taken care of Shias more?" On being asked if the Shia clerics also support the BJP, he smiled, "They wouldn't say that in public!"[26] In addition to these public silences and private confessions, a handful of Shia political leaders and clerics in Lucknow have never shied away from openly supporting the BJP. They do it either to support their own political endeavors, or to maintain patrimonial relationships with the state and central government.

These claims and the way they are framed emphasize how the Shia identified yet another change in the larger sociopolitical context that puts Muslims in general at a disadvantage, and responded to it strategically for self-preservation. Interviews also demonstrate how the Shias have responded by casting themselves as a separate community that is peaceful, patriotic, and has "nothing" to do with the Sunnis whom they have bundled within the Wahhabi/Salafi category. In the process, they also reproduce parts of the cultural-nationalist narrative of Hindutva, where Muslims are seen as suspects within the discourse of Islamophobia. This recent phase involves a cultural-nationalist public, as the default majority, and a range of public spaces where the collective Shia self was presented. These spaces included: the mass media, where Shias used strategic silences about the Babri mosque and Ram Temple controversy; private spaces, where Shia clerics and leaders disassociated from the larger Muslim resistance to the RSS and its affiliates; and public offices, such as police stations, where interpersonal interactions between Shia individuals and police officers took place. The larger Muslim community was stigmatized by the cultural-nationalist public, first as intolerant invaders and later as Islamist terrorists, against which the Shia cast themselves positively as a religiously tolerant, peaceful, and patriotic community that conform to the cultural-nationalist imagination of the RSS and its affiliates.

Conclusion

The case of Shias in modern India show how a small community of a politically insignificant size perform in, in regards to, and to the public – as arena, actor, and audience – to create a positive edifice of their collective self in response to stigmatization. The Shia undertake boundary work to present their collective self in relation to Sunni Muslims as the other, and the public in a triangular scheme. I study Shia identity by bringing together concepts from Goffman's work on performance, scholarship on the public sphere, and boundary making. I use the historical-sociological method to interpret my evidence, which lets me study meaning-making at specific moments embedded within a longer period of time.

While public spheres or arenas may be suitable places for contentious politics between comparable groups and communities that compete to become the abstracted notion of the public (Freitag, 1990; Mah, 2000; Gilmartin, 2015) the possibilities for small groups are limited. My evidence shows how Shia presentations of their collective self have been shaped by the limitations of their group size that increasingly became a liability with the rise of modern politics, especially representative democracy. Driven by aspirations rooted in a politically powerful past and hindered by the insignificance of their voting power, they found alternative ways of self-preservation. Shias do not present themselves simply in contrast to the Sunni Muslims as other, but also in relation to a third party who holds sway in the process. This third party is the public, or the default majority, which shifts over time across three historical periods in India. This public was constituted of British sovereignty in the first period, the anticolonial nationalists in the second period, and an emergent cultural-nationalist zeitgeist in the third period. This public, or the third party, acts not only as audience, but also as judge under whose gaze Shias aspire to be accepted as a desirable group. This emphasizes the extraordinary influence that the public has over the Shia, under the force of which they compromise and adjust their collective self. I argue that the public denotes not only a sphere, arena, state action, or self-directed individuals, as scholars of the public sphere have suggested, but also an independent actor that exerts its own force on the processes that take place in these public arenas and spheres. I also show how the public as independent actor forces small minority groups to adjust their collective self under its force.

Finally, studying performances or word-acts as the mechanism for constructing and reconstructing religious or sectarian identity in the public also helps reinterpret religion in general, and religious identity in particular. Traditional understanding assumes religious beliefs, rituals, and experiences to be the primary shapers of religious identity. However, the fact that the construction and transformation of Shia collective identity takes place primarily in public emphasizes the porosity of religious boundaries, and the malleability of its content. The public in my case is eminently political, as it is saturated with conceptual labels such as rights, subjecthood, loyalty, nationalism, and citizenship. It is these profane ideas and aspirations that primarily drive the many transformations of Shia collective identity, thus disrupting the monopoly of religious roots of religious identity. At the broadest level, this chapter also helps question the artificial distinction between interest and identity that we so often engage with in debates about identity politics. Indeed, identity and interest are much closer than they may deceptively appear.

Notes

1 "Mr. Radice's remarks"/Uttar Pradesh State Archives (UPSA)/General Administration Department (GAD)/1911/File No. 366/p. 1.
2 "Mr. Radice's remarks"/Uttar Pradesh State Archives (UPSA)/General Administration Department (GAD)/1911/File No. 366/p. 1.
3 "Final report of the Piggot Committee," January 1909/ Uttar Pradesh State Archives (UPSA)/ General Administration Department (GAD)/1908/File No. 591.
4 "Muhammadan Feelings in India vis a vis Turko-Egyptian Frontier"/ National Archives of India (NAI)/Foreign/Secret-E/1907/May/764–96.
5 "Letter"/ National Archives of India (NAI)/Foreign/Secret-C/1907/May/764–96/p. 4.
6 "Memo – Muhammadan Feelings in India"/ National Archives of India (NAI)/Home-Political/1913/March/45–55/Part A.
7 "Memo – Muhammadan Feelings in India"/ National Archives of India (NAI)/Home-Political/1913/March/45–55/Part A, p. 29.
8 "Memo – Muhammadan Feelings in India"/ National Archives of India (NAI)/Home-Political/1913/March/45–55/Part A, pp. 10–57.
9 "Resolutions Adopted at a Meeting Held at Dacca Regarding the Formation of a Political Association Styled the 'All India Moslem League'"/ National Archives of India (NAI)/Home/Public/1907/Feb/71–4/p. 181.
10 "Resolutions Passed by the AISC Regarding the Mussalman Wakf Act 1923"/ National Archives of India (NAI)/Home-Judicial/1925/Part B/Deposit/Proceedings/234.
11 "Resolution on the Oudh Bequest," 8th October 1913/ National Archives of India (NAI)/Foreign-General/1914/July/1–13/Part A/p. 18.
12 "Khilafat Day"/Bombay Chronicle, 18th October 1919/Native Newspapers/ National Archives of India (NAI)/1919.
13 "Transcript of public speech delivered by Muhammad Ali at Town Hall, Banaras, 16th November, 1920"/ National Archives of India (NAI)/Home-Political/1921/11/p. 6.
14 "Khilafat Conference Address to the Viceroy, Delhi, 19th January, 1920." Reproduced in: Aziz, K.K. (1972) *The Indian Khilafat Movement, 1915–1933: A Documentary Record*, Karachi: Pak Publishers, p. 70.
15 "CID report on Khilafat speeches and resolutions"/Uttar Pradesh State Archives (UPSA)/ General Administration Department (GAD)/Police/1920/513.
16 "Transcript of Speech by Syed Agha Hasan, Noncooperation speeches"/ Uttar Pradesh State Archives (UPSA)/ General Administration Department (GAD)/1920/16/16/pp. 125–6.
17 "Transcript of speech by Syed Dilawar Husain, Noncooperation speeches"/ Uttar Pradesh State Archives (UPSA)/ General Administration Department (GAD)/1920/16/16/p. 137.
18 "Transcript of speech by Syed Dilawar Husain, Noncooperation speeches"/ Uttar Pradesh State Archives (UPSA)/ General Administration Department (GAD)/1920/16/16/p. 137.
19 "Resolution passed by the All Parties Shia Conference, 25th December, 1945"/ National Archives of India (NAI)/Home-Public/1946/File No. 289/p. 17.
20 "Representations from the All Parties Shia Conference, February, 1946"/ National Archives of India (NAI)/Reforms Department/1946/41/3/46-R/pp. 4–24.

21 "Telegram, Patel to Hooseinbhoy, APSC Resolutions, 12th February, 1946"/ National Archives of India (NAI)/Reforms Department/1946/41/3/46-R/p. 3.
22 Interview/Lucknow/Sunni respondent/Police personnel/No. 13.
23 Interview/Lucknow/Hindu respondent/Police personnel/No. 7.
24 Interview/Lucknow /Shia respondent/Cleric/No. 2.
25 Interview/ Lucknow /Sunni respondent/Journalist/No. 3.
26 Interview/ Lucknow /Shia respondent/Community member/No. 11.

References

Published works

Andersen, W.K., and Damle, D.S. (2018) *The RSS: A View to the Inside*, Gurgaon: India Penguin Viking.

Birrell, S. (1981) "Sport as Ritual: Interpretations from Durkheim to Goffman," *Social Forces*, 60(2): 354–76.

Brass, P.R. (2011) *The Production of Hindu-Muslim Violence in Contemporary India*, Seattle: University of Washington Press.

Brubaker, R., and Cooper, F. (2000) "Beyond 'identity," *Theory and Society: Renewal and Critique in Social Theory*, 29(1): 1–47.

Brunner, R., and Werner E. (2001) *The Twelver Shia in Modern Times: Religious Culture & Political History*, Leiden: Brill.

Calhoun, C. (1992) *Habermas and the Public Sphere*, Cambridge, MA: MIT.

Cerulo, K.A. (1997) "Identity Construction: New Issues, New Directions," *Annual Review of Sociology*, 23: 385–409.

Chakrabarty, D. (1991) "Open Space/Public Place: Garbage, Modernity and India," *South Asia: Journal of South Asian Studies*, 14(1): 15–31.

Clark, T.N., and Lipset, S.M. (2001) *The Breakdown of Class Politics: A Debate on Post-Industrial Stratification*, Washington, DC: Woodrow Wilson Center Press.

Cole, J.R. (1988) *Roots of North Indian Shi'ism in Iran and Iraq: Religion and State in Awadh, 1722–1859*, Berkeley: University of California Press.

Devji, F.F. (1991) "Gender and the Politics of Space: The Movement for Women's Reform in Muslim India, 1857/1900," *South Asia*, 14 (1): 141–53.

D'Souza, D. (2014) *Partners of Zaynab: A Gendered Perspective of Shia Muslim Faith*, Columbia, SC: The University of South Carolina Press.

Eley, G. (1997) "Nations, Publics, and Political Cultures," in C.J. Calhoun (ed) *Habermas and the Public Sphere*, Cambridge, MA: MIT Press, pp. 289–339.

Fraser, N. (1992) "Rethinking the Public Sphere: A Contribution to the Critique of Actually Existing Democracy," in C.J. Calhoun (ed) *Habermas and the Public Sphere*, Cambridge, MA: MIT Press, pp. 109–37.

Freitag, S.B. (1990) *Collective Action and Community: Public Arenas and the Emergence of Communalism in North India*, Delhi: Oxford University Press.

Gilmartin, D. (2015) "Rethinking the Public through the Lens of Sovereignty," *South Asia*, 38(3): 371–86.

Goffman, E. (1961) *Asylums: Essays on the Social Situation of Mental Patients and Other Inmates*, Harmondsworth: Penguin.

Goffman, E. (1963) *Stigma: Notes on the Management of Spoiled Identity*, Englewood Cliffs, NJ: Prentice Hall.

Greil, A., and Davidman, L. (2007) "Religion and Identity," in J.A. Beckford, and J. Demerath (eds) *The Sage Handbook of the Sociology of Religion*, Los Angeles: Sage, pp. 549–65.

Habermas, J. (1992) *The Structural Transformation of the Public Sphere: An Inquiry into a Category of Bourgeois Society*, Cambridge: Polity.

Habermas, J. (2006) "Religion in the Public Sphere," *European Journal of Philosophy*, 14 (1): 1–25.

Hardy, P. (1972) *The Muslims of British India*, London: Cambridge University Press.

Hauser, G.A. (2010) *Vernacular Voices: The Rhetoric of Publics and Public Spheres*, Columbia, SC: University of South Carolina Press.

Hollister, J.N. (1953) *The Shi'a of India* , London: Luzac.

Johnston, E. (2016) "The Enlightened Self: Identity and Aspiration in Two Communities of Practice," *Religions*, 7(7).

Jones, J. (2012) *Shi'a Islam in Colonial India: Religion, Community and Sectarianism*, Cambridge: Cambridge University Press.

Koller, A. (2010) "The Public Sphere and Comparative Historical Research: An Introduction," *Social Science History*, 34 (3): 261–90.

Lamont, M. (2008) *Money, Morals, and Manners: The Culture of the French and American Upper-Middle Class*, Chicago: University of Chicago Press.

Lamont, M. and Molnár, V. (2002) "The Study of Boundaries in the Social Sciences," *Annual Review of Sociology*, 28(1): 167–95.

Lichterman, P. (2008) "Religion and the Construction of Civic Identity," *American Sociological Review*, 73(1): 83–104.

Mah, H. (2000) "Phantasies of the Public Sphere: Rethinking the Habermas of Historians," *Journal of Modern History*, 72(1): 153–82.

Masselos, J. (1991) "Appropriating Urban Space: Social Constructs of Bombay in the Time of the Raj," *South Asia: Journal of South Asian Studies*, 14 (1): 33–63.

McCallum, R. (2011) "Micro Public Spheres and the Sociology of Religion: An Evangelical Illustration," *Journal of Contemporary Religion*, 26 (2): 173–87.

Mead, G.H. (1934) *Mind, Self, and Society*, Chicago: University of Chicago Press.

Minault, G. (1982) *The Khilafat Movement: Religious Symbolism and Political Mobilization in India*, New York: Columbia University Press.

Moinuddin, K., Rao, V.V., and Vedantam, T. (1977) *A Monograph on Muharram in Hyderabad City*, Delhi: Controller of Publications.

Mukherjee, M. (2009) *India in the Shadows of Empire: A Legal and Political History (1774–1950)*, Delhi: Oxford University Press.

Negt, O., and Kluge, A. (1993 [1972]) *Public Sphere and Experience: Toward an Analysis of the Bourgeois and Proletarian Public Sphere*, Minneapolis: University of Minnesota Press.

Pinault, D. (1992) *The Shiates: Ritual and Popular Piety in a Muslim Community*, New York: St. Martin's Press.

Qureshi, M.N. (1999) *Pan-Islam in British Indian Politics: A Study of the Khilafat Movement, 1918–1924*, Leiden: Brill.

Rizvi, S.A.A. (1986) *A Socio-Intellectual History of the Isnā 'Asharī Shī'īs in India*, New Delhi: Munshiram Manoharlal Publishers.

Robinson, F. (1974) *Separatism Among Indian Muslims: The Politics of the United Provinces' Muslims, 1860–1923*, London: Cambridge University Press.

Ryan, M. (1997) "Gender and Public Access: Women's Politics in Nineteenth-Century America," in C.J. Calhoun (ed) *Habermas and the Public Sphere*, Cambridge, MA: MIT Press, pp. 259–88.

Schubel, J.V. (1993) *Religious Performance in Contemporary Islam: Shi'i Devotional Rituals in South Asia*, Columbia, SC: University of South Carolina Press.

Sundar, N. (2004) "Teaching to Hate: RSS' Pedagogical Programme," *Economic and Political Weekly*, 39(16): 1605–12.

Udayakumar, S.P. (1997) "Historicizing Myth and Mythologizing History: The 'Ram Temple' Drama," *Social Scientist,* 25(7–8): 11–26.

Warner, M. (2014) *Publics and Counterpublics*, New York: Zone Books.

Wilkinson, S. (2006) *Votes and Violence: Electoral Competition and Ethnic Riots in India* (Cambridge Studies in Comparative Politics), Cambridge: Cambridge University Press.

Archival sources

National Archives of India, Delhi (NAI)
Government of India (GoI), Foreign Department Files (Foreign)
Government of India (GoI), Home Department Files (Home)
Government of India (GoI), Home- Political Department Files (Home-Political)
Government of India (GoI), Ministry of States Files (States)
Government of India (GoI), Political Department Files (Political)
Native Newspapers

Uttar Pradesh State Archives (UPSA), Lucknow
Government of United Provinces (GoUP), General Administration Department Files (GAD)

Government of United Provinces (GoUP), Home Department Files (Home)

Government of United Provinces (GoUP), Home-Political Department Files (Home-Political)

Government of United Provinces (GoUP), Political Department Files (Political)

6

The Power of Meaning: Toward a Critical Discursive Sociology of Religion

Titus Hjelm

Peter L. Berger, the now-departed prickly doyen of the sociology of religion, was characteristically upfront when discussing the debates over different definitions of religion: "I must confess that I find this question sublimely uninteresting" (Berger, 2014: p. 17). On the one hand, I heartily agree. There is no shortage of academic work that takes a definition of religion and uses it as a template for assessing whether something counts as "religion." Lužný (2020), for example, argues that Czech Jediism and the Czech Church of Beer do not count as religions using a choice of (mostly functional) definitions. While he makes the valuable point that academic definitions may function to legitimate state decisions, it is less clear how the attempt to fit a religious group into a definitional box contributes to knowledge. Finding yet another case study to challenge a familiar definition is not a sign of sociological imagination, but rather of misunderstanding the function of definition. Consequently, it is only a small step to the other prevalent practice in the field, namely the infinite loop of metatheoretical discussion over the scholarly uses of "religion" (Saler, 1993; McCutcheon, 1997). Indeed, an expanded definition of religion is what Lužný recommends as a way out of the problem of accounting for "invented religions" like Jediism and the Church of Beer. Why I find both endeavors, with Berger, "sublimely uninteresting," is simple: While we need working definitions of religion for many types of research, these definitions are – and should be – given as pragmatic ways to demarcate the field of vision rather than more or less accurate depictions of reality. The question, then, is not about truthfulness, but usefulness.

However, on the other hand, definitions are the *most* interesting question in the sociology of religion – just not in the way the field has traditionally considered it. To give you an example: my PhD student Helmi Halonen analyzes the ways in which the Finnish immigration authority (Migri) decides whether an asylum seeker's conversion to Christianity is genuine enough to warrant asylum based on religious discrimination in the country of origin. These can be literally life and death decisions. However, instead of challenging Migri's decisions by assessing whether the asylum seekers' faith counts as a "real" religion by contrasting their stories with substantive (what religion is) and functional (what religion does) definitions, Halonen focuses on the definition process itself. What is it that Migri accomplishes by defining "genuine" religion in particular ways? "Religion" is constantly – increasingly, some would say – invoked, challenged, and redefined in public discourse all over the world. The issue for the sociology of religion is, then, not so much about whether a phenomenon fits either main definition (substantive/functional) – or if these definitions should be updated and complemented – but on what is being *done* when "religion" is talked about in a particular way. Indeed, this is what Jim Beckford suggested already some time ago: "It would be better to abandon the search for, and the assumption that there are, generic qualities of religion and, instead, to analyze the various situations in which religious meaning or significance is constructed, attributed or challenged" (Beckford, 2003: p. 16).

Consequently, I would like to propose two things: First, that instead of definitions that try to capture the reality of "religion" in its myriad forms, we should talk about *approaches* to studying religion sociologically (Hjelm, 2021). A substantive or functional approach defines which questions to ask, which data to use, and which method would be appropriate for research – without the burden of trying to fit myriad phenomena under one definition of religion. Substantive approaches, for example, are required for research on secularization, where we need a clear definition of what religion *is* in order to measure whether there is less of it over a period of time. Functional definitions, in turn, are used when the point is to examine, for example, which social institutions contribute to social cohesion. The important point, then, is what religion *does*. Thinking of these as *approaches* helps us focus on what these different definitions allow us, as scholars, to do and ask about religion.

Second, and following from the above, I would add another approach to the above, a "third way" of doing sociology of religion, namely a constructionist one:

> Constructionist approaches ask *what passes for religion in society*. Instead of trying to come up with a definition of religion in order to focus the research questions and appropriate data, constructionist approaches

concentrate on the act of definition itself. Thus, the focus is on how people construct the meaning of "religion" in different contexts, and what the social consequences of these constructions are. The analytical term for studying this is *discourse*, that is, the ways in which we talk about "religion." (Hjelm, 2021: p. 138. Emphasis in the original.)

In this chapter, I want to examine how a focus on discourse changes the questions we ask and the overall orientation of research. Further, as I have argued elsewhere (for example, Hjelm, 2014a), discursive approaches to religion have so far paid insufficient attention to issues of power. My aim here, therefore, is to construct a framework, which takes the prompt "what passes for religion in society" seriously, with particular focus on how different constructions of religion reproduce – or transform – power relations in society. I call this approach *critical discursive sociology of religion* (CDSR).

The chapter is divided into two main sections. In the first, I will present the broad parameters of what I consider the key elements of CDSR, discussing "discourse" as theory and method, and how power features in the framework of CDSR. In the second part, I will apply the framework provided to the case of "national churches" in Europe. Using Finland as a case study, I analyze how defining the historical state church as a "folk church" does ideological work in reproducing religious privilege.

Discourse as social practice

"Social construction" came, saw, and conquered the social sciences from the 1970s onward. Berger and Luckmann's *The Social Construction of Reality* (1967 [1966]) made little impact at its time of publication, but three decades later was considered the fifth most important work in 20th century sociology by the members of the International Sociological Association (Hjelm, 2018: p. 157). Social constructionism has its detractors, but the idea of social construction has become common fare in sociology.

Owing to academic contingencies, "discourse" has made much less of an impact on social science, especially in North America, despite the close association with the idea of social construction. Instead, discourse theorists can primarily be found in philosophy and literature departments. This is embodied in the most pre-eminent theorist of discourse in North America at the moment, Judith Butler, who is perhaps best characterized as a feminist philosopher, but who is affiliated with the Department of Comparative Literature at University of California, Berkeley. This disciplinary history is, I would say, partly to blame for the suspicion some still harbor toward using discourse in sociological analysis. Even when the concept is used, it is not necessarily used in the sense of world-constructing text and talk. As I have argued earlier (Hjelm, 2014a; 2021), a "third way" discursive approach to the sociology of religion assumes – explicitly or implicitly – two things: (1) discourse constructs social reality, and (2) things are done with discourse. The former attribute I refer to as *constitutiveness*, the latter as *action orientation*.

Constitutiveness signifies the basic premise of social constructionism, that is, that our ways of talking and writing about the world – a succinct definition of "discourse" – do not simply "reflect" how the world is, but actively construct it as well. We can tell the truth and nothing but the truth, but we can never tell the whole truth (Barker, 2011: p. 200). It is the choice of *which* truth gets told that is the constitutive element. Our discourse is by definition partial in both senses of the word. It is partial because it is always incomplete and it is partial because it is filtered through our interests and interpretations of what is important. This is why one person's new religious movement is another person's dangerous, brainwashing cult.

This much is usually agreed within the broad framework of constructionist research. The second aspect, action orientation, is sometimes less well understood and explicated. Taking action orientation seriously means that the analyst cannot stop at mapping the variety of discourses. Showing the variety of ways in which people talk about an issue shows the constructedness of social reality very well, but it says little about what is being accomplished by constructing social reality in a particular (partial) way. Already in 1940, C. Wright Mills talked about how "the differing reasons men [sic] give for their actions are not themselves without reasons" (Mills, 1940: p. 904). That is why discourse is never just constitutive, but has a functional side as well. It enables or constrains interpretations, which in turn may lead to further actions. We cannot deduce these outcomes from the discourse itself – Thompson (1990: pp. 24–5) calls this "the fallacy of internalism" – but taking into account contextual factors, we can map the reasonable options available for different audiences. Words have consequences, even if we cannot deduce *which* consequences from the words themselves. Calling an action "sinful," for example, is not simply a statement. It may also be a warning and an exhortation to cease acting in that way.

Meaning in the service of power

Already almost four decades ago, Jim Beckford (1983) exhorted sociologists of religion to bring power back into the center of inquiry. Despite numerous citations and reprints of his article, the field as a whole has taken little heed. It is still fair to say (see: Hjelm, 2014a), that a self-identifying critical sociology of religion – one that would foreground power in the study of religion – does not currently exist (even if brilliant individual studies and scholars in that vein do, for example, McKinnon, 2006; Josephsohn and Williams, 2013). This chapter, then, is a follow-up to my previous contributions toward that kind of critical sociology of religion.

Narrowing down the complexity of the world is, in a way, required for effective functioning in society. We cannot stop to think about the mechanics of alarm clocks every morning if we want to wake up in time for work or school. But narrowing down interpretive horizons is also a function of power. In late modernity, power is less about coercion and more about consent. Consent, in turn, is achieved by constructing a selective – partial, as already mentioned – view of the world through discursive persuasion.

My choice of term for analyzing the processes in which this narrowing down happens is *ideology*. Although influential theorists of discourse, such as Michel Foucault, have talked about discourse and power without reference to ideology (Cousins and Hussein, 1984: p. 172), I think it best captures the social impact of language use.

A now-dated survey (Hamilton, 1987) found 27 different meanings for "ideology." Although the key elements in these varying definitions can be condensed, it is likely that an updated survey would find ever-new ways of using the concept. For our purposes, however, we can settle with a distinction between two definitions, the neutral and the critical. I have referred to the former as the *noun-type* definition. That is, ideology is seen as an equivalent of a "worldview" and it is manifested in political ideologies like nationalism and socialism, for example. The point is that ideology is treated as a noun, like an "ism" (although not always explicitly so) with a substantive content, which people endorse and act upon. This is the everyday language version of "ideology" and one most often encountered in political science textbooks.

What I am more interested in is the latter, critical, definition. This is best captured, I think, by John B. Thompson's (1990: p. 7) succinct characterization of ideology as "meaning in the service of power," that is, "the ways in which meaning serves, in particular circumstances, to establish and sustain relations of power which are systematically asymmetrical." This is the *adjective or adverb-type* definition. Discourse is ideological or functions ideologically when it contributes to the imbalance in power relations by ironing out alternative, competing accounts of the physical world, social relations, and social identities (Fairclough, 1992: p. 87; Chouliaraki and Fairclough, 1999: p. 26). Although not a novel phenomenon (Said, 1997), the media coverage of Islam in the post-9/11 world is the most obvious example of a discourse where Muslims are afforded only a narrow choice of roles as terrorists or victims of a patriarchal religion (for example, Poole, 2002; Poole and Richardson, 2006; Farris, 2017). It also means Islamophobia becomes not only an understandable, but also an acceptable response to Muslims in the eyes of many Westerners. It is not an automatic response – remember "the fallacy of internalism" – but becomes more plausible when stoked by people with political, economic, or cultural power and something to gain from it.

There are, however, four important qualifications to "meaning in the service of power" (see, for example: Fairclough, 1992). First, the focus on meaning prioritizes the *content* of discourse. Indeed, examining the meaning of words is central to the critical discourse analyst's toolkit (Richardson, 2007: pp. 47–9). However, many aspects of the *form* of language also function ideologically. One classic example is the way in which human agency, and hence responsibility, is obfuscated by sentence structure. In what I consider the best available practical guide to doing critical discourse analysis, Richardson (2007: p. 56) analyzes a late-1990s British government policy paper on "the knowledge economy," which says, "capital is mobile, technology can migrate quickly and goods can be made in low cost countries and shipped to developed markets." In this sentence capital (as Marx had already observed) acts on its own, as does technology. Presumably, human agents are involved in the making and shipping of goods, but we never learn who these people are. It is no wonder that many people today feel that they have been robbed of agency, and that politics is useless. The function of this kind of political discourse is to construct a view where the political process (humans acting in concert) is powerless to influence the independent force of capital. Whether intended or unintended, this kind of discursive cloaking of agency functions ideologically by reproducing a world in which "there is no alternative" to current neoliberal economic policies. A similar process could be said to have happened with public debates concerning Islam and violence: "Islam is a violent religion" is a common refrain among Right-wing media, especially. What this masks is that religions do not commit violent acts, only people do. What it conversely accomplishes is that if Islam is the agent, then every Muslim is potentially violent.

Second, although "meaning in the service of power" is a useful shorthand, discourse functions ideologically also through absence. What is said (and how it is said) obviously matters, but equally important for the critical analyst is what is *not* said. What is the story that is not told? What is the perspective that is not voiced? Importantly, absence may signal naturalization, that is, that a particular version of the world is taken as so commonsensical that it does not even need to be mentioned. The focus on absences and silences also points to an epistemological issue in CDSR: in order to know what we might be missing, we need to have a solid understanding of the contexts of discourse. A potentially infinite number of alternative constructions are available in most instances, but only a limited number will make sense in particular contexts. As I argue in the second part of this chapter, that only a handful of the members of the 200-strong Finnish Parliament took part in a debate on freedom of religion signals that in the context of advanced secularization this is not a topic that inspires many politicians. The silence of the majority of MPs also signals that the current privileged position of the Evangelical Lutheran Church of Finland (ELCF) is a state of things that is considered politically unproblematic (Hjelm, 2014b).

Third, we need to expand Thompson's definition regarding how meaning is used to "establish and sustain" unequal power relations. The focus is often on "narrowing down," as I put it earlier. The theoretically more refined term would be *reproduction*. Bourdieu and Passeron's (1990) analysis of the French school system as the arena where middle-class "habitus" is reproduced is a classic in the field. Even earlier, Otto Maduro (1982) used Bourdieu's ideas to show how Catholic clergy in Latin America actively reproduce social inequalities by giving the class system a divine legitimation. Although this is not necessarily a conscious narrowing down of interpretive horizons, it has the consequence of perpetuating elite dominance. Much research in the critical tradition (Marxist, feminist, queer, decolonial, and so on) is concerned with exactly that. This has led to the common refrain that critical social science, and critical discourse studies in particular, is overly concerned with negative topics, things that are generally considered – or at least seen by the analyst – as problematic (Breeze, 2011: pp. 516–17).

There is, however, another way of approaching discourse and power. Fairclough (1992: p. 65) usefully reminds us that discourse is never just about reproducing ("establishing and sustaining") oppressive social structures, but always has a transformative side as well. Instead of narrowing, discourse can be thought of as expanding interpretive horizons. For example, the constitutional changes in 19th and 20th century Europe, which led to the legal recognition of religious pluralism and secularity – in contrast to the confessional state – were at heart discursive debates about the definition of religion and the appropriate boundaries of religion in modern states (Rémond, 1999: pp. 130–9). Literally, this meant churches losing ground to politicians debating freedom of religion in parliaments. The analyzed transformations may be progressive or regressive (as defined in each context) but what is common is that the status quo is discursively challenged and the challenge leads to changes in legislation or culture, for example.

A final issue is what could be called the dual nature of discursive power. Critical discourse studies commonly take the Foucauldian view that power permeates all discourse. It is the discourse that does the persuading, regardless of the persuader. Ideological (although that is not the term that Foucault would use) language can be found in many texts and interactions where the avowed point is not to "establish and sustain relations of power which are systematically asymmetrical" (Thompson, 1990: p. 7). Discourse works ideologically, regardless of the intentions of the producers. This could be called the "power in discourse" position. In a discussion in the British parliament, a House of Lords representative argued that current legislation is sufficient for dealing with terrorism, because: "… if the home secretary thinks Mohammad el-Smith wants to do something and is planning to do something and has talked to others about doing something nasty, that is not conspiracy?" (quoted in Richardson, 2007: p. 50). By referring to the imaginary terrorist as "Mohammad el-Smith" – the most common Muslim male name and the most common British family name – the implication is that the speaker "believes the average terrorist suspect to be Muslim" (Richardson, 2007: p. 51).

I do not think, however, that we should abandon the more traditional, Weberian view of domination in CDSR. This is famously and concisely expressed by Lukes's (1974: p. 27) formulation: "A exercises power over B, when A affects B in a manner contrary to B's interests." In this conceptualization, power – or more accurately, domination (Hearn, 2012: p. 21) – is anchored in actors. These actors are, in turn, embedded in social positions that grant them more or less power over others. A good example is the classroom: when a teacher asks a question, pupils "do not have the option to reply, 'I'd rather not answer that question,' or 'I think I'll turn that over to Sammy; it's more in his line'" (Chimombo and Roseberry, 1998: p. 11). In the classroom context at least, the teacher has power to narrow down the actions conceivable to pupils by virtue of her social position within that context. To give an example from the world of religion, it is likely that the words of the Pope weigh more in the eyes of the global Catholic communion than those of a lay member. The more powerful the source of discourse doing the narrowing, the more powerful the effect. This is what I refer to as the "power of discourse." Where power *in* discourse refers to the capacity of language itself to influence our action, the power *of* discourse points to the authority of the speaker and the receptivity of the audience. CDSR is interested in both.

The "folk church" as ideology[1]

The idea of a "national church" goes as far back as the Peace of Augsburg in 1555, when Catholic and Lutheran (but not Calvinist) forces in Europe agreed that "their locality determined the faith of subjects who perforce embraced the religion of their monarch" (Rémond, 1999: p. 21). Although freedom of religion has since been established, albeit at various levels, all over Europe, the connection between religion and nation is retained in many countries. This is reflected in the official names of national churches, such as the Church of Greece, Church of England, and Church of Sweden.

Often a "national church" is associated with the state, either in practice or in people's perceptions. Indeed, Fox's (2008: pp. 111–12) global survey ranks several churches in Europe as "active state religions," that is, countries where "the state has one or more official religions *and* the state actively promotes the state religion [through various measures]." This is a rather uncomfortable position for the relatively liberal national churches, such as those in the Nordic countries. Hence, there has been an attempt to downplay the church-state connection. The preferred term is "folk church," which associates the church with the people of a nation rather than the state. In Denmark, this is enshrined in the official title of the majority Lutheran church, the Danish Folk Church (*Den Danske Folkekirke*). What looks on the surface like harmless semantics is, I argue, very much what is at stake when analyzing meaning in the service of power. Using the Evangelical Lutheran Church of Finland (ELCF) as an example, I argue that "folk church" works ideologically by downplaying the church-state connection and, in so doing, reproduces the privileged position of the ELCF.

The German term *Volkskirche* can be traced to the writings of Friedrich Schleiermacher (1768–1834) and appears in Finnish sources from the late 19th century. A proper genealogy of the term's Finnish uses is yet to be written and beyond the scope of this chapter (for a fuller view, see: Hjelm, 2019), but suffice it to say it became common in Finnish usage from the mid-1950s at the latest. This is partly explained by the increasing post-war pressure to consider and present the ELCF as separate from the Finnish state. Interestingly, academic theology played a key part in this, as terminology trickled down to church practice and from there to policy. It would not be an exaggeration to say that the contemporary discourse on the ELCF as a folk church can be traced back to one source, namely church historian and Archbishop Mikko Juva's 1960 book *Valtiokirkosta kansankirkoksi* (*From State Church to Folk Church*). Not only did the title canonize the term "folk church," but it also naturalized the idea that the church moved from one status to another. More interesting for my current purposes, however, is the contemporary usage of the term. I will discuss two examples: the self-presentation of the ELCF and a parliamentary debate regarding the privileged status of the ELCF.

Church and state, according to the Church

In international comparison, the ELCF retains many of the trappings of a state church. Fox (2008: pp. 115–16), for example, places Finland in the abovementioned "active state religions" category. It is the only religious community mentioned in the Finnish constitution and retains multiple legal privileges not afforded to the other religious communities (with the exception of the Orthodox Church of Finland, which is closer to holding state church status than other minority religions). But since we are talking about discourse and perceptions, I will analyze the official ELCF website (evl.fi) and its self-presentation.

The current ELCF Finnish-language webpages have a dedicated page titled "The Church as Part of Society," in which the church-society relationship is described as follows:

The church is connected to Finnish society and culture in many ways
... Although the actual state church system was dismantled already in
the 19th century, the church still has official connections with society,
and the church's operation is legislated by the Church Act.[2]

Interestingly, the connection made here is to *society* (*yhteiskunta*) rather than
to the state, although the "actual" state church system is said to have already
been dismantled in the 19th century. This is a reference to the 1870 Church
Act, which made the ELCF autonomous from the state, but which had no
effect on its privileged status. The hedging word "actual" implies – quite
rightly – that some sort of state connection remained.

A subpage titled "State and Church" tackles the question of state versus
folk church explicitly:

The state church system has been dismantled in Finland in 1870.
The state and the church are separate actors and the church makes its
decisions independently ... The ELCF is better characterized by the
word *folk church*. Majority of Finns are members of the church and it
takes care of many important social functions. Lutheran culture and
customs appear in many ways in Finnish culture.[3]

Unlike the starting page, the dedicated text on church and state is
unambiguous about the ELCF *not* being a state church but a folk church
instead. Indeed, it is as if the introductory paragraph is a pre-emptive
comment on comparative studies such as Fox's: "In every country, the
relations between the majority religion and the state have been organized
differently, and the systems are incomparable."[4] In turn, the "folkness" of
the church is justified by numbers and by the ELCF's role in culture. The
latter is further reinforced on the page titled "Cultural Heritage":

Church environments are a central part of our cultural landscape. The
rhythm of ordinary days and celebration, work, and rest is based on
the Christian tradition. The churchly cultural heritage is present on
every day of the year.[5]

Despite majority membership numbers, so few Finns attend the regular
Sunday mass weekly that the church's own research prefers to present the
number as people who visit at least once a month, which was nine per cent
in 2015 (Ketola et al, 2016). Rhetorically, then, it is the latent aspects of
our "*churchly* cultural heritage" that matter more – indeed so much so, that
these are present on *all* days of the year for the *volk*.

Analyzing the English-language pages of the ELCF is interesting, because
when writing for an international audience, the church cannot assume the

same contextual knowledge that makes "folk church" a meaningful term for Finns. The English-language version of the current ELCF website is sparse, to say the least. The page titled "Lutheranism in Finland" says only the following: "Prayer has been at the heart of many people's lives in Finland through the centuries, but – and this is a very Finnish characteristic – faith is a largely private matter."[6] Church and state are not mentioned at all. Religion is private and comes close to some sort of nature mysticism: "Even today, many Finns seek God in nature and the wilderness: in a forest, by a lake or at the seashore."[7] The sub-pages titled "History" and "Worship in Diversity" do mention key dates but without explanation of their meaning.

The silence on the church and state issue is interesting in light of the previous homepages of the ELCF. I did an illustrative analysis of those pages for a conference paper in 2013, but I do not know when the page changed. Thanks to the Wayback Machine archive, the pages can still be found. The Finnish and English language pages resemble each other much more than the current pages. The English version is not, however, a direct translation. It is worth looking at the pages side by side:

Translation from the Finnish:	English Original:
Finland does not have a state church system, but the church can be called a folk church. The church and state *cooperate* in many ways. ... [The Church] is an integral part of the people's history and culture. Majority of Finns belong to the church. The church's ceremonies, from baptism to funerals, and its customs are part of the Finnish tradition.[8]	The Evangelical Lutheran Church of Finland has traditionally been labelled in two different ways: some speak of it as a state church, while others call it a folk church. Both labels are somewhat misleading and susceptible to propagandistic use ... These days Finland no longer has a state-church structure in the precise sense of the term. The system has been dismantled step by step so as to give greater internal independence to the Lutheran Church.[9]

In Finnish, the question of state church versus folk church is unambiguous. Finland does not have a state church. But there is – in bold – cooperation (*yhteistyö*), which is further explained in subsequent subpages. The text then repeats how the ELCF is hegemonic numerically and culturally.

In English, by contrast, there is a whole paragraph of what Fairclough (1992: p. 112) calls "hedging," in this case, the "some say, others say" structure. Neither "state church" nor "folk church" is entirely correct and, significantly, both are "susceptible for propagandistic use." It is as if the ELCF is admitting the ideological nature of both terms! Furthermore, the English page also admits, in a way that Finnish pages do not, that:

[Both terms] remain useful in that they still give a rough picture not only of the position of the church in Finnish society, but also of the relationship between the church and the state. In order to understand the current religious situation and church politics in Finland, it is important to bear in mind the country's strong state–church oriented tradition. This tradition is so long-standing and influential that the current situation is difficult to understand outside this context.[10]

The brief analysis here suffices to demonstrate the point about naturalization made above: "folk church" (*kansankirkko*) in Finnish is the shorthand for "not state church." The old webpages at least go into detail about the basis for the conceptual change – although the end of state–church status is always measured by the ELCF's autonomy from the state, never by its perpetual privileged status – but the complicated situation is only implied on the current pages. Silences matter.

"Folk church" in parliamentary politics

My second case is a plenary session in the Finnish parliament on 15 February 2006. The Members of Parliament (MPs) debated a Members' Initiative (diary number LA157/2005) regarding the equality of religious communities in Finland and proposed amendments to the constitution and several laws legislating the privileged status of the ELCF and the Orthodox Church.[11] There was never a vote for its passing because a new parliament was voted in while the proposal was doing the rounds in legislative committees. In Finland, proposals do not carry over to the next parliament. The case is nevertheless important because, as both discourse analysts and scholars of parliamentary democracy have noted, speeches in plenary sessions are about displaying MPs' political credentials to their voters, media, and the broader public, while hammering out the details of initiatives happens in parliamentary committees (for example, Wodak, 2008). Hence, the dominant type of research into religion and politics that focuses on the content of constitutions and legislation, or their impact, misses a whole world of sociologically significant material.

The initiative LA157/2005 was signed by Irina Krohn and Rosa Meriläinen, two Finnish Green Party MPs, but only Krohn sat in session when the proposal was brought to debate, bearing the brunt of the debate. The opposition to the proposal was unanimous – even the then Chair of the Green Party undermined it by stating that this was not a party initiative. Importantly, the focus on the "folk church" nature of the ELCF comprised only one aspect of the analyzed debate, but the connection between the ELCF and national identity is ideologically significant in light of what has been already discussed. The parliamentary discourse shows how academic discourse, beginning with Archbishop Juva's work and filtered through the ELCF's self-understanding, is a major factor in reproducing religious inequality in Finland.

The construction of the ELCF as "folk church" is explicit in the opening speech of the plenary session. In it, Christian Democrat MP Päivi Räsänen said: "The state is not denominational in itself, even though the Lutheran Church and also the Orthodox Church have the status of folk church." The "folkness" of the ELCF is achieved in three distinct ways: symbolically, through an appeal to democracy, and by equating "Finnish values" with the values of the church. The first type equates the church with other national symbols, most explicitly in Räsänen's already quoted opening speech:

"Quickly going through this list, it seems like just about the only things that are forgotten is a proposal to abandon the flag with the blue cross, and changing religious holidays into working days. In my opinion, the best part of this bill is its short list of signatories."

Räsänen is here equating the stripping of the ELCF of its constitutionally privileged status with getting rid of the Finnish national flag. Rhetorically, this is an obvious expansion of the original issue, as the flag – possibly the most potent symbol of national identity – is of interest even to MPs indifferent to the politics of religion.

The MPs opposing the initiative also played the numbers game: the privileged status of the ELCF is justified because, in a democracy, it is the will of the people. Räsänen again summarized the discourse: "In legislative work, it is justified to take into consideration the prevailing religious circumstances. It is justified for a religious community's legal status to reflect the community's real status in society, and *this is how democracy works*" (emphasis added). She continued: "84 per cent of Finns belong to the church and of them 73 per cent have never considered leaving the church. The juridical status of the Lutheran church reflects the religious situation in the country and its religious-cultural history." Finally, she repeated the idea in her closing statement: "Based simply on the *principles of democracy*, it is quite right that the influence of Christian values, Christian cultural heritage is visible" (emphasis added). The "democratic will" discourse was echoed in the responses of two Center Party MPs – incidentally, both were also ordained Lutheran ministers. MP Lauri Oinonen said, somewhat incoherently, "The laws are in harmony with the fact that citizens, who are both citizens of the state, inhabitants of municipalities and mostly members of the Evangelical Lutheran Church, can live with a legislation which is in harmony with itself." MP Simo Rundgren repeated the sentiment, while defending religious education in state-funded schools: "About 85 per cent of Finns belong to the Lutheran church … This is just the way our will is."

In addition to national symbols and democratic will, MPs linked the privileged status of the church with Finnish values, the logic being that losing one would lead to the erosion of the other. This is not always expressed explicitly, but since the Christian values that Finnish society is putatively built upon are manifested in the church, changing the existing arrangement would be detrimental. Social Democrat MP Esa Lahtela argued that:

"Finnish society is in any case built on this Christian value base. From that one could of course immediately say that when in Rome, do as the Romans do (*maassa maan tavalla*), which means that certain foundations have existed. Our legislation is built on a particular value base and it draws its strength from these values, which come from biblical doctrines, Christian doctrine."

Lahtela's Social Democrat colleague. MP Kalevi Olin, made the point that values are not just fancy dressing, but have material effects:

"That equality is realized is surely a modern aspiration, but, dear Mr. Speaker, according to research, the success of Finnish society, for example in working life, is based on exactly the Protestant ethic, especially in agricultural but also in industrial society, on work ethic, and in this case it is worth asking whether there is a reason to abandon this kind of Lutheran viewpoint."

Olin's point is telling, because his statement implies that the work ethic is not only a Lutheran value, but an effect of the privileged status of the ELCF, which is, after all, the topic of the debate. Aspiring to equality is a commendable goal, but the price in this case would be too high.

Krohn's Green colleague, Erkki Pulliainen, made explicit that the values are institutionally manifested in the ELCF (and the Finnish Orthodox Church), hence reproducing the idea that touching the ELCF's privileged status means, ultimately, tampering with the "ultimate things" in Finnish society:

"Values belong to Finnish society as a very important element. Those particular values, specifically Christian values, whether they are realized (*toteutuivatpa ne*) in the Evangelical-Lutheran church or the Orthodox church, are very important things. They are downright ultimate things."

Discourse works ideologically when it obfuscates and misdirects. The intent of the initiative – explained and defended on several occasions by MP Krohn during the debate – was to make all religious communities equal in the eyes of law. It was not an attack on the ELCF as such, as Krohn had to remind her colleagues. However, the other MPs' responses switch the focus of discussion from a question of religious equality to a question of national identity. Few politicians oppose equality as a political principle, but even fewer want to undermine the central symbols of national identity. The equation of *volk* and church in the debate sealed the fate of the proposal.

As I have noted, for critical discursive research, absence is as important presence. Finnish church–state legislation has remained mostly untouched since the drafting of the first constitution and the original Freedom of Religion Act in the immediate years after Finland's independence in 1917. Hence, one could have expected the LA157/2005 initiative to generate heated debate in the parliament. The debate that emerged was loud at times, but the silence was louder: of the 200 MPs in the Finnish parliament, *eight* took part in the debate, including Irina Krohn, one of the initiative's signatories. Now, we cannot get into the minds of these MPs in order to study their motivations, but it says *something* that so few – markedly, two of them Lutheran ministers and one known for her religious activism in parliament – bothered with any response at all. My thesis is that the same folk church ideology articulated by the several MPs present was manifested as absence among the rest: changing the status quo was met by indifference or refusal to even debate the issue. Although it is obviously impossible to "prove" direct causal links, it is completely plausible to argue that the parliamentary discourse and the silence of the majority of MPs is a function of the established "folk church" discourse espoused by scholarship and the church itself. The difference is that in the parliament the discourse has more immediate and direct consequences – in this case the preservation and reproduction of the status quo. Freedom of religion legislation in Finland might be robust from an individual's perspective, but debates and silences such as those discussed here perpetuate the inequality of religious communities.

Conclusion

To go back to where I started, how would the analysis of the ELCF as a "folk church" have been different from a substantive or functional approach to sociology of religion? Substantively speaking, the focus of analysis would have been on the accuracy of "state church" in designating the ELCF. This is indeed what much of the writing on the subject does (Hjelm, 2019: pp. 300–7). However, as the same writing has shown, different authors end up with different answers even with the same criteria. The goalpost can always be moved. A functional approach, such as that of Sundback (1984), who is inspired by Robert Bellah, avoids the substantive problem of fitting a definitional box by focusing on the putative functions of "civil religion." However, where Bellah situates civil religion in practices outside institutional religion, such as the singing of national anthems and presidential speeches, Sundback equates civil religion with the ELCF. Finnish national identity, according to this discourse, is so intimately tied up with the institution of the ELCF that the church simply becomes an institutional manifestation of civil religion.

CDSR approaches the question differently. In fact, the question whether the ELCF *is* a state church or a "folk church" is not even very relevant. It is arguably both. But what the other approaches miss is what is being *done* when the ELCF is talked about as a "folk church." As the above analysis has demonstrated, whatever we think of the ELCF substantively and functionally speaking, "folk church" works ideologically by downplaying constitutional and legal church-state connections and consequently, reproduces the privileged position of the ELCF. Identifying the ELCF with the nation or people not only constructs the institution from a particular perspective – this is a discourse that would be impossible for any one denomination to pull off in the North American context – but also makes it difficult to challenge the privileged position, because such challenges become not only anti-church, but unpatriotic. The action orientation aspect of "folk church" is to minimize criticism. The terms of debate in each of the countries with a "national" church are different, of course, but the Finnish case works as an example of how definitions of "church" may work ideologically.

For the purposes of this chapter, I have focused on "what passes for religion in society," but I want to emphasize that CDSR is not just about defining religion. It certainly is not just about the "category of religion," which is the focus of much of discursive work in religious studies. A critical discursive approach could examine, for example, how discourses and silences have perpetuated a culture of sexual abuse in the Catholic Church, but also how alternative discourses and new voices have challenged and called that culture into account. This is about "religion," conventionally understood, but it is not about the definition of religion as such. CDSR is a much broader endeavor.

It is also worth saying that CDSR is applicable on multiple levels of analysis. "What passes for religion in society" tends to focus the analysis on institutions, like courts, parliaments, media, and so on. But the discursive approach is equally valid and useful in examining how group and individual identities are constructed and how ideological discourse enables or constrains communities and individuals. I have consistently talked about religion in this chapter, but there is no reason why the principles of CDSR could not be applied to spirituality, secularity, or nonreligion.

My presentation of critical discursive sociology of religion in this chapter is made with humility (sometimes lacking in the enthusiasm for the "interpretive turn," "cultural turn," and other "turns" in earlier decades). It is not offered as an approach that will solve all of the discipline's problems – or even as one that can answer many of its key questions. Nevertheless, the focus on the constitutive and functional properties of text and talk is something that I see as having potential to expand the horizons of our endeavor at the moment. This is especially so in light of the mainstream of North American sociology of religion, which tends to be rather provincial in terms of theories and methodologies (Bender et al, 2013). European and North American theoretical framings have in many ways colonized alternative ways of looking at religion (Spickard, 2017), but even between the two, there are significant differences. Methodologically, the appropriation of "discourse" into the sociologist's conceptual toolkit has been much more advanced in Europe. The second aspect of this expansion, as I have argued above, would be to incorporate the analysis of power into our studies. Despite periodically recurring exhortations, there are few systematic approaches that do so in the sociology of religion (one would be well advised to read feminist, decolonial and queer work in this regard). In this chapter, I have only been able to outline the principles of one possible approach. The encouraging news is that there is an emerging corpus of empirical analyses and theoretical refinements in the discursive sociology of religion – and plenty of room for further expansion of the field. Even that "sublimely uninteresting" practice of defining religion may be rewarding if we rethink how to go about it.

Notes

[1] Parts of this section have been reworked from Hjelm, 2019.
[2] "Church as Part of Society," accessed 23 April 2019, evl.fi/tietoa-kirkosta/kirkko-ja-yhteiskunta?OpenDocument&lang=FI.
[3] "State and Church," accessed 23 April 2019, evl.fi/tietoa-kirkosta/kirkko-ja-yhteiskunta/valtionkirkko-ja-kansankirkko. Emphasis in the original.
[4] "State and Church," accessed 23 April 2019, evl.fi/tietoa-kirkosta/kirkko-ja-yhteiskunta/valtionkirkko-ja-kansankirkko. Emphasis in the original.
[5] "Cultural Heritage," accessed 23 April 2019, evl.fi/tietoa-kirkosta/kirkko-ja-yhteiskunta/kulttuuriperinto.
[6] "Lutheranism in Finland," accessed 23 April 2019, evl.fi/our-faith/lutheranism-in-finland.
[7] "Lutheranism in Finland," accessed 23 April 2019, evl.fi/our-faith/lutheranism-in-finland.
[8] "Valtiokirkko purettu kansankirkoksi," accessed 23 April 2019, web.archive.org/web/20131030173059/http://evl.fi/EVLfi.nsf/Documents/85BBFB4816F713BEC2256FEA0 03A7232?OpenDocument&lang=FI. Emphasis in the original.
[9] "Church and State," accessed 23 April 2019, web.archive.org/web/20130312072427/http://evl.fi/EVLen.nsf/Documents/A47B48B9B3B2188AC22572B400213 CE6?OpenDocument&lang=EN.
[10] "Church and State," accessed 23 April 2019, web.archive.org/web/20130312072427/http://evl.fi/EVLen.nsf/Documents/A47B48B9B3B2188AC22572B400213 CE6?OpenDocument&lang=EN.
[11] All quotes from the parliamentary debate refer to diary number LA 157/2005. *Laki Suomen perustuslain 76 §:n kumoamisesta sekä eräiden siihen liittyvien lakien kumoamisesta ja muuttamisesta.* The initiative and a transcript of the debate are available at: www.eduskunta.fi/FI/Vaski/sivut/trip.aspx?triptype=ValtiopaivaAsiakirjat&docid=ptk+8/2006, accessed 23 April 2019. All speeches quoted here can be found under "keskustelu" on this page. For a full analysis of the debate, see: Hjelm, 2014b.

References

Barker, E. (2011) "The Cult as a Social Problem," in T. Hjelm (ed) *Religion and Social Problems*, New York: Routledge, pp. 198–212.

Beckford, J.A. (1983) "The Restoration of 'Power' to the Sociology of Religion," *Sociological Analysis*, 44(1): 11–31.

Beckford, J.A. (2003) *Social Theory and Religion*, Cambridge: Cambridge University Press.

Bender, C., Cadge, W., Levitt, P., and Smilde, D.A. (2013) "Introduction: Religion on the Edge: De-Centering and Re-Centering the Sociology of Religion," in C. Bender, W. Cadge, P. Levitt, and D.A. Smilde (eds) *Religion on the Edge: De-Centering and Re-Centering the Sociology of Religion*, New York: Oxford University Press, pp. 1–20.

Berger, P.L. (2014) *The Many Altars of Modernity: Toward a Paradigm for Religion in a Pluralist Age*, Boston and Berlin: De Gruyter.

Berger, P.L., and Luckmann, T. (1967 [1966]) *The Social Construction of Reality: A Treatise in the Sociology of Knowledge*, Garden City, NY: Anchor Books.

Bourdieu, P. and Passeron, J-C. (1990) *Reproduction in Education, Society and Culture* (2nd edn), London: SAGE.

Breeze, R. (2011) "Critical Discourse Analysis and its critics," *Pragmatics*, 21(4): 493–525.

Chimombo, M.P.F., and Roseberry, R.L. (1998) *The Power of Discourse: An Introduction to Discourse Analysis*, Mahwah, NJ: Lawrence Erlbaum.

Chouliaraki, L., and Fairclough, N. (1999) *Discourse in Late Modernity*, Edinburgh: Edinburgh University Press.

Cousins, M. and Hussain, A. (1984) "The question of ideology: Althusser, Pecheux and Foucault," *The Sociological Review*, 32(1): 158–79.

Fairclough, N. (1992) *Discourse and Social Change*, Oxford: Polity Press.

Farris, S.R. (2017) *In the Name of Women's Rights: The Rise of Femonationalism*, Durham and London: Duke University Press.

Fox, J. (2008) *A World Survey of Religion and the State*, Cambridge: Cambridge University Press.

Hamilton, M. (1987) "The Elements of the Concept of Ideology," *Political Studies*, 35(1): 18–38.

Hearn, J. (2012) *Theorizing Power*, Basingstoke: Palgrave Macmillan.

Hjelm, T. (2014a) "Religion, Discourse and Power: A Contribution towards a Critical Sociology of Religion," *Critical Sociology*, 40(6): 855–72.

Hjelm, T. (2014b) "National Piety: Religious Equality, Freedom of Religion and National Identity in Finnish Political Discourse," *Religion* 44(1): 28–45.

Hjelm, T. (2018) "Assessing the Influence of *The Sacred Canopy*: A Missed Opportunity for Social Constructionism?" in T. Hjelm (ed) *Peter L. Berger and The Sociology of Religion: 50 Years after " The Sacred Canopy,"* London: Bloomsbury Academic, pp. 157–74.

Hjelm, T. (2019) "One *Volk*, One Church: A Critique of the 'Folk Church' Ideology in Finland," *Journal of Church and State*, 62(2): 294–315.

Hjelm, T. (2021) "Sociology of Religion," in R.A. Segal and N.R. Roubekas (eds) *The Wiley Blackwell Companion to the Study of Religion* (2nd edn), Oxford: Wiley Blackwell, pp. 135–51.

Josephsohn, T.J., and Williams, R.H. (2013) "Possibilities in the critical sociology of religion," *Critical Research on Religion*, 1(2): 123–8.

Juva, M. (1960) *Valtiokirkosta kansankirkoksi*, Helsinki: Suomen kirkkohistoriallinen seura.

Ketola, K., Hytönen, M., Salminen, V.-M., Sohlberg, J., and Sorsa, L. (2016) *Osallistuva luterilaisuus: Suomen evankelis-luterilainen kirkko vuosina, 2012–2015* , Tampere: Kirkon tutkimuskeskus.

Lukes, S. (1974) *Power: A Radical View*, London: Macmillan.

Lužný, D. (2020) "Invented Religions and the Conceptualization of Religion in a Highly Secular Society: The Jedi Religion and the Church of Beer in the Czech Context," *European Journal of Cultural Studies*, published online 23 May 2020, doi.org/10.1177/1367549420919876.

Maduro, O. (1982) *Religion and Social Conflicts*, translated by R.R. Barr, Maryknoll, NY: Orbis Books.

McCutcheon, R.T. (1997) *Manufacturing Religion: The Discourse on Sui Generis Religion and the Politics of Nostalgia*, New York: Oxford University Press.

McKinnon, A.M. (2006) "Opium as Dialectics of Religion: Metaphor, Expression and Protest," in W.S. Goldstein (ed) *Marx, Critical Theory, and Religion*, Chicago: Haymarket Books, pp. 11–29.

Mills, C.W. (1940) "Situated Actions and Vocabularies of Motive," *American Sociological Review*, 5(6): 904–13.

Poole, E. (2002) *Reporting Islam: Media Representations of British Muslims*, London: I.B. Tauris.

Poole, E., and Richardson, J.E. (eds) (2006) *Muslims and the News Media*, London: I.B. Tauris.

Rémond, R. (1999) *Religion and Society in Modern Europe*, Oxford: Blackwell.

Richardson, J.E. (2007) *Analysing Newspapers: An Approach from Critical Discourse Analysis*, Basingstoke: Palgrave Macmillan.

Said, E. (1997) *Covering Islam: How the Media and the Experts Determine How We See the Rest of the World* (revised edn), New York: Vintage Books.

Saler, B. (1993) *Conceptualising Religion. Immanent Anthropologists, Transcendent Natives, and Unbounded Categories*, Leiden: Brill.

Spickard, J.V. (2017) *Alternative Sociologies of Religion: Through Non-Western Eyes*, New York: New York University Press.

Sundback, S. (1984) "Folk Church Religion – A New Kind of Civil Religion?" in B. Harmati (ed), *The Church and Civil Religion in the Nordic Countries of Europe*, Geneva: Lutheran World Federation, pp. 35–40.

Thompson, J.B. (1990) *Ideology and Modern Culture*, Stanford: Stanford University Press.

Wodak, R. (2008) "Introduction: Discourse Studies – Important Concepts and Terms," in R. Wodak and M. Krzyzanowski (eds), *Qualitative Discourse Analysis in the Social Sciences*, Basingstoke: Palgrave, pp. 1–29.

7

The Religion of White Male Ethnonationalism in a Multicultural Reality

George Lundskow

White supremacy in the United States

This chapter argues that the true religion of the United States is white male ethnonationalism, often but not always polished with a Christian veneer (Lundskow, 2020). The essential doctrine of faith is white supremacy, and the essential rite is restorative violence against those perceived as the "Evil Other" – Black people in particular, although others often stand in as well, such as Mexicans and other Latinx, and various Muslim ethnicities. Post-Civil War Reconstruction, and the 20th century labor movement, respectively, offer two sociohistorical moments when the faith of white male ethnonationalism thwarted racial reconciliation and material social progress. My approach uses contemporary empirical research to establish the concept and broad social impact of white male ethnonationalism. Concurrently, the two historical periods represent decisive moments when the social forces of the Civil War and rapid industrialization challenged racial and gender hierarchies. The goal is not to chronicle the periods in question, but to highlight the enduring dominance of white male ethnonationalism and demonstrate how it played the role of religion, over and against material concerns. More specifically, I argue that as wealthy and powerful whites pursue ever more wealth and power, they also need whites of all classes to embrace their acquisition as a legitimate and moral conquest, and that this requires validation that transcends economic interests and exacts willing personal sacrifice from the white 'servant classes' (those with minimal to no upward mobility) – in other words, religious validation.

What is American white supremacy? People of white European descent can embrace diverse ethnic heritages, including German, Dutch, French, English, Swedish, and many others. Yet these are particular *European* heritages, not *American white* heritage. Immigrants were English, German, and so on, not specifically white. Rather, whiteness developed in the first Thirteen Colonies in America as a justification for enslavement and genocidal annihilation (Allen, 1994), such that initially, only Anglo-Saxon Protestant men of property counted as white (Roediger (2018 [2005])). Many southern, eastern, and Catholic European groups started as denigrated ethnicities and gradually joined the white hegemony – more or less – such as Italians (Guglielmo and Salerno, 2003), Greeks (Kaloudis, 2018), Poles (McCook, 2011), Irish (Ignatiev, 2009 [1995]) and Jews (Ratskoff, 2020), although in the process all of them and many others faced widespread ethnocentric discrimination and exclusion (Lee, 2019). The reasons for ethnocentric xenophobia might be skin color, but non-Protestant religion and any language except English also excluded immigrant groups from the white hegemony. Although almost everyone of European heritage can now identify as white, I argue that American whiteness is something else entirely – it is a claim of divine supremacy. European cultures have contributed much to science, art, literature, music, cinema, cuisine, and many other positive things. While most of those people were and are white, those accomplishments are not white specifically, nor inherently restricted only to white people.

Whiteness as religion

Although not a formally established religion, white male ethnonationalism inspires strong emotional commitment to the belief that God ordained white superiority over all others (Berry, 2017; Davis and Perry, 2020), rejects any notion of racial equality (Perry and Whitehead, 2015; Rodriguez, 2018), and equates "Christian" with "white" (Baker, Perry, and Whitehead, 2020; Posner, 2020). Whether perceived as specifically religious commitment or not, white supremacy evokes both the emotional passion and existential life and death commitments of religious faith, which shapes perception of social issues as well as worldview. If a set of beliefs and practices feature divine imagery, explain the order of existence, supersede material reality, call people to fulfill moral obligations, and require acceptance based on faith, then it's a religion, formally or not. Most importantly, white supremacy demarcates the sacred and the profane and sets the center point that creates and legitimates all of society – all of reality, for that matter – and thus completes the social-psychological connection between the individual, society, and existence. As Mircea Eliade (1987 [1957]) explains it: "... primary religious experience precedes all reflection on the world. For it is the break effected in space that allows the world to be constituted, because it reveals the fixed point, the central axis for all future orientation" (p. 21). White supremacy stands on the pre-reflective (taken for granted) notion that white men and patriotic violence constitute the essential sacred foundation of the American nation and of the world.

This sacred expression distinguishes the eternal and perfect divine reality from the fluctuating and flawed reality of the profane (common) world. Because profane transience always threatens to disrupt the divine perfection of white male domination, then the more devoutly religious a person feels, the more alertly they must detect and aggressively thwart anything that threatens the divine order, because, "… religion is the paradigmatic solution to every existential crisis … because it is believed to have a transcendental origin and hence is valorized as a revelation received from a transhuman world" (Eliade 1987 [1957]: p. 210). Whether society and the world change slowly or rapidly, humans cannot live without sincere religious faith, and even atheism is a devout faith. Once humans evolved self-awareness, we cannot live without meaningful answers to the four great existential questions that Peter Berger (1990 [1967]) identified: Who am I? Why am I here? How should I live? What happens when I die? Following Erich Fromm (1997 [1976]), I argue that nearly anything can serve as an object of worship and also, following Eboo Patel (2018), that irrespective of doctrine, religion derives essentially from either love or hate – what he calls the faith line. Either will create social unity and a sense of purpose.

White supremacists in both overt and mainstream forms have historically and continue to embrace hate in brutal simplicity; they must oppose or suppress every social and political change in the profane world and enforce conformity to religious perfection, because white male ethnonationalism consists only of the most simplistic possible belief – divine whiteness – realized through violent oppression of non-whiteness. This simplicity most closely resembles the remote and supreme gods of creator/annihilator religions (the great makers are also the great destroyers) that have absolute power of creation and destruction, sometimes united in the same one god as with Yahweh in the Old Testament (Eliade 1987 [1957]: pp. 121–8). Found typically in the most rigidly hierarchical warrior societies (Benedict, 2005 [1934]), they rely on brutality and oppression, but also appear when the ruling powers are in actual or perceived decline, such that a sense of crisis prefigures the rise of "strong gods" (Reno, 2019) who will restore the old order through death and destruction – both symbolically and literally. Therefore, as multicultural reality transforms the US, those devoted to white male ethnonationalism must oppose it, because the fall of whiteness as the center of American culture, economics, and politics inherently means an end to white superiority and the meaning of life based on it.

As a religion then, white male ethnonationalism relies on the faith that God has made white people inherently superior to all others, and restorative violence as a sacred act against perceived Evil Others to restore what the impure have stolen or corrupted. This serves four definitive social-psychological purposes: (1) publicly proves one's own faith and purity; (2) exploits or eliminates perceived evil transgression, (3) reinforces the in-group's exalted status, and (4) demonstrates white manhood as an indicator of privilege. This religion guides self-avowed white supremacists, but white male ethnonationalism also constitutes the center of mainstream white culture as a basic orientation to social life, and thus it encompasses and benefits white people generally unless they actively oppose it. Based entirely on the hatred and demonization of non-whiteness to reinforce faith in white superiority, I assert that white male ethnonationalism has no affirmative center, only a negative fear and simultaneous hatred for non-whites (Simi et al, 2017), whom whites in general perceive as grounded in a unique, present, and different culture, which emotionally exposes their own cultural emptiness. Intolerant and fearful (MacWilliams, 2017), they longingly persecute cultural transgressors (Thomsen, Green, and Sidanius, 2008) and envision their hatred in a judgmental and violent patriarchal god who demands aggression as a sacrament, and instills a doctrine of hate in place of hope. Even as a broad culture of white supremacy protects white people in general from racist prejudice and persecution, it provides no emotional comfort beyond the moment of aggression (Beck and Plant, 2018). Yet for most white people, the consolation of whiteness, as we will see, has been enough historically to maintain racist discrimination and violence that otherwise could have led to a common human identity and socioeconomic progress for a broad multitude. At decisive periods in US history, many whites chose a violent white supremacy and a majority chose to at least tolerate it, even if it meant lower income and quality of life for themselves as well.

Five social facts intersect to construct the religion:

- the sociocultural forces of racism (Hughey, 2010);
- sexism-homophobia (Jones, 2019);
- political-economic-cultural domination at the level of the family (Speed, 2019), at the national level (Bergin and Rupprecht, 2018; Gibbons, 2018), and the global level (Golash-Boza, Duenas, and Xiong, 2019);
- an authoritarian character structure (Bret et al, 2017; Parker and Towler, 2019); and
- belief in an Evil Other (Knitter, 2019).

Each element arose from its own sociohistorical relations, but each also reinforces the others. Taken together, white American culture posits a divine hierarchy of superior and inferior races that mandates strict social and cognitive boundaries. Any deviation or unpunished challenge evokes intense fear of hierarchical collapse in the believers, and consequently they project anger and aggression toward even the smallest perceived transgressions, which precludes rational consideration of alternatives or of self-reflection. All racial and other status groups must accept the natural and divine hierarchy on faith and vigorously enforce its laws. In this manuscript, I consider only two essential features – sociocultural racism (white supremacy) and restorative violence against the Evil Other.

Next, I analyze historical moments that challenged white ethnonational hegemony, and then how those moments shaped the present crisis of American democracy.

Decisive moments when white people embraced racism

Reconstruction after the American Civil War

The main reason that Reconstruction utterly failed was because the culture of white supremacy in the South remained dominant – and crucially, the North obliged. Robert E. Lee surrendered the bulk of the Confederate forces to Ulysses Grant on 9 April 1865 at Appomattox Courthouse, although several other rebel generals continued fighting until the final military surrender on 23 June. Union general Ulysses Grant hoped that lenient surrender terms would encourage the rebels to more readily assimilate into a reconstructed South. On the contrary, white soldiers and civilians overwhelmingly refused to acknowledge the end of the war, accepting only the end of the current fighting. Whites immediately suppressed Black celebrations of Union victory and their newfound freedom, and Southern elites schemed to undermine the Union occupation and to devise means to restore slavery, if not in name, then in effect (Varon, 2014). As the former President of the Confederacy Jefferson Davis declared a few years later:

> "Nothing fills me with deeper sadness than to see a Southern man apologizing for the defense we made of our inheritance. Our cause was so just, so sacred, that had I known all that has come to pass, had I known what was to be inflicted upon me, all that my country was to suffer, all that our posterity was to endure, I would do it all over again." (Cooper, 2003)

No Confederate officers or politicians ever stood trial for treason or taking up arms against the United States. Although the Confederate armies surrendered, the South did not. Union general William Tecumseh Sherman predicted that racist virulence so permeated Southern identity that the Union would ultimately win only if they could break Southern culture (O'Connell, 2015). History proved Sherman correct.

The image of the genteel 'Southern gentleman' and refined 'Southern belle' derive from the antebellum social conventions of the wealthy slave-owning elite, who viewed themselves as sophisticated and superior even to their European progenitors; they were Roman patricians reborn in the New World (Fox-Genovese, 2008). Given family lineage and notions of racial hierarchy, wealthy white Southerners built the belief of white superiority through a strict social hierarchy and principles of violent domination, both through slavery and patrimonialism, under which common white people lived mostly as subsistence tenant farmers dependent on the patronage of wealthy whites. Patrimonial class-culture relations governed Southern institutions so thoroughly that most of the Confederate army consisted of poor whites risking life and limb to defend slavery for their patrons. Wealthy plantation owners owned the arable land, controlled the courts, the banks, the press, and suppressed public education even when some localities attempted to establish accessible public schools. Inequality within white society was so great, and poor whites so completely dependent on wealthy slave-owners, that "the biggest danger to Southern society was neither Northern abolitionists nor Black slaves, but the masterless white men of servile laborers, whom they deemed unfit for self-government yet clothed with the attributes and powers of citizens" (Merritt, 2017: p. 161). White elites banned all abolitionist publications and anything else that challenged the slave system, and so thoroughly censored news and prohibited public education that at least 70 per cent of the Southern white population was completely illiterate (compared to about 30 per cent in the North), and another 15 per cent could do little more than write their own name and read simple sentences (Merritt, 2017). Much like in feudal Europe, religion enforced this patrimonial servitude as a moral obligation in the antebellum South (Fox-Genovese and Genovese, 2008). Wealthy plantation owners rented land to poor whites, either as tenant farmers or sharecroppers, and also provided some semblance of justice, much as a feudal lord held dominion over all matters within their territory. Like their European peasant counterparts, poor white Southerners practiced a kind of fealty to their plantation masters, pledging their loyalty and support in times of war. This elevated them to one notch above the slaves, but also ensured their continued subservience. Tenant farming never allowed enough surplus to move up in the world because elites grew and traded the cash crops, especially cotton and tobacco, while poor whites supported themselves with subsistence food crops (White, 2017: pp. 226–8). By the 1850s, the plantation elite overwhelmingly and publicly rejected democracy in favor of hereditary aristocracy as the divine order of American society (Merritt, 2017: p. 171). During the same period, this extended to the slaughter of Mexicans when whites invaded and carved out Texas (Ortiz, 2018), and the genocide of Native Americans rivals antebellum slavery in both magnitude and brutality (Dunbar-Ortiz, 2014).

Of course, Black emancipation after the war threatened the plantation owners who owned the vast majority of slaves. At the same time, it also threatened the patrimonial bond between rich and poor whites, and so elites pushed a strong sense of "pride of race" and "social exclusiveness," specifically to prevent poor whites from uniting with freed slaves (Isenberg, 2016: p. 183). That is, white male ethnonationalism slightly elevated the impoverished white tenant farmer above the Black former slave, and they clung tenaciously to their sense of racial superiority. Otherwise, the impoverished white Southerner would truly have nothing. Overall then, southern white supremacy consisted of three mutually reinforcing aspects: economic dependency, authoritarian domination-submission, and religious sanctification. Like Grant at Appomattox, radical Reconstructionists such as Thaddeus Stevens and Charles Sumner similarly underestimated the type and extent of change necessary (Foner, 2014 [1988]: pp. 271–80). White southerners broadly came to despise anything that in any way threatened their social, psychological, and religious commitment to "heritage." The reality of freed slaves empowered with the vote and equality under the law challenged all three aspects of white supremacy because it broke the economic power of plantation elites, split the rich–poor white patrimonialism, and demonstrated that God did not inherently bless whites with superiority.

Consequently, whites chose to violently enforce the old ways, rather than to move forward alongside freed slaves. Six months after the Appomattox surrender, the former rebel general Nathan Bedford Forrest and five other Confederate officers founded the Ku Klux Klan in Pulaski, Tennessee on 24 December 1865, specifically to thwart Northern post-war occupation and to terrorize and murder Black people. Chapters quickly arose throughout the South. They murdered thousands of African Americans, burned down homes and Freedmen's schools, and occupied many political offices to create the Negro Laws that essentially re-enslaved African Americans (Alexander, 2015). Recognizing his mistakes with the terms of surrender at Appomattox, now President Grant in 1871 deployed Major Lewis Merrill to destroy the so-called 'invisible empire'. Not surprisingly, Merrill discovered that wealthy whites overwhelmingly constituted Klan leadership, but that whites of all social classes joined enthusiastically, which made infiltration especially difficult. Experienced in counter-terrorism during the Civil War, Merrill employed local intelligence networks to infiltrate the Klan's so-called invisibility, pre-empt Klan violence, expose its leaders, and then used his troops to defeat their murder gangs (Pearl, 2016). Through Merrill's combination of legal prosecutions and military force, Grant successfully crushed the first version of the Klan by 1873. Force temporarily stopped the lynchings, but not faith in white supremacy. The Klan reformed in 1915 at Stone Mountain, Georgia, inspired by the very popular movie *Birth of a Nation*, directed by D.W. Griffith, which portrays Black people as vicious animals and the Klan as the heroes of Reconstruction. More than any other source, this first-ever blockbuster movie provided visual imagery with which to construct Black people as the Evil Other, the eternal predator that lies in wait to rob, rape, and kill unsuspecting whites. As Hunter (2000) argues, white Southerners demonized Black people, and simultaneously deified a mythical vision of the Old South that turned Dixie into a kind of immortal holy land of grace for true white believers in the Lost Cause, now risen from the fields of military defeat. They wrote new church hymns, canonized people like Robert E. Lee and Jefferson Davis, erected monuments, worshipped the gray jacket and Lee's "stars and bars" battle flag as sacred symbols, invented "traditional" holidays to commemorate the eternal spirit of the antebellum South, and embarked on countless literary and historical endeavors to restore Southern heritage and "vindicate it in the language and structure of religion" (Hunter, 2000: p. 186). The South lost the war, but increasingly dominated popular memory through cultural religious fervor.

What of the North? President Grant remained steadfast, determined to neutralize the culture of white supremacy in the South and to reconstruct its culture and economy through public education and economic development (Brands, 2012). He believed that economic investment would benefit any impoverished person, white and Black both, but the Northern white population nevertheless felt that military occupation and federal administration of the South were not worth the cost (White, 2017), because they seemed to benefit Blacks more than whites (Foner, 2014 [1988]). Although Grant remained widely popular going into his second term, he lacked both elite and popular political support for Reconstruction. Consequently, Congress withdrew resources and forced him to abandon Reconstruction for alleged economic reasons (Brands, 2012: pp. 528–35), but crucially, this maneuver included a particular political component to accept an "agreement between the men of quality" and to acknowledge former plantation owners, Confederate officers, and Klan members as part of the legitimate Southern leadership (Foner, 2014 [1988]: 502–3). This political-economic agreement consequently retained and promoted the cultural values and social relations of slave society (Richardson, 2001), such that white supremacy flourished with full political, economic, and cultural support that reinforced authoritarian hate of the Other among white Southerners as Black people struggled to improve their lives. As Eric Foner (2014 [1988]) documents, Black people who achieved even the slightest degree of economic success offended white Southerners the most, from the highest elites to the most impoverished tenant farmer, and most of all when Black owners employed white workers (p. 429) – a clear violation of profane material interests over sacred order.

The post-war South gradually worsened the condition of Blacks as new laws excluded freed Black men from work except as prison labor, stripped away ownership rights, and empowered any white man to kill any Black person – who was no longer the valuable property of a wealthy white man – at will. Although most people in the North opposed slavery, they never accepted the radial abolitionist/Reconstruction position of people like Charles Sumner and Thaddeus Stevens that all people, including Black people, where equal under God. After the war, wealthy Southerners and former Confederate leaders (Jefferson Davis, Robert E. Lee, Braxton Bragg, and Jubal Early foremost among them) openly proclaimed their love of the Confederacy, their hatred of the North, and called for a new, allegedly benign stewardship of freed Blacks as perpetual serfs (Varon, 2014: pp. 222–3). Southerners overwhelmingly embraced the justification for renewed servitude by equating Christianity with whiteness, and that whites carried a divine mission to subjugate – and thus redeem – the entire world under a godly America, which fit comfortably with Northern religious asceticism of self-discipline and moral purity. Blacks and other non-Anglo-Saxons had no place in this mission except to serve whites (Jewett and Lawrence, 2003: pp. 67–9). Northerners increasingly viewed the multitude of Black people migrating North to escape mass persecution and murder as simply lazy, ignorant, and disgruntled workers with a propensity for violence that would only add to the increasing industrial labor discontent and undermine the nation's sacred mission to civilize the world (Richardson, 2001: pp. 214–17). The heroic former slaves who contributed 30,000 troops to the Union army had now become "un-American negroes" whom Northerners vilified in general, while simultaneously accepting the equality of a few select (token) individuals, such as Frederick Douglass.

During the war, both sides thoroughly believed they were fighting a war of deliverance from evil (Varon, 2019), and these initially disparate missions of Southern white supremacy and Northern religious asceticism merged by the late 1870s to create contemporary white male ethnonationalism. Cognizant of this development, Douglass lamented on Memorial Day in 1878 that white people had already forgotten that there was a right and wrong side to the war, and that the South had never repented. Douglass called upon Southerners to "take some steps by way of reconciliation … and not glory in their atrocities and boast of their non-repentance" (in Varon, 2019: p. 433). "We are neither fully freed from Egypt, nor have we reached the promised land," Douglass continued (in Varon, 2019: p. 434), so long as Southerners and their ever-increasing Northern sympathizers regarded Black people as subhuman and outside the grace of God, deliverance from slavery would fail.

Unfortunately, Northern capitalists and speculators looking for opportune investments in the South united with the landed Southern elites against broad principles of racial equality and the extensive government intervention necessary to ensure it, and this disenfranchised Blacks in the South almost completely. By 1903, every Southern state was permitted to enact racial segregation and subordination laws on education, property, public space, and voting (Richardson, 2001: p. 224). In other words, the mainstream North rebuked their own radical Reconstructionists and instead venerated white male ethnonationalism as moral justification for economic exploitation, accumulation, and the sacred mission to redeem the earth. To the extent that white supremacy ruled both the South and the North, although in different ways, this complicity of whiteness and capital prefigured the industrial labor struggles of the 20th century.

Twentieth-century labor movements

As a result of a failed Reconstruction, the South elected many former Confederates to public office and, as the years wore on, their racist descendants built the Lost Cause of the Confederacy mythology, which claimed that Confederate rebellion was about states' rights to self-determination and not about slavery at all (see, for example: Pollard, 1867). This mythology of states' rights, Southern nobility, and innocent agrarian conflict with an overbearing industrial North quickly replaced the truth of slavery and the oppressiveness of Southern life in popular imagination, and even widely among academics until the late 20th century (Gallagher and Nolan, 2010). The Lost Cause narrative of a "lost Eden" and alleged social harmony in the Old South fit more comfortably with the emerging doctrine of American industrial progress and international ascension as a continuation of God's will. In place of the divine right of a landed plantation aristocracy arose the prophets of business and industry – racist capitalists such as Henry Ford and Walt Disney. This new American success inspired a new generation of white supremacists and the Ku Klux Klan, violent mobs, and sweeping segregation laws that quickly incarcerated large numbers of Black men for violating laws written so as to be impossible not to violate at some point. Sentenced to a farm system labor force, they occupied an economic class position very similar to the slave system. Yet the rise of industrial capitalism also brought the hope that emerging economic solidarity in Northern labor unions around improved pay, benefits, and working conditions would expose the irrational hold of white supremacy and unite workers around economic justice. Instead, whites broadly chose racism, and these racial divisions instilled an inherent weakness in the US labor movement that capitalists consistently exploited to weaken organized labor and eventually, by the early 1980s, to break it.

Industrialization brought numerous Black people to the North, as well as immigrants from throughout Europe. The so-called 'melting pot' existed mostly in the industrial cities of the Midwest, where no one particular immigrant ethnicity predominated, and industrial production required a vast army of workers as mining, steel, and mechanical assembly grew exponentially. No less than Reconstruction, the labor movement of the 20th century opened a crucial historical period to radically challenge the race, class, and gender relations of the US, but also like Reconstruction, white people embraced the familiar racial (and gender) relations of the past, now worshipped as "heritage." By the 20th century, everyone wanted economic progress, but the failure of Reconstruction only intensified the clash between American white "heritage" against racial reconciliation and labor unity in the US.

How did class conflict and racial oppression fail to unite, and instead become adversaries? As the civil rights movement gained strength in the 1960s, the white-controlled labor movement often opposed it (Korstad and Lichtenstein, 2007), such as when industrial and construction workers went berserk and tore through a peaceful anti-war and civil rights rally of about 1,500 local high school and some college students in New York City on 8 May 1970. Known as the "hard hat rebellion," the workers beat the protestors with various industrial tools and chased them through the city for several blocks while the police did nothing. The major labor unions endorsed the violence as appropriately standing up for America (Perlmutter, 1970). In other words, white male union workers beat young and racially mixed protestors to defend white male ethnonationalism.

In 1938, the labor movement was poised to take control of national politics. Unfortunately, the two major national unions (the leftist IWW was a minor player) held very different views on race. As the standard of white male ethnonationalism, the American Federation of Labor (AFL) supported racial segregation and opposed the more progressive Congress of Industrial Organizations (CIO), which sought racial integration as a necessary first step in unifying labor to oppose the power of capital (Hinshaw, 2002: pp. 42–60). In contrast, the AFL collaborated with management to exclude minorities from union jobs in exchange for easier contract negotiations; this ultimately undermined the labor movement because it maintained an auxiliary supply of workers to replace union workers as necessary to break strikes (Arnesen, 2007). By the time the AFL and CIO merged in 1955, the CIO had lost half its members due to purges of alleged communists and other 'un-American' radicals, including civil rights activists. By 1960, the AFL-CIO had fully institutionalized racial discrimination (Hinshaw, 2002: pp. 200–22).

One of the largest and most powerful AFL-CIO unions in the single most economically important industry, the United Auto Workers (UAW), did accept Black workers, but only for unskilled jobs, and barred them from promotion and union leadership positions. To combat this, Black workers formed the Trade Union Leadership Council (TULC) in 1957 (Thompson, 2017: pp. 49). For several years, the TULC negotiated carefully within the union to change policies and wage structures, but the UAW leadership had yielded little by the late 1960s. Given widespread discontent among white workers with seniority and gender rules, various Revolutionary Union Movements (RUMs) formed within individual plants and regions – the Detroit-RUM was the largest – and these groups inspired numerous wildcat strikes by the early 1970s. Women, junior workers, and more or less everyone except senior white males walked off the job (Thompson, 2017: pp. 182–91). These more aggressive and unpredictable tactics gradually earned some concessions, but by 1979, plant closures and outsourcing rendered many issues moot as layoffs reduced UAW membership from a high of 1.5 million in 1969 to 477,000 in 1982 (Thompson, 2017: p. 216). Despite overt support for Black and women's rights and opportunities in the workplace, the UAW leadership, like the AFL-CIO national leadership, catered to white males and consistently limited actual gains for women and minorities. Political power slipped away regionally and nationally as senior white males maintained the old racial, gender, and seniority hierarchies that ultimately broke the union. Like almost all of the other unions in the AFL-CIO, the UAW integrated far too late to sustain the labor movement or even to maintain sufficient political cover to protect its own interests.

So, just as the union leadership felt secure in US politics, ownership replaced their jobs with mechanization, automation, and, by the 1980s, outsourcing and offshoring. In response, they fought ever more vehemently to reserve the best jobs for white workers and not to organize the emerging service workers, who were mostly Black and Latinx. All too willing to subordinate class unity to white supremacy, the labor movement consistently excluded minority workers and settled for pay and benefits far below the increasing rate of profits, all in the name of patriotism throughout the First and Second World Wars, the Korean War, and the war in Vietnam (Fantasia and Voss 2004; Aronowitz 2014;). This confluence of white supremacy and patriotism led most unions to strongly support Ronald Reagan in the 1980s (Kimeldorf, 1988), even as he dismantled the labor movement through legislation, executive orders, changing regulations, and racially divisive politics (Frymer, 2008). By the time unions realized the fatal mistakes of racism and patriotism, union membership had dropped from a high of 33 per cent of the workforce in 1979 to a mere 7.1 per cent in 2020 (Bureau of Labor Statistics, 2020). While the UAW still exists today, and has corrected the mistakes of the past, it has only 398,829 members – over half of which are the long-excluded clerical, educational, and service workers (Howard, 2020) – and has been unable to organize in any of the Japanese, Korean, or German plants in the US. Although effectively integrated since the early

2000s and generally on the side of progressive politics, the labor movement is far too small to exert substantive change in work relations or in national politics. Given the choice between a much stronger union movement politically and economically, they embraced white male ethnonationalism and lost most of their collective bargaining power and livelihood. White sacredness so permeated the 20th century labor movement as an entrenched religious faith that it prevailed over material economic interests. With a racially divided labor movement, union leadership maintained the familiar patrimonial unity with management through a sense of racial affinity, but like the tenant farming from earlier times, it also ensured subservience to and dependence on wealthy and powerful patrons. Willing to use American white nationalism to subdue workers, modern capitalist enterprises proved much less faithful in return as they freely relocated facilities to low-wage locations, or replaced workers with automation. Perhaps diminished in terms of the percentage of adherents, white supremacy and ethnonationalism has lost none of its virulence for the believers, and configures present-day ethnonational assaults to overthrow democratic government, just as Southern plantation owners rejected democracy in the 1850s. As in the past, white ethnonationalism depends first and foremost on demonization of and aggression against the perceived Evil Other.

The Evil Other

White supremacy correlates strongly with religiosity (Whitehead, Perry, and Baker, 2018), and although it overtly embraces Christianity as the only legitimate religion (Riaz and Qadir, 2018) and condemns all others as racialized affronts to God (Taras, 2013; Considine, 2017), white supremacist Christianity is not the worship of Jesus and his values of peace and love, but rather, the worship of a judgmental and punitive God who annihilates all who oppose him. This god rewards loyal warriors with any and all of status, money, power, and this acquisition proves God's favor for both the individual and the nation, as the vast military-industrial complex projects righteous American power around the globe. This power requires eternal vigilance in order to maintain God's grace, vigilance all the way from global political-economic-cultural dominance to suppressing the everyday transgressions of those types who either don't believe or can never be real men – women, LGBTQ people, and the many non-white infiltrators. These people are not just different, but an absolute perversion of ideal men – they are the Other – and therefore their very existence constitutes an inherent threat. Real Americans do not negotiate with inherent evil; they eradicate it.

Multiculturalism, feminism, and other movements premised on inclusion and mutual respect challenge worldly white male ethnonationalism and also usurp the divine order, because people of color and women will never be white and male. Consequently, as people of the Other improve their lives through work and education, as they organize to represent their interests in the cultural sphere and in the socially salient institutions of the economy and government, white supremacists imagine that people of color are not joining the system or building a more egalitarian America; they are invading and destroying God's order. As Eric Hoffer (1963 [1951]) argued, "Mass persecutions can rise and spread without belief in a god, but never without belief in a devil" (p. 95). The existence of the Evil Other focuses the collective hatred of the dominant group, "and like an ideal deity, the ideal devil is omnipotent and omnipresent" (Hoffer 1963 [1951]: 97). The purpose of the dominant identity thus becomes oppression – and in the more extreme cases – annihilation. Negation of Others animates white collective identity, rather than affirming a uniquely white identity and culture. In other words, whiteness is defined by what it is not, and therefore whites must curtail or eradicate all of those people and things they perceive as non-white. This includes *inter*-racial difference that positions whites as essentially superior to those marked as non-whites, and second, *intra*-racial distinction and marginalization that subordinates whites who fail to exemplify white racial dominance and success (Hughey, 2018: p. 214). Consequently, some whites can effectively lose their whiteness and join the ranks of the inferior through poverty, criminality, or race betrayal. This correlates with the fact that white Americans in general do not understand social inequality in class terms (Newman, Johnston, and Lown, 2015; Rhodes, Shaffner, and McElwee, 2017), but as personal and inherent moral strength or weakness.

The demonization of the Other – whether by race, culture, gender, language, body size, or whatever else – depends inherently on illusions. Demonization requires illusions because demons do not really exist. In order to understand persecution and violence on a small or large scale, we must include but also look beyond political-economy, culture, and upbringing. The scale of the Holocaust, or Stalin's purges, or the killing fields in Cambodia, or the genocide of Native Americans, police murdering people of color on the streets in the US, or law enforcement and voter suppression that target ethnic communities, all developed from the fundamentally irrational belief in the Evil Other. However, the Evil Other never exists in reality, and crucially, can never exist. The Jews, Native Americans, counterrevolutionaries, and modern liberal urbanites are real people, but the aggressors construct them as a transcendent evil with supernatural evil powers. The enemy is lazy, corrupt, dirty, sexually wild – a teeming mass of vermin – yet simultaneously skillfully manipulative and capably discreet enough to hide their manipulation and invasion in order to dominate the good people. They are brutish yet clever, simple-minded yet fiendishly intelligent, morally degenerate, and wild yet self-sacrificing and disciplined – all at the same time. They are everywhere yet nowhere, blatantly obvious yet simultaneously waiting in ambush. Such contradictory monsters can only exist as illusions.

Most of the time though, the haters know they hate certain types of people, and they are always on guard to detect them, keep them in line, punish, and eliminate them. For this reason, I think arguments about hidden or unintentional racism are wrong. White people know they at least fear, and frequently hate people of color (Banks and Hicks, 2016; Tate and Page, 2018). The only difference between overt and allegedly unintentional racism is how capably a hater masks their true feelings. The Evil Other doesn't leave their awareness because they may be out of sight at any given moment. Moreover, social-psychological resentment intensifies when whites believe that people of color appear to achieve far more in life with allegedly little effort. Contrary to public proclamations about the value of hard work, white males in particular feel entitled to what they believe minorities have stolen from them – success with little effort (Feldman and Huddy, 2005; Knuckey and Kim, 2015; Filindra and Kaplan, 2016; LeCount, 2018). Most whites today believe that low-income labor is really for Black and Brown people (or fallen whites), and thus whites generally oppose any policy or program that benefits non-whites, even if it would benefit themselves as well (Wetts and Willer, 2018), and they perceive any minority gains as an inherent loss for white people (Banks, 2014; Duina, 2018). In place of political-economic analysis, the dominant white culture substitutes the illusory racial Other, such that whites who have the least contact with non-whites hate them the most (Cramer, 2016).

Overall then, racially authoritarian white people – and non-whites who identify with whiteness – resent the decline of white male ethnonational domination, and they derive great satisfaction by hurting, or supporting other people or groups, who inflict harm on non-white people (Karenga, 2018; Womick et al, 2018). They especially fear and hate increasing ethnic diversity in the US (Major, Blodorn, and Blascovich, 2018), and, in the 2016 election, people voted for Trump overwhelmingly because he speaks to their belief that white people are widely persecuted, and they believe he will punish non-whites (Smith and Hanley, 2018). They embrace the illusion that people of color have swarmed into the country as illegal and morally degenerate immigrants (Ramirez, 2016), and that Black people reproduce in huge numbers and consume resources in gluttonous quantities through lazy abuse of welfare handouts (Roberts, 2017 [1997]; Strings, 2019), and this has eliminated opportunities for whites (McVeigh and Estep, 2019; Metzl, 2020). White supremacist religion amplifies these longstanding illusions into vast ethnic conspiracies and subversion. Just as many Northerners imagined free Blacks swarming into and undermining Union states after the Civil War, many whites today believe that massive numbers of illegal immigrants supposedly voted in the 2016 election (Edelson et al, 2017;

Udani and Kimball, 2018), that people of color consume the majority of the federal budget through welfare cheating (Bjorklund, Davis, and Pfaffendorf, 2018), and that foreign-born citizens and permanent residents are a kind of counterfeit citizen unless they are white and speak English (DeJesus et al, 2018; Dowling, Ellison, and Leal, 2012). Because most whites perceive non-white immigrants who don't speak English as lazy, degenerate, and criminal (Harell et al, 2012; Valentino, Brader, and Jardina, 2013) and therefore inherently threatening (Harell, Soroka, and Iyengar, 2017; Tsukamoto and Fiske, 2018), many whites feel that non-whites can never be trusted citizens under any circumstances (Perry and Whitehead, 2019). As white male ethnonationalism teaches, only vigilance and ready violence can protect the nation from infiltration and collapse.

The rite of white American restorative violence

Alongside the faith in white supremacy, white male ethnonationalism depends on violence to enforce illusions of divine providence and cannot exist independently of violence. Hegemonic white politics, economics, culture, and identity were built on, require, and enforce legal and cultural segregation and exploitation over a racial and gendered Other (Birnbaum, 2019; Richardson, 2020; Shor, 2020), which in the US has consisted of, from the earliest colonial settlements, Black people (Blackmon, 2009; Bloom and Martin, 2016; Rothstein, 2018), Native Americans (Dunbar-Ortiz, 2014), Latinx (Ortiz, 2018), and women (Block, 2006; Crane, 2011). The foundational beliefs of white American culture – manifest destiny and American exceptionalism – teach that God appointed strong white males to rule, whether that authority covers only a single family (Bjork-James, 2020), an encounter in public (Milner, George, and Allison, 2016), the workplace (McLaughlin, Uggen, and Blackstone, 2012; Smith, 2012), or confrontations between armies and nations (Duriesmith, 2016). Research shows that the more a person deviates from white, male, wealthy, average height, and physically fit, the more public suspicion they acquire and the more readily people will inflict insults, social stigma, and exclusion (Whitesel, 2017). While body size, fitness, gender, and race all prove statistically significant and each intensifies the others in multivariate regression analysis, race retains the most explanatory power in nearly all social contexts of inequality and aggression (Nawyn and Gjokaj, 2014 ; Harnois, 2017).

Restorative violence as a sacred rite in the American spiritual mind arose from the mythology that religiously devout white people built the United States from nothing, through self-sacrifice, hard work, and patriotic service of sacred violence against non-whites (Slotkin, 2000 [1973]). This success requires eternal vigilance and violence against non-whites, who will corrupt and destroy American godliness (Hughes, 2018). The history of the US is a history of self-proclaimed righteous conquest ("manifest destiny"), enslavement, and slaughter of Black people, Native Americans, Mexicans, and other Latinx in the service of white male ethnonationalism. Although the frontier in which the mythology of restorative violence arose ended long ago, white supremacists still learn it from parents and peers who articulate it as "heritage" and a doctrine of faith, the mythical paradise that was the Old South, the good manufacturing jobs reserved for white men, which various media, including online sites and Fox News reinforce. This adds a sense of transcendent legitimacy to bend reality to fit their doctrine (Whitehead, Perry, and Baker, 2018) and precludes any sort of dynamic adaptation to social change, hence today for example the rejection of science in all its forms, especially something as universal as climate change (the scientific reality of the global heat trap) or the reality of an ever more ethnically diverse United States. Only restorative violence can restore divine order and halt such widespread transgressions against the faith.

Therefore, when armed militants stormed the Michigan Capital on 30 April 2020 (Egan, 2020), they were following a long tradition of white male ethnonational religious fervor. Many wearing and carrying Confederate flags, they filled the spectator galleries as legislators conducted the affairs of the state under the menacing glare of armed racists, Trumpists, Q-Anon fanatics, and various other Right-wing conspiracy enthusiasts. Ostensibly about "liberty" and standing up to "tyranny," the real issue, I contend, is a perceived decline in white male hegemony. In this case, the female governor, Gretchen Whitmer, had dared to order white men to stay at home, maintain social distancing, and various other protocols to decrease the spread of the COVID-19 virus. As white males, no namby-pamby medical experts, a woman governor, or sissy intellectuals have any right to order the conduct of their lives during a pandemic or any other time. Instead, might makes right. Even if the COVID-19 threat is real, a real white man is better off strong and wrong than weak and right. Their guns, symbols of white power, and threat of violence prove their strength, which God has bestowed upon them since white Europeans first invaded North America, stole the land, slaughtered the indigenous people, and enslaved Africans. white women can join the cause as well, by the way, as long as they remember the real issue: the divinity of white male power.

Aren't people who cannot work from home upset about not being able to earn a paycheck? Maybe, but most of the protestors were still employed or retired (Baldas, 2020). And why the effigies in nooses, and Confederate flags? Why do all the signs pertain to "liberty" and "freedom" (Hutchinson, 2020), and not a right to return to work or unemployment benefits? Why do they need to carry automatic weapons at all times? More than half of the Democratic $3 trillion package passed in the House of Representatives on 15 May 2020 would have gone to state governments, public schools, and unemployed people – substantial infusions of cash that would immediately benefit individuals, including the Right-wing protestors in Michigan and other states (*New York Times*, 2020). The Republican-controlled Senate and the Trump administration resolutely opposed and blocked this bill (although it later passed with a new democratic President and Congress, with no Republican votes in favor). From the white male ethnonational perspective, government aid is un-American because it benefits inherently un-American people of color, even if it also benefits white people. Instead, guns, hate symbols, and righteous rage will redeem the good (white) people from the pandemic. As with all simplistic creator/annihilator religions, the gods will directly intervene and save the chosen people (hence Trump's belief that the virus will magically vanish if we hold faith in him as the great white male patriot). Therefore, whites should never weakly submit to wearing a mask and should hit back relentlessly against perceived attacks on white superiority.

Shortly after white racist militants stormed the Michigan legislature, a sudden new racial awareness exploded. On 25 May 2020 in Minneapolis, Minnesota, white male police officer Derek Chauvin murdered George Floyd, a Black man, for allegedly attempting to pass a counterfeit $20 bill. For several minutes, Chauvin kneeled on Floyd's neck, as Floyd pleaded that he couldn't breathe. In an act of restorative violence against a perceived Evil Other, Chauvin asphyxiated Floyd as he lay handcuffed on the ground, and kept his knee on Floyd's neck for about two minutes after Floyd was dead. In full awareness of his actions, Officer Chauvin smirked several times at the phone cameras as bystanders videoed the murder, in broad daylight, in front of numerous witnesses. This incident closely resembled the earlier murder of Eric Garner on 1 August 2014, when white police officer Daniel Pantaleo choked Eric Garner to death for standing outside a convenience store. Like Floyd, Garner pleaded that he couldn't breathe. Also like Floyd, the police murdered Garner in broad daylight in front of numerous witnesses. The State of New York filed no criminal charges against Pantaleo, and having delayed for years about whether Pantaleo violated Garner's civil rights, the US Justice Department under William Barr ordered the case dropped (Benner, 2019). In the last ten years, US police have choked at least 70 people to death, 47 of whom were Black (who are only 13 per cent of the population), and the majority of them had been stopped or held over nonviolent infractions, 911 calls about suspicious behavior, or concerns about their mental health (Baker et al, 2020).

The murder of George Floyd was not the first or last time the police would murder a Black man for a minor or nonviolent crime, or for no crime at all. For example, on 12 June 2020 in Atlanta, Georgia, the white police officer Garrett Rolfe shot and killed Rayshard Brooks for running away (*Washington Post*, 2020). Although Brooks had earlier failed a sobriety test and had struggled as police attempted to arrest him for something never determined, Rolfe shot

Brooks four times in the back as he fled (Fausset, Diaz, and Bogel-Burroughs, 2020). Although police kill unarmed white people also, they kill Black people at 2.5 times the rate (Fatal Force, 2020), and empirical research shows that white supremacy is in fact a core element of police training (Beliso-De Jesús, 2019) and in American police culture (Hirschfield, 2015; Hester and Gray, 2018). For nearly all officers who murder a Black person, the worst fate they typically suffer is to be fired from their current force and hired somewhere else (Garza, 2020). Police or not, white men with guns in general feel free to kill Black men at will. On 23 February 2020, in Glynn County, Georgia, Travis and Gregory McMichael, and William Bryan, murdered a Black man, Ahmaud Arbery, for jogging near their Satilla Shores neighborhood near Brunswick, Georgia. The local white prosecutor filed no charges, and the State Attorney General only picked up the case two months later when Bryan's boasting video of the murder went viral and drew national attention. The restorative religious aspect is clear – if a Black person turns their back on or disobeys the orders of any white man, their disobedience is punishable by death. The divine order must remain in control.

Most recently, a racist mob stormed the US Capitol building on 6 January 2021, following the belief that mysterious forces had stolen the election from Donald Trump. They intended to hang Vice President Mike Pence (a Republican) and Nancy Pelosi (a Democrat) as traitors. As Jeffrey Goldberg (2021) discovered, talking with the insurrectionists as the siege unfolded, they essentially created a "mass delusion" event, based on ramblings from various Q-Anon aligned websites and social media. They believed that Pence, Pelosi, and others were part of a conspiracy to steal the election from Donald Trump, who they believed had won by a landslide. Online chats and racist groups such as the Proud Boys and the Three Percenters invoked a longstanding white ethnonational identity that deifies people like Donald Trump (white, male, rich, racist, and aggressive) and cannot imagine how their living god lost the election. Consequently, they violently seized the Capitol to restore white ethnonationalism.

Conclusion

In order to create any sort of dramatic and long-lasting change, the majority white population will need to recognize the intersecting hierarchies of race and class (as well as of gender and sexuality). In American history, almost no movement has emphasized economic class as a real hierarchy, and not for very long. In both the Reconstruction period and the 20th century labor movement, whites refused to admit a broad commonality with people of all races, religions, and national origins, because white national supremacy remained the decisive priority. Quite simply, the vast majority of white people have historically chosen a faith in racial superiority over broadly collective gains in the quality of life and political power. As long as the clear majority of capitalists and politicians are white, then the white male ethnonational god still reigns, and all is well, even for whites who work tirelessly for a declining quality of life, and those who work for poverty wages.

In order to save the US from its own dysfunction and self-destruction, white people will need to join the revolution. In 1973, Black Panther People's Party co-founder Huey Newton argued that, "Black people, American Indians, women ... and homosexuals are the most revolutionary because they are the most oppressed" (Newton, 2009 [1973]: pp. 153–4), but they can't win unless the white multitude joins as well. Joshua Bloom and Waldo E. Martin similarly argue in *Black Against Empire* that, although the US has seen large-scale mobilizations in the 2000s, none envisioned anything beyond immediate issues such as fair housing, living wages, or removing guns in schools (Bloom and Martin, 2016: pp. 398–9).

Until a revolutionary movement can seize the political imagination of large segments of the people and create a broad insurgent alliance that is difficult to repress or appease, there will be no transformational social change. For Bloom and Martin (2016), this has not happened since the heyday of the Black Panther People's Party, "and may not happen again for a very long time" (p. 401). For broad and meaningful social change, diverse groups must unite to collectively oppose racial, class, gender, and sexual injustice and oppression, and for that matter, to oppose environmental, ageist, ableist, cultural origin, religious, and any other form of despoliation, oppression, and injustice we can discern. Most importantly, white people must renounce the wicked cant of white male ethnonationalism, actively challenge white supremacy, and struggle for a future premised on egalitarianism and justice. Otherwise, broad social progress may not happen for a very long time.

References

Alexander, S. (2015) *Reconstruction Violence and the Ku Klux Klan Hearings: A Brief History with Documents*, New York: St. Martin's Press.

Allen, T.W. (2014 [1994]) *The Invention of the White Race, Vol 2*, New York: Verso.

Arnesen, E. (2007) "The Quicksands of Economic Insecurity: African Americans, Strikebreaking, and Labor Activism in the Industrial Era," in E. Arnsesen (ed), Urbana and Chicago: University of Illinois Press.

Aronowitz, S. (2014) *The Death and Life of American Labor: Toward a New Worker's Movement*, New York: Verso Press.

Baker, J.O., Perry, S.L., and Whitehead, A.L. (2020) "Keep America Christian (and White): Christian Nationalism, Fear of Ethnoracial Outsiders, and Intention to Vote for Donald Trump in the 2020 Presidential Election," *Sociology of Religion*, 81(3): 272–93.

Baker, M., Valentino-DeVries, F., Fernandez, M., and LaForgia, M. (eds) (2020) "Three Words. 70 Cases. The Tragic History of 'I Can't Breathe,'" *The New York Times* [online], available at www.nytimes.com/interactive/2020/06/28/us/i-cant-breathe-police-arrest.html?searchResultPosition= 2 [Accessed 28 March 2021].

Baldas, T. (2020) "Age of Resistance: How A Virus Riled Up Michigan And Spawned A Rebellion," *Detroit Free Press* [online], available at www.freep.com/in-depth/news/local/michigan/2020/05/17/how-coronavirus-riled-up-michigan-and-spawned-resistance-movement/5185632002/ [Accessed 28 March 2021].

Banks, A.J. (2014) *Anger and Racial Politics: The Emotional Foundation of Racial Attitudes in the United States*, New York: Cambridge University Press.

Banks, A.J., and Hicks, H.M. (2016) "Fear and Implicit Racism: Whites' Support for Voter ID Laws," *Political Psychology*, 37 (5): 641–58.

Beck, C.L., and Plant, E.A. (2018) "The Implications of Right-Wing Authoritarianism for Non-Muslims' Aggression Toward Muslims in the United States," *Analyses of Social Issues and Public Policy*, 18(1): 353–77.

Beliso-De Jesús, A.M. (2019) "The Jungle Academy: Molding White Supremacy in American Police Recruits," *American Anthropologist*, 122(1): 143–56.

Benedict, R. (2005 [1934]) *Patterns of Culture,* Boston and New York: Mariner Books.

Benner, K. (2019) "Eric Garner's Death Will Not Lead to Federal Charges for N.Y.P.D. Officer," *The New York Times* [online], available at www.nytimes.com/2019/07/16/nyregion/eric-garner-case-death-daniel-pantaleo.html [Accessed 12 January 2021].

Berger, P. (1990 [1967]) *The Sacred Canopy: Elements of a Sociological Theory of Religion*, New York: Anchor Books.

Bergin, C., and Rupprecht, A. (2018) "Reparative Histories: Tracing Narratives of Black Resistance and White Entitlement," *Race & Class*, 60(1): 22–37.

Berry, D.T. (2017) *Blood and Faith: Christianity in American White Nationalism*, Syracuse, NY: Syracuse University Press.

Birenbaum, A. (2019) *A Nation Apart: The African-American Experience and White Nationalism*, New York: Routledge.

Bjork-James, S. (2020) "White Sexual Politics: The Patriarchal Family in White Nationalism and the Religious Right," *Transforming Anthropology*, 28(1): 58–73.

Bjorklund, E., Davis, A.P., and Pfaffendorf, J. (2018) "Urine or You're Out: Racialized Economic Threat and the Determinants of Welfare Drug Testing Policy in the United States, 2009-2015," *Sociological Quarterly*, 59(3), 407–23.

Blackmon, D.A. (2009) *Slavery by Another Name: The Re-Enslavement of Black Americans from the Civil War to World War II*, New York: Anchor Books.

Block, S. (2006) *Rape and Sexual Power in Early America*, Chapel Hill, NC: University of North Carolina Press.

Bloom, J., and Martin, W.E. (2016) *Black against Empire: The History and Politics of the Black Panther Party*, Oakland, CA: University of California Press.

Brands, H.W. (2012) *The Man Who Saved the Union: Ulysses Grant in War and Peace*, New York: Doubleday.

Bret, A., Beffara, B., McFadyen, J., and Mermillod, M. (2017) "Right Wing Authoritarianism Is Associated with Race Bias in Face Detection," *PLoS ONE*, 12(7): e0179894.

Bureau of Labor Statistics (2020) "Union Members Summary," Washington, DC: US Bureau of Labor Statistics [online], available at www.bls.gov/news.release/union2.nr0.htm [Accessed 28 March 2021].

Considine, C. (2017) "The Racialization of Islam in the United States: Islamophobia, Hate Crimes, and Flying while Brown," *Religions*, 8 (9): 165–83.

Cooper, W.J. (2003) *Jefferson Davis: The Essential Writings*, New York: Random House.

Cramer, K. (2016) *The Politics of Resentment: Rural Consciousness in Wisconsin and the Rise of Scott Walker*, Chicago: University of Chicago Press.

Crane, E.F. (2011) *Witches, Wife Beaters, and Whores: Common Law and Common Folk in Early America*, Ithaca, NY: Cornell University Press.

Davis, J.T., and Perry, S.L. (2020) "White Christian Nationalism and Relative Political Tolerance for Racists," *Social Problems*, spaa002, [online], available at doi.org/10.1093/socpro/spaa002 [Accessed 28 March 2021].

DeJesus, J.M., Hwang, H.G, Dautel, J.B, and Kinzler, K.D. (2018) "American = English Speaker Before American = White: The Development of Children's Reasoning About Nationality," *Child Development*, 89(5): 1752–67.

Dowling, J.A., Ellison, C.G., and Leal, D.L. (2012) "Who Doesn't Value English? Debunking Myths About Mexican Immigrants' Attitudes Toward the English Language," *Social Science Quarterly*, 93(2): 356–78.

Duina, F. (2018) *Broke and Patriotic: Why Poor Americans Love Their Country*, Stanford: Stanford University Press.

Dunbar-Ortiz, R. (2014) *An Indigenous Peoples' History of the United States*, Boston, MA: Beacon Press.

Duriesmith, D. (2016) *Masculinity and New War: The Gendered Dynamics of Contemporary Armed Conflict*, New York: Routledge.

Edelson, J., Alduncin, A.A., Christopher, K., Sieja, J.A., and Uscinski, J.E. (2017) "The Effect of Conspiratorial Thinking and Motivated Reasoning on Belief in Election Fraud," *Political Research Quarterly*, 70(4), 933–46.

Egan, P. (2020) "Capitol Protesters Urge an End to Michigan's State of Emergency," *Detroit Free Press* [online], available at www.freep.com/story/news/local/michigan/2020/04/30/capitol-protesters-urge-end-michigan-state-of-emergency/3055294001/ [Accessed 28 March 2021].

Eliade, M. (1987 [1957]) *The Sacred and the Profane: The Nature of Religion*, New York: Harcourt Brace Jovanovich.

Fantasia, R., and Voss, K. (2004) *Hard Work: Remaking the American Labor Movement*, Berkeley and Los Angeles, CA: University of California Press.

Fatal Force (2020) Database on Police Violence, *The Washington Post* [online], available at www.washingtonpost.com/graphics/investigations/police-shootings-database/ [Accessed 28 March 2021].

Fausset, R., Diaz, J., and Bogel-Burroughs, N. (2020) "Atlanta Police Chief Resigns After Officer Shoots and Kills a Black Man," *The New York Times* [online], available at www.nytimes.com/2020/06/13/us/atlanta-police-shooting-rayshard-brooks.html [Accessed 28 March 2021].

Feldman, S., and Huddy, L. (2005) "Racial Resentment and White Opposition to Race-Conscious Programs: Principles or Prejudice?" *American Journal of Political Science*, 49(1): 168–83.

Filindra, A., and Kaplan, N.J. (2016) "Racial Resentment and Whites' Gun Policy Preferences in Contemporary America," *Political Behavior*, 38(2): 255–75.

Foner, E. (2014 [1988]) *Reconstruction: America's Unfinished Revolution, 1863–1877*, New York: HarperCollins.

Fox-Genovese, E., and Genovese, E.D. (2008) *Slavery in White and Black: Class and Race in the Southern Slaveholders' New World Order*, New York: Cambridge University Press.

Fromm, E. (1997 [1976]) *To Have or to Be?*, New York: Bloomsbury Academic.

Frymer, P. (2008) *Black and Blue: African Americans, the Labor Movement, and the Decline of the Democratic Party*, Princeton, NJ: Princeton University Press.

Gallagher, G.W., and Nolan, A.T. (2010) *The Myth of the Lost Cause and Civil War History*, Bloomington, IN: Indiana University Press.

Garza, A., Goff, P.A., Gupta, V., Sinyangwe, S., and Thomson, J.S. (2020) "Police Reform is Necessary, but How do We Do It?" *The New York Times Magazine* [online], available at www.nytimes.com/interactive/2020/06/13/magazine/police-reform.html [Accessed 28 March 2021].

Gibbons, A. (2018) "The Five Refusals of White Supremacy," *American Journal of Economics and Sociology*, 77(3–4): 729–55.

Golash-Boza, T., Duenas, M.D., and Xiong, C. (2019) "White Supremacy, Patriarchy, and Global Capitalism in Migration Studies," *American Behavioral Scientist*, 63 (13): 1741–59.

Goldberg, J. (2021) "Mass Delusion in America: What I Heard from Insurrectionists on their March to the Capitol," *The Atlantic Online*, www.theatlantic.com/politics/archive/2021/01/among-insurrectionists/ 617580/ [Accessed 12 January 2021].

Guglielmo, J., and Salerno, S. (2003) *Are Italians White? How Race is Made in America*, New York: Routledge.

Harell, A., Soroka, S., and Iyengar, S. (2017) "Locus of Control and Anti-Immigrant Sentiment in Canada, the United States, and the United Kingdom," *Political Psychology*, 38 (2): 245–60.

Harell, A., Soroka, S., Iyengar, S., and Valentino, N. (2012) "The Impact of Economic and Cultural Cues on Support for Immigration in Canada and the United States," *Canadian Journal of Political Science*, 45(3) (09): 499–530.

Harnois, C.E. (2017) "Intersectional Masculinities and Gendered Political Consciousness: How Do Race, Ethnicity and Sexuality Shape Men's Awareness of Gender Inequality and Support for Gender Activism?," *Sex Roles*, 77(3–4): 141–54.

Hester, N., and Gray, K. (2018) "For Black Men, Being Tall Increases Threat Stereotyping and Police Stops," *Proceedings of the National Academy of Sciences – PNAS*, 115(11): 2711–15.

Hirschfield, P.J. (2015) "Lethal Policing: Making Sense of American Exceptionalism," *Sociological Forum*, 30(4): 1109–17.

Hinshaw, J. (2002) *Steel and Steelworkers: Race and Class Struggle in Twentieth-Century Pittsburgh*, Albany, NY: SUNY Press.

Hofer, E. (1963 [1951]) *The True Believer: Thoughts on the Nature of Mass Movements*, New York: Time Incorporated.

Howard, P.W. (2020) "Many of UAW's Newest Members Aren't Traditional Autoworkers," *Detroit Free Press* [online], available at www.freep.com/ story/money/cars/2020/04/14/uaw-membership-2019/2923908001/ [Accessed 28 March 2021].

Hughes, R.T. (2018) *Myths America Lives By: White Supremacy and the Stories That Give Us Meaning*, Champaign-Urbana, IL: University of Illinois Press.

Hughey, M.W. (2010) "The (Dis)Similarities of White Racial Identities: The Conceptual Framework of Hegemonic Whiteness," *Ethnic and Racial Studies*, 33(8): 1289–309.

Hughey, M.W. (2018) "Hegemonic Whiteness from Structure and Agency to Identity Allegiance," in S. Middleton, D.R Roediger, and D.M. Shaffer (eds) *The Construction of Whiteness: An Interdisciplinary Analysis of Race Formation and the Meaning of a White Identity*, Jackson, MS: University Press of Mississippi.

Hunter, L.A. (2000) "The Immortal Confederacy: Another Look at Lost Cause Religion," in G.W. Gallagher and A.T. Nolan (eds) *The Myth of the Lost Cause and Civil War History*, Bloomington, IN: Indiana University Press.

Hutchinson, B. (2020) "Operation Gridlock: Convoy in Michigan's Capital Protests Stay-At-Home Orders," *ABC News* [online], available at abcnews. go.com/US/convoy-protesting-stay-home-orders-targets-michigans-capital/story?id=70138816 [Accessed 28 March 2021].

Ignatiev, N. (2009 [1995]) *How the Irish Became White*, New York: Routledge.

Isenberg, N. (2016) *White Trash: The 400-year Untold History of Class in America*, New York: Viking Press.

Jewett, R., and Lawrence, J.S. (2003) *Captain America and the Crusade Against Evil*, Grand Rapids, MI: William B. Eerdemans.

Jones, H. (2019) "More in Common: The Domestication of Misogynist White Supremacy and The Assassination of Jo Cox," *Journal of Ethnic and Racial Studies*, 42 (14): 2431–49.

Kaloudis, G. (2018) *Modern Greece and the Diaspora Greeks in the United States*, Lanham, MD: Lexington Books.

Karenga, M. (2018) "Trump's Mind, Mouth and Fecal Matters: Racism's Red Meat and Raw Sewage," *Journal of Pan African Studies*, 11(4): 4–16.

Kimeldorf, H. (1988) *Reds or Rackets? The Making of Radical and Conservative Unions on the Waterfront*, Berkeley and Los Angeles, CA: University of California Press.

Knitter, P. (2019) "Symbiotic Supremacies: Racial and Religious," *Buddhist-Christian Studies*, 39(1): 205–15.

Knuckey, J. and Kim, M. (2015) "Racial Resentment, Old-Fashioned Racism, and the Vote Choice of Southern and Nonsouthern Whites in the 2012 US Presidential Election," *Social Science Quarterly*, 96 (4): 905–22.

Korstad, R. and Lichtenstein, N. (2007) "Opportunities Found and Lost: Labor, Radicals, and the Early Civil Rights Movement," E. Arnesen (ed) *The Black Worker*, Urban and Chicago: University of Illinois Press.

LeCount, R.J. (2018) "Visualizing the Increasing Effect of Racial Resentment on Political Ideology among Whites, 1986 to 2016," *Socius: Sociological Research for a Dynamic World*, 4, doi: http://dx.doi.org.ezproxy.gvsu.edu/10.1177/2378023118801096

Lee, E. (2019) *America for Americans: A History of Xenophobia in the United States*, New York: Hachette Group.

Lundskow, G. (2020) "The Necessity of Progressive Religion to Foment Progressive Change: A Frommian Argument," in J. Braun and K. Durkin (eds) *Erich Fromm's Critical Theory: Hope, Humanism, and the Future*, London and New York: Bloomsbury Press.

MacWilliams, M.C. (2017) "Intolerant and Afraid: Authoritarians Rise to Trump's Call," in M. Fitzduff (ed) *Why Irrational Politics Appeals: Understanding the Allure of Trump*, Santa Barbara, CA: Praeger Group.

Major, B., Blodorn, A., and Blascovich, G.M. (2018) "The Threat of Increasing Diversity: Why Many White Americans Support Trump in the 2016 Presidential Election," *Group Processes & Intergroup Relations*, 21(6): 931–40.

McCook, B. (2011) *The Borders of Integration: Polish Migrants in Germany and the United States, 1870–1924*, Athens, OH: Ohio University Press.

McLaughlin, H., Uggen, C., and Blackstone, A. (2012) "Sexual Harassment, Workplace Authority, and the Paradox of Power," *American Sociological Review*, 77(4): 625–47.

McVeigh, R. and Estep, K. (2019) *The Politics of Losing: Trump, the Klan, and the Mainstreaming of Resentment*, New York: Columbia University Press.

Merritt, K.L. (2017) *Masterless Men: Poor Whites and Slavery in the Antebellum South*, New York: Cambridge University Press.

Metzl, J.M. (2020) *Dying of Whiteness: How the Politics of Racial Resentment is Killing America's Heartland*, New York: Hachette Group.

Milner, A., Brandon, N., George, J., and Allison, D.B. (2016) "Black and Hispanic Men Perceived to Be Large Are at Increased Risk for Police Frisk, Search, and Force," *PLoS ONE*, 11(1): e0147158.

Nawyn, S.J., and Linda, G. (2014) "The Magnifying Effect of Privilege: Earnings Inequalities at the Intersection of Gender, Race, and Nativity," *Feminist Formations*, 26(2): 85–106.

Newman, B.J., Johnston, C.D., and Lown, P.L. (2015) "False Consciousness or Class Awareness? Local Income Inequality, Personal Economic Position, and Belief in American Meritocracy," *American Journal of Political Science*, 59 (2): 326–40.

Newton, H. (2009 [1973]) *Revolutionary Suicide*, New York: Penguin Group.

New York Times (2020) "House Passes $3 Trillion Relief Bill Seen as Democrats' Opening Bid," *The New York Times* [online], available at www.nytimes.com/2020/05/15/us/coronavirus-updates.html?searchResultPosition=8 [Accessed 28 March 2021].

O'Connell, R.L. (2015) *Fierce Patriot: The Tangled Lives of William Tecumseh Sherman*, New York: Random House.

Ortiz, P. (2018) *An African American and Latinx History of the United States*, Boston, MA: Beacon Press.

Parker, C.S., and Towler, C.C. (2019) "Race and Authoritarianism in American Politics," *Annual Review of Political Science*, 22(1): 503–19.

Patel, E. (2018) *Out of Many Faiths: Religious Diversity and the American Promise*, Princeton, NJ: Princeton University Press.

Pearl, M. (2016) "K-Troop: The Story of The Eradication of the Original Ku Klux Klan," *Slate Magazine* [online], available at www.slate.com/articles/news_and_politics/history/2016/03/how_a_detachment_of_u_s_army_soldiers_smoked_out_the_original_ku_klux_klan.html [Accessed 28 March 2021].

Perlmutter, E. (1970) "Head of Building Trades Unions Here Says Response Favors Friday's Action," *The New York Times* [online], 12 May 1970, available at timesmachine.nytimes.com/timesmachine/1970/05/12/issue. html [Accessed 28 March, 2021].

Perry, S.L. and Whitehead, A.L. (2015) "Christian Nationalism and White Racial Boundaries: Examining Whites' Opposition to Interracial Marriage," *Ethnic and Racial Studies*, 38(10): 1671–89.

Perry, S.L., and Whitehead, A.L. (2019) "Christian America in Black and White: Racial Identity, Religious-National Group Boundaries, and Explanations for Racial Inequality," *Sociology of Religion*, 80(3): 277–98.Pollard, E. (1867) *The Lost Cause: A New Southern History of the War of the Confederates*, New York: E.B. Treat Publishers.

Posner, S. (2020) *Unholy: Why White Evangelicals Worship at the Altar of Donald Trump*, New York: Random House.

Ramirez, M., Argueta, N.L., Castro, Y., Perez, R., and Dawson, D.B. (2016) "The Relation of Drug Trafficking Fears and Cultural Identity to Attitudes Toward Mexican Immigrants in Five South Texas Communities," *Journal of Borderlands Studies*, 31 (1): 91–119.

Ratskoff, B. (2020) " 'Improbable Spectacles': White Supremacy, Christian Hegemony, and the Dark Side of the *Judenfrage*," *Studies in American Jewish Literature*, 39(1): 17–32.

Reno, R.R. (2019) *Return of the Strong Gods: Nationalism, Populism, and the Future of the West*, Washington, DC: Regnery Gateway Publishing.

Rhodes, J.H., Schaffner, B.F., and McElwee, S. (2017) "Is America More Divided by Race or Class? Race, Income, and Attitudes among Whites, African Americans, and Latinos," *The Forum*, 15(1): 71–91.

Riaz, H. and Qadir, S. (2018) "A Critical Enquiry of Racism 'within the Idioms of Religion' in America," *FWU Journal of Social Sciences*, 12 (2): 12–28.

Richardson, H.C. (2001) *The Death of Reconstruction: Race, Labor, and Politics in the Post-Civil War North*, Cambridge, MA: Harvard University Press.

Richardson, H.C. (2020) *How the South Won the Civil War: Oligarchy, Democracy, and the Continuing Fight for the Soul of America*, New York: Oxford University Press.

Roberts, D. (2017 [1997]) *Killing the Black Body: Race, Reproduction, and the Meaning of Liberty*, New York: Vintage Books.

Rodríguez, R.R. (2018) "Do Black Lives Matter to White Christians?," *Cross Currents*, 68(1): 112–34.

Roediger, D. (2018 [2005]) *Working Toward Whiteness: How America's Immigrants Became White: The Strange Journey from Ellis Island to the Suburbs*, New York: Hachette Group.

Rothstein, R. (2018) *The Color of Law: A Forgotten History of How Our Government Segregated America,* New York: W.W. Norton.

Shor, F. (2020) "The Long Life of US Institutionalized White Supremacist Terror," *Critical Sociology*, 46(1): 5–18.Simi, P., Blee, K., DeMichele, M., and Windisch, S. (2017) "Addicted to Hate: Identity Residual among Former White Supremacists," *American Sociological Review*, 82(6): 1167–87.

Slotkin, R. (2000 [1973]) *Regeneration Through Violence: The Mythology of the American Frontier, 1600–1860*, Norman, OK: University of Oklahoma Press.

Smith, D.N. and Hanley, E. (2018) "The Anger Games: Who Voted for Donald Trump in the 2016 Election, and Why?," *Critical Sociology*, 44(2): 195–212.

Smith, R.A. (2012) "Money, Benefits, and Power: A Test of the Glass Ceiling and Glass Escalator Hypotheses," *The Annals of the American Academy of Political and Social Science* 639(1): 149–72.

Speed, S. (2019) "The Persistence of White Supremacy: Indigenous Women Migrants and the Structures of Settler Capitalism," *American Anthropologist*, 122(1): 76–85.

Strings, S. (2019) *Fearing the Black Body: How the Female Body Has Been Racialized for over Two Hundred Years*, New York: New York University Press.

Taras, R. (2013) "Islamophobia Never Stands Still: Race, Religion, and Culture," *Ethnic and Racial Studies*, 36(3): 417–33.

Tate, S., A. and Page, D. (2018) "Whiteliness and Institutional Racism: Hiding Behind (Un)Conscious Bias," *Ethics and Education: Critical Philosophy of Race and Education*, 13(1): 141–55.

Thompson, H.A. (2017) *Whose Detroit? Politics, Labor, and Race in a Modern American City*, Ithaca, NY: Cornell University Press.

Thomsen, L., Green, E.G.T., and Sidanius, J. (2008) "We Will Hunt Them Down: How Social Dominance Orientation and Right-Wing Authoritarianism Fuel Ethnic Persecution of Immigrants in Fundamentally Different Ways," *Journal of Experimental Social Psychology*, 44 (6): 1455–64.

Tsukamoto, S., and Fiske, S.T. (2018) "Perceived Threat to National Values in Evaluating Stereotyped Immigrants," *The Journal of Social Psychology*, 158(2): 157–72.

Udani, A., and Kimball, D.C. (2018) "Immigrant Resentment and Voter Fraud Beliefs in the US Electorate," *American Politics Research*, 46(3): 402–33.

Valentino, N.A., Brader, T., and Jardina, A.E. (2013) "Immigration Opposition Among US Whites: General Ethnocentrism or Media Priming of Attitudes About Latinos?," *Political Psychology*, 34(2): 149–66.

Varon, E. (2014) *Appomattox: Victory, Defeat, and Freedom at the End of the Civil War*, New York: Oxford University Press.

Varon, E. (2019) *Armies of Deliverance: A New History of the Civil War*, New York: Oxford University Press.

Washington Post (2020) "What Video Shows Happened Before and After the Death of Rayshard Brooks," *The Washington Post* [online], 14 June 2020, available at www.washingtonpost.com/video/national/what-video-shows-happened-before-and-after-the-death-of-rayshard-brooks/2020/06/14/18d922aa-3b76-4bf0-a183-f5390d80451d_video.html [Accessed 28 March 2021].

Wetts, R., and Willer, R. (2018) "Privilege on the Precipice: Perceived Racial Status Threats Lead White Americans to Oppose Welfare Programs," *Social Forces*, 97(2): 793–822.

White, R. (2017) *The Republic for Which it Stands: The United States During Reconstruction and the Gilded Age, 1865–1896*, New York: Oxford University Press.

Whitehead, A.L., Perry, S.L., and Baker, J.O. (2018) "Make America Christian Again: Christian Nationalism and Voting for Donald Trump in the 2016 Presidential Election," *Sociology of Religion*, 79 (2): 147–71.

Whitesel, J. (2017) "Intersections of Multiple Oppressions: Racism, Sizeism, Ableism, and the 'Illimitable Etceteras' in Encounters with Law Enforcement," *Sociological Forum*, 32 (2): 426–33.

Womick, J., Rothmund, T., Azevedo, F., King, L.A., and Jost, J.T. (2018) "Group-Based Dominance and Authoritarian Aggression Predict Support for Donald Trump in the 2016 US Presidential Election," *Social Psychological and Personality Science*, 10(5): 643–52.

8

Totalitarianism as Religion

Yong Wang

Introduction

There have appeared two lines of inquiry concerning the relationship between religion and modernization. The first line runs on the decline of religion driven by the intensification of modernization, which can be termed the 'secularization thesis'. As we know, most of the founding fathers of sociology such as Karl Marx, Émile Durkheim, and Max Weber argued along this line. Most well-known is probably Weber's observation of the shift from value-oriented and tradition-based rationalities to instrumental rationality (Weber, 1992 [1930]). This school of inquiry treats religions as the object of negation that allowed for the rise of science, reason, historical laws, namely all "oracular voices"[1] of modernity as Milbank calls them (Milbank, 1990). Unbeknownst to the gesture of negation is the erection of ideological forms and new deities that often entail the reshaping of finite historical contingencies into inevitabilities. Various formulations of the Marxian 'historical Law' and the rise of the nation-state attest to modernity's own need for the sacred.

Following a more specific inquiry, Raymond Aron recognizes the homology between totalitarian social-political ideologies and religion, and gives such ideological systems a seemingly self-contradictory name: secular religion (Aron, 1957).[2] In characterizing what he calls secular religions, Raymond Aron argues that "such doctrines set up an ultimate and quasi-sacred goal and define good and evil in relation to this ideal" (Aron, 2003: p.178). In his illustrative example, Aron points out that Hitler and his Germany functioned as the common foundation for the secular religion of fascism (Aron, 2003). Addressing the supposedly emancipatory impact of such secular religions, Aron further argues, "But every advance in liberation carries the seed of a new form of enslavement" (Aron, 1957: p. 21). Along a similar but ambiguous line, Bellah (1967) examines the elements in US political discourse, and argues that already present in the founding documents of the United States are the notion of God and its selected aspects. This notion of God is "… much more related to order, law, and right than to salvation and love" (Bellah, 1967: p. 7). Bellah's analysis points to a tendency in US political discourse to draw on a properly religious tradition to sacralize civic political values, goals, and missions. What is noteworthy is that inquiries such as Aron's and Bellah's maintain the distinction between the religious and the quasi-religious; and their analyses of modern social-political ideological systems rely on the very distinction.

This leads us to the other line of inquiry, whose initial focus was on the seemingly inevitable homology between religions understood as a remainder of progressing history. Carl Schmitt was probably the first to notice that, "All significant concepts of the modern theory of the state are secularized theological concepts …" (Schmitt, 2005: p. 36). As a jurist, Schmitt's focus was largely on the development of the sovereign in the modern state as the exception: a founding agent of the law that hides itself in plain daylight and its acts mystified (Schmitt, 2005). For Schmitt, the founding exception is no less than a parallel to the miracle in theology, and the mysterious lawgiver, God. Schmitt's argument demystifies the modernist assumption that the modern state and society are founded rationally, suggesting that the rational has to sweep its miraculous founding gesture under the carpet. If the differences between religion and secular ideological systems are tacitly maintained in Aron, Bellah, and even Schmitt, Berger's "sacred canopy" as "a meaningful order" that "… is imposed upon the discrete experiences and meanings of individuals" and "a world-building enterprise" (Berger, 1967) further blurs the boundaries of the distinction. More recently, the Hegelian-Lacanians point out that in the founding moment of law, a (violent) act has to be concealed as miraculous agent-act and an exception (Žižek, 2006a) or that the law and its institutions, ancient and modern, are always sustained by some "central imaginary" (Castoriadis, 1987: p. 129) that is mythical, nonfunctional, and ahistorical, resistant to any causal integration in any rational manner. This erasure of the boundaries between the religious and the pseudo-religious presents a moment for sociological inquiry on the rise and falls of ideological systems to reverse the Durkheim thesis that "the religious is social" to "the social is religious."

This chapter is not intended for the untangling of the tremendous dialectical process of the conceptual and theoretical evolution in the sociological studies of religion. Arguably, a minimal distinction between the religious proper and the secular ideological may be more effective in our enterprise. This chapter relies on the tools in the repertoire of sociological inquiry of religion to examine one species of modern totalitarianism, namely communism, and its experiment in China, focusing on the founding moment, its structuring of experiences and members of the Chinese society, and its transition to a post-totalitarian order. This chapter does suggest that the distinction between the religious proper, however it is defined, and the secular ideological can only be maintained by subsuming the secular ideological under the religious as one of its species.

My inquiry in this chapter is largely based on a singular case: China and its communist revolution in the 20th century, which resulted in a totalitarian system whose ramifications and metamorphoses still define what the country is and does in the 21st century. While the homology between theology and secular religions is largely visible in the West or further in the territories dominated by the Abrahamic religions, in countries like China where religions functioned as sites of retreat from the social-political, sites of spiritual comfort for either the disillusioned elites or the desperate commoners, the need of a political ideology for a religious underpinning, at least structurally, is never clear. My question is: What have been the forms of the Chinese Communist political theology after this tired, secluded, and confused empire was dragged into the modern era? In other words, how did the modern Chinese, the Communists in particular, create a political ideology that bears any resemblance to a theology or religion in a tradition where religious doctrines and practices had been largely asocial in the two dominant religions of Buddhism and Daoism? In addition, I focus on the basic coordinates of the ideological systemic shifts entailed by the social and economic exhaustion as consequences of the very political acts to sustain the system. My goal is not to offer a full-fledged analytical framework but to repeat one more time the attempt at making sense of the process, through which behaviors of a totalitarian regime emerged and unfolded.

The founding act and the constitution of a new world

Durkheim's analysis of the religious (Durkheim, 1982 [1915]) focuses on the routinized practices and is mostly silent on the founding moment or gesture of religious orders and communities, which seem always already there out of some unmentioned or unmentionable acts. The rise and fall of several of the ideological attempts at reordering the world in the modern era have allowed us to witness their inception and demise. Admittedly, the new world of modernity is driven by the mandate that the society as an amorphous entity that generates excesses all the time must be reined in by some rational forces, communism and fascism, the two species of modern totalitarianism paradoxically bear the most uncanny resemblance to religion proper in both the collective sentiments they generate and the forms of human association. However, fascism and communism are often treated as special cases – of personality cult in the case of fascism, or as lost causes whose beautiful soul needs to be saved in the case of communism. Looking closely, one does not fail to see that at the center of the incarnations of the two systems is the state, which is supposed to embody reason, and thus must be granted power over all domains of social, economic, and cultural life so that the excesses generated by modernization can be tamed. A crucial difference between the two is their choice over the past: communism features a radical break with the past, and fascism a reconnection with it. The most well-known analyses of totalitarianism have strong predilection for historicism; Arendt's (1973) work may be one of the best examples of this approach. However, the search in historical circumstances for the origins of totalitarianism necessarily pushes the ahistorical and transcendental aspects of totalitarianism into the background and renders them invisible. History, for instance, is not only a source of causes of totalitarianism, but also a category to be shaped and reshaped by the totalitarian regimes. This is particularly important for understanding the Chinese case, or perhaps, the communist cases in general.

Inherent to the communist experiments in the 20th century was a violently forced break of history. China was no exception. If the past has to be radically negated, the future has to be asserted. In a culture that had meticulously kept historical records for over two thousand years and a tradition that had been oriented toward and obsessed with its past, this was no easy task. That is to say, the rise of communism in China can hardly be associated with any historical traces already existent in the Chinese tradition waiting for its chance to be activated. The absence of cause, one is tempted to argue, is precisely the cause. After eight years of war with the Japanese (1937–45), and three bloody years of civil war between the Communists and the Nationalists (Kuomintang) (1946–49), China was a chaos in 1949 ready to be reshaped into anything that might represent order and meaningfulness. As Mao Zedong later admitted, "A clean sheet of paper has no blotches, and so the newest and most beautiful pictures can be painted on it" (MacFarquhar and Schoenhals, 2008, p. 1). So, China in 1949 was ripe for a historical break; the only thing to be done was proclaim it.

Forty days after Mao declared that "The Chinese people have stood up," in Tiananmen Square on 1 October 1949, Hu Feng, one of the leading figures of the Leftist literary movement in post-Qing China (post-1911) announced that "Time has begun!" in a poem of a much exaggerated Mayakovskian style, if that is literarily possible at all. However, the sentiments feel authentic even today. This is evidence that at least some members of the educated elite experienced this moment, the symbolic founding gesture as a true break with everything past: the slate was wiped clean, let's start anew. Hu Feng and the educated elite, however, were totally oblivious to what was about to come, not knowing that they were precisely the elements to be swept under the carpet of history. In less than five years, he and anyone who was perceived even remotely sympathetic to him were condemned as counterrevolutionaries. Hu Feng then spent close to thirty years in imprisonment. The cruel irony is not that the one who declared this break became one of its first victims, but the break itself was not what Hu Feng had imagined, even though he indeed captured the sentiments of the moment.

A closer look at the poem reveals that, in Hu Feng's declared new era, Mao was already placed outside Time and space as its commander: "at the mountaintop, Mao, standing like a statue, ... issuing a command to Time, 'March'". The first stanza itself presents a very hyperbolical but nonetheless ontologizing image:

> Time has begun!
> At the center of the platform,
> Mao Zedong, standing,
> On the surface of the Earth,
> In front of China's landscape,
> like a statue!
> Applauds and cheers recede into silence!
> (Hu, 1949)

Is this not an instance of an exception of the universal: everyone is subject to the universal march of history except the One that issues the command? Furthermore, Hu Feng's poem performs a truly miraculous feat that brings all the dead, the martyrs and the oppressed, to life by announcing that "in the warm embrace of the fatherland, they have all come to life" (Hu, 1949). In the place of "rest in peace" for the dead, this gesture that brings the dead to life was a Christian one, one that would appear peculiar to the Chinese traditional religious sensibility. Furthermore, a radical break from the past itself was an alien notion for the masses whose history repeated in cycles for over two thousand years, with any break but a new beginning for its recycling. The idea that history is but repetition is not new in the Chinese collective consciousness of history. What is new is the sense that history, through a miraculous break, does not have to repeat, and that history has a direction that necessarily points to an end. Although some late Qing reformists had already realized that Qing China was then facing a great transformative force that China had not seen in three millennia,[3] their goal was to conserve the dynastic system through economic reform by introducing science and technology from the West without real change of the structure of governance. The Nationalist revolution in 1911 and onwards was largely a political revolution; social revolution was gradual and intermittently interrupted by conflicts among the warlords, and later violently disrupted by the war against the Japanese and the civil war against the communists from 1946 to 1949. Therefore, the new era announced by Hu Feng was the first instance of a self-consciousness that the future would be radically different from what China had gone through – a future full of promises.

However, the moment ushered in by this founding gesture, or more precisely, the moment of a radical historical break, never really opened the possibility the gesture itself "imagines" or promises. Indeed, the poetic discursive gesture itself was a moment full of possibilities; but, at the same time, this moment of radical negation also opened an abyss whose force might be actualized precisely by the acts to cover it up. In other words, this opening must be positivized by "the Object," as Žižek would put it (Žižek, 1989)[4]. Is this not the founding moment of the Durkheimian "sacred:" a moment whose emptiness coincides with its positivization through the image of Mao as a giant statue, which, at the same time, appears to be the subject of knowing? One could easily discern that the negation of time made a clearing for the positive "sacred" whose existence is sustained only by a chain of ceaseless signifiers. This is already clear between the lines of Hu Feng's poem, through the double images of "time begins" and the "giant on the mountaintop:" the emptiness in time is immediately filled in by an image (almost infinitely spatial in the imaginary) of the giant who is "the oceans, … that wants to embrace everything … and to purify everything;" "whose grips hold all the rivers … and commands them to march with him;" and "who wants to light up the infinite universe with its shining waves, happy and pure" (Hu, 1949).

If we follow strictly Durkheim's definition of religion as "… a unified system of beliefs and practices relative to sacred things, that is to say, things set apart and forbidden …" (Durkheim, 1982, p. 129), the moment can be called the pre-religious, a mythical moment when the distinction between the sacred and the profane was emerging or being delineated. The moment was later crystalized in Mao's proclamation of "The Chinese people have stood up!"; and has been repeated in all possible media until today. Already in the moment, it was not hard to glimpse the early signs of the sacred: the leader and the Law of History.

On the other hand, this moment of hope and promise was accompanied by the "real" of the symbolic, by the campaign to suppress counterrevolutionaries (1951–2), Sufan (purge of counterrevolutionaries) movement (1955), and the movements against the "three evils" and the "five evils" (1952–4), which targeted the Nationalist military and government personnel left on mainland, dissidents within the Communist Party, and urban business owners respectively. The campaign to suppress counterrevolutionaries was also the first in post-1949 China where quotas of execution were issued formally and informally to various cities and regions, resulting in at least 700,000 executions. If the long years of wars before 1949 cleared the ground for the moment of historical break, the break itself had to be sustained as the appearance of revolution, which entailed more violence. The violence at the founding moment of the modern totalitarian system seems to be a general rule in both fascism and communism. Arguably, this is entailed by

185

the modern secular theology's central tenet on the state. The very imagery of an omnipotent state (Taylor, 2003), a state as the solution to all problems, functions as the very support for the symbolic order of modern secular deities such as the Nation, Race, Equality, and Laws of History.

The sacred

Any Freudian or Lacanian knows that the repressed returns and that it returns with a vengeance (Freud, 1939; Lacan, 2006). Undoubtedly, the 20th century bore the brunt of such vengeance in its most violent, relentless, and insidious form. One thing we have learned from the 20th century is that a symbolic–ideological break from the past was almost always executed with violence, and that its ideological foreclosure was sustained by the state's monopoly and often arbitrary exercise of violence. The break itself seems fleeting, trivial, and ineffectual in its impacts compared with the gravity of what really happened afterwards, as the act to "realize the symbolic"[5] (Fink, 1995). At least with regard to the Chinese case, one is tempted to say that the real of the power of history's repetition, what Karatani (2008, 2012) calls the "repetition compulsion," overshadows the symbolic gesture. Already in 1916, merely four years after the Nationalist revolution that toppled the Qing Empire, Yuan Shikai, a Qing military general turned revolutionary, had declared himself the Emperor, one last time, the real last emperor of China. This Chinese Empire only lasted for 86 days, which, at first sight may appear as a perfect example for "a dead emperor who does not know he is dead." Or perhaps it is history repeating itself as farce, if one regards the collapse of the Qing Dynasty as a tragedy. As much as this interpretation is appealing to many, Chinese history of the 20th century may be viewed differently from the framework of repetition of history without the deployment of the oft quoted Marxian saying "first time a tragedy and then a farce."

According to the standard discursive deployment, the second repetition that is the farce marks the end of what is repeated. The farce itself is a sign that demonstrates the impotence and death of the power or structure to be repeated. Karatani, as a good materialist and a faithful interpreter of Marxism, insists that "... repetition is possible only in terms of form (structure) and not event (content)." (Karatani, 2012: p. 2) However, as an incisive philosopher, Karatani is not restricted by his faithful adherence to materialism by further including the forms of power that dictate "exchange relations" (Karatani, 2014), namely, the superstructure and the representation, or the political and the ideological as forms of possible repetition. Following this line of argument, the new sacred realm whose deities included the leader, the party, and the mysterious Laws of History that emerged in the early days of the Chinese Communist regime to be imposed onto the much baffled masses whose cultural and cognitive dispositions had been largely shaped by a long past. What was to be repeated?

What emerged from the "blank sheet of paper" in the early years in Communist China were two sets of signifiers that not only signaled the advent of new deities in a new cosmos but prepared the possibility of the return of China's stubborn past. The first set contained abstract notions such as the Laws of History, class struggle, the universal Truth of Marxism and Leninism, and the inevitable communist utopia, whereas the second set featured more concrete images such as the Leader (Mao) as an all-knowing commander of the Laws of History, the Party as the vanguard during class struggles, and the "People" as both the source of Party members and paradoxically the entity led by the Party. The first set, due to its unfamiliarity and abstractness, needed education camps and labor camps to render it real, which only culminated in their destructive explosion of the Great Cultural Revolution 16 years later, after a whole generation of indoctrination. The second set of images included a supreme and impeccable leader who now lived in the Imperial Palace (the West Wing of the Forbidden City), and an all-knowing party, whose high-rank officers had occupied the mansions of the princelings of yesteryears. More importantly, already in the early 1950s any critical comment of members of the Party was considered counterrevolutionary and the Party's power appeared arbitrary in its exercise and in its violence, which often surpassed that of many emperors that belonged to a seemingly irretrievable past. While the two sets of symbols and images comprised the new domain of the sacred, the first set had to be anchored on the second, which provided the imaginaries.

To address the relations between the symbolic and the imaginary, there seems a need to take a detour through Žižek to Lacan. The Lacanian world is structured in three dimensions (or registers): the symbolic, the imaginary, and the real. Without delving too much into the relations between the three registers, it suffices here to refer to Žižek's brilliant and succinct explication using the chess game as his prompt. If all the rules that define a chess game constitutes the symbolic, the naming of the chess pieces as king, queen, and bishop and so on adds the imaginary layer to the game (Žižek, 2006b, p.8). This imaginary element is not superfluous. On the contrary, it is constitutive: it constitutes and supports the chess game as a "battle" between two kingdoms. Without the support of the imaginary, the chess game becomes dry mathematical calculation; without the naming of king, queen, and so on, the symbolic, or the big Other, or the system itself, loses its ideological grip.

Therefore, the symbolic in the sacred domain of the Chinese Communist ideological universe, the master signifiers such as the Leader, the Party, and the people, were sustained by a set of imaginaries that belonged to the past. This is not to argue that there is any resemblance or homology between communism and the Chinese traditional imperial secular theology. What is proposed here is that the imaginaries that sustained the new symbolic order had origins in the past, despite the future-oriented ideological universe. Without the familiarity of the Emperor and his minions, the master signifiers such as the Leader and the Party would lose its ideological efficacy. A true revolution has to undermine the very imaginary support of the symbolic. This, of course, didn't happen in China. In fact, the Chinese regime, including Mao himself, exploited the odd coupling of a "progressive" ideology and a traditional imaginary. Allegedly, it was Mao himself who sanctioned the slogan "Long live Chairman Mao!" for one of the early large parades in Beijing.

It was at the imaginary level that the Chinese Communists repeated, and still repeat, the dynastic shifts with which the Chinese were too familiar, and which seemed cognitively palatable to the Chinese masses. Many signs pointed to such a repetition: the so-called "democratic parties," namely the non-communist bourgeois parties that were yet to be subjected to the control of the new regime in the early 1950s, voluntarily submitted their petitions following the imperialist Confucian vocabulary and procedure; Mao and his state-ranked comrades moved into the Forbidden City, which served as the royal palace for two dynasties; and the regional, ethnic, and religious leaders such as the Dalai Lama were called upon to present themselves at an audience with Mao. Even in the early 1970s, the official slogans issued to instigate people in preparation for a (possible) war with the Soviet Union were almost literal quotes of the first Ming Emperor. Despite the socialist ideological façade, Mao and his comrades understood and conducted their relations and interactions largely in terms of a model of the emperor and his officials.

There were signs of something "new" in the repetition. The real paradoxical situation occurred during the Cultural Revolution, seventeen years after the Communist regime came to power, when the masses were pressured and, in many cases, ordered to perform a "loyalty dance" on a daily basis. The daily rituals were designed to show the masses' love for and loyalty to Mao himself, in front of Mao's portrait-shrine, and to confess their fleeting thoughts of "selfishness." These rituals appeared new since they bore more resemblance to the liturgical performances of, say, the Catholic Church than to the traditional Confucian rites and ceremonies. The Chinese emperors were never treated as gods or God in principle. Instead, they were construed as sons of God, humans to be obeyed, but never worshipped. They could be enlightened or benighted, wise or ignorant, mature or childish, good or evil; they only embodied power and authority, but not divinity. Mao and his Party, however, were not only to be obeyed but to be worshipped. The emperor's subjects and officers only needed to follow the Confucian etiquettes in the presence of the emperor; however, one had to sincerely "want" to grant Mao and his Party not only proper respect but also sincere willingness to make the ultimate sacrifice. It is indeed true, as Žižek points out several times, that within the communist ideological universe the Leader and the Party embody "historical necessity" (Žižek 1989, 2001, 2005); but the real of the Chinese characteristic lies somewhere else – in the imaginary underpinning of the Leader as an emperor more than an emperor. The excess of the communist ideology is that the Leader demands sincere love and loyalty, not merely obedience and formal etiquettes.

The underside of the sacred

In his *The Elementary Forms of Religious Life*, Durkheim (1982 [1915]) already notices the ambiguity of the sacred. He points out that there are two kinds of sacred, the auspicious and the inauspicious, and an object or figure can pass from one to the other domain (Durkheim, 1982 [1915]). More recently, Agamben connects the dots between the ancient *homo sacer*, the sovereign as the exception, and biopolitics. Agamben's *homo sacer* is a crucial juridical figure who "is reduced to bare bodily life and at the same time an embodiment of the originary juridico-political dimension" (Agamben, 1998: p. 19). To examine the Chinese Communist system as religion, one needs to examine the categories the regime uses to classify the members of Chinese society, and the ways in which such categories are maintained in relation to the law or the lack thereof. These categories corresponded to the delineation of the sacred, the profane, and the *homo sacer*, the last of which was the underside of the sacred.

Already in the early days of the Chinese Communist regime, a distinction between the "People" and the "masses" emerged as an element of the communist doctrine to draw the boundaries between the sacred and the profane. The regime started to contrive a categorial scheme based on supposedly Marxist class analysis to classify the Chinese people even before its takeover. The Marxian grand narrative of human history is homologous to the Christian story of "fall-and-salvation" mediated by a savior, in which the emergence of private property marks the fall, the communist world society is the salvation, and the mediating savior is the Communist Party. This narrative, plus Lenin's revision based on Russian society in the early 20th century, served as the social classification system of the Chinese Communist regime. This scheme recognized the lack of capitalist development in China, and consequently sizable classes of urban workers and bourgeoisie; but it nonetheless asserted the vanguard status of the workers, and the Party being a worker's party. Therefore, it appeared ideologically inevitable that the regime had to create three large categories: the trinity of Leader-Party-People, the masses, and the elements to be eradicated.

Thus, the "People" began to signify the supporters of the revolution, and "the masses" a category that included the backward classes such as the peasantry and urban small business owners. The exploitative classes, on the other hand, had to be abolished. In a largely agricultural society, the landowners were defined as an exploitative class, thus likely to be counterrevolutionary; whereas the peasants were allies who needed to be led and educated. Guided by such a system, the regime had finished land reform in the north during the civil war (1946–49), then implemented the same scheme in the rest of the country in the early 1950s. According to Teiwes (1997), "The major steps were a class identification of all village inhabitants, followed by the confiscation and redistribution of landlord land and other productive property" (Teiwes, 1997: p. 35). In addition to 200,000 to 800,000 executions (a higher estimate places the number at 1.5 million) (Tweiwes, 1997, p. 36), an estimated 1.5 to 5 million landowners were sent to labor camps. The ensuing "movements" and purges that ended in 1956 resulted in another million executions targeting the "counterrevolutionaries" (mostly peoples who were employed in the Kuomintang government and military forces). The three-year "socialist reconstruction" (1953–6) not only nationalized most private businesses but also made members of the urban bourgeoisie into a pariah class, a class of parasites. Finally, the "People" could arrive at the scene to legitimize the existence of the Party, which in turn represents "the People;" and Mao, as a marginal member of the first National Party Congress back in 1921, was elevated as the founding father of the Party, who embodied the will of the Party and the "People."

The sacred that emerges from the process features a trinitarian structure with Mao as the creator-father, the Party as the executive team of vanguards, and the People as the revolutionary community. Anything that disturbs the trinitarian structure is regarded as excessive. The trinitarian structure is one of class purity, which paradoxically relies on the excesses the system generates: the exploitative classes and the counterrevolutionaries. The "masses," however, was a precarious and open category, whose boundaries and extension had to be continually redelineated and redefined. Thus, the sacred trinity is sustained by the anti-sacred, which is also part of the sacred, but the inauspicious side of the sacred (Durkheim, 1982 [1915]). Durkheim's treatment of the "impurely sacred" or the "sacredly inauspicious" already recognizes "the inequalities and incompatibilities between sacred things" (Durkheim, 1982 [1915], p. 301). The "masses" in the Chinese Communist categorial system then functions as a category of the profane, the nonsacred: as if the sacred needs a buffer between its own splits. There never appeared an overall category that refers to the set of the anti-sacred sacred, the excess to the socialist appearance. They were of their own specific kinds: the landlord, the rich peasant, the counterrevolutionary, the Rightist (after 1957), and the bad element. Note that "the bad element" is not a general category, and it only refers to criminals, who could be of any class background. As the regime mounts more movements to sustain the appearance of historical progress, more categories were invented with each movement generating its own excesses. In the early years of the Cultural Revolution (1966–8), new categories such as the capitalist liner and the class traitor became official categories to target people of "good" background but perceived as being allied with the wrong fractions.

Symbolically, these categories of excess are necessary to the ideological façade. In the "real" of the symbolic, or the implementation of such an unstable societal program, the inauspicious sacred has to be "set apart and forbidden" (Durkheim, 1982 [1915]: p. 129). It should come as no surprise that the totalitarian systems in the 20th century, both fascist and communist, had to rely on their invention of the camp. In the Chinese case, a person identified by one or more of the categories of excess carries the branding all the time and everywhere. S/he is either in prison if sentenced by the court, or in a labor or reeducation camp if the local public security office sees fit. If s/he survives the prison or camps, s/he is constantly monitored by the "masses" and the local public security office. In the heat of a social movement such as the Cultural Revolution, they become the targets of the "masses," unprotected by the juridical system. During the notorious Red August (August 1966, also known as the Red Terror), 1,772 people in the city of Beijing alone were murdered by mobs of Red Guards. During the same month, in Beijing and Shanghai, the two largest cities in China, the homes of over 100,000 families labeled as members of the bourgeoisie were looted, the spoils of which were later used to fund the expense of the Red Guards with the approval from the highest-ranked leaders (MacFarquhar and Schoenhals, 2008, p.124 and p. 117). This is probably a case whose victims were the closest to Agamben's *homo sacer*: outside any legal protection, economic means stripped away, and killed "*impune occidi,*" without punishment (Agamben, 1998, p. 72).

The communist ideological program and the real of its experiment requires that the "Leader" be the only constant that presided over the purity of the Party and the People. Inherent to the program is a need for the appearance of historical progress, which in turn relies on the very excesses it generates, namely the "bad elements" that belong to the past. As a result, it produced two forms of the inauspicious sacred: the outcast in labor camps and the "*incast*" who lives among and is monitored by the "masses." In his only work solely devoted to the examination of modern totalitarianism, Žižek (2001: pp. 73–5) offers two distinctions between the Nazi concentration camps and the Soviet gulag: in Soviet gulags prisoners were economically exploited out of some pragmatic considerations of the regime; (minimal) resistant acts were still possible in the gulags, but in Nazi concentration camps such acts only existed as a fantasy. Such analysis may be "accurate" but verges on preferring, if not justifying, one to the other. The real reason for the minimal difference between Nazi and communist camps perhaps lies in the differences in their ideological systems: the one based on racial purity had to remove and exterminate the impure; while the one based on the marching of History had to create a minimal semblance of a temporal order in the social space. The presence of the *incast* in China thus functioned to sustain the appearance of historical progress, the "rubbish of history" had to be made visible so that History could march on.

From the sublime to the grotesque: the transition

Because the all-knowing leader is at the center of the whole ideological program, the death of the stand-in of the Master-Leader necessarily destabilizes the regime. Arguably, the downfall of the Soviet Union began in 1956 when Khrushchev condemned Stalin, a moment when the "father" was removed from the trinitarian structure. The mystery of the stability of a trinitarian structure is beyond the scope of this chapter. But empirically at least, once "the Leader" collapses, the "Party" as the instrument of the Leader loses its grip on the masses. The death of the Leader seems to be a crucially dangerous moment for all communist regimes that have existed. Žižek (1989, p. 193) points out that Stalin's claim that the communist is made of special stuff places the communist body in the interspace of its symbolic and bodily deaths, the interspace between the sublime and the real or the grotesque.

Unlike the Soviet Union, the "father" in the Chinese case never really dies. In an act that resembled not only how the Soviets treated Lenin's dead body but also the first Chinese Emperor's (Shi Huang Di) dream of eternal life, and the Pharaonic attempt at resurrection, Mao's body was processed for preservation and placed right in the center of Tiananmen Square, a symbol of the power center not only for the Communist regime but also for the last two dynastic empires. Since Mao was judged "as his coffin lid was closed," as the Chinese would say, as "a flawed but nonetheless great leader," his body was never removed. As Lenin's body was only removed from the Red Square after the collapse of the Soviet regime, Mao's body remains in-between the dead and the living; it functions as the undead in maintaining the regime, a shadow that reminds of the violent past, and paradoxically, a shaky foundation of the power, a figure that shifts between the sublime body of special stuff and the grotesque human carcass.

A fundamental difference between the religion proper and a "secular religion" is that the "sacred" in the religion proper belongs to a different realm from the profane. The profane has its this-worldliness as a defense against the expansion and intrusion of the sacred; as Durkheim makes clear, the "sacred" is often manipulated through acts in the profane for pragmatic reasons and kept away in distance to avoid excessive intrusion. With secular religions such as communism and fascism, the sacred itself is invited to take over this world, only postponed in time. In order to sustain the sacred, its postponedness has to be translated into expansion in space. Just as the 1995 Nikita Mikhalkov movie *Burnt by the Sun* suggests, it is no use to stay away from the Sun, the Sun is everywhere; and it burns everything. What is at stake in the human embodiment of the sacred is the unpredictable shifting in the collective perception between the sacred and the profane: for instance, the sublime of a revolution perceived from a distance could quickly turn into senseless violent acts and demonstration of cruelty if witnessed closely. That is why the perceptions of the preserved bodies of the communist leaders[6] are emblematic of the perceptions of the regimes themselves. The display of Stalin's body in Red Square ended in 1961, marking the beginning of the post-totalitarian phase of the Soviet regime. If we borrow Kantorowicz's (1957) notion of the King's two bodies – a body natural and a body political, the latter of which symbolizes the office divined by God – what was preserved in 1953 was Stalin's political body, or the sublime. What was moved to and buried in a public cemetery in 1961 was the natural body, the grotesque. This shift in perception was a shift in perception of the regime itself.

The Chinese Communist regime repeated the same act. Merely one month after Mao's death, his successor, Hua Guofeng, announced that Mao's body was to be preserved and a mausoleum built in Mao's name. In addition to his gesture of loyalty and the proclaimed assurance that everything would remain the same, he tries to shape his own image after Mao through the propaganda apparatus: another case of a "dead" emperor who didn't know he was dead and an attempt at keeping the dead undead. His public appearance often exposed his desperate and clumsy mimicking of Mao's mannerisms. The shift of Hua's image from a semblance to Mao to a stern-faced grumpy old man happened almost overnight. Two years after Mao's death, everyone except Hua himself seemed to know that he had to go. His removal was gentle and polite compared with the purge in Mao's time, and in compliance with the Party bureaucratic procedures, almost a perfect replication of Khrushchev's removal in 1964. This repetition only arrived when factions within the Party, created by the ruthless and violent purges in the past controlled and managed by the supreme leaders such as Mao or Stalin, emerged after the death of the leader to negotiate for their new places in the power structure. All factions needed to maintain the structure more or less intact. In both the Soviet and the Chinese cases, the factions reached a deal, oftentimes explicitly, on their political safety. That is why no bloody purge happened during the second or third generations of the communist regimes. The challenge, of course, is to conceal the "hole" left by the rejection and condemnation of the supreme leader. A minimal sense of continuity and legitimacy is maintained by the Leader's body. This is why Stalin's body was not removed until 1961, five years after Khrushchev condemned him at the 20th Party Congress; Mao's body remains in his mausoleum to this day.

To conceal the empty place opened in the ideological coordinates by the death of the Leader is no easy task. What happened next is what Weber describes as "disenchantment": the world is no longer "a great enchanted garden" (Weber, 1963: p. 270). Books such as *Mao Zedong Off the Altar*, started to appear in bookstores. However, the political elite, no longer threatened by arbitrary and unchallenged power, had finally reached some equilibrium and started in their collaboration to maintain the façade of the power structure. This is often characterized as the moment of post-totalitarianism, a mode of control that no longer needs sincere passion and loyalty; it merely relies on voluntary dutiful performance of the official rituals. Vaclav Havel (1985) illustrates this mode of power most accurately and succinctly in one image: a greengrocer dutifully hangs out official banners on national holidays but complains about the bureaucracy all the time. As Žižek (1989, 1991) points out repeatedly, the cynical attitude, the distance from the official ideology is the distinctive feature of post-totalitarianism. The display of Mao's body is at best perceived with ambiguity: despite crowds of visitors to the Mausoleum, many out of curiosity, Mao's body is often mentioned as "smoked pork" on private occasions. Arguably, this phase of the post-totalitarian regime features the collapse of the sacred, making the regime's foundation precarious and opening a space for new ideological formulations long suppressed by the regime. The resurgence of the Catholic Church in Poland in the late 1970s and early 1980s and the official narrative of the Chinese nation and Chinese civilization are two such examples.

From inevitability to eternity: the rise of the new deity

To the Chinese Communist regime, the 1980s was an ideological disaster. The Chinese political elite realized that the ideological black hole left by Mao's death had to be patched up with new deities. The economic reform that started in 1978 was an attempt to shift its legitimacy based on revolution to a form based on economic development. Economic reform, however, entailed a rejection of the previous official ideology. In the early years of reform, Deng Xiaoping had to resort to "Four Cardinal Principles," which came with a threat: don't challenge the power of the regime. This threat later became action, in the Tiananmen Square crackdown in 1989. If in the early years of the reform the educated elite was allowed to indulge in some form of examination and criticism with regard to China's politics and Chinese culture, the crackdown in 1989 totally foreclosed the ideological space that was hesitantly and half-heartedly permitted earlier. What is worth noting is that, already in the 1980s, the rise of patriotism-nationalism (like all nationalism, the Chinese version is also termed patriotism) had already intensified through promotion by official media. After the 1989 crackdown ended all the discussions of possible roads, concepts such as "land of the ancestors," the "Chinese nation," and later "the Chinese civilization" replaced the Leader as the new god. By the mid–1990s, a new trinitarian structure had been instated, one that placed the "Nation" at the center, and the Party as the representative of the People and their interests.

This ideological shift, of course, required replacing the Party in relation to the master signifier. The new trinitarian structure features the "land of the ancestors" or "the Nation" as the sacred source of everything Chinese; the Party is now redefined as the vanguard of modernity, representing people's interest most broadly. A noticeable change is that the category of "People" is closed, at least symbolically, to include all Chinese people; and the "Party" became an open category ready to include private business owners and educated elite, who used to be identified as members of the bourgeoisie. The "Leader" retires from the ideological domain and the new generation of leaders are depicted as effective technocrats in promoting economic development. Between 1998 and 2012, the Chinese regime bore more resemblance to a single-party authoritarian system such as Lee Kuan Yew's Singapore or Pinochet's Chile than its own previous incarnation.

Timothy Snyder's (2018a, 2018b) examination of "tyranny" provides two analytical categories of totalitarianism: politics of inevitability and politics of eternity. Although his argument that US politics has been, in a progressive version at least, the politics of inevitability is problematic, the true politics of inevitability is that of the communist experiments in the 20th century: a politics anchored on the inevitable historical progress that promises a perfect end. The fundamental paradox of the communist politics of inevitability is that history, governed by its Law, inevitably leads to the communist world society; but at the same time, historical movement needs to be pushed by the Party. Fascist politics is one of eternity: a nation's eternal cycling of rise and fall. This is perhaps the underlying affinity between the two forms of totalitarianism: both are constituted by placing the sacred in a historical trajectory. The difference is that the sacred for fascism, and Nazism in particular, is the nation or race, which undergoes eternal rises and falls; the sacred for communism is the end of history in the form of a communist utopia. According to Snyder (2018b), Russia has transitioned from the politics of inevitability to one of eternity, where the turning point hinged on the power relay from Yeltsin to Putin. Although the Chinese Communist regime took a different route, the similarity to that of Russia's is uncanny, as if both regimes abide by some mysterious historical law that dictates their historical destiny. The irony is that the historical law imposed by the two largest communist regimes has never manifested even the faintest signs of actualization; but their histories seem to suggest that another mysterious and powerful historical "Law" is at work.

Of course, we must reject the existence of such a historical Law. The transition from politics of inevitability (communism, for instance) to politics of eternity (nationalism) is an outcome of the political elite's success in transforming themselves into a new economic elite. The specter of the totalizing state still haunts both China and Russia. In comparison, the Putin regime has been much more successful in severing its connection with the 70-year horror of the Soviet regime and connecting with an older Russia. In spite of its spectacular economic growth, the Chinese regime appears more vulnerable, because it had proudly presented itself for close to 30 years as the destroyer of the past and tradition. The Party has never comfortably repositioned itself in a nationalistic ideology because of its doctrinal faithfulness to Marxism, a Western worldview.

Modernity, despite its insistent rejection of religion in the names of reason and science, has populated the world with its own deities, and created its own spheres of the sacred and the profane. Paradoxically, the true "secularizing act" was performed by the rise of Protestantism, which erased the difference between the sacred and the profane through a gesture of universal sacralization: everything is always already sacred. Classical liberalism simply continued this gesture: since everything in this world is always already sacred, let us focus on this-worldly affairs. Weber (1992 [1930]) was probably the first to notice the dialectic process of universal sacralization and secularization in his *The Protestant Ethic and the Capitalist Spirit*, albeit implicitly. Modern totalitarianism, at least in its species of communism, reversed this gesture within the domain of the sacred: everything is "inauspiciously sacred" or evil in the world, and a radically new world must be brought about where the distinction between the sacred and profane on longer exists, that is, a classless society. Furthermore, the catastrophe of modern totalitarianism is also a consequence of a century-long obsession (early 1800s to early 1900s) with the fantasy that the state is the solution to all problems, among which economic inequality resulting from capitalist economy is perceived as the evil of all evils. Its ideological deep structure, however, is not new. Modern totalitarianism is not the heir to the truly revolutionary universal sacralization performed by the early Protestants. Instead, it repeats a millennium-old attempt to bring heaven to earth: that is, to bring the sacred to an evil (not profane) world. One consequence of this attempt is an obsession with purity, as there is a constant need to separate the sacred and the profane and to sort out the profane from the evil. Thus, in the cases of "really existed communist societies," the endeavor to bring the sacred into this world turned into obsessive and violent acts of eliminating "demons and monsters" from the profane.[7]

Notes

[1] Milbank, 1990: p.1. Here Milbank draws the distinction between the word of "the Creator God" and the voices of the "finite idol."

[2] Aron (1957) explicitly names Stalinism as a secular religion.

[3] This assessment first appeared in a "Memorial to the Throne" by the then Qing prime minister Li Hongzhang in 1873.

4   The Lacanian object takes different forms in its Žižekian interpretations: an *objet-petit-a*, for instance, refers to the object of desire, which is the excess and the leftover of a symbolic operation. Here the object is understood as a discursive ideological excess that fills in the emptiness of a historical break in relation to a subject.

5   It was Bruce Fink (1995) who injects life into the Lacanian registers of the real, the symbolic, and the imaginary by using terms such as "realizing the symbolic," or "symbolizing the real" in a series of truly brilliant footnotes in his book *The Lacanian Subject*.

6   In the 20th century, the bodies of four communist leaders were preserved. These leaders are Lenin, Stalin, Mao, and Ho Chi Minh.

7   "Demons and Monsters" is a term to refer to counterrevolutionaries, members of the bourgeoisie and so on, during China's Cultural Revolution, namely people who try to resist the movement of the "wheel of history."

References

Agamben, G. (1998) *Homo Sacer Sovereign Power and Bare Life*, translated by Daniel Heller-Roazen, Stanford: Stanford University Press.

Arendt, H. (1973) *The Origins of Totalitarianism*, New York: Harcourt Brace Jovanovich.

Aron, R. (1957) *The Opium of the Intellectuals*, New York: W.W. Norton & Company, Inc.

Aron, R. (2003) *The Dawn of Universal History: Selected Essays from a Witness to the Twentieth Century*, New York: Basic Books.

Bellah, R.N. (1967) "Civil Religion in America," *Daedalus*, Winter, 1967, Vol. 96, No. 1, 1–21.

Berger, P.L. (1967) *The Sacred Canopy: The Social Reality of Religion*, Harmondsworth: Penguin Books.

Castoriadis, C. (1987) *The Imaginary Institution of Society*, translated by K. Blarney, Malden, MA: Polity Press.

Durkheim, É. (1982 [1915]) *The Elementary Forms of the Religious Life*, London: George Allen and Unwin Ltd.

Fink, B. (1995) *The Lacanian Subject: Between Language and Jouissance*, Princeton, NJ: Princeton University Press.

Freud, S. (1939) *Moses and Monotheism*, translated by K. Jones, London, UK: The Hogarth Press and the Institute of Psychoanalysis.

Havel, V. (1985) "The Power of the Powerless," *International Journal of Politics* 15(3–4): 23–96.

Hu, F. (1949) *Time Has Begun: First Chapter*, originally published in *People's Daily*, November 1949, available at www.douban.com/group/topic/4794992/.

Kantorowicz, E.H. (1957) *The King's Two Bodies: A Study in Mediaeval Political Theology*, Princeton, NJ: Princeton University Press.

Karatani, K. (2008) "Revolution and Repetition," *Umbr(a): Utopia A Journal of the Unconscious*, 2008: 133–49.

Karatani, K. (2012) *History and Repetition*, New York: Columbia University Press.

Karatani, K. (2014) *The Structure of World History: From Modes of Production to Modes of Exchange*, translated by M.K. Bourdaghs, Durham: Duke University Press.

Lacan, J. (2006) *Ecrits: The First Complete Edition in English*, translated by B. Fink, New York: W.W. Norton & Company.

MacFarquhar, R., and Schoenhals, M. (2008) *Mao's Last Revolution*, Cambridge, MA: The Belknap Press of Harvard University Press.

MacFarquhar, R. (2011) (ed) *The Politics of China: Sixty Years of the People's Republic of China* (3rd edn), New York: Cambridge University Press.

Milbank, J. (1990) *Theology and Social Theory: Beyond Secular Reason*, Oxford: Blackwell Publishing.

Scheidel, W. (2017) *The Great Leveler: Violence and the History of Inequality from the Stone Age to the Twenty-First Century*, Princeton, NJ: Princeton University Press.

Schmitt, C. (2005) *Political Theology: Four Chapters on the Concept of Sovereignty*, Chicago: University of Chicago Press.

Snyder, T. (2018a). *The Road to Unfreedom*, New York: Tim Duggan Books.

Snyder, T. (2018b), "Vladimir Putin's Politics of Eternity," in *The Guardian* [online], 16 March 2018, available at www.theguardian.com/news/2018/mar/16/vladimir-putin-russia-politics-of-eternity-timothy-snyder [Accessed 28 March 2021].

Taylor, C. (2003) *Modern Social Imaginaries*, Durham, NC: Duke University Press.

Teiwes, F.C. (1997) "The Establishment and Consolidation of the New Regime, 1949–57," in R. MacFarquhar (ed) *The Politics of China: The Eras of Mao and Deng*, Cambridge: Cambridge University Press, pp. 5–86.

Weber, M. (1963) *The Sociology of Religion*, London: Methuen & Co. Ltd.

Weber, M. (1968) *Economy and Society: An Outline of Interpretive Sociology*, Berkeley: University of California Press.

Weber, M. (1992 [1930]) *The Protestant Ethic and the Spirit of Capitalism*, translated by T. Parsons, London: Routledge. Žižek, S. (1989) *The Sublime Object of Ideology*, London: Verso.

Žižek, S. (1991) *For They Know Not What They Do: Enjoyment as a Political Factor*, London: Verso.

Žižek, S. (2001) *Did Somebody Say Totalitarianism? Five Interventions in the (Mis)use of a Notion*, London: Verso.

Žižek, S. (2005) *Interrogating the Real*, R. Butler and S. Stephens (eds), London: Bloomsbury Academic.

Žižek, S. (2006a) *The Universal Exception: Selected Writings*, R. Butler and S. Stephens (eds) New York: Continuum.

Žižek, S. (2006b) *How to Read Lacan*, New York: W.W. Norton & Company.

9

The Heritage Spectrum: A More Inclusive Typology for the Age of Global Buddhism

Jessica Marie Falcone

The seeds for the Foundation for the Preservation of the Mahayana Tradition (FPMT) were planted in the late 1960s when an eccentric Russian American woman traveling in India asked the Tibet-born Lama Yeshe (and his young Nepali-born disciple Lama Zopa Rinpoche) to teach her about Tibetan Buddhism. Lama Yeshe and his disciple – who were in India due to the Chinese occupation of Tibet – soon began taking on students, mostly American and European hippies, backpackers, and other searchers. Since FPMT officially incorporated in 1975, it has grown into something of a transnational Buddhist empire with over 150 centers and projects all over the world. I did fulltime ethnographic research on FPMT between 2005–7 and periodically thereafter (mostly in India, but also at centers and events in the US).[1] FPMT's transnational breadth invites us to dwell upon the issue of enculturation and identity in global Buddhism, and this chapter will address the puzzle of how scholars ought to refer to an increasingly diverse slate of people and practices.

FPMT is currently running study centers for all ethnic groups, monasteries and nunneries for non-Western (for example, Tibetan, Mongolian, Nepali) *sangha* (Buddhist communities), voluntary charitable projects, giant construction projects, educational initiatives, language training efforts, a college in the US, as well as a magazine, and other projects. Although the organization is very diverse, the very large majority of FPMTers are practitioners who were not enculturated into Buddhism growing up. These FPMTers chose Buddhism as adults and thus I would call them "nonheritage Buddhist practitioners" of FPMT's unique transnational Buddhism. As I wrote about FPMT's diverse transnational Buddhist practitioners, I was obligated to engage and struggle with extant categories of Buddhists and Buddhisms in the West. Buddhist scholars have long agonized about how to write about communities of Buddhists, especially outside of Asia, and how to categorize different kinds of Buddhist informants and interlocutors – some of our previous categories are fraught, exclusionary, or inaccurate.

This chapter's critical reflection on Buddhist categories was primarily born from a place of self-criticism and doubt about my own early writing on this topic. While noting its limitations, I used Nattier's three-pronged distinction among Buddhists – "elite," "ethnic," and "evangelical" (1998) – throughout my dissertation on FPMT and its ill-fated Maitreya Project (Falcone, 2010). After doing a talk for a dream job at a public liberal arts college in 2009, I was asked a question that went something like this: "So, you have said that the Buddhist practitioner terminology you are using is imperfect, but you keeping using it anyway. Why haven't you figured out something better?" I remember trying to helpfully explain why Jan Nattier's terminology was at least more precise than many previous terms, but inwardly I cringed, and for years I was haunted by that very sharp, very fair question. How can we write about very different types of Buddhists in the so-called West without holding our noses as we use terms that over-determine ethnicity and race, or rely on other imprecise and problematic terms like "elite" or "convert"? As I slowly edited my dissertation into a book (Falcone, 2018), I challenged myself to work toward a more inclusive and more sensitive way to identify disparate Buddhist practitioners. The "heritage spectrum" is the result of that effort. When I began other projects on transnational Buddhists and Buddhisms that required engaging with the differences acknowledged by the categories – working with Buddhists in Second Life (2010–12 and 2018–20), and a project on a Soto Zen temple in Hawai'i (2015-present) – I found that the heritage spectrum could be usefully applied to other case studies; later in this chapter I explain how this terminology is generalizable and useful for discussing religious practitioners in the context of contemporary global flows.

I am far from the first person troubled by the challenges of categorizing types of Buddhist persons. If not an "ethnic Buddhist" in opposition to an "elite Buddhist," then what? In *Luminous Passage*, Prebish (1999) details and acknowledges some of the complexities of various terminologies. In *Zen in Brazil*, Cristina Rocha spends a section discussing the inadequacies of the existing terminologies, but reverts to using "ethnic" and "convert" (Rocha, 2006: p. 192); that she herself puts these words in quotation marks reinforces the fact that she remains uncomfortable with the terms. Before settling on "Asian immigrant" and "American converts," in reference to Theravada congregants in the US, Paul David Numrich wryly noted, "There is perhaps no completely satisfactory terminology for distinguishing the dichotomous groups in these temples" (Numrich, 1996: p.63). Yet as academics it is our duty to critique ourselves toward more perfect categories. Feminist and decolonial scholarship has long demanded the kind of inclusive rethinking that leads to better, truer work (Smith, 1999).

In his excellent treatise, *Crossing and Dwelling: A Theory of Religion*, Thomas Tweed is vexed by the need to define and categorize "religion," and yet he deems this work a scholarly obligation (Tweed, 2006, p.29). He writes, "... we are called to the task of defining – and to contesting definitions. We are called to offer self-conscious sightings from where we stand, reflexive surveys of the disciplinary horizon. We're called to 'exegetical fussiness'" (p. 33). While much ink has been spilled considering the question, "Who is Buddhist?," that is not the question that keeps me up at night. Like Thomas Tweed (1999), I accept that someone who purports to practice Buddhism is a Buddhist;[2] however, the spectacular diversity of practitioners and practices that are then under that big tent means that in order to comprehensibly and meaningfully write about Buddhists, we must make analytical sense of emergent variation, and we must do so with care. It is not pedantic to listen when the people you hope to write about say that you must choose your words more carefully, lest you write them out of the story by accident.

The first half of this chapter is a detailed assessment of how scholars have engaged with these differences in the past, which takes pains to show why many of these categorizations remain unsatisfying. I will then posit a preferable way forward: instead of the binaries usually used, I propose that we use a heritage spectrum – which can be applied to people and/or institutions – which arrays the signified across a spectrum from heritage through semiheritage to nonheritage by looking at the holistic personal, historical, and cultural context of their engagements. Finally, I turn to the epistemological questions involved with challenging and creating categories as a key aspect of representing others in our scholarly writing.

Categorical erasure

In 1991, nonheritage American Buddhist Helen Tworkov frustrated many readers by suggesting in an editorial that Americans who converted to Buddhism should be credited with doing the work toward founding an authentic "American Buddhism" (Tworkow, 1991). Furthermore, Tworkov went on to later assert that Asian Americans participated in "Buddhism in America," but should not be considered a part of "American Buddhism" (cited in Ames, 1994). These exclusive statements were understandably troubling to many Asian Americans, such as Ryo Imamura, who protested that they should be lauded for also contributing to many forms of "American

Buddhism," and should not be pushed out from under the big tent of American Buddhism writ large in this way (Ames, 1994).

While examining the Buddhist studies literature set outside of Asia, it is not uncommon to see scholars establish a simple differentiation between "Eastern Buddhism" in opposition to "Western Buddhism" (Humphreys, 1977: p. 28), even when both are being practiced in the West: for example, when Prebish contrasts the "Oriental American" Buddhist with "Westerners" (Prebish, 1979: p. 68) or when Skennar distinguishes between Buddhists by calling heritage Buddhists in Australia "migrants" while referring to nonheritage Buddhists as "western adherents" (Skennar, 2010: p. 87). All of the aforementioned definitions exclude Asian immigrants in the West from the category of "Western." As I read through G. Victor Sogen Hori's (1998) discussion of the difference between Zen in Japan and Zen in America, I was flabbergasted to realize that throughout his chapter on "Japanese Zen in America," he was exclusively referring to nonheritage groups of Zen practitioners in the US. Many Zen temples in the US were overlooked in statements like this: "Though there was some literary and academic interest in Zen in the first half of the twentieth century, the first of the serious Zen practice communities did not open in North America until 1959" (Hori, 1998: p. 52). Hori states that no real Zen was practiced in the US until Robert Aitken Roshi – a white, nonheritage, convert to Zen – founded the Diamond Sangha in 1959, but this would doubtless come as a shock to members of the Daifukuji Soto Zen community in Hawai'i whose temple was founded in 1914, or practitioners at the Zenshuji Soto Mission in Los Angeles, California, founded in 1922. In effect, Hori erases older Zen communities like Daifukuji and Zenshuji – which both happened to be majority Asian American – from the "Zen in America" story.

In contrast, in 2001 Coleman distinguishes the two strands of "Western Buddhism" rather more inclusively by noting an "ethnic Buddhism" in contrast to a "new Buddhism" (Coleman, 2001: p. 7), yet he relapses in his narrative exposition when he imprecisely equates "Westerner" with those of European descent (pp. 20–1, 25). Sometimes in Buddhist studies, immigrants and people of color are not explicitly written out, but they are implicitly erased by careless language all the same. For example, Ruth Fitzpatrick wrote a book chapter about "Australian women" doing Green Tara Pujas, but it took five pages for the reader to learn that the make-up of the group was all of "Anglo-Saxon Australian background, except one" (Fitzpatrick, 2010: p. 53) and we never learn if the exception was an Aboriginal person, an Asian Australian, an ethnic Tibetan immigrant, or a woman of some other background entirely. From an anthropological perspective, their enculturation and background matters as we read about the cultural practices at hand.

In Justin von Bujdoss's chapter in *Buddhism and Whiteness*, he very skillfully criticizes structural racism in the West, but arguably his language inadvertently does the work of categorical erasure. He writes:

> It seems that American Vajrayana Buddhism lacks the means of thorough self-reflexive internal theological debate. Perhaps this is partially due to the fact that as a relatively new faith in the United States it has not been fully claimed with authority by its Western practitioners/teachers who worry about having the authority to do so, and the reluctance of Asian lineage holders to let go of the reins and trust their students to self-govern and attend to the needs that exist her on the ground. (von Bujdoss, 2019: p. 220)

As he refers to both "American Vajrayana Buddhism" there, and "American Buddhism" later on the page (p. 220), he is very clearly referring to relatively nonheritage practices as opposed to heritage ones; but as we know there are plenty of Tibetan Americans in the US who practice relatively heritage Vajrayana practices. Why should they be thus excluded? And he clearly means nonheritage practitioners/teachers when he writes "Western practitioners/teachers," which to be fair, is common albeit problematic parlance. I recognize that it is highly likely that I have previously used the category of "Western Buddhists" before in the same way – certainly in speaking, if not in writing – and like von Bujdoss, I did not immediately see the implicit exclusions of such terminology.

There are plenty of writers who have quite understandably bristled when people of color are written out of big tent definitions (Quli, 2009; Hu, 2019), for example, when "[excluding] Asian-Americans from the American 'we'" (Hu, 2019: p. 298). Scholars should be more vigilant that the terms qualifying and regionalizing our Buddhist informants – "Australian," "Western," "American," "British," for that matter – ought never to be written as if they are speaking only of the white majority. Once a reader becomes attuned to the frequency of this imprecise and exclusionary language, one finds that it stymies much writing about Buddhism outside of Asia. Working determinedly toward more inclusive language is our responsibility, and so in the next sections I will dig deeper into problematic Buddhist terminologies, many of which are still in use by scholars today.

Typologies of Buddhist practitioners outside Asia and their shortcomings

While some terminologies differentiate between Buddhists in the West without inherently placing immigrants outside of general definitions like "Western" or "American" Buddhism, even these approaches fail to capture the diversity of Buddhists in non-Asian locales. This section shows that too often race/ethnicity or socioeconomic class are used as the major determining factors of extant Buddhist practitioner typologies. While I acknowledge that such differentiations can have some broad-strokes utility, they are just as often misleading or even offensive.

The language of distinction used in Table 9.1 shows scholars working to make visible substantive sociocultural differences in Buddhist practice. The distinctions are not cosmetic, they are cultural; utterly erasing difference, and just saying, "a Buddhist is a Buddhist is a Buddhist" would be entirely unhelpful from a scholarly point of view. However, if we can be more attentive to the language we use to differentiate between major subcultures of Buddhist practitioners in the era of global Buddhism, it can help us to ask better questions in the future.

Race and ethnicity are often used as categorical markers of Buddhist identity, for example, the categorical use of "ethnic Buddhist" when a writer wants to point toward racial ancestry as a shorthand for differences in belief and practice. In Chandler's work, he notes that Charles Prebish first differentiated between "ethnic" versus "elite" Buddhists in the West (Prebish, cited in Chandler, 1998: p. 24). Jan Nattier, writing about Buddhism in America in 1998, differentiated three major types of practitioners: "ethnic Buddhists," "elite Buddhists" and "evangelical Buddhists" (Nattier, 1998: p. 193). "Ethnic" Buddhists – those whom I would call heritage Buddhists – are "Asian immigrant" (p. 190) Buddhists and their families, and Nattier tells us that this category is defined "primarily by their ethnicity" (p. 190).

Racism in Buddhist spaces is widespread (Suh, 2019). While addressing racism in Buddhism in the US, Jan Willis wrote, "… racism or white supremacy is like the water in which we all swim: some of us are aware of it, others do not notice it or are in denial of its existence. We are all fish swimming in white supremacy" (Willis, 2019: p. viii). Thus, Buddhist studies scholars ought to work harder to make sure that we not compounding this problem in our work by erasing non-white, nonheritage Buddhists in our terminologies. First, the use of "ethnic" to denote heritage practitioners suggests that ethnicity is the sole domain of Asian immigrants and their progeny. The existence of an "ethnic" category implies troubling assumptions: nonheritage practitioners are then presumed "non-'ethnic'" (as if the category is all white, *and* as if all white people lack ethnicity). Wakoh Shannon Hickey astutely made this argument in her work critiquing Buddhist terminologies: "But taxonomies that include an 'ethnic Buddhism' category apply the term 'ethnic' *only* to people who are not white, to presume that whiteness is the norm against which 'ethnic' is measured is another example of unconscious white privilege" (Hickey, 2010: p. 14). "Non-'ethnic'" is often just implied, but religious studies scholar Baroni explicitly designed the

Table 9.1: The "who": some terminologies for practitioners of Buddhism outside Asia

---

"Asian" vs. "American" (Layman, 1976: p. 262)

"Japanese"/ "American-born individuals of Japanese ancestry" vs. "non-Orientals"/ "Americans coming from a Judeo-Christian background" (Layman, 1976: p. 43)

"Orientals" vs. "Caucasians and Black Americans" (Layman, 1976: p. 252)

"Oriental American" vs. "Westerners" (Prebish, 1979: p. 68)

"Asian Buddhists" (p. 369) vs. "white Buddhists" (p. 83)/"Western Buddhists" (p. 368)/ "new American Buddhists" (p. 374)/ "American Buddhists" (p. 379) (Fields, 1992)

"ethnic" vs. "occidental" (Ellwood and Pilgrim, 1985)

"immigrant Buddhist" vs. "Euro-American" (Eck, 1997)

"Asian immigrants" vs. "American converts" (Numrich, 1996)

"Asian immigrants" vs. "(mostly) Euro-Americans" (Prebish, 1998: p. 7)

"ethnic" vs. "elite" (Prebish cited in Chandler, 1998: p. 24)

"ethnic Buddhist" vs. "white Buddhist" (Fields, 1998: p. 196)

"ethnic Tibetan" vs. "American Vajrayana student" (Lavine, 1998: p. 110)

"ethnic Buddhist" vs. "evangelical" vs. "elite Buddhist" (Nattier, 1998: p. 193)

"ethnic"/ "Asian-American" vs. "Euro-American" (Tanaka, 1998: p. 288)

"Asian immigrants" vs. "Caucasian Americans" (early Prebish cited in Prebish, 1999, p. 61)

"Asian American" vs. "Western" (p. viii)/ "non-Asian" (p. 61) (Prebish, 1999)

"Asian immigrant Buddhist" vs. "American convert" (Prebish, 1999: p.63)

"Asian American Buddhists" vs. "new Buddhists" (Queen, 1999: p. xix, p. xxiv)

"Immigrant" (1st generation) & "oldline" ("... Asian Americans, primarily from Chinese or Japanese backgrounds, who have practiced Buddhism in this country for four or five generations") vs. "convert" (Seager, 1999: pp. 9–10)

"cradle Buddhists" vs. "convert Buddhists" (Tweed, 1999: p. 84)

"Eastern" vs. "Western"/"American" (Coleman, 2001: pp. 191–4)

"Asian Buddhists" vs. "convert Buddhists"/ "Western Buddhists"/"Western followers" (Baumann, 2001)

"Asian Australian" vs. "Anglo-Australian"/"convert" (Rocha and Barker, 2010)

"ethnic"/ " 'immigrant,' born Buddhists'" and "western converts" (Bubna-Litic and Higgins, 2010: p. 27)

"immigrant Buddhists" in Australia vs. "Anglo-Australians (that is, those of Anglo-Celtic or European descent)" (McAra, 2010: p. 65)

"migrants" vs. "western adherents" (Skennar, 2010: p. 87)

"Asian Buddhists" vs. "Australia Buddhists" (Rinpoche, 2010)

"Nisei" and "Euro-American" (Ama, 2011: p. 97)

"ethnic or immigrant Buddhists" vs. "convert or white Buddhists" (Cheah, 2011: p. 7)

"Tibetan Buddhist" vs. "non–Tibetan Buddhist convert"/"Western Tibetan Buddhist devotees" (Jacoby and Terrone, 2012: p. 106)

"raised/immigrant" [includes foreign-born converts] vs. "American-born convert" (Leamaster, 2012: pp. 149–50)

"ethnic" vs. "convert" (Leamaster, 2012: pp. 152–3)

"modern Soto Zen Buddhists in Japan and Hawai'i" vs. "American Zen Buddhists" (Tanabe and Tanabe 2013: p. 13)

"traditional" vs. "non-traditional" (Dessi, 2014)

"heritage" vs. "non-heritage" (Falcone, 2015)

"heritage" vs. "nonheritage" [across a spectrum that includes a "semiheritage" category as well] (Falcone, 2018)

"*Tibetan* Tibetan Buddhist teacher" vs. "Anglo- or European teacher of Tibetan Buddhism" (Moeller, 2019: p. 192)

"Asian American heritage communities" vs. "American Buddhist convert groups" (many, but not all, of the latter are deemed "meditation-based convert lineages" (Gleig, 2019: pp. 7-8)

"Immigrant Buddhist communities" vs. " 'American' Buddhist communities" (Vesely-Flad, 2019: p. 79)

---

group "non-ethnic" Buddhists in contrast with "ethnic" Buddhists (Baroni, 2000). There are many non-white, nonheritage practitioners outside of Asia – and there are many white people with meaningful ethnic identities too (Swedish, Italian, Russian, Greek, and so on) – so the use of "ethnic" as an identifier in this context is problematic.

The "ethnic Buddhist" category also oversimplifies the experience of Buddhists of Asian descent. Since some people of Asian heritage in the diaspora were not enculturated as Buddhists, but embrace the tradition later in life, talking of "Asian" or "immigrant" Buddhism is suggestive of kind of selective amnesia about the diversity of Buddhists in the world. Of those who espouse religious identity in Korea today, more self-identify as Christian than Buddhist (Koo, 2010), and thus it is just as likely as not that a particular Korean-American Buddhist is a nonheritage Buddhist. I have met and interviewed many people of Asian descent that chose Buddhism despite the fact that it was not their heritage tradition; they should not be lumped into an amorphous "Asian-American Buddhist" category based solely on their ethnicity, as this undermines the sociological import behind making a differentiation in the first place.

Stuart Chandler's research on Chinese Buddhists in America shows that it is unhelpful to assume that Chinese Buddhists were acculturated into the tradition as the "ethnic" Buddhist category infers, because many Chinese Buddhist immigrants embraced Buddhism only after immigrating to the US (Chandler, 1998). Chandler notes:

Dr. Ted T'ang of the Buddhist Association of Compassion and Wisdom estimates that over half of the Chinese who actively participate in Buddhist associations took the Five Precepts Vow only *after* arriving in America ... A sampling of the membership in several typical organizations indicates that at least a significant minority of Chinese American Buddhists, and probably a majority, had negligible knowledge of Buddhist teachings before reaching the United States ... First-generation Chinese Americans who become Buddhist are not maintaining a directly inherited identity so much as reconstructing one. (Chandler, 1998: pp. 23–4)

Chandler rightly observes that, given the cultural-historical context, the dominant terminologies fail: neither Prebish's "ethnic"/"elite" binary, nor Nattier's ethnic-elite-evangelical terminology works effectively in the case of many Chinese Americans.

I have met many informants in fieldwork settings who reinforced my strong views on the limitations of ethnically determined categorizations. For example, I met with a Korean-American woman at an FPMT center whose relatives were all practicing Christians. Since she was not enculturated into Buddhism, she would best be thought of as a nonheritage Buddhist; her forays into Buddhist practice represented a complex, fraught rupture from her Christian religious upbringing. There are too many people who do not fall neatly into the box suggested by their skin color and ethnic identity to consider these cases irrelevant outliers.

When race matters, such as when critiquing racist practices – when Moeller writes powerfully about structural racism in Buddhist institutions, including her own (Moeller, 2019), for example – it makes sense to discuss race. When racial identity is actually being addressed, such as when a writer is referring to a person's or group's social identity – for example, when saying that Jan Willis, a Black Buddhist, has written about questions that arose during an "African American Buddhist Retreat" (Willis, 2004) – then one must refer to race/ethnicity markers.[3] My point here is simply that racial/ethnic identity should no longer be routinely misused to make overwrought assumptions about the nature and character of a particular Buddhist's beliefs and practices.

Since Jan Nattier's second category, "Elite Buddhists" (Nattier, 1998: p. 193), was predicated on "class background" (p. 189), it is no surprise that it over-determines socioeconomic status. "Elite" carries the baggage of socioeconomic class, as well as the unfortunate association with the notion of "superiority." Are nonheritage Buddhists really best categorized as "elite"? Even if many nonheritage Buddhists are middle-class or wealthy, there are those from socioeconomically disadvantaged backgrounds who find their way to Buddhism too. And is it not just as problematic to use language that implies that "Asian-American" heritage Buddhists are then, by definition, "non-'elite'" Buddhists? There are many economically well-off heritage Buddhists of Asian descent in the US; defining them in opposition to the category of "elite" has some awkward, unintended linguistic consequences. Several Asian Americans I interviewed voiced concern that Asian Buddhists were being defined in opposition to the "elite" category. "'Elite' means better," one Korean American told me with frustration, "so of course they don't want to include us in that."

Some readers may suggest that nonheritage practitioners should just be called "converts." However, the term "convert" is misleading and, more importantly, it has been rejected as a designation by many supposed "converts." For example, many of my nonheritage Buddhist informants were concerned that the term "convert" carries the insinuation that they have given up all other religious activities, which was often not the case. Buddhist informants who were born into Jewish families, for example, generally eschewed the term "convert," as they felt the term would suggest that they have repudiated their Jewish heritage. For example, one of my FPMT informants, a "Buddhist Jew" (or "JewBu"), said that she feels deeply committed to Buddhism and yet balked at saying that she had "converted to" it (as she felt that it would suggest that she had converted away from Judaism). I heard this same argument from a Jewish woman who had become a nun in FPMT; she was ordained and yet, by virtue of her heritage and identity, she firmly rejected the notion that she was a "convert" to Buddhism. I met similar resistance against the use of the word "convert" with a newly ordained FPMT nun from Latin America who was from a Catholic background, and many others like her.

Although Ann Gleig ultimately chooses to use the term "convert" in reference to nonheritage Buddhists, she does so with regret, writing, "The category of convert Buddhism should be adopted cautiously as it has appropriately come under critical academic scrutiny..." (Gleig, 2019: p. 6). Although Thomas Tweed also uses the term "convert Buddhists" in contrast to "cradle Buddhists," he acknowledges the complexity of that appellation by elaborating on the "diverse characters in the story," such as the "not-just-Buddhist, who (if asked) would openly acknowledge dual or multiple religious identities: the Vietnamese refugee who says she is Confucian and Buddhist, the American Zen convert who claims to be both a practicing Buddhist and a religious Jew" (Tweed, 1999: p. 84). In addition, the use of "convert" as a synonym for "nonheritage" erases the experience of those born into nonheritage Buddhist families. The children born to nonheritage Buddhist parents and thus themselves raised in Buddhism – those who may be more accurately called "semiheritage" Buddhists – did not themselves then convert to Buddhism, yet those individuals are often miscategorized as "converts."

Typologies of Buddhist institutions and their shortcomings

Since there are countless divergent kinds of Buddhism being practiced in the West, how do we even begin to parse the institutional differences? There are newer forms of Buddhism that are being vigorously transformed (and sometimes even returned eastward), and those that are more consistent with their antecedents. Categorical distinctions must be understood as simplistic placeholders in deference to the quickly changing landscape of global Buddhism today, but I acknowledge that the differences present a meaningful pattern, and we must write them as such.[4] As an anthropologist, it is intractable to deem any Buddhism more real or authentic than another. Yet scholars have a responsibility to discuss divergent practices and institutions without flattening difference by limply saying, "Buddhism is Buddhism is Buddhism." As one can see from Table 9.2, scholars have been wrestling with how to delineate the difference between Buddhist institutions outside of Asia for years. So how might we write about Buddhist institutions that are different in terms of their relationships to their antecedents? And again, how do we write about difference with care and inclusivity? This section explores the issues with institutional categorizations used in the past in order to think about best practices for inclusively discussing Buddhist institutions outside of Asia moving forward.

First, it would be helpful to elucidate why the institutional differences are anthropologically meaningful. There are many syncretic, hybrid Buddhisms that would be conceived of as quite distinct and alien from their antecedents. For example, "Neobuddhism" is a particular kind of relatively nonheritage Buddhism that works to erase some or all of the traditional elements by separating out the desirable philosophical elements from the cultural elements that some Neobuddhists find objectionable. In Abraham Zablocki's exposition of so-called "Protestant Buddhism," for example, he cites a white European informant who claims a transnational Tibetan Buddhist teaching lineage, yet simultaneously works to instruct his students in a Buddhism that he has cleansed of ritual and culture. Zablocki's informant, "Sven," feels that his modern Tibetan Buddhism is superior to traditional forms, and yet he also claims that he can discern truth through his meditative experiences, including the fact that he knows he was a Khampa warrior in a previous life, and that holy objects have important magical properties (Zablocki, 2008). Zablocki's "Sven" has constructed a type of Protestant Buddhism that Zablocki fairly compares to the classic Orientalist perspective, since both views find merit in a version of Buddhism that tries to extract a philosophy and practice from their cultural moorings.

Neobuddhism has at its root in the Orientalist romanticization of Buddhism by mostly nonheritage Westerners that has emphasized the

Table 9.2: The "what": some terminologies for Buddhist institutions and practices outside Asia

"Eastern Buddhism" vs. "Western Buddhism" (Humphreys, 1977: p. 28)

"Japanese American ethnic" vs. "interethnic" (Kashima, 1977: p.198)

"places primary emphasis on sound, basic doctrines, shared by all Buddhists, and on solid religious practice"/ "stable" vs. "attraction to something new"/"unstable" (Prebish, 1979)

"Asian Buddhism" vs. "emerging American Buddhism" (p. 375)/"American Buddhism" (p. 379) (Fields, 1992)

"Tibetan Buddhism" vs. "American Vajrayana" (Lavine, 1998: p. 107)

"ethnic Buddhism" ("baggage religion") vs. "evangelical Buddhism" ("export religion") vs. "elite Buddhism" ("import religion") (Nattier, 1998: pp. 189–90)

"meditative" vs. "church" and "evangelical" (Albanese cited in Nattier, 1998: p. 321)

"Buddhism in America" vs. "American Buddhism" (Tworkov, 1991)

"ethnic Buddhism" vs. "white Buddhism" (Fields, 1998)

"ethnic Buddhism" vs. "new Buddhism" (Coleman, 1999: p. 92)

"Asian Buddhist group" vs. "non-Asian Buddhist group" (McLellan, 1999)

"ethnic Asian American Buddhism" vs. "Euro-American Buddhism" (Prebish, 1999)

"Asian immigrant Buddhist community" vs. "American convert community" (Prebish, 1999: p. 63)

"Japanese American Zen temples" vs. "Euro-American Zen centers" (Asai and Williams, 1999: pp. 28–9)

"ethnic Buddhist communities" vs. "non-ethnic Buddhist communities"/"haoli Zen" (Baroni, 2000)

"ethnic Buddhism" vs. "new Buddhism" (Coleman, 2001: p.7)

"ethnic Buddhism of migrant enclaves" vs. "new Western Buddhism" (Coleman, 2001: p. 12)

"traditional" vs. "new" (Coleman, 2001, p. 20)

"traditionalist" vs. "modernist" [with the developing possibilities of a third category: a "post-modernist" strand that is nigh "non-Buddhist"] (Baumann, 2001)

"Asian Buddhist communities" vs. "American Buddhist communities" (Steele, 2004: p.76)

"Asian Buddhism" vs. "western Zen"/"Australian Zen" (Barzaghi, 2010)

"Relatively heritage Buddhism" vs. "relatively semiheritage Buddhism" vs. "relatively nonheritage Buddhism" across a spectrum (Falcone, 2018) philosophical and textual aspects of Buddhism, while simultaneously ignoring the way that Buddhism was actually practiced (Said, 1978; Lopez, 1995; Lopez, 1998; Faure, 2004). "Neobuddhist enthusiasts avert their eyes from prayer wheels and other embarrassing signs of 'popular superstition,' raising them up toward spiritual realities of a more sublime nature" (Faure, 2004: pp. 15–16). A Neobuddhist, in Faure's terms, evokes the type of Buddhist who would try to strip away the Tibetanness from Tibetan Buddhism or try to scoop the Japanese culture out of Rinzai Zen. Neobuddhists remain vulnerable to criticism that their judgments about what is "true" or "real" Buddhism smack of Orientalism. On the other extreme, some have misrepresented Tibetan Buddhism by emphasizing only its supposed mysticism or positing that Tibetans are all innately spiritual and peace-loving,[5] or romanticizing only classical Tibetan institutions as "real" Tibetan Buddhism.

While some newer forms of Buddhist practice exist in the extremes, it is far more often a more mixed bag. There are many types of newer Buddhism that represent ruptures from their predecessors that are not blatantly Orientalist. For example, the FPMT may represent a relatively nonheritage form of Buddhism, but it is not strictly Neobuddhist in Faure's terms, since the institutional literature, practices, and discourse are demonstrably supportive of much (though certainly not all) of the aesthetics, ritual, and cultural artifacts of Tibetan Buddhism. Still, in my years of research with FPMT practitioners, it was clear that there were many students in the FPMT family who held Neobuddhist views and sought to take only the philosophical-meditational wheat and leave what they saw as the cultural chaff. When an institution asserts that their singular type of Tibetan Buddhism is the "truer" kind of Buddhism, anthropologists of religion should report that cultural view without conceding the analytical point.

How can we write in legible, meaningful broad analytical strokes about these three very different Tibetan institutions that exist in the state of New York, for example: (1) the Dalai Lama's Namgyal monastery, the seat of the institution in the US that is manned by heritage Tibetan Buddhist monks, and serves "parallel congregations" (Numrich, 1996); (2) an FPMT center that substantially translates and transforms traditional Gelukpa Tibetan Buddhist practice, even while preserving certain cultural phenomena like altars and Tibetan art; (3) Sven's group – as per Zablocki's work (2008) – that has tried to utterly shed Tibetan "culture" from their version of Tibetan Buddhism. Since the differences could not be greater between these many variants of Tibetan Buddhism, we need to be able to represent that in our writing.

Would it work to rely on a modern–traditional binary? Baumann has shown that it is also problematic to view the temples and monasteries of immigrant communities as if they are rigidly traditional. He writes:

Although a marked emphasis is placed on the retention of the transplanted ritual forms of devotional acts such as prostration and chanting, and on the maintenance of the monk versus lay hierarchy, changes and adaptations have nevertheless taken place. This applies to the times of rituals, the performance of festivals, the role of the laity, and much more. Also, more and more, the use of language in gatherings and religious services has become an issue of discussion, especially when the up-and-coming generation is fluent to a large extent in the language of the host country ... Far from being an "object" unchanged and frozen in time, these diasporic Buddhist communities reluctantly or willingly change. They create new, adapted forms of traditionalist Buddhism. (Baumann, 2001)

His solution: focus on type of institution – traditionalist or modernist – rather than the type of practitioner. As his quote shows, he knows very well how complex this is to neatly bifurcate, even on the face of things, and he does note some exceptions (as when some nonheritage Tibetan Buddhists embrace devotional practices or the cultural "mystique" of their lama). I concur with Baumann that understanding institutional norms is a significant factor in working to understanding the contemporary Buddhist landscape. The substantial sociological differences must be distinguished with workable categories in our writing, so in the next section I posit a heritage spectrum along two axes: institutions and practitioners.

The heritage spectrum

A heritage spectrum could serve as a more accurate, complex, and inclusive typology of diverse Buddhist practitioners in America according to the specific contemporaneous cultural context one is representing in their academic writing. Based on their specific "positioned sightings" (Tweed, 2006: p. 167), Buddhist studies researchers can array their interlocutors along two axes: one which evaluates the practitioner and another which tracks the institution. I view the variables as being context specific and flexible enough to accommodate macro and micro comparisons (from global to regional or local levels). The heritage spectrum is flexible enough to be defined anew within the cultural parameters of a particular ethnographic study, but I have defined a "heritage spectrum prime" for the purposes of demonstrating the utility of this heuristic.

On one end of a spectrum, for the purposes of this chapter, a "heritage" practitioner is someone who is enculturated into a particular tradition from at least one side of the family raising them. On the other end of the spectrum, one finds a "nonheritage" practitioner who has adopted a tradition they were not raised in. There are often some people that fall in between whom we could consider "semiheritage." The heritage spectrum for Buddhist practitioners evaluates the extent to which someone was taught their Buddhism by their family, and is therefore focused more on enculturation than ethnicity.

The heritage spectrum allows us to appreciate the variability in the Buddhist enculturations of Rena, Rachel, and Rinchen. Rena is a teenager in Philadelphia who was raised in a Jewish household and practices Buddhism in a relatively nonheritage Tibetan Buddhist institution. I would call Rena a nonheritage Buddhist. Rachel is a woman born in Wisconsin to white parents who studied, prayed and meditated regularly at Deer Park with a Tibetan teacher throughout her childhood. However, Rachel and her family had other religious and cultural influences (for example, Christian grandparents on both sides), and thus, I would call Rachel a semiheritage Buddhist. Rinchen was born in New York City to an ethnically Tibetan family who are dedicated Tibetan Buddhist practitioners, and she had no other meaningful religious influences; thus, insofar as she continues to practice, Rinchen is a heritage Tibetan Buddhist. The heritage spectrum, with its "semiheritage" appellation, makes space for the children of nonheritage parents without awkwardly trying to shoehorn them into "heritage" or "nonheritage" categories (see Table 9.3). Also note that these categorizations are contextual: if Rinchen were to move to Korea and live in a Buddhist nunnery there, then she would still be a heritage Buddhist, but in that context, we might say that she is a nonheritage practitioner of Korean Buddhism.

Along the institution axis (see Table 9.4), one is attentive to the rate of innovation and change within a particular tradition. Anthropologically, I recognize that it is useful to differentiate between a congregation that is teaching newer material – a congregation in the process of figuring things out, making up rules, deciding on institutional rules for laity and sangha – and a congregation that is more or less offering continuity and endurance in the form of a transplanted institution. While I also see the axis definition as a flexible one (so that scholars could zoom in or out, and redefine the

Table 9.3: Heritage spectrum prime: parameters for *practitioner* axis

Heritage: significant cultural-religious enculturation in this particular tradition (in terms of family influences and upbringing)

Semiheritage: relatively partial cultural-religious influence in this particular tradition through family ties or other early life experience, to the extent that one was partially, but never fully, enculturated

Nonheritage: no cultural-religious background/legacy/early enculturation into this particular tradition

Table 9.4: Heritage spectrum prime: parameters for *practice/ institution* axis

---

Heritage: full cultural-religious influence from this particular tradition (with minimal changes over the past hundred years; and if major changes, then still popularly perceived as the mainstream or core form of this particular tradition)

Semiheritage: substantive cultural-religious changes from the precursor tradition have occurred over the past hundred years, and the institution and its practices are somehow seen as being inside the tradition, but outside of the mainstream

Nonheritage: an innovation of the practice that draws upon cultural-religious precursors, but diverges in clear ways from the past, in a manner that it is popularly perceived as being new and/or peripheral to its mainstream antecedent

---

spectrum parameters accordingly), for the purposes of this chapter (and as an institutional heritage spectrum prime), one could define "heritage Buddhism" as a set of institutional practices that have gone through relatively little change over the past 100 years (and/or viewed as mainstream or core versions of that particular strand of a tradition). A relatively nonheritage Buddhist institution would be one that is so innovative that it is popularly perceived as a new Buddhism. Semiheritage Buddhisms would be types arrayed in between and could be seen as institutions or groups that have substantively changed or altered precursor Buddhisms; while they may not be mainstream, they are not seen as so peripheral to be altogether, jarringly, new.

Many Buddhists and Buddhist institutions fit neatly into the "heritage" or "nonheritage" categories, and the rest fall into a "semiheritage" space, which gives researchers and readers the opportunity to learn more, to gain a fuller picture of the social landscape of Buddhist spaces. Semiheritage institutions are comprised of hybrids and mixtures. When an institution does both relatively heritage and relatively nonheritage work, it behooves us to look at the patterns of practice in general terms; in toto, they could be deemed a relatively semiheritage Buddhist institution. For example, I might call the Namgyal Institute, in Ithaca, NY, a relatively semiheritage institution. As I knew it as a practitioner (2002–5 and 2007–9), the Namgyal Institute occupied a charming older home in a residential neighborhood. Its altar rooms were flanked by teaching and gathering spaces, and heritage monks lived in the upper apartments. The Namgyal Institute supported both heritage and nonheritage Buddhisms simultaneously with a schedule that included both *pujas* (acts of worship) that were frequented primarily by the area's relatively robust Tibetan-in-exile community, as well as lectures and meditation sessions that were almost exclusively attended by their nonheritage Buddhist congregants.[6] In this case, the two sets of congregations, heritage and nonheritage, were usually fairly separate, but they did comingle for particular events; though they may have coexisted and occasionally practiced side by side, the two broadly defined sets of "parallel" (Numrich, 1996) congregations made quite different spiritual, cultural, linguistic and educational demands of the resident monastics.

At the home institution – which in this case could be the central Namgyal Monastery in Tibet or the main Namgyal Monastery in exile in India – most monks are heritage Tibetan Buddhists practicing a relatively heritage Tibetan Buddhism. As a fairly new foreign extension of an old Tibetan institution, it was markedly distinct from its antecedents. I learned this from a monk stationed at the Ithaca branch of Namgyal where we met regularly for my Tibetan language lessons. He had lived in Ithaca for several years at that time, but he found the work there to be rather strange and exotic compared to the routines and rhythms of life in the central branch in India where he had been enculturated. Other Tibetan refugees and migrants in Ithaca also told me how very different it was from the temples they had grown up with in Asia: different activities, different schedules, different administration, different programs, and so on. That said, those heritage Buddhists were surely far more comfortable at Ithaca's relatively semiheritage Tibetan Buddhist institution than they would have been at Sven's relatively nonheritage Tibetan Buddhist institution.

The heritage spectrum: zooming out at the big picture

A wide lens view of the heritage spectrum (see Figure 9.1) allows a fuller look at the wide array of transnational Buddhist practice. In my writing, I will try to specify where a practitioner sits in relation to their practice. Since a person might practice at multiple institutions in their life, it is important to take note of the specific context in which a person is practicing when writing about them.

A. When a Cambodian-American woman is practicing at a Cambodian Buddhist temple in Oregon that is very close to what she was enculturated into, she is a heritage practitioner at a relatively heritage Cambodian Buddhist institution.

B. When a Vietnamese-American woman raised in a Christian home (but who has always had a close relationship with her Buddhist grandparents who took her to their temples) embraces Buddhism and begins participating actively at a relatively heritage Vietnamese Buddhist institution, she is a semiheritage Buddhist participating at a relatively heritage Buddhist institution.

C. When Richard – a white American man who was born into a Catholic home – joins the Namdroling Tibetan monastery in Bylakuppe, India, he is a rare nonheritage Buddhist practicing at a relatively heritage Tibetan Buddhist institution.

Figure 9.1: Heritage spectrum – wide lens: practitioner spectrum across the horizontal axis and institutional spectrum along the vertical axis

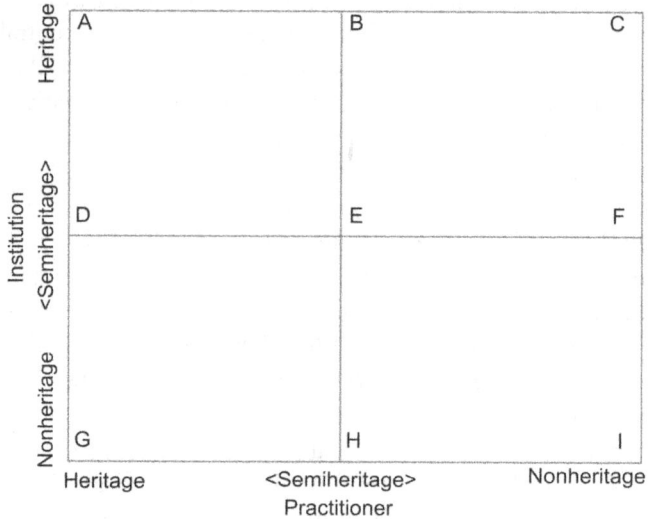

D. When Lobsang, a Tibet-born, Buddhist-raised man currently living in Ithaca, NY, goes to an English-language hybrid puja at the Namgyal Institute in Ithaca, he is a heritage Tibetan Buddhist practitioner engaging in a relatively semiheritage Tibetan Buddhist institutional practice.

E. Katie, an eleven-year-old American, whose parents are both nonheritage Buddhist (born into Christian families), has been brought up regularly attending the Namgyal Institute in Ithaca as her primary exposure to religion. When Katie is practicing at Namgyal, she is a semiheritage Buddhist practitioner at a relatively semiheritage Tibetan Buddhist institution.

F. Raphaella, a woman born into a Jewish family, lives in Ithaca, and attends the Namgyal monastery meditation sessions and guru pujas whenever she can; she considers herself Buddhist and Jewish. Raphaella is a nonheritage Buddhist practicing at a relatively semiheritage Buddhist institution.

G. When Lama Zopa Rinpoche is teaching a highly edited set of practices in English to nonheritage Buddhist students at a US center, the Nepali-born spiritual teacher is a heritage Gelukpa Tibetan Buddhist practicing at a relatively nonheritage Tibetan Buddhist institution.

H. When Soo-hyun, a Korean-American woman who was primarily raised Protestant Christian, but had extensive contact with Buddhist extended family and grew up doing Buddhist rituals, embraces Buddhism as an adult by practicing Buddhism at the Diamond Sangha in Honolulu, she is a semiheritage Buddhist practicing in a relatively nonheritage Buddhist institution.

I. Alex, raised in a Christian family in North Carolina, took refuge at an ecumenical Buddhist center in Asheville; Alex is a nonheritage Buddhist practicing at a relatively nonheritage Buddhist institution.

The macro view is useful for showing that, in the era of global Buddhism, it is important to look at context when describing and writing about Buddhists. In addition, the heritage spectrum can be deployed productively in more narrow contexts by tightening the heritage terminology, for example, to map the diversity of practitioners and practices within a single institution. In the next section, I will demonstrate the utility of the heritage spectrum with a detailed case study of a particular relatively nonheritage Tibetan Buddhist institution FPMT.

The heritage spectrum: zooming in on FPMT

There is a wide variety of practices at FPMT, but taken as a whole (and in contrast to other, more conventional Tibetan Buddhist communities) I deem FPMT a relatively nonheritage Buddhist institution (Falcone, 2018). There are a handful of fairly heritage institutions within the FPMT institutional family – that is, a few separate monastic institutions funded by FPMT – but Buddhist practice in the large majority of the 150-plus FPMT centers is innovative, transformed, and translated. This institutional designation was reinforced to me when talking to heritage Tibetan Buddhists about how alien FPMT events and spaces felt to them. I had countless conversations with Tibetan refugees and their adult children in India (in Delhi, Dharamshala, and Bodh Gaya, in particular), and in the US (in California, North Carolina, and New York) about their involvement with, or opinions about, FPMT; they noted that they were not unwelcome at FPMT centers, yet they tended to find them bewildering, exotic, and strange. In most centers, while a teacher may be a heritage Tibetan Buddhist, the large majority of the devotees were nonheritage Buddhist learners. Occasionally I brought heritage Tibetan Buddhists (usually bilingual, English- and Tibetan-speaking, Indian-born Tibetan refugees), friends, and acquaintances to an FPMT center in India where I was doing research; FPMT's spaces and practices were jarringly unfamiliar to those raised in more heritage Tibetan Buddhist contexts.

In its organizational literature and rhetoric, FPMT's institutional Buddhism often aligns itself with the romantic notion of Tibetan Buddhism as a powerful and mystical tradition but, while some Tibetan culture is welcomed, much of the prayer so central to traditional Tibetan Buddhist practice is rigorously backgrounded in favor of meditation work. While FPMT's version of Tibetan Buddhism is a new tradition, it is no more or less Buddhist than what is practiced in the heritage institution of Sera Je monasteries today (either the one near Lhasa, or the one in south India).[7] The gender-segregated monks at Sera Je in Bylakuppe, India, are learning in the traditional mode, according to "the three acumens,"[8] in which one needs to perfect one's understanding long before engaging in meditation practice. On the other hand, during retreats for its nonheritage clientele, FPMT's Kopan near Lhasa is full of laity (women and men together at that!) learning basic philosophy and doing meditation immediately without first doing any of the prerequisite teachings, memorization, or scholastic debate. FPMT's focus on meditation for laity is a major rupture with mainstream Gelukpa practice.

However, for a scholar writing about a single institution or tradition, there is utility in showing the diversity of practice across the organization. Taken as a whole, FPMT is a relatively nonheritage Buddhist institution, but zooming in shows crucial detail both in terms of practitioner and institutional settings.

J. A Nepali nun practicing Buddhism at the FPMT-funded Khachoe Ghakyil Ling Nunnery is a heritage practitioner at a relatively heritage Buddhist institution.

K. A young Spanish boy, known as Osel today, was born to nonheritage Buddhist parents in Spain and subsequently recognized as a reincarnate lama; while Osel was training at a Tibetan monastery in India, he was a semiheritage Buddhist practicing at a relatively heritage Buddhist institution.

L. When Sally, a Catholic-raised American woman working in Nepal with a rural health nonprofit, goes to the local nunnery funded by FPMT and occasionally practices with them, she is nonheritage Buddhist practicing at a relatively heritage Tibetan Buddhist institutional situation.

M. A Mongolian student, Jargal, who grew up Buddhist who practices at the FPMT center in Ulaanbaatar is a heritage Tibetan Buddhist practitioner engaging in a relatively semiheritage Tibetan Buddhist institutional practice.

N. When Lissie – whose parents took her to FPMT sessions as a kid, in addition to exposing her many other religious groups, like a Hindu ISKCON community, in addition to services at her grandparents' Christian churches – went to Nepal to study at Kopan, she was a semiheritage Buddhist practitioner in a relatively semiheritage Tibetan Buddhist institutional situation.

O. Marianna, the American anthropologist who was not raised as a Buddhist, but practiced at the FPMT center in Ulaanbaatar while doing research, is an example of a nonheritage Buddhist practicing at a relatively semiheritage FPMT context.

Figure 9.2: Heritage spectrum for FPMT: practitioner spectrum across the horizontal axis and institutional spectrum along the vertical axis

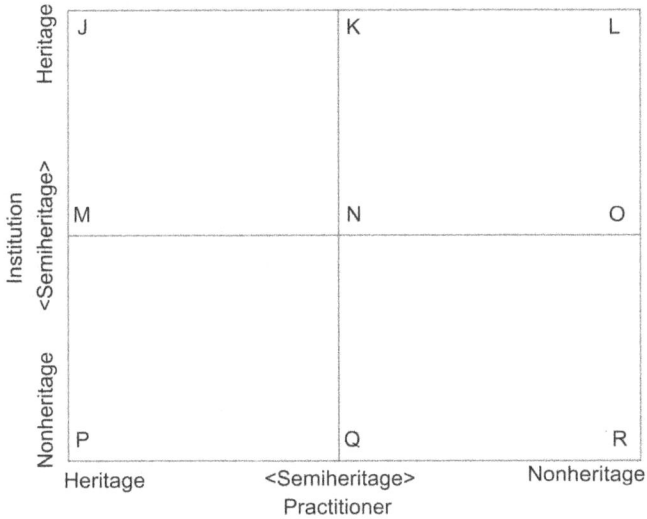

P. When he is practicing with FPMT's Maitripa College in Portland Oregon, Yangsi Rinpoche is a heritage Gelukpa Tibetan Buddhist practicing in a relatively nonheritage Tibetan Buddhist institutional milieu.

Q. When Susan, a Korean-American woman who was raised Protestant Christian, but had extensive enculturation with Korean Buddhist family on her mother's side, fully embraces Buddhism as an adult and heads to a Buddhist retreat at FPMT's Tushita Institute in Dharamshala, she could be deemed a semiheritage Buddhist practicing in a relatively nonheritage Buddhist institutional space.

R. Matt, born into a family of nonpracticing Protestant Christians in Chicago, took refuge with FPMT and goes to regular sessions at their branch in San Francisco, where he lives. Matt is a nonheritage Buddhist practicing in a relatively nonheritage Tibetan Buddhist context.

The large majority of FPMT religious practice aligns with Matt in the R zone of the heritage spectrum laid out in in Figure 9.2, but it would be anthropologically inaccurate to gloss the diversity of practice in this transnational Buddhist community. Even as a relative nonheritage Buddhist institution in sum, the diversity of practices and practitioners is best acknowledged by looking deeper at the case study through the lens of enculturation and innovation. The heritage spectrum is an analytical framework that incorporates, and makes space for, lived religious diversity.

Conclusion

> Categorization is a fundamental and universal process precisely because
> it satisfies a basic need for cognitive parsimony. (Hogg and Abrams,
> 1988: p. 72)

I did not start using the terminology "nonheritage Buddhist" or "semiheritage
Buddhist" while in the field with FPMTers; my categories emerged after
the fact while I tried to accurately represent what I had experienced in
the field. Later, I deployed the heritage spectrum in other contexts – with
Buddhists practicing ecumenical Buddhisms in a virtual community in
Second Life, and at a temple in Hawai'i where I have interlocutors who
fall across the Buddhist heritage spectrum – and it has served me well. My
collaborators have never challenged the heritage spectrum labels I have used
when talking with them, but I find that my interlocutors still tend to call
themselves "Buddhists" full-stop. This self-categorization is perfectly fine ...
until Buddhist scholars start writing about meaningful variation. My hope
is that with the heritage spectrum we have a scholastically useful, culturally
contextualized terminology that would not be deemed exclusionary by
those we hope to fairly represent in our writing.

Defining our terms is one of the most common and fundamental aspects
of academic writing. Who is actually being written about? This can be
surprisingly opaque and fluid: "Even national and provincial censuses
amazingly show that the categories into which people fall change every
ten years. Social change creates new categories of people ..." (Hacking,
1986: p. 163). For example, in academic writing should one use the term
"Hispanic" or "Latino" or "Latinx" (Meraji, 2020)? Should we use the term
"Brown" or "Desi" or "South Asians" or focus on national ancestry (Indian
or Pakistani or Sri Lankan) only (Sircar, 2020)? Anthropologists often trace
the categorical "folk taxonomies" (Fish, 1995) of constructed cultural
categories: race, ethnicity, caste, and even what counts as a fruit as opposed
to a vegetable, for as Ian Hacking rightly observes, "each category has its own
history" (Hacking, 1986: p. 168). In fact, "The very existence of a social,
intersubjective world presupposes our sharing a common vision of objects in
it as 'similar' to or 'different' from one another" (Zerubavel, 1996: p. 431), yet
in each discrete culture we learn through "cognitive socialization" (Zerubavel,
1996: p. 427) precisely how to sort people, things, and ideas in a given time.

Of course, there are different categories of categorization. Richard Jenkins
theorizes that: "There are thus two ideal-typical modes of identification: *self-*
or *group identification* and the *categorization* of others (externally-oriented)"
(Jenkins, 2000: p. 8). As academics writing about culture, anthropologists
conventionally acknowledge two perspectives on their cultural foci: the
emic (the internal sociologics of a culture) and the etic (externally observed

perspectives about a culture). Hacking bifurcates the viewpoints on categorization thus: "One is the vector of labeling from above, from a community of experts who create a 'reality' that some people make their own. Different from this is the vector of the autonomous behavior of the person so labeled, which presses from below, creating a reality every expert must face" (Hacking, 1986: p. 168). The etic vantage point of an anthropology of Buddhism must take into consideration the emic realities of our interlocutors to ensure that our external, "expert" terminologies are cohesive and true, as well as inoffensive and inclusive.

Moreover, as I have asserted that the heritage spectrum is contextual and site-specific, it is more flexible than a typical etic framing. In *Crossing and Dwelling*, Tweed (2006) spends a chapter exploring other people's definitions of "religion" before then pitching his own. As he wrings his hands about the very act of categorization, Tweed thinks through a typology of categories as first defined by Robert Baird: (1) "lexical" definitions that are based on popular usage; (2) "real" definitions as based on empirical truths; (3) "functional (or stipulative)" definitions which are contextual: "stipulative definitions cannot be true or false; they can be only more or less useful" (Tweed, 2006: pp. 33–4). It is in a "stipulative" vein then that I offer the heritage spectrum categories as a flexible corrective to more popular and empirical Buddhist terminologies that have so far disappointed scholars as they have tried to represent transnational Buddhists in the era of global Buddhism. As a functional taxonomy, the heritage spectrum offers contextual value for terms and serves to "cease to think of [them] as the name for a thing and to come to view [them] instead as a *placeholder* for a set of inquiries – inquiries which may be destined never to be resolved" (Nomi Maya Stolzenberg, cited in Tweed, 2006: p.36).

Precision and comprehensibility are only part of what is at stake when academics demand of one another that we define our terms with care. Words have always mattered. There are fascinating disparate experiences, histories, and practices at play in various Buddhist settings that ought not be erased or overlooked, and so we need categories that enable every Buddhist to feel that they are not being carelessly written out of the global Buddhist narrative.

While religion has always already been on the move, globalization and new technologies have sped up the process of religious practices shifting and morphing across boundaries. As Vikash Singh states in the Afterword of this volume, "Religion is also change, responsive to the times and to changing obligations. We see this history happening right in front of our eyes … ." If ever there was a time that religious practitioners could be meaningfully sorted primarily according to racial or national identities, then that time is long past. Inclusivity in terminology is not just an imperative for Buddhist studies: the global flows of religiosity – the movement of religious ideas and people across borders, the establishment of diasporic religious institutions of all kinds, and the changing demographics of various congregations – make this a generalizable lesson for the scholarship of contemporary religious practice. Because reframing toward inclusivity is a part of precise, careful scholarship, religious studies scholars should embrace a more flexible typology of practitioners for the age of globalization, such as the heritage spectrum or another terminology proposed in the future that takes similar care.

Notes

[1] My research was primarily funded by the American Institute for India Studies although Cornell University's Anthropology and South Asia Program made contributions as well. I did participant observation at several FPMT centers in India and followed the planning – and subsequent resistance movement against – FPMT's giant statue plan, the Maitreya Project. I offered collaborators confidentiality so all proper names of interviewees have been changed. Human subjects authorization was granted through the Cornell University IRB process.

[2] Why not use their definitions? It is not that Buddhists have no folk taxonomies – Theravada/Mahayana/Vajrayana, or various schools of thought within a region, such as the Tibetan schools like Geluk, Kagyu, Sakya, and Nyingma – it is that the distinction between Buddhists across the spectrum is often glossed by practitioners themselves. When I was in the field interviewing FPMT devotees and students – those who I here deem nonheritage Buddhists – they usually said something like, "I'm a Buddhist," "Just call me a Buddhist," or "I'm a Tibetan Buddhist."

[3] Scholars must strive toward comprehensibility and accuracy both. As a reader, I get confused when a writer does not make the distinction between the background of the person they are writing about and the type of Buddhism that that person is practicing. For example, when Mushim Ikeda-Nash once wrote, "… the teacher, a Korean Zen monk, occasionally resorted to what he termed 'irritation Zen,' and he would say insulting things to his students" (Ikeda-Nash, 2004: p. 108). Did the "Korean" descriptor refer to type of Buddhism ("Korean Zen"), or rather to the "Korean" ethnicity (and/or nationality?) of the person? Or both? The context of the passage afforded no clues. On the other hand, while clunky, when Moeller referred to a teacher as a "*Tibetan* Tibetan Buddhist" (Moeller, 2019: p. 192), it did serve to more clearly represent the person she was writing about to her readers.

[4] Peter Gregory was on the right track when he protested the provisional use of the two types of American Buddhisms (Gregory, 2001). However, I am less than convinced by his argument that the boundaries would be inevitably blurred to the point that there is no distinction at all; at least for the foreseeable future, we have to wrestle with these distinctions.

[5] These distortions, especially as regards the trope of the Dalai Lama as the embodiment of Tibet, are myths forwarded by nonheritage practitioners and media, but at the same time these fallacies have also been usefully deployed for the benefit of Tibetans working to get the support of the international community as they wait in exile (Dodin and Rather, 2001). The myth is itself is a double-edged sword; it has served to both forward the sociopolitical causes of Tibetan refugees, and simultaneously boxed Tibetan exiles into certain tightly prescribed notions of Tibetan identity (Falcone and Wangchuk, 2008).

[6] My observations of Namgyal in Ithaca are based on my involvement as a practitioner, student, and sometimes community member on and off from 2002–8. I never officially studied Namgyal as an anthropologist; that is to say, Namgyal was not itself a field site.

However, as a graduate student I took intermediate Tibetan lessons there, and attended public talks, events, meditation sessions, and community gatherings.

[7] For more on the variability of monastic traditions over time, please see: Dreyfus, 2003, and Sopa, 1983.

[8] The three acumens (*prajnas*) – "acumen arising from listening," "acumen arising from thinking," and "acumen arising from meditation" – that structure traditional Tibetan Buddhist pedagogy in the Gelukpa tradition (and elsewhere) explain that meditation is just one level of reflection, which must be preceded by other important steps in learning and comprehension (Dreyfus, 2003). The third acumen, actually practicing meditation, is generally deferred indefinitely, or at least until the monk has reached a very senior status.

References

Ama, M. (2011) *Immigrants to the Pure Land: The Modernization, Acculturation, and Globalization of Shin Buddhism, 1898–1941*, Honolulu: University of Hawaii Press.

Ames, D.P. (ed) (1994) *The Wider Shin Buddhist Fellowship Newsletter*, Berkeley: Wider Shin Buddhist Fellowship.

Asai, S., and Williams, D.R. (1999) "Japanese American Zen Temples: Cultural Identity and Economics," in D.R. Williams and C.S. Queen (eds) *American Buddhism: Methods and Findings in Recent Scholarship*, Surrey: Curzon, pp. 20–35.

Baroni, H. (2000) "Haoli Zen: Ethnic and Non-ethnic Zen Communities in Hawaii," for "Lotus in Paradise: Buddhism and Japanese American Identity" event at the Japanese Cultural Center, 31 March 2000.

Barzaghi, S. (2010) "The Journey of a Lay Zen Teacher: 'On a Withered Tree a Flower Blossoms'," in C. Rocha and M. Barker (eds) *Buddhism in Australia: Traditions in Change*, New York: Routledge.

Baumann, M. (2001) "Global Buddhism: Developmental Periods, Regional Histories, and a New Analytical Perspective," *Journal of Global Buddhism*, 2: 1–44.

Bubna-Litic, D., and Higgins, W. (2010) "The emergence of secular insight practice in Australia," in C. Rocha and M. Barker (eds) *Buddhism in Australia: Traditions in Change*, New York: Routledge.

Chandler, S. (1998) "Chinese Buddhism in America: Identity & Practice," in C.S. Prebish and K.K. Tanaka (eds) *The Faces of Buddhism in America*, Berkeley: University of California Press, pp. 13–30.

Cheah, J. (2011) *Race and Religion in American Buddhism: White Supremacy and Immigrant Adaptation*, New York: Oxford University Press.

Coleman, J.W. (1999) "The New Buddhism: Some Empirical Findings," in D.R. Williams and C.S. Queen (eds) *American Buddhism: Methods and Findings in Recent Scholarship*, Surrey: Curzon, pp. 91–9.

Coleman, J.W. (2001) *The New Buddhism: The Western Transformation of an Ancient Tradition*, New York: Oxford University Press.

Dessi, U. (2014) "Religious Change as Glocalization: The Case of Shin Buddhism in Honolulu," in L. Kalmanson and J.M. Shields (eds) *Buddhist Responses to Globalization*, Lanham, MD: Lexington Books, pp. 33–49.

Dodin, T., and Rather, H. (2001) *Imagining Tibet*, Boston: Wisdom Publications.

Dreyfus, G. (2003) *The Sound of Two Hands Clapping: The Education of a Tibetan Buddhist Monk*, Berkeley: University of California Press.

Eck, D. (1997) "Two Buddhisms or One?," in *On Common Ground*, CD-ROM, New York: Columbia University Press.

Ellwood, R.S. and Pilgrim, R. (1985) *Japanese Religion: A Cultural Perspective*, Englewood Cliffs, NJ: Prentice-Hall Inc.

Falcone, J. (2010) "Waiting for Maitreya: Of Gifting Statues, Hopeful Presents and the Future Tense in FPMT's Transnational Tibetan Buddhism," PhD diss., Cornell University.

Falcone, J. (2015) "Our Virtual Materials: The Substance of Buddhist Holy Objects in a Virtual World," in D. Veidlinger and G. Grieve (eds) *Buddhism, The Internet and Digital Media: The Pixel in the Lotus*, New York: Routledge, pp. 173–90.

Falcone, J. (2018) *Battling the Buddha of Love: A Cultural Biography of the Greatest Statue Never Built*, Ithaca, NY: Cornell University Press.

Falcone, J. and Wangchuk, T. (2008) "'We're not Home': Tibetan Refugees in India in the Twenty-First Century,'" *India Review*, 7(3): 164–99.

Faure, B. (2004) *Double Exposure: Cutting Across Buddhist and Western Discourses*, Stanford: Stanford University Press.

Fields, R. (1992) *How the Swans Came to the Lake* (3rd edn), Boston: Shambala Press.

Fields, R. (1998) "Divided Dharma: White Buddhists, Ethnic Buddhists and Racism," in C.S. Prebish and K.K. Tanaka (eds) *The Faces of Buddhism in America* , Berkeley: University of California Press, pp. 196–206.

Fish, J.M. (1995) "Mixed Blood," *Psychology Today*, November–December, 28(6): 55–61, 76, 80.

Fitzpatrick, R. (2010) "Green Tara in Australia: Reassessing the Relationship between Gender, Religion, and Power Relations," in C. Rocha and M. Barker (eds) *Buddhism in Australia: Traditions in Change*, New York: Routledge.

Gleig, A. (2019) *American Dharma: Buddhism Beyond Modernity*, New Haven, CT: Yale University Press.

Gregory, P. (2001) "Describing the Elephant: Buddhism in America," *Religion and American Culture: A Journal of Interpretation*, 11(2): 233–63.

Hacking, I. (1986) "Making up people," in T.C. Heller, M. Sosna, and D.E. Wellbery (eds) *Reconstructing Individualism*, Stanford: Stanford University Press.

Hickey, W. (2010) "Two Buddhisms, Three Buddhisms, and Racism," *Journal of Global Buddhism*, 11: 1–25.

Hogg, M.A. and Abrams, D. (1988) *Social Identification: A Social Psychology of Intergroup Relations and Group Processes*, London: Routledge.

Hori, G.V.S. (1998) "Japanese Zen in America: Americanizing the Face in the Mirror," in C.S. Prebish and K.K. Tanaka (eds) *The Faces of Buddhism in America*, Berkeley: University of California Press, pp. 50–78.

Hu, H. (2019) "The White Feminism of Rita Gross' Critique of Gender Identities and Reconstruction of Buddhism," in E. McRae and G. Yancy (eds) *Buddhism and Whiteness: Critical Reflections*, Lanham, MD: Lexington Books, pp. 193–208.

Humphreys, C. (1977) *Zen Comes West: The Present and Future of Zen Buddhism in Western Society*, London: Curzon Press.

Ikeda-Nash, M. (2004) "Birthing and Blooming: Reflections on the Third Noble Truth," in H. Gutiérrez Baldoquin (ed) *Dharma, Color, and Culture: New Voices in Western Buddhism*, Berkeley: Parallax Press, pp. 107–10.

Jacoby, S. and Terrone, A. (2012) "Tibetan and Himalayan Buddhism," in D.L. McMahan (ed) *Buddhism in the Modern World,* New York: Routledge.

Jenkins, R. (2000) "Categorization: Identity, Social Process, and Epistemology," *Current Sociology*, July, 48(3): 7–25.

Kashima, T. (1977) *Buddhism in America: The Social Organization of an Ethnic Religious Institution*, Westport, CT: Greenwood Press.

Koo, S. (2010) "Religions of Korea Today and Yesterday," *SPICE Digest* [online], Freeman Spogli Institute for International Studies at Stanford, Fall, available at spice.stanford.edu [Accessed 12 December 2019].

Lavine, A. (1998) "Tibetan Buddhism in America: The Development of American Vajrayana," in C.S. Prebish and K.K. Tanaka (eds) *The Faces of Buddhism in America* , Berkeley: University of California Press, pp. 100–15.

Layman, E.M. (1976) *Buddhism in America*, Chicago: Nelson-Hall.

Leamaster, R.J. (2012) "A Research Note on English-Speaking Buddhists in the United States," *Journal for the Scientific Study of Religion,* 51(1): 143–55.

Lopez Jr., D.S. (ed) (1995) *Curators of the Buddha: The Study of Buddhism Under Colonialism*, Chicago: University of Chicago Press.

Lopez Jr., D.S. (1998) *Prisoners of Shangri-La: Tibetan Buddhism and the West*, Chicago: University of Chicago Press.

McAra, S. (2010) "Buddhifying Australia: multicultural capital and Buddhist material culture in rural Victoria," in C. Rocha and M. Barker (eds) *Buddhism in Australia: Traditions in Change*, New York: Routledge.

McLellan, J. (1999) *Many Petals of the Lotus: Asian Buddhist Communities*, Toronto: University of Toronto.

Meraji, S.M. (2020) "Hispanic, Latino, or Latinx? Survey says …" *Code Switch* [online], 11 August 2020, available at www.npr.org/sections/codeswitch/2020/08/11/901398248/hispanic-latino-or-latinx-survey-says [Accessed 19 January 2021].

Moeller, C.J. (2019) "bell hooks Made Me a Buddhist," in E. McRae and G. Yancy (eds) *Buddhism and Whiteness: Critical Reflections*, Lanham, MD: Lexington Books, pp. 181–205.

Nattier, J. (1998) "Who is a Buddhist? Charting the Landscape of Buddhist America," in C.S. Prebish and K.K. Tanaka (eds) *The Faces of Buddhism in America*, Berkeley: University of California Press, pp. 183–95.

Numrich, P.D. (1996) *Old Wisdom in the New World: Americanization in Two Immigrant Theravada Buddhist Temples*, Knoxville: University of Tennessee.

Prebish, C.S. (1979) *American Buddhism*, North Scituate, MA: Duxbury Press.

Prebish, C.S. (1998) "Introduction," in C.S. Prebish and K.K Tanaka (eds) *The Faces of Buddhism in America*, Berkeley: University of California Press, pp. 1–10.

Prebish, C.S. (1999) *Luminous Passage: The Practice and Study of Buddhism in America*, Berkeley: University of California Press.

Queen, C.S. (1999) "Introduction," in D.R. Williams and C.S. Queen (eds) *American Buddhism: Methods and Findings in Recent Scholarship*, Surrey: Curzon, pp. xiv–xxxvii.

Quli, N.E. (2009) "Western Self, Asian Other: Modernity, Authenticity, and Nostalgia for 'Tradition' in Buddhist Studies," *Journal of Buddhist Ethics*, 16: 15–18.

Rinpoche, L.C. (2010) "Challenges of Teaching Buddhism in Contemporary Society," in C. Rocha and M. Barker (eds) *Buddhism in Australia: Traditions in Change*, New York: Routledge.

Rocha, C. (2006) *Zen in Brazil: The Quest for Cosmopolitan Modernity*, Honolulu: University of Hawaii Press.

Rocha, C., and Barker, M. (2010) "Introduction," in C. Rocha and M. Barker (eds) *Buddhism in Australia: Traditions in Change*, New York: Routledge.

Said, E.W. (1978) *Orientalism*, New York: Vintage Books.

Seager, R.H. (1999) *Buddhism in America*, New York: Columbia University Press.

Sircar, A. (2020) "Is the Term 'Desi' Offensive? Some South Asian Americans Think So," *Scroll* [online], 8 December 2020, available at scroll.in/global/975071/is-the-term-desi-offensive-some-south-asian-americans-think-so [Accessed 19 January 2021].

Skenner, J. (2010) "Sydney, A City Growing Within: The Establishment of Buddhist Centres in Western Sydney," in C. Rocha and M. Barker (eds) *Buddhism in Australia: Traditions in Change*, New York: Routledge.

Smith, L.T. (1999) *Decolonizing Methodologies: Research and Indigenous Peoples*, New York: Zed Books.

Sopa, G.L. (1983) *Lectures on Tibetan Religious Culture*, Dharamsala: Library of Tibetan Works and Archives.

Steele, R.M. (2004) "A Teaching on the Second Noble Truth," in H. Gutiérrez Baldoquin (ed) *Dharma, Color, and Culture: New Voices in Western Buddhism*, Berkeley: Parallax Press, pp. 75–80.

Suh, S.A. (2019) " 'We Interrupt your Regularly Scheduled Programming to Bring You This Very Important Public Service Announcement...': aka Buddhism as Usual in the Academy," in E. McRae and G. Yancy (eds) *Buddhism and Whiteness: Critical Reflections*, Lanham, MD: Lexington Books, pp. 1–19.

Tanabe, G., and Tanabe, W.J. (2013) *Japanese Buddhist Temples In Hawaii: An Illustrated Guide*, Honolulu: University of Hawaii Press.

Tanaka, K.K. (1998) "Epilogue: The Colors and Contours of American Buddhism," in C.S. Prebish and K.K. Tanaka (eds) *The Faces of Buddhism in America*, Berkeley: University of California Press, pp. 287–98.

Tweed, T.A. (1999) "Night-Stand Buddhists and Other Creatures: Sympathizers, Adherents, and the Study of Religion," in D.R. Williams and C.S. Queen (eds) *American Buddhism: Methods and Findings in Recent Scholarship*, Surrey: Curzon, pp. 71–90.

Tweed, T.A. (2006) *Crossing and Dwelling: A Theory of Religion*, Cambridge, MA: Harvard University Press.

Tworkov, H. (1991) 'Many is More', *Tricycle*, Winter, 1(2).

Vesely-Flad, R. (2019) "Racism and *Anatta*: Black Buddhists, Embodiment, and Interpretations of Non-Self," in E. McRae and G. Yancy (eds) *Buddhism and Whiteness: Critical Reflections* , Lanham, MD: Lexington Books, pp. 79–97.

von Bujdoss, L.J. (2019) "Excoriating the Demon of Whiteness from Within: Disrupting Whiteness through the Tantric Buddhist Practice of Chöd and Exploring Whiteness from Within the Tradition," in E. McRae and G. Yancy (eds) *Buddhism and Whiteness: Critical Reflections*, Lanham, MD: Lexington Books, pp. 207–27.

Willis, J. (2004) "Dharma has no color," in H.G. Baldoquín (ed.) *Dharma, Color, and Culture: New Voices in Western Buddhism*, Berkeley: Parallax Press, pp. 217–24.

Willis, J. (2019) "Foreword", in E. McRae and G. Yancy (eds) *Buddhism and Whiteness: Critical Reflections*, Lanham, MD: Lexington Books, pp. vii–xi.

Zablocki, A. (2008) *After Protestant Buddhism: Beyond the Modern / Traditional Binary in the Anthropology of Contemporary Buddhism*, Conference Paper from 15th Congress of the International Association of Buddhist Studies (IABS), unpublished.

Zerubavel, E. (1996) "Lumping and Splitting: Notes on Social Classification," *Sociological Forum*, September, 11(3): 421–33.

10

Interpreting Nonreligion

Evan Stewart

What does it mean to be nonreligious? One of the most notable trends in the study of religion today is the growing number of people who claim no religious affiliation. In the early 1990s, only about 7 per cent of respondents to the US General Social Survey would choose "none of the above" when asked to pick a religion. In 2018, about 23 per cent of respondents chose this option.

This trend toward religious disaffiliation has spurred interest across the social sciences – in sociology (Zuckerman, 2011; Hout and Fischer, 2002, 2014; Manning, 2015; Edgell et al, 2006, 2016; Schnabel and Bock, 2017; Frost, 2019; Smith and Cragun, 2019; Thiessen and Wilkins-Laflamme, 2020), political science (Layman and Weaver, 2016; Brockway, 2018), psychology (Silver et al, 2014; Gervais and Najle, 2018), and history (Schmidt, 2016). It is also more than an academic curiosity. When I tell people that I study this group I am often met with a knowing nod or an excited "That's me!" as people realize their own personal experiences fit into a larger social fact.

The unaffiliated are also entering public life, and many different interest groups want to claim them. Organizations like American Atheists and the American Humanist Association talk about this trend as if their ranks are swelling. Faith-based groups take it as evidence they need to redouble their efforts to welcome back disaffected believers who are unsatisfied with religious institutions. The unaffiliated are a substantive portion of the Democratic Party, but some have strong ties to independent or libertarian politics (Cimino and Smith, 2014). One of the most notable nonreligious advocacy groups was even run by a former Republican staffer and center-Right lobbyist.[1]

This wide-ranging research base and public conversation create a challenge for studying the unaffiliated: being nonreligious means many different things to different people. This is an interpretive problem. There are many specific subgroups to study, including atheists, agnostics, people who say they are "spiritual but not religious," and those who call themselves "nothing in particular." There are many traits to study, including demographic and personality characteristics, beliefs, practices, and political views. Finally, there are a range of public frames for making sense of this trend in larger social context. With all this variation, researchers risk making contradictory claims about the unaffiliated that are not harmonized across disciplinary subfields. This makes public commentary about the group increasingly fraught, as any particular framing is likely to be contradicted by new findings from another specific subgroup.

This chapter focuses on how we can improve the study of nonreligion by integrating the interpretive insights of cultural sociology with survey research. We often associate the interpretive sociological tradition with qualitative methods, using interviews and observations to trace out patterns in how people reason through their lives. In contrast, survey questions often face criticism because they seem to lack meaning – probing issues where people lack strong opinions and therefore creating the very attitudes that they claim to measure (Blumer, 1948; Bourdieu, 1979). A new synthesis in public opinion research (Perrin and McFarland, 2011), paired with the insights of interpretive cultural sociology, shows us a way to use survey methods to more accurately reflect the meaning that people experience in their lives. The idea is not to replace qualitative methods with quantitative measurement, but to identify a way that scholars can better use the insights of qualitative findings to substantively improve their quantitative measures.

First, I summarize literature on religious disaffiliation to show how nonreligion means different things to different people. Second, I review the most common approach to addressing this problem in survey research: data disaggregation into subgroups of different kinds of nonreligious people. Disaggregation creates new categories, but problems with the interpretation of those categories can lead to misclassifying nonreligious people in surveys. Third, I propose a different approach using the interpretive tradition that addresses these problems, and I show the benefits of this approach with nationally representative survey data. Drawing on research using cultural approaches to study lived religious practice (Edgell, 2012; Ammerman, 2013), I argue that measuring differences of *magnitude*, rather than differences in *kind*, can better identify respondents who are substantively nonreligious regardless of how they self-identify. Finally, I provide some concluding thoughts about using the interpretive tradition in survey research more broadly.

The interpretive challenge for nonreligion

The study of nonreligion is a complicated terrain of concepts and terms. A few definitions can help. By "secular" I mean things that are part of the finite, contingent, material world. The important challenge for scholars is that people have different definitions for the term "secular," and groups use them interchangeably for their own pragmatic ends (Blankholm, 2014). As a result, "secular" comes to mean everything from a perspective that explicitly rejects religion, to one that relegates it to the private sphere, to one that is simply disinterested in religion altogether.

These varied definitions of secular call for more interpretive attention to nonreligion. By "nonreligion" and "nonreligious," I mean the way that people make sense of their social position outside of, but in relation to, religious institutions, religious authority, and religious belief systems. Following earlier work in the field (Quack, 2014; LeDrew, 2015; Lee, 2012, 2015; Sumerau and Cragun, 2016), this approach highlights the distinctly sociological way that people construct their beliefs and identities in relation to others, rather than assuming that nonreligious people have no engagement with religion at all.

People combine secularity and nonreligion in different ways. We could imagine a person who lives a largely secular life and also develops a nonreligious worldview concerned with larger questions of meaning and moral order (Taves, 2018) outside of religious experiences, groups, and authority (Hägglund, 2019). Another person could become "spiritual, but not religious" (Ammerman, 2014; McClure, 2017), pursuing a sense of transcendence through practices that are not secular. This person could still be nonreligious by maintaining a critical distance from existing religious institutions, even if they combine this nonreligion with practices that indicate lower secularity.

Research examining why people leave religion highlights two patterns that produce different combinations of secular and nonreligious experiences. One treats religious disaffiliation as an active ideological choice, specifically a form of political backlash. Here, people in the US who hold liberal and progressive political views and moderate religious commitments see the close relationship between conservative politics and conservative faith forged by the religious Right and decide that religion is simply not for them (Hout and Fischer, 2002; Putnam and Campbell, 2012; Margolis, 2018). The backlash theory sees disaffiliation as a symptom of political and cultural polarization where social identities increasingly fall in line with partisan preferences (Baldassarri and Goldberg, 2014; DellaPosta et al, 2015; Iyengar and Westwood, 2015; Mason, 2018).

The other pattern treats religious disaffiliation as a more passive process linked to declining participation in civic institutions. While many make the choice to leave religious groups, a growing number of people simply stop attending or never join in the first place. More people in the US are being raised outside of religious groups and growing up with more secular peers, such that each birth cohort appears less religious than the last (Manning,

2015; Voas and Chaves, 2016; Thiessen and Wilkins-Laflamme, 2017). In this way, religious involvement goes the way of volunteering, political activism, and other kinds of civic engagement as people adapt to other structural changes in social life, such as precarious labor and solitary living (Putnam, 2001; Klinenberg, 2013; Pugh, 2015; Kalleberg, 2018). People can leave religious groups without necessarily *opposing* religious groups. They may retain some previous religious beliefs and practices, or they may never develop those beliefs and practices in the first place. The result is a population that is more secular, but neither necessarily nor uniformly nonreligious.

Both accounts are true, but neither tells a complete story. This raises an interpretive problem for researchers. Stories about people who have broken up with religious groups will inevitably clash with stories about those who drifted away, because they result from different experiences. To avoid this problem, most research uses data disaggregation to separate people with different nonreligious experiences.

The typical solution: disaggregation

Much of the current research on religious disaffiliation treats the unaffiliated as a category, the way we would separate different religious denominations. This approach calls for data disaggregation – splitting the broad category of "none" or "nothing in particular" into more finely grained categories that can highlight different kinds of nonreligious experiences and attitudes.

Early work on the topic began with a simple categorical measure: those who select "none" on survey items inviting religious identification (Hout and Fischer, 2002; Vargas and Loveland, 2011). More comprehensive studies include a variety of measures for low religious belief, belonging, and behavior (Keysar, 2014), and later work focused on using these measures to create more categories for different types of unaffiliated respondents. Hout and Fischer's (2002, 2014) analysis of religious disaffiliation finds many people who choose no religious affiliation, yet express belief in God or other religious commitments, leading them to describe a subgroup of "unchurched believers." Baker and Smith (2015) build on this category and find many substantive differences between unchurched believers, atheists, and agnostics. The contrast between identities and beliefs also overlaps. Self-identified atheists exhibit different sociodemographic traits from nonbelievers who do not call themselves atheists (Stewart, 2016; Edgell et al, 2017; Baker, 2020).

Researchers have also studied people who self-identify as "spiritual, but not religious" (SBNRs) (Ammerman, 2013; McClure, 2017). While SBNRs and unchurched believers share a similar skepticism of religious institutions, SBNRs also pursue spiritual practices and meaningful community ties that can provide comparable social goods to conventional religious communities (Besecke, 2014; Mercadante, 2014; Kucinskas, 2019).

Other work focused on the political mobilization of nonreligious people raises a distinction between "active" or "committed" seculars and "passive" seculars (Layman and Weaver, 2016; Brockway, 2018). Here, active seculars treat nonreligion as an "affirmative identification with and commitment to secular views of the world" (Layman and Weaver 2016: p. 276), agreeing with survey items that emphasize the role of factual evidence, philosophy, science, and reason in making moral decisions. Passive seculars exhibit low engagement on conventional measures of religious belief, belonging, or behavior without expressing these ideological affinities.

Integrating many of these findings, Thiessen and Wilkins-Laflamme (2020: p. 78) use five categories to map variation among the unaffiliated: involved seculars, inactive nonbelievers, inactive believers, the spiritual but not religious, and religiously involved believers. The advantage of this approach, as they note, is that it is more substantive – more able to map the rich variation in how people who are religiously unaffiliated understand themselves and their experiences. There are also two persistent challenges to the disaggregation approach, however, and both stem from the interpretive challenge in studying nonreligion.

First is a theoretical problem: new categories create a complicated group of terms to categorize nonreligion that are not harmonized across social science subfields (Lee, 2012). For example, survey items indicating "active secularism" for Layman and Weaver (2016: p. 280) and Brockway (2018) include prompts such as "factual evidence from the natural world is the source of true beliefs," and "the great works of philosophy and science are the best source of truth, wisdom, and ethics." Other work on secular social movements (Cimino and Smith, 2014; Kettell, 2014; LeDrew, 2015) supports this measurement strategy, but with one important caveat: these statements come from *movement atheism*. "Active secularism" can be a useful proxy for this kind of group affinity and ideology, but it does not necessarily capture the considerations that the majority of nonreligious respondents may bring to their political decisions. Putting research on the nonreligious from sociology and political science into conversation shows us how different categories risk capturing only a limited subset of the full range of nonreligious respondents. Social science benefits from research that synthesizes these fine-grained distinctions to provide clear concepts that work coherently across disciplines (Steensland, 2009; Guhin, 2014).

Second is an empirical problem: categorical approaches create classification problems where people who are substantively nonreligious sort into unexpected categories. For example, anti-atheist sentiment is persistent and durable, and research demonstrates that negative attitudes toward atheists "spill over" into attitudes about nonreligion more broadly (Edgell et al, 2016). Researchers have long suspected that many kinds of nonreligious identification, especially atheism, are underreported. Basic descriptive statistics bear this out; in the 2014 Pew Religious Landscape study, about 10 per cent of the US population reported that they do not believe in God, while only about 4 per cent of the population identified as an atheist. One study estimates that the actual proportion of people who do not believe in God could be as high as 26 per cent (Gervais and Najle, 2018). Other work shows that women and people of color are more likely to take on a less-stigmatized nonreligious identity, such as "nothing in particular" or "spiritual but not religious," than a more stigmatized identity like atheist (Edgell et al, 2017; Hutchinson, 2020). Studies that rely on self-identification questions risk missing or misclassifying respondents, even if their substantive beliefs or behaviors match up with more stigmatized identity categories.

Classification problems also happen in the gap between categories that are researcher-defined (etic) and respondent-defined (emic). One example is debate about the validity of "spiritual, but not religious." Nancy Ammerman (2013) challenges this category with interview data that shows people combine spiritual and religious considerations in different ways. Other work defines SBNRs by their skepticism toward organized religious institutions (Besecke 2014; Mercadante 2014). In contrast, McClure (2017) finds SBNR-identified respondents do exhibit unique views of "god" and moral authority that distinguish them from respondents with other religious identifications. Researchers can use the category SBNR meaningfully, but they need to carefully consider the use of this term, rather than assuming both they and their respondents agree on what it conveys.

Finally, classification problems arise from religious switching and what researchers call "liminal nones" (Hout, 2017; Lim et al, 2010). Liminals change their identification from affiliated to unaffiliated over time and across waves of survey panel data. Hout (2017) estimates that liminals comprise up to 20 per cent of the US population because of both actual religious switching (Sherkat, 2014) and error in respondents' reporting of their religious identities. It may not always be appropriate to classify the nonreligious as a coherent group the way one would speak about Catholics or Mormons with this liminality, because categorical typologies risk missing the contingent nature of how these respondents take up religious and nonreligious perspectives.

Categorical typologies are useful for studying nonreligion as a new and growing set of identities. They also create challenges for researchers who are interested in the full range of people who do not affiliate with religious institutions. Not everyone who disaffiliates develops a coherent identity around that disaffiliation. A categorical approach leads to continued debates about definitions and the misclassification of respondents. A different approach grounded in the interpretive tradition provides a way to avoid these problems.

A different solution: the interpretive approach

Following cultural approaches to the sociology of religion, we can avoid problems with meaning and misclassification by treating nonreligion not only as a *difference in kind* the way one would discuss denominational affiliation, but also as a difference of *magnitude*. Quantitative survey research can better reflect the insights of qualitative research by focusing on continuous measures of high and low engagement with different facets of the nonreligious experience.

Cultural approaches to the sociology of religion focus on how people develop a shared sense of meaning in their lives (Swidler, 1986; Sewell, 1992; Lamont and Thévenot, 2000; Eliasoph and Lichterman, 2003). In this perspective, culture is not a static doctrine to which people adhere, but a set of available repertoires of action that they can apply in different social contexts. Research on lived religion, for example, focuses on the way people enact their religious identities and perspectives in everyday life, sometimes inconsistently applying beliefs, behaviors, and identities (for example, Ammerman, 2020). Other research brings in work on culture and cognition to argue that this inconsistency in religious expression is the norm, and that it is a fallacy to expect consistency between religious beliefs, affinities, and practices (Chaves, 2010). Theories of religious complexity argue that religion intersects with other social locations – such as race and social class – and that these intersections change religious expression in social life (Wilde and Glassman, 2016; Yukich and Edgell, 2020). Penny Edgell (2012) calls these approaches a "cultural sociology of religion" – one that foregrounds how people package together different combinations of religious beliefs, affinities, and practices into repertoires of action that fit their social locations.

Interpretive cultural approaches are valuable because they allow us to measure different combinations of intensity at the same time. They allow us to integrate different measures of religiosity into a spectrum of certainty in religious beliefs, frequency of behaviors such as prayer and attendance at religious services, and strength of commitments through personal salience and religious belonging (Davidson and Knudsen, 1977; Cornwall et al, 1986; Wimberley, 1989; Marshall, 2002; Pearce and Denton, 2011). More recently, additional work on Christian nationalism and the public expression of religion has also introduced a new measurement dimension that attends to how people feel religious authority should be integrated into public life (Stewart et al, 2018; Delehanty et al, 2019; Whitehead and Perry, 2020). The important point for my interpretive approach is that any given category (whether Catholic, evangelical, or atheist), will obscure different combinations of high and low intensity that are important for researchers to understand how religion works in the world.

This approach is especially useful for the study of nonreligion. Quantitative research recognizes the need to treat nonreligion as a spectrum, but it often cuts that spectrum into discrete categories and typologies. In contrast, qualitative interview and ethnographic work in nonreligious communities focuses on different practices through which nonreligious individuals take on a variety of identities and act them out in social life (Zuckerman, 2011; Smith, 2013; Beaman and Tomlins, 2015; Cotter, 2015; LeDrew, 2015; Lee, 2015). This work has identified multiple ways that nonreligious people perceive religious others (Guenther et al, 2013; Guenther, 2014; Sumerau and Cragun, 2016), grapple with uncertainty in life (Frost, 2019), develop collective identities through group interaction, and advocate for a secular public sphere (Blankholm, 2014; Kettell, 2014). Across all of this work, researchers have identified how some people fiercely advocate for nonreligious worldviews, preferring a confrontational or combative stance against religion in the public sphere. Others are more accommodating of religious differences and view their nonreligion as secondary to other identities and social commitments. And while many people do develop tangible, discrete identity categories, this work finds that the heterogeneity in meaning systems within each of those categories often makes comparisons across the categories more strained and tentative then we would like to admit.

Focusing on magnitude gives us a window into the meaning people make of their nonreligious experiences. Current typologies of nonreligion often capture differences in personal secularity through beliefs and behaviors, but they often talk around the distinction between those personal aspects and the public implications of nonreligion identified in qualitative work. A person may never outwardly self-identify with any of the nonreligious categories presented, and yet they may neither believe in any god or higher power nor accept the legitimacy of religious claims in the public sphere. Another person may want to maintain a degree of spirituality in her personal life and may welcome the government support of religious charities, but also strongly support the separation of church and state when it comes to legislation over issues such as school prayer. It is possible and necessary for research to map this complexity and avoid the potential classification errors that would exclude any of these people from analysis.

Next, I show the stakes of this approach using two survey datasets. First is the 2014 Boundaries in the American Mosaic Survey (BAM), fielded by the University of Minnesota American Mosaic Project in partnership with GfK with funding from the National Science Foundation (grants numbers: 1258926 and 1258933) and the Edelstein Family Foundation. GfK's KnowledgePanel recruitment is based on online, probability-based sampling (Couper, 2017), which assures that multiple sequential samples drawn from this rotating panel membership will each reliably represent the US population (Yeager et al, 2011). The BAM survey sample was drawn from panel members using a probability proportional to size weighted sampling approach oversampled for African Americans and Hispanics, with a final N of 2,521 respondents.

Second is a 2016 multi-investigator election panel study conducted by the University of Minnesota Center for the Study of Political Psychology (CSPP), fielded by Survey Sampling International (SSI). SSI employs a similar panel methodology to GfK, but recruits participants through online communities and social networks by focusing on demographic groups that are difficult to reach. The CSPP developed a raked survey weight to bring this sample in line with nationally representative benchmarks on race, age, ethnicity, income, gender, and educational attainment. I treat this dataset as a diverse national sample meant to supplement the representative probability sample drawn for the BAM 2014 survey. SSI sampled 6,320 individuals to complete the study, with 3,557 successfully completing Wave One between 1 and 18 July 2016.

Both surveys include the same set of items designed to measure both personal and public nonreligion. To capture personal dimensions of nonreligion, I use Pearce and Denton's (2011) example of the "avoider" repertoire – a common pattern among religiously unaffiliated respondents who disengage from participating in religious groups and no longer see religion as relevant to other spheres of their social lives. I use three items to capture this repertoire: personal religious salience ("How important is your religious identity to you"), attendance at religious services ("How often do you attend religious services?"), and belief in God (in BAM 2014: "Do you believe in god or a universal spirit?," in CSPP 2016: "Which statement comes closest to expressing what you believe about god?"). All of these items use Likert-type response scales, with the exception of the BAM 2014 "belief in god" question, which used Gallup's dichotomous question wording. To improve on this wording and provide a measure that is easier to standardize, the CSPP 2016 survey used the General Social Survey's six-point scale for "certain belief in god."

To capture public dimensions of nonreligion, I use three survey items adapted from Stewart et al's (2018) and Delehanty et al's (2019) studies of public religious expression to capture whether respondents disagree that religion should play a role in fostering good political leadership, good citizenship, and good social interaction with others. Each of these items employed a four-point Likert-type scale ranging from strongly agree to strongly disagree for the following statements: "Religion is important for being a good American," "A president should have strong religious beliefs," and "Society's standards of right and wrong should be based on God's laws." In the analysis below, higher values on all measures indicate stronger *nonreligious* perspectives.

Table 10.1 presents descriptive statistics for all of these individual measures, as well as the proportion of respondents in each survey sample who selected

Table 10.1: Description of nonreligion measures

	CSPP 2016				BAM 2016			
	N=3482				N=2364			
	Min	Max	Mean	SD	Min	Max	Mean	SD
Personal Nonreligion (High values – Low religion)								
Church attendance	1	7	3.27	2.15	1	7	3.50	2.21
Belief in God	1	6	4.81	1.66	1	2	1.11	0.32
Religious salience	1	5	2.59	1.43	1	4	1.91	1.07
Public Nonreligion (High values – Disagree with each)								
Important for being good American	1	4	2.50	1.09	1	4	2.42	1.03
A president should have strong religious beliefs	1	4	2.67	1.02	1	4	2.28	0.93
Society's standards of right and wrong should be based on God's laws	1	4	2.72	1.08	1	4	2.33	1.06
Religious identification								
Affiliated			0.74				0.70	
Spiritual, but not religious (SBNR)			0.06				0.08	
Atheist			0.04				0.03	
Agnostic			0.05				0.03	
Nothing in particular			0.11				0.16	

different options on the question, "What is your current religious preference, if any?" (Response options to this item included Protestant, Catholic, Eastern Orthodox, Mormon, Jewish, Muslim, Buddhist, Hindu, some other religion, spiritual but not religious (SBNR), atheist, agnostic, or nothing in particular). I created composite measures for personal nonreligion and public nonreligion using each set of three items, generating predicted scores from a confirmatory factor analysis model. Both of these scales are centered at the mean, so that each person in each survey sample has a positive score if they express higher than average public and personal nonreligion, and a negative score if they have lower than average personal and public nonreligion. Additional analyses indicated that separating these scores into two composite scales, rather than a single scale for religiosity, is an appropriate choice that fits the data well.[2]

How do these two continuous measures map onto the typical categories that researchers use to measure different kinds of nonreligion? Figure 10.1 compares affiliated and unaffiliated respondents using jittered scatterplots. These plots place each respondent according to their composite scores for personal and public nonreligion. People who selected any religious affiliation are shaded in gray, while people who selected atheist, agnostic, spiritual but not religious, or "nothing in particular" are highlighted in black. We would expect to see a fairly clean break in the plots, with black points clustered in the upper-right hand corner of each plot for respondents who score above the mean in both personal and public nonreligion. This is not entirely the case in Figure 10.1. Instead, we see substantive overlap in affiliation across these scores.

The upper-right quadrant contains respondents who scored above the mean on both factors – those who appear to be substantively nonreligious in terms of their personal preferences and in the vision of the public sphere. It is important to note that many of the respondents in this quadrant maintain some kind of religious affiliation, despite expressing preferences that are ostensibly secular and nonreligious. It may be the case that people maintain a religious affiliation that they were raised in, despite not practicing frequently. They could also be avoiding an explicitly nonreligious identity label due to the social desirability biases discussed above. Or, they may exhibit a pattern of religious expression where they "belong without believing" by maintaining

Figure 10.1: Variation across affiliated and unaffiliated respondents

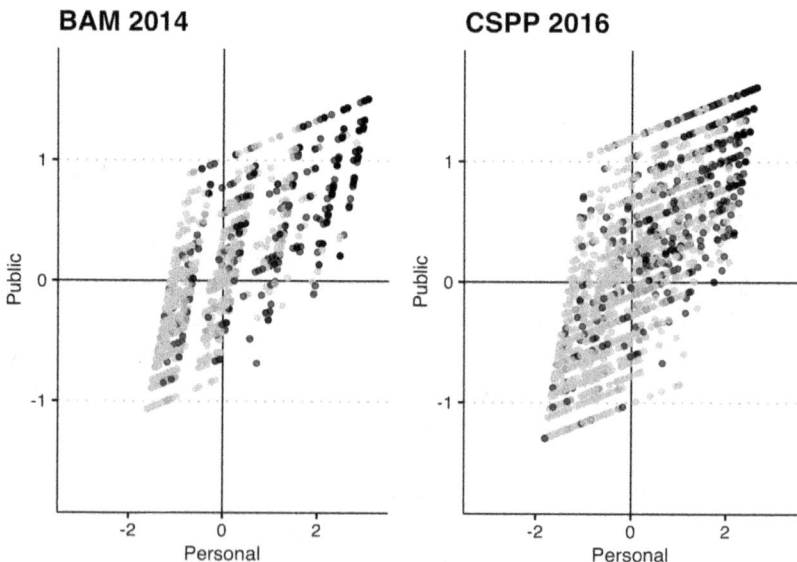

religious ties for community reasons despite their own skepticism of religious authority or doctrine (Kasselstrand, 2015).

Conversely, the bottom-left corner contains respondents who express stronger religious commitments on the factor scores, and here we see a smaller proportion of respondents who report no religious affiliation. For some people, this could be due to simple errors in question response. However, it may also indicate a pattern where people who express strong religious commitments, but prefer a nondenominational affiliation, reject the available identity options in the survey item. In the upper-left hand corner, we see another important subgroup of respondents who report both affiliation and nonaffiliation – those who score below the mean on personal nonreligion (indicating higher religious salience and practice), but above the mean on public nonreligion (indicating a stronger rejection of religious authority in the public sphere). This quadrant indicates the presence of people who appear to have stronger personal religious commitments, but also support a stronger implicit separation of church and state in their views on religious authority.

While the unaffiliated are concentrated in the upper-right hand corner, as we would expect, they are much more evenly dispersed across these three quadrants than the literature typically expects. Overall, Figure 10.1 provides preliminary evidence for the presence of different nonreligious repertoires within the unaffiliated *and within the affiliated,* as each option for identification contains respondents who combine their personal and their public views on religion in different ways. Analyses that focus only on the categorical difference between the affiliated and the unaffiliated risk missing this underlying variation.

Figures 10.2 and 10.3 take these original scatterplots and spread them out across each of the nonreligious categories commonly used by research in the field: atheists, agnostics, spiritual but not religious respondents, and "nothing in particular" respondents. Two important additional patterns persist in these figures. First, there are many respondents who choose "spiritual but not religious" and "nothing in particular" who nevertheless give answers to the religion items that place them in the lower-left quadrant for stronger personal and public religious commitments. While work disaggregating these groups does note that they are more similar to religiously affiliated respondents than to atheists and agnostics (for example, Baker and Smith, 2015), these results show they are part of a second, deeper problem with classification: a substantive proportion of religiously affiliated respondents nevertheless score high enough on each of the nonreligion scales to place themselves in the upper-right quadrant. These are respondents who would be missed in analyses that use a conventional categorical approach; because they picked a religious affiliation, they would be placed into a "religious" comparison group despite the fact that their response patterns are comparable to others in the nothing in particular and spiritual but not religious category. Categorical

Figure 10.2: Variation across nonreligious typologies, 2014

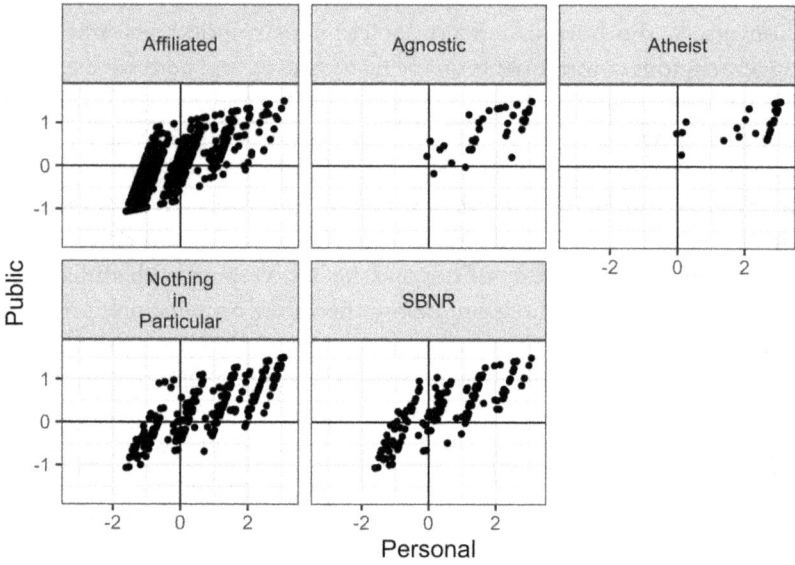

Figure 10.3: Variation across nonreligious typologies, 2016

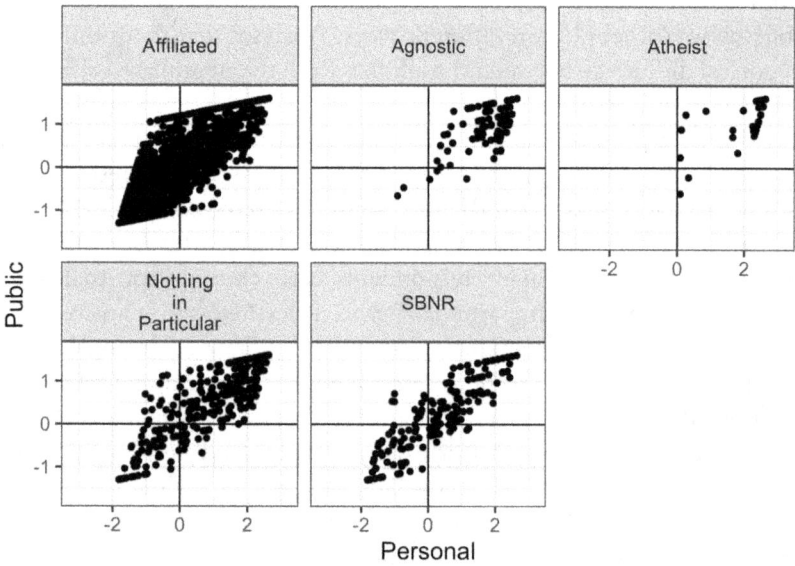

analyses are missing the extent to which low religion is substantively similar to no religion. Only atheists and agnostics, the two smallest groups in the samples, exhibit the kind of codified identities and coherent secular and nonreligious preferences that we would expect from the literature. These results show that their preferences are not reflected in the larger population of religiously unaffiliated people.

Conclusion

These results show the stakes of classification problems for studying nonreligion. The typical approach to sorting nonreligious respondents into categories risks overlooking people who select one identification category but have a response profile that matches another. The result is a muddied comparison between groups where people in the "religious" baseline are substantively nonreligious, and vice versa. A stronger interpretive approach, in contrast, does not assume that researchers and respondents agree on what category labels mean on a survey. By treating personal and public religious commitments as differences in magnitude or intensity, rather than differences in kind, survey researchers can adjust for this interpretive gap in three ways.

First, intensity lets researchers separate distinct measurement constructs and better capture multiple meanings to which interpretive sociology attends. Here, we see the difference in terms of secularism and nonreligion. The unaffiliated in these surveys have both higher and lower scores on measures of personal religious practice (secularity) and public religious expression – a measure of nonreligion focused on how they view the relationship between religious authority in public life. Recent research focusing on this dimension of public religion, both for religiously affiliated and unaffiliated respondents, demonstrates that it has unique explanatory power independent of personal religious commitments (Stewart et al, 2018; Delehanty et al, 2019; Whitehead and Perry, 2020). This research would not have identified this measurement construct had it continued to focus simply on measures of religious belief and practice, rather than engaging in interpretive work to understand what people mean when they invoke religious claims in public life and how that differs from other kinds of religious practice.

Second, this approach helps us better explain in-group variation, which is important for understanding the religiously unaffiliated because they emerge from different processes of active disaffiliation and passive socialization. Interview and ethnographic research shows how unaffiliated people vary widely in their origin stories (Zuckerman, 2011), how they process uncertainty (Frost, 2019), and their demand for meaningful community (Ammerman, 2013). Most importantly, these results show how relatively few unaffiliated people, especially those with stronger personal religious engagement, embrace the strong, consistent identity provided by movement atheism (LeDrew, 2015). In contrast, categories lead us to focus on between-group comparisons, asking questions like "How will the unaffiliated vote?" Interpretive work reminds us that the unaffiliated are not a single category, nor are they necessarily just one or two meaningful subcategories. While we can certainly make between-group comparisons, we also have to validate them to make sure they are not actually better explained by within-group variation.

Finally, interpretive approaches remind us of the value of good sampling and the use of survey research for cultural sociology. Because of high public attention to the New Atheist movement in the early 2000s, influential interview and ethnographic work grounded in the interpretive tradition studied atheism first (for example, Smith, 2013; Cimino and Smith, 2014; Kettell, 2014; LeDrew, 2015) and then broadened to nonreligion in general. Now, larger-sample survey research is demonstrating which insights from this work are generalizable to the larger group of unaffiliated Americans and which are not (Baker and Smith, 2015). Researchers now need to be much more cautious about convenience and respondent-driven sampling through social networks. These results demonstrate unexpected and unexplored pockets of respondents who appear in nationally representative samples but would never be recruited to participate in studies of atheist and secular affinity groups. Unfortunately, those affinity groups are also the easiest to target for sampling and recruitment through nonreligious advocacy groups and social networks, and sometimes preferred as a more affordable alternative to conducting nationally representative surveys.[3] These results show how conventional survey research is particularly useful for interpretive analysis and validating a plurality of different cultural repertoires in the general population (Martin and Desmond, 2010; Perrin and McFarland, 2011).

Research has identified a wide range of nonreligious meanings. If future work does not attend to this variation and continues to focus only on categorical measures of religious disaffiliation, it risks misclassifying respondents due to respondent switching, social desirability bias, and measurement error. One solution to this problem is to treat different aspects of the nonreligious experiences as differences in magnitude, rather than differences in kind. My cultural, interpretive approach to the study of religion and nonreligion considers many kinds of magnitude simultaneously so that we can specify different repertoires of nonreligion – packages of beliefs, practices, and affinities that people develop at different rates of intensity in their lives. It also reminds us that different religious and nonreligious repertoires are not interchangeable. People who are staunchly committed to their personal religious standpoints may not necessarily translate those views into support for religion in the public sphere, while moderately nonreligious partisans who do not attend church often may nonetheless show stronger support for a political candidate with strong religious commitments. Research needs to map out the full range of cultural repertoires of nonreligion to better understand the growing nonreligious population in the US.

Here, I selected two examples of a personal nonreligious repertoire of avoidant religion (Pearce and Denton, 2011) and a public nonreligious repertoire of support for secular authority in the public sphere (Delehanty et al, 2019). There are of course other repertoires of personal and public religion and nonreligion present in the US and around the world that suggest different combinations of beliefs and practices. Some examples include the cultural work in religious progressive movements (Delehanty, 2016; Braunstein, 2017), secular organizing for racial justice (Hutchinson, 2020), a trend toward mindfulness in personal spiritual practice (for example, Kucinskas, 2019) and a focus on the religious provision of social services that motivates religiously affiliated political movements (Davis and Robinson, 2012). Future research should focus on the conceptualization and measurement of these repertoires, but here the focus on avoidant nonreligion and secular public expression provides a measurement strategy for two of the most common nonreligious repertoires among the religiously unaffiliated in the US identified by the literature.

Finally, this work points the way toward a broader synthesis of qualitative and quantitative insights that can improve survey research. In the case of people who are nonreligious, qualitative work tapping different attitudes about the relationship between religious authority and the public sphere highlights an important measurement dimension that improves our quantitative understanding of the uses and limitations of researcher-defined categories. By extending this approach to other fields of research, cultural sociology grounded in the interpretive tradition can do much more to bring disparate methodologies together and improve our understanding of the social world.

Notes

[1] Edwina Rogers, former director of the Secular Coalition for America from 2012 to 2014, has also worked in policy positions for Presidents George H.W. Bush and George W. Bush, and Senator Jeff Sessions, among others.

[2] At issue is whether these items are all informed by the same latent construct for low religiosity or whether they are better measured as two different latent constructs for personal and public nonreligion. I modified an approach by Layman and Weaver (2016) to test this using confirmatory factor analysis. I tested differences in fit between two CFA models. The two-factor model provided a substantively better fit to the data in each survey. While the single-factor model provides a reasonable fit to the data according to the CFI

and SRMR, the two-factor model improves the TLI and the RMSEA past the threshold for what the literature considers an excellent model fit (CFI & TLI > .96, RMSEA & SRMR < .09). Factor loadings across these models also showed how separating personal and public nonreligion provides improved internal consistency on each measure.

3   See here, for example, the United States Secular Survey (secuarsurvey.org) that was a large-sample survey of about 34,000 respondents but recruited through secular social networks. The result is a very large sample that is only representative of people active in these networks (McFarland and McFarland, 2015; Meng, 2018).

References

Ammerman, N.T. (2013) *Sacred Stories, Spiritual Tribes: Finding Religion in Everyday Life*, Oxford and New York: Oxford University Press.

Ammerman, N.T. (2020) "Rethinking Religion: Toward a Practice Approach," *Am. J. Sociol.*, 126(1): 6–51, doi.org/10.1086/709779.

Baker, J.O. (2020) "Race, Gender, and Avowing (or Avoiding) the Stigma of Atheism," in P. Edgell and G. Yukich (eds), *Religion Is Raced*, New York: New York University Press, pp. 58–73.

Baker, J.O., and Smith, B.G. (2015) *American Secularism: Cultural Contours of Nonreligious Belief Systems*, New York: NYU Press.

Baldassarri, D., and Goldberg, A. (2014) "Neither Ideologues nor Agnostics: Alternative Voters' Belief System in an Age of Partisan Politics," *Am. J. Sociol.*, 120(1): 45–95, doi.org/10.1086/676042.

Beaman, L.G., and Tomlins, S. (2015) *Atheist Identities-Spaces and Social Contexts*, Cham: Springer.

Besecke, K. (2014) *You Can't Put God in a Box: Thoughtful Spirituality in a Rational Age*, Oxford and New York: Oxford University Press.

Blankholm, J. (2014) "The Political Advantages of a Polysemous Secular," *J. Sci. Study Relig.*, 53(4): 775–90 doi.org/10.1111/jssr.12152.

Blumer, H. (1948) "Public Opinion and Public Opinion Polling," *Am. Sociol. Rev.*, 13(5): 542–9.

Bourdieu, P. (1979) "Public Opinion Does Not Exist," in A. Mattelart, and S. Siegelaub (eds), *Communication and Class Struggle*, New York: Bagnolet, pp. 124–30.

Braunstein, R. (2017) *Prophets and Patriots: Faith in Democracy Across the Political Divide*, Oakland, CA: University of California Press.

Brockway, M. (2018) "Home on Sunday, Home on Tuesday? Secular Political Participation in the United States," *Polit. Relig.*, 11(2): 334–63, doi.org/10.1017/S175504831700061X.

Chaves, M. (2010) "SSSR Presidential Address Rain Dances in the Dry Season: Overcoming the Religious Congruence Fallacy," *J. Sci. Study Relig.*, 49(1): 1–14, doi.org/10.1111/j.1468-5906.2009.01489.x.

Cimino, R., and Smith, C. (2014) *Atheist Awakening: Secular Activism and Community in America*, (1st edn), New York: Oxford University Press.

Cornwall, M., Albrecht, S.L., Cunningham, P.H., and Pitcher, B.L. (1986) "The Dimensions of Religiosity: A Conceptual Model with an Empirical Test," *Rev. Relig. Res.*, 27(3): 226–44, doi.org/10.2307/3511418.

Cotter, C.R. (2015) "Without God Yet Not Without Nuance: A Qualitative Study of Atheism and Non-religion Among Scottish University Students," in *Atheist Identities – Spaces and Social Contexts, Boundaries of Religious Freedom: Regulating Religion in Diverse Societies*, Cham: Springer, pp. 171–93, doi.org/10.1007/978-3-319-09602-5_11.

Couper, M.P. (2017) "New Developments in Survey Data Collection," *Annu. Rev. Sociol.*, 43: 121–45, doi.org/10.1146/annurev-soc-060116-053613.

Davidson, J.D., and Knudsen, D.D. (1977) "A New Approach to Religious Commitment," *Sociol. Focus*, 10(2): 151–73, doi.org/10.1080/00380237.1977.10570284.

Davis, N.J., and Robinson, R.V. (2012) *Claiming Society for God: Religious Movements and Social Welfare Egypt, Israel, Italy, and the United States*, Bloomington: Indiana University Press.

Delehanty, J., Edgell, P., and Stewart, E. (2019) "Christian America? Secularized Evangelical Discourse and the Boundaries of National Belonging," *Soc. Forces*, 97(3): 1283–306, doi.org/10.1093/sf/soy080.

Delehanty, J.D. (2016) "Prophets of Resistance: Social Justice Activists Contesting Comfortable Church Culture," *Sociol. Relig.*, 77(1): 37–58, doi.org/10.1093/socrel/srv054.

DellaPosta, D., Shi, Y., and Macy, M. (2015) "Why Do Liberals Drink Lattes?" *Am. J. Sociol.*, 120(5): 1473–511, doi.org/10.1086/681254.

Edgell, P. (2012) "A Cultural Sociology of Religion: New Directions," *Annu. Rev. Sociol.*, 38: 247–65, doi.org/10.1146/annurev-soc-071811-145424.

Edgell, P., Frost, J., and Stewart, E. (2017) "From Existential to Social Understandings of Risk: Examining Gender Differences in Nonreligion," *Soc. Curr.*, 4(6): 556–74, doi.org/10.1177/2329496516686619.

Edgell, P., Gerteis, J., and Hartmann, D. (2006) "Atheists as 'Other': Moral Boundaries and Cultural Membership in American Society," *Am. Sociol. Rev.*, 71(2): 211–34.

Edgell, P., Hartmann, D., Stewart, E., and Gerteis, J. (2016) "Atheists and Other Cultural Outsiders: Moral Boundaries and the Non-Religious in the United States," *Soc. Forces* , 95(2): 607–38, doi.org/10.1093/sf/sow063.

Eliasoph, N., and Lichterman, P. (2003) "Culture in Interaction," *Am. J. Sociol.*, 108(4): 735–94, doi.org/10.1086/367920.

Frost, J. (2019) "Certainty, Uncertainty, or Indifference? Examining Variation in the Identity Narratives of Nonreligious Americans," *Am. Sociol. Rev.*, 84(5): 828–50, doi.org/10.1177/0003122419871957.

Gervais, W.M., and Najle, M.B. (2018) "How Many Atheists Are There?" *Soc. Psychol. Personal. Sci.*, 9(1): 3–10, doi.org/10.1177/1948550617707015.

Guenther, K.M. (2014) "Bounded by Disbelief: How Atheists in the United States Differentiate themselves from Religious Believers," *J. Contemp. Relig.*, 29(1): 1–16, doi.org/10.1080/13537903.2014.864795.

Guenther, K.M., Mulligan, K. and Papp, C. (2013) "From the Outside In: Crossing Boundaries to Build Collective Identity in the New Atheist Movement," *Soc. Probl.*, 60(4): 457–75.

Guhin, J. (2014) "Religion as Site Rather Than Religion as Category: On the Sociology of Religion's Export Problem," *Sociol. Relig.*, 75(4): 579–93.

Hägglund, M. (2019) *This Life: Secular Faith and Spiritual Freedom* (1st edn), New York: Pantheon Books.

Hout, M. (2017) "Religious Ambivalence, Liminality, and the Increase of No Religious Preference in the United States, 2006–2014," *J. Sci. Study Relig.*, 56(1): 52–63, doi.org/10.1111/jssr.12314.

Hout, M., and Fischer, C.S. (2002) "Why More Americans Have No Religious Preference: Politics and Generations," *Am. Sociol. Rev.*, 67: 165–90, doi.org/10.2307/3088891.

Hout, M., and Fischer, C.S. (2014) "Explaining Why More Americans Have No Religious Preference: Political Backlash and Generational Succession, 1987–2012," *Sociol. Sci.*, 1: 423–47, doi.org/10.15195/v1.a24.

Hutchinson, S. (2020) "Intersectional Politics among Atheists and Humanists of Color," in: P. Edgell and G. Yukich (eds), *Religion Is Raced*, New York: New York University Press, pp. 58–73.

Iyengar, S., and Westwood, S.J. (2015) "Fear and Loathing across Party Lines: New Evidence on Group Polarization," *Am. J. Polit. Sci.*, 59(3): 690–707, doi.org/10.1111/ajps.12152.

Kalleberg, A.L. (2018) *Precarious Lives: Job Insecurity and Well-being in Rich Democracies*, Cambridge, UK and Medford, MA: Polity Press.

Kasselstrand, I. (2015) "Nonbelievers in the Church: A Study of Cultural Religion in Sweden," *Sociol. Relig.*, 76(3): 275–94.

Kettell, S. (2014) "Divided We Stand: The Politics of the Atheist Movement in the United States," *J. Contemp. Relig.*, 29(3): 377–91, doi.org/10.1080/13537903.2014.945722.

Keysar, A. (2014) "Shifts Along the American Religious-Secular Spectrum," *Secul. Nonreligion*, 3 doi.org/10.5334/snr.am.

Klinenberg, E. (2013) *Going Solo: The Extraordinary Rise and Surprising Appeal of Living Alone*, New York: Penguin.

Kucinskas, J. (2019) *The Mindful Elite: Mobilizing from the Inside Out*, New York: Oxford University Press.

Lamont, M., and Thévenot, L. (eds) (2000) *Rethinking Comparative Cultural Sociology: Repertoires of Evaluation in France and the United States, Cambridge Cultural Social Studies*, Cambridge and New York: Cambridge University Press.

Layman, G.C., and Weaver, C.L. (2016) "Religion and Secularism among American Party Activists," *Polit. Relig.*, 9(2): 271–95.

LeDrew, S. (2015) *The Evolution of Atheism: The Politics of a Modern Movement*, New York: Oxford University Press.

Lee, L. (2012) "Research Note: Talking about a Revolution: Terminology for the New Field of Non-religion Studies," *J. Contemp. Relig.*, 27(1): 129–39, doi.org/10.1080/13537903.2012.642742.

Lee, L. (2015) *Recognizing the Non-religious: Reimagining the Secular* (1st edn), Oxford: Oxford University Press.

Lim, C., MacGregor, C.A., and Putnam, R.D. (2010) "Secular and Liminal: Discovering Heterogeneity Among Religious Nones," *J. Sci. Study Relig.*, 49(4): 596–618.

Manning, C. (2015) *Losing Our Religion: How Unaffiliated Parents are Raising their Children, Secular Studies*, New York: NYU Press.

Margolis, M.F. (2018) *From Politics to the Pews: How Partisanship and the Political Environment Shape Religious Identity, Chicago Studies in American Politics*, Chicago and London: University of Chicago Press.

Marshall, D.A. (2002) "Behavior, Belonging, and Belief: A Theory of Ritual Practice," *Sociol. Theory*, 20(3): 360–80.

Martin, J.L., and Desmond, M. (2010) "Political Position and Social Knowledge," *Sociol. Forum*, 25(1), 1–26, doi.org/10.1111/j.1573-7861.2009.01154.x.

Mason, L. (2018) *Uncivil Agreement: How Politics Became Our Identity*, Chicago and London: University of Chicago Press.

McClure, P.K. (2017) Something Besides Monotheism: Sociotheological Boundary Work Among the Spiritual, but not Religious," *Poetics*, 62: 53–65, doi.org/10.1016/j.poetic.2017.01.001.

McFarland, D.A., and McFarland, H.R. (2015) "Big Data and the Danger of Being Precisely Inaccurate," *Big Data Soc.*, 2(2), doi.org/10.1177/2053951715602495.

Meng, X.-L. (2018) "Statistical Paradises and Paradoxes in Big Data (I): Law of Large Populations, Big Data Paradox, and the 2016 US Presidential Election," *Ann. Appl. Stat.*, 12(2): 685–726, doi.org/10.1214/18-AOAS1161SF.

Mercadante, L.A. (2014) *Belief without Borders: Inside the Minds of the Spiritual but not Religious*, New York: Oxford University Press.

Pearce, L., and Denton, M.L. (2011) *A Faith of Their Own: Stability and Change in the Religiosity of America's Adolescents*, New York: Oxford University Press.

Perrin, A.J., and McFarland, K. (2011) "Social Theory and Public Opinion," *Annu. Rev. Sociol.*, 37: 87–107, doi.org/10.1146/annurev.soc.012809.102659.

Pugh, A.J. (2015) *The Tumbleweed Society: Working and Caring in an Age of Insecurity*, New York: Oxford University Press.

Putnam, R.D. (2001) *Bowling Alone: The Collapse and Revival of American Community*, New York: Simon & Schuster.

Putnam, R.D., and Campbell, D.E. (2012) *American Grace: How Religion Divides and Unites Us*, New York: Simon & Schuster.

Quack, J. (2014) "Outline of a Relational Approach to 'Nonreligion,'" *Method Theory Study Relig.*, 26(4–5): 439–69.

Schmidt, L.E. (2016) *Village Atheists: How America's Unbelievers Made Their Way in a Godly Nation*, Princeton: Princeton University Press.

Schnabel, L., and Bock, S. (2017) "The Persistent and Exceptional Intensity of American Religion: A Response to Recent Research," *Sociol. Sci.*, 4, 686–700, doi.org/10.15195/v4.a28.

Sewell, W.H. (1992) "A Theory of Structure: Duality, Agency, and Transformation," *Am. J. Sociol.*, 98(1): 1–29.

Sherkat, D. (2014) *Changing Faith: The Dynamics and Consequences of Americans' Shifting Religious Identities*, New York: NYU Press.

Silver, C.F., Coleman III, T.J., Hood Jr, R.W., and Holcombe, J.M. (2014) "The Six Types of Nonbelief: A Qualitative and Quantitative Study of Type and Narrative," *Ment. Health Relig. Cult.*, 17(10): 990–1001, doi.org/10.1080/13674676.2014.987743.

Smith, J.M. (2013) "Creating a Godless Community: The Collective Identity Work of Contemporary American Atheists," *J. Sci. Study Relig.*, 52(1): 80–99, doi.org/10.1111/jssr.12009.

Smith, J.M., and Cragun, R.T. (2019) "Mapping Religion's Other: A Review of the Study of Nonreligion and Secularity," *J. Sci. Study Relig.*, 58(2): 319–35, doi.org/10.1111/jssr.12597.

Steensland, B. (2009) "Restricted and Elaborated Modes in the Cultural Analysis of Politics," *Sociol. Forum*, 24(4): 926–34, doi.org/10.1111/j.1573-7861.2009.01145.x.

Stewart, E. (2016) "The True (Non)Believer? Atheists and the Atheistic in the United States," in R. Cipriani, and F. Garelli (eds), *Annual Review of the Sociology of Religion*, Leiden: Brill, pp. 137–60.

Stewart, E., Edgell, P. and Delehanty, J. (2018) "The Politics of Religious Prejudice and Tolerance for Cultural Others," *Sociol. Q.*, 59(1): 17–39, doi.org/10.1080/00380253.2017.1383144.

Sumerau, J.E., and Cragun, R.T. (2016) "'I Think Some People Need Religion': The Social Construction of Nonreligious Moral Identities," *Sociol. Relig.*, 77(4): 386–407, doi.org/10.1093/socrel/srw031.

Swidler, A. (1986) "Culture in Action: Symbols and Strategies," *Am. Sociol. Rev.*, 51(2): 273–86.

Taves, A. (2018) "What is Nonreligion? On the Virtues of a Meaning Systems Framework for Studying Nonreligious and Religious Worldviews in the Context of Everyday Life," *Secul. Nonreligion*, 7(1): 1–6, doi.org/10.5334/snr.104.

Thiessen, J., and Wilkins-Laflamme, S. (2017) "Becoming a Religious None: Irreligious Socialization and Disaffiliation," *J. Sci. Study Relig.*, 56(1): 64–82, doi.org/10.1111/jssr.12319.

Thiessen, J., and Wilkins-Laflamme, S. (2020 *None of the Above: Non-religious Identity in the US and Canada, Secular Studies*, New York: New York University Press.

Vargas, N., and Loveland, M.T. (2011) "Befriending the "Other": Patterns of Social Ties between the Religious and Non-Religious," *Sociol. Perspect.*, 54(4): 713–31.

Voas, D., and Chaves, M. (2016.) Is the United States a Counterexample to the Secularization Thesis?" *Am. J. Sociol.*, 121(5): 1517–56, doi.org/10.1086/684202.

Whitehead, A.L., and Perry, S.L. (2020) *Taking America Back for God: Christian Nationalism in the United States*, New York: Oxford University Press

Wilde, M., and Glassman, L. (2016) "How Complex Religion Can Improve Our Understanding of American Politics," *Annu. Rev. Sociol.*, 42: 407–25, doi.org/10.1146/annurev-soc-081715-074420.

Wimberley, D.W. (1989) "Religion and Role-Identity: A Structural Symbolic Interactionist Conceptualization of Religiosity," *Sociol. Q.*, 30(1): 125–42, doi.org/10.1111/j.1533-8525.1989.tb01515.x.

Yeager, D.S., Krosnick, J.A., Chang, L., Javitz, H.S., Levendusky, M.S., Simpser, A., and Wang, R. (2011) "Comparing the Accuracy of RDD Telephone Surveys and Internet Surveys Conducted with Probability and Non-Probability Samples," *Public Opin. Q.*, 75(4): 709–47, doi.org/10.1093/poq/nfr020.

Yukich, G., and Edgell, P. (eds) (2020) *Religion is Raced: Understanding American Religion in the Twenty-first Century*, New York: New York University Press.

Zuckerman, P. (2011) *Faith No More: Why People Reject Religion*, New York, NY: Oxford University Press.

Afterword: Approaching Religions – Some Reflections on Meaning, Identity, and Power

Vikash Singh

An explanation of the puzzle that is religion has been one of the more notable challenges, and perhaps achievements, of sociological knowledge. The collective representations of religion, Durkheim told us, provided a systematic and comforting explanation of the universe, rendering it simultaneously cognizable to the mind and somewhat compliant to the will (see: Durkheim, 1995 [1912]).[1] Religion not only helped to represent and understand the world, but also to get a measure of control through personifying it and instituting rituals, incantations, and sacrifices to influence fate. The divine representations at once helped explain, console, and regulate human life. Sigmund Freud further noted in this personification of divine as God the adult version of the child's need as much as fear of the power of the father. Making a phylogenetic comparison, Freud equated religious ideas to childhood neuroses – ideas motivated by wish-fulfillment that help to repress dangerous thoughts. Important though these ideas that met "our wishes and illusions half-way" were in making civilization possible, Freud believed that the blind faith, sectarian identity, and dogmatic practice that religion encouraged made it a burden on cultural progress (Freud, 1939: p. 204; Freud, 1961).

For both these doyens of sociological thought, religion was the bedrock, the possibility of meaning (intellectual, moral) to human existence and society. But while Durkheim attempted to be morally agnostic, Freud was unequivocal that religion eventually be replaced by civic morality. The trajectory would be tortuous, no less than a neurotic working through his repressed content, but it was a moral necessity (Freud, 1961: p. 55). Freedom from the mythical clouds that had shadowed humans in all their diverse histories looked imminent – whether conceptualized as the sanguine outcome of the unrelenting progress of the world spirit to absolute

250

knowledge in Hegelian speculative philosophy (Hegel, 1998 [1807]), or the dismal colonization of the world by the forces of rationalization (Weber, 1948). Berger (1967) went even further and located humanity's secular destiny in the birth of the Jewish religion itself. Thus, these eminent voices heralded the death of religion and of God with resounding conviction.

But perhaps it is here, after the universalizing voice of Reason – such contemplation from a distance with its big picture perspective, the consideration of beings or things from a distance as present-at-hand as Heidegger (1962) [1927] would have said – has spoken the last word that the hermeneutic task begins. The task of a hermeneutics of religion would be precisely to bracket these pre-notions (always temporarily) and jump once again, every time, to address the acts of religion in the thickets of everyday life, politics, or economics, and the finite lives of the subjects. And yet insofar as this teleology, this theory, this "progress" is written into History and hence the histories of individuals and communities, any interpretive project must always return to these historical effects of rationalist interpretations, their closures and openings. This volume presents an ensemble of acts and experiences of religion, with authors bringing different traditions and methodologies – which are as tactical as they are ontological – to throw light on the effects and subjects of religion in a variety of cultural and social contexts. And the first upshot of these exercises is precisely that the religious, alive or in its ghosts, yet looms over us as much a feature of collective memories, institutions, and practices as it is embedded in people's self-identities and moral obligations. Methodologically, the chapters in this volume remind us, if such a reminder was indeed needed, that the most fruitful challenge of the hermeneutic exercise is still "to hear," for it is here in the legacy of language, where generations past continue to whisper their ministrations as it were that alterity trusts itself to the researcher.[2] Furthermore, as language but mirrors the world in its historicity, no other subject dominates this medium as religion does. In the societies of the past, since everything was so imbued with religion, everything "a sign of, a factor in, or the reflection of, divine forces," the Indo-European ancients did not even have a separate word for "religion" (Benveniste, 1973: p. 516). And to this day, it appears that the past perseveres its penchant for and holds us accountable in the religious medium.

This intergenerational religious communion could not be more semantically pregnant than in the transference of trauma among the survivors of the Holocaust and their descendants. We see them in Jacobs's chapter (Chapter 2), for example, as communities and selves agonizingly swing between enraged accusations against God for his terrible betrayal, and gratitude for helping them survive where so many others had perished. The generations –parents, children, grandparents – accordingly quarrel and oscillate between the strictest adherence to religious rituals and conventions, and complete disavowal of God. This discord is particularly poignant on Yom Kippur, the Day of Atonement. What must the self that has suffered the most grievous assault or the descendants who have inherited their pain be accused of? How should they respond and address this insane ritual command in the wake of such history? As may be expected, often a "religious schizophrenia" takes over, with characters divided between bitter rage and fear of God, between keeping alive the ritual legacy which marked the departed and had been dear to them, and trying to block the traumatic repetition. These rituals may seem untimely and yet it is through such material practices and symbols – whether, as Jacobs expertly narrates, it is the special relationship with the Shabbat candles, or the cuisine in which memories are relived, or the prayers, the fasting, and the feast that recollect and condense experiences over several millennia – that religion keeps memories alive, and institutes a higher truth, say of unquestioning forgiveness, into command.

Religion is also change, responsive to the times and to changing obligations. We see this history happening right in front of our eyes, as the survivors' descendants graduate to alternate or modified practices. Many choose practices defined by the moral commands of our own time (say, gender equality, interfaith tolerance, spiritual seeking) foraying into "other" religions and more therapeutic forms such as yoga, Tibetan Buddhism, or mystical Judaism, or indeed reinterpreting the Biblical God as the sacred feminine.

> But what if God was not with the killers … If God was present at Auschwitz, it was in the mother, in her words, in her emotions, in the instinct that kept her from abandoning her child … God permeated every Jew who held a dying parent, or a brother or sister, or a friend, or even a stranger. (Rosensaft, 2001: pp. 190–1)

The most important lesson, Jacobs exhorts us, is to listen and be an empathetic witness to the account. And, must we add, hear what goes unsaid, or in the silences. Some of these silences, as Gould in her environmental ethnography notes (Chapter 4), are marked by a sense of awe, "an appreciation of beauty and a profound feeling of connection: to God, to the quiet lake, to the pine tree in the backyard extending its branches toward the sun." But equally common are the fraught silences, the blockades in communication that fall with a thud when the words of different religious (or secular) communities run into one another's worlds. Despite their shared appreciation of the environment or care for the earth or creation, these discursive interruptions have all the significance of the violent religious breaches that have defined human history – making "history come alive" as Gould recognizes. Often it is a battle of interpretation, about what may be legitimately projected onto the Earth or nature. Thus, for example, where for the secular or even the religious liberal, the Earth may be by itself sacred and processes such as composting or felling of trees may develop a theological import, for an avid evangelical such talk is pagan heresy. And even where a devout Catholic such as Teresa recognizes the spiritual side of her environmentally conscious gardening, she firmly rejects any environmental revisionism of her Catholic identity, which is "defined by her commitment to traditional doctrine and the fulfillment of Catholic duties, including strict observance of the holy days of obligation, praying the rosary and regularly attending Mass with her children."

> But as far as my religious background and the garden, no. No. No. I'm a Catholic and my children are Catholic. ... And the environment doesn't really fit into Catholicism for me. (Baugh, 2017, cited in Gould, Chapter 4)

These conflicts are as much expressions or continuations of the cultural and political antagonism between liberal pluralists and conservative Christians in the US as they repeat and perform the *longue durée* contests between religious groups. The turn to individual spiritualism is perhaps the reconciliation, the denouement (sublimation, in Freud's language) we would have expected from the long and violent historical contestations between different religious worldviews. And yet as we can "feel" in Gould's ethnography, inside this dialectic of "reconciliation" or civil silence throbs a true Hegelian tension. "It is one thing to know that history and another to *feel* that history." But histories are manifold, devious, and often self-contradictory. The scholar must watch against succumbing to wishful teleological illusions, for histories are quick to violently remind us of the importance of chance, or that what we perceived as sublated or sublimated had indeed only been repressed.

In a searing theological analysis of the Chinese Communist Party and state (Chapter 8), Wang illustrates the repetition compulsion structuring the project. Building on Carl Schmitt's theory of exception, Wang argues that the communist project was shaped by two exceptions, one the sacred in the form of Mao and the communist utopian vision, and the other, the antipodal counterpart of the sacred, the pariah classes including primarily the landowners but also variously small business owners, party dissidents, and former Kuomintang officials. It was through continuous purging of the latter (millions executed, many more condemned to labor camps) that the Party cultivated, restored and replenished faith in the communist doctrine. Ritual condemning and sacrifice of the pariah groups, a baptism of the society by blood so to speak, was how the Party sought to validate and realize (in terms of political expediency and belief-wise) communist rule and vision; and conspicuously pay homage to the sacred sovereign exception, which was the figure of Mao –first as the living emperor, later his preserved body on public display at Tiananmen!

The communists proclaimed a clean break from the past, and the writing of a new history beginning with a blank slate. Yet this historical progression and its new symbolic order both in its promise and politics, argues Wang, were sustained precisely on the back of the imaginaries of China's stubborn past. The communist transition performatively repeated the dynastic transitions with which the Chinese were all too familiar. "Mao and his comrades understood and conducted their relations and interactions largely in terms of a model of the emperor and his officials": moving into the Forbidden City; asking regional ethnic and religious leaders to present themselves before Mao; using literal quotes from the emperors to incite the masses; expecting and ordering "loyalty dances"; and so on.

Wang carefully sketches a fundamental homology between a religious order and a secular juridical system insofar as they are both founded on a sovereign exception. Thus, not only is the religious social as Durkheim observed but the social is religious; fueled, energized and bounded by the same types of dark secrets and repressed content that we usually associate with the domain of religion and magic. More ominously, while religion keeps a clear wall between the sacred and the profane, totalitarian ideology insists on the colonization of the profane by the sacred resulting in an incessant demand to purify, to purge. This ideological system thus "paradoxically relies on the excesses" it generates: "the exploitative classes and the counterrevolutionaries."

It was a failed revolution, as the communists' new future-oriented symbolic order was unable to cast off the imaginary support of the past. In fact, Wang argues that the Protestant Reformation, insofar as it proclaimed the otherwise profane world itself as God's work and hence sacred, was much more radically transformative. Obviously, the Protestant dogma of "work is worship," and the manner in which it has been employed to legitimize the most glaring wealth inequalities, racial discrimination, and the condemning and criminalization of the poor, in particular "the colored poor," using a just deserts rationale has its fair share of detractors (Emerson and Smith, 2001). One may instead argue, following Kristeva (1982), that the Protestant Reformation was a turnabout after the Christian revolution, which transformed the notion of external impurity (the leper, deformed, diseased, the shabby/impoverished), heretofore an object of disgust, into a state to be embraced and loved. Witness the overflow of love in a Francis of Assisi "who visits leproseries, stays with the people there, bathing their wounds, sponging pus and sores, to leave only after kissing each leper on the mouth" (Singh and Torkelson, 2020: p. 262). Thus, Christianity was revolutionary in relation to the Jewish faith, precisely because it elevated and incorporated this abject into the body proper of the society, to instead turn the focus to the moral impurity within. The Protestant reformation then, as Berger (1967) argues to a separate end, was indeed a return to the Jewish past.

It is to the underside of Christian religiosity in the US that Lundskow's chapter directs our attention (Chapter 7). In a provocative statement, Lundskow argues the encompassing religious significance of white male ethnonationalism premised on hatred toward the Evil Other in US society. The divinity of this group is the white man, God's chosen for the promised land of America. This sacred covenant between land, man, and God must be protected from transgressions by the Evil Other – Blacks, Latinos, LGBTQ, at other times Jews. In the lack of any positive integrating historical factors, contempt for these morally degenerate, lazy, welfare cheating, and illegal "colored" people is essential for the coherence of the white male identity. The Evil Other must be imagined into being:

> The enemy is lazy, corrupt, dirty, sexually wild – a teeming mass of vermin – yet simultaneously skillfully manipulative and capably discreet to hide their manipulation and invasion in order to dominate the good people. They are brutish yet clever, simple-minded yet fiendishly intelligent, morally degenerate and wild yet self-sacrificing and disciplined – all at the same time. They are everywhere yet nowhere, blatantly obvious yet simultaneously waiting in ambush. Such monsters can only exist as illusions. (Lundskow, Chapter 7)

And periodic regenerative violence against this Evil Other is essential to sustain this ideological structure. Such a religious imperative of the white man has meant that at crucial junctures in US history, such as after the Civil War, during the period of industrialization, and after the civil rights movement, this group – and thereby US society – has been led by hate, fear, and distrust at the cost of inclusive possibilities. Lundskow locates the failure of reconstruction and of the 20th century labor movement in the fact that the white male, including those of the working class or tenant farmers, repeatedly chose racial status entitlement and brutalities against minorities over the moral good and their own politico-economic interests.

If the *homines sacrii* of the communist system were the landlords and small businesses, Blacks, LGBTQ, and others are the exceptions constitutive of the American system. It is in the exclusion of these groups ("lazy, degenerate, cunning, sinner") through their negative reference that the society based on hard work and God's moral law recognizes itself. Note here the 8 minutes and 46 seconds for which a smirking Officer Chauvin kept his knee on George Floyd's neck (BBC, 2020). Hardly a sacrifice worth mentioning, the Black man must be mercilessly persecuted to preserve the sacred law and good order (Correll et al, 2007; Alexander, 2010). It is a moral duty, and one must be able to perform it with impunity. On the other side of this is the sovereign exception, whether Mao or the white man, the true citizen whose divinely ordained status cannot be challenged, whether by an epidemiological administration, a female governor of Michigan, or the authority of the Capitol (Graham, 2020; Harper, 2021). Instead, the sovereign is the constitutive externality whose pleasure precedes the law and declares it into existence. He has the right to destroy the capital or government itself if he should *feel* ill-served by it; this, in the words of Walter Benjamin (1996), is "lawmaking violence."

Yet, religion continues to be the site and discursive source of subaltern resistance and contention too, of a call and calling for divine law, the law of the body or of the book of nature as inherent in the lived experiences of faith and polymorphous desire as opposed to narrowly interpreted biblical dogma. In a powerful text (Chapter 1), O'Brien narrates a heroic tale of queer renegotiation and reclaiming of churches, which have otherwise cast queer people as "sinful" or at best, "afflicted." These are people trapped in the "contradiction" of deep belonging in congregations and yet being cast aside by the official discourse and practices of the church, exiles " 'spun off' with no hope of redemption." While some have prioritized their love for and belonging in the church and chosen to be celibate, others (including many a pastor) have sought to actively reform Christianity and return it to its revolutionary roots. Wasn't Jesus on the side of the homeless, the sick, the poor, the downtrodden?, they ask. These actors and congregations argue that LGBTQ people as the most mistreated people of our time are the most deserving of Christian love. In fact, they are the chosen ones sent to bring back to Christians, the Gospel's message of love, forgiveness, and unquestioning acceptance, a message forgotten in narrow dogmatic interpretations of the Bible. Their life and experience at the margins of the society, in the lack of protections, status, their suffering, and their trans bodies most resemble the transubstantiation of Christ's own body, and his amorphous times.

O'Brien tells us that the elective virtual communities of the internet age were a major factor in the heightened political consciousness and consolidation of opinion on issues of homosexuality beginning the 1990s. Equally important was the provocation from the "moral majority" movement based on the alliance between Christian conservativism and the Republican Party under Reagan and Bush; the scandal of the government response to the AIDS epidemic is an object lesson of this repressive alignment (Petro, 2015). In an interesting turnabout, LGBTQ activism used the sacred status of marriage in the Bible and in the discourse of the religious Right to campaign for marriage equality laws, leading to the landmark 2015 Supreme Court judgment legalizing same-sex marriage in all 50 states.

The AIDS epidemic, and the relentless attack on LGBTQ communities in general, is a rather grim reminder of the continuing influence of religion in politics. Conversely, political participation and popular vindication is no less important to religious groups, even more so in a democratic polity. This aspect is particularly conspicuous in India where many different religious identities must expertly maneuver their communities, alliances, and public performances to defend interests and compete for legitimation. Some identities are favored, others stigmatized – but fortunes can change, and one cannot let go one's guard. Stakes could not be higher. In Chapter 5, Hasnain tells the gripping rollercoaster of how the Shia Islamic sect of India performed and represented itself over the last century to uphold its identity and standing, and safeguard its interests in humoring inconstant dominant parties. The Shias made subtle shifts in their self-representations – performed through speech acts, rallies, religious demonstrations, delegations – to indulge the dominant "public." This "public" was variously conceived, first through the law and order discourse of the British colonial government, followed by the nationalist movement in the Empire's waning years, and Hindu majoritarianism that has dominated Indian polity for the last few decades. The Shias emphasized their distinct identity compared to the mainstream Sunni sect's characterizations as "jihadi," or Ottoman sympathizers when the patron was the British government, but took a pan-Islamic turn when Sunni Islamic politics was in favor during the 1920s. In current politics, when Hindu nationalism dominates and Muslims are often characterized as "outsiders," "invaders", jihadis, and anti-nationalists, the Shias have been at pains to show their nonfanaticism, patriotism, and affinity with the Hindus.

The public sphere, scholars of South Asia have argued, is best conceived as a public arena where contesting claims are *performed* through rallies, demonstrations, religious processions, and other dramatized speech acts and assemblies (Freitag, 1989). Even more so, argues Hasnain, the public is an addressee, a court of hegemonic opinion to which addresses are to be made. A community – represented by and often representing only its elite – demonstrates the legitimacy of its claims in reference to hegemony. Such machinations are particularly conspicuous with a religious minority such as the Shias, who enjoyed much clout as a professional class in pre-colonial times (in particular during the Mughal era) but have a precarious status in a democratic polity owing to their numerical disadvantage.

A few things are clear from these exercises of interpretation of religious phenomena, groups, and of the effects of religion on social processes. First, while causal, moral, and teleological abstractions have their place, sociology must continue to prioritize religion as a social fact. Insofar as the phenomenon exists, it has real effects and it affects people and social groups. Second, these effects are so intricate and existentially significant, so diversely immersed in the life of the society and people's minds and relationships, for good or for bad, that to suggest they could be flattened into numbers and measured is confounding. Statistics, just like speculative thinking, tell their own interesting stories but there is no replacing the color and density of interpretations that allow full and free play to the linguistic and inter-subjective creativity of the trained scholar.

In this volume, Evan Stewart thoughtfully shows the potentials and pitfalls of quantitative analysis in his chapter on layers of often contradictory, transient, and highly subjective meanings and stances of "nonreligious" identification in survey research (Chapter 10). Using two respected national level surveys, the author establishes how people who deny a religious affiliation using the identifiers "spiritual but not religious" or "nothing in particular" are closer in several measures of personal and public religiosity to the religiously affiliated than to self-avowed atheists and agnostics. Their nonreligiosity is not a qualitative difference in political and personal values from the religiously affiliated but a difference of magnitude. While nonreligion is often attributed to secular socialization and as moral and political pushback against the imposition of the dominant group's religiously inflected values on civic life, a closer analysis of the survey data shows that people attribute a variety of meanings to their disavowal of religious identity. People who are categorized as nonreligious often adhere to a substantively religious packages of beliefs and values, while those that claim religious affiliation in turn often betray substantive nonreligiosity. Parsing out these apparent contradictions, Stewart expertly argues for complementing survey data with interpretive qualitative methods to explore the continuities among subjects by exploring the various repertoires that account for their ways of making sense of the world.

The misrecognitions emanating from the artifices and limits of survey-based research of nonreligion have important consequences for public perception and politics, perpetuating a possible "reign of error" to use Merton's (1948) characterization of the tautological social structure of the self-fulfilling prophecy. Yet, mischaracterizations can exist, and are no less disconcerting in qualitative narratives of religion. In a sweeping study of Buddhisms in the US (Chapter 9), Falcone illustrates the racial overload on descriptions of Buddhist practitioners, temples, and monasteries. Falcone's account shows the pervasive erasure of the distinctions between traditional or heritage practitioners and temples, and relatively new, Westernized Buddhist institutions and their mostly US-born members. Such erasure is a form of "Whitewashing" that habitually excludes not only immigrant heritage practitioners but also forms of praying, rituals, incantations, clerical forms, and material and cultural artifacts in favor of a rational core – as Falcone says, "to take only the philosophical-meditational wheat and leave what they saw as the cultural chaff."

Finding no easy path out of this apparent fait accompli of racial, material and ideological domination, Falcone insists on the marking of difference. Just as Stewart makes a case for studying nonreligiosity in magnitude as opposed to a dichotomous understanding, Falcone argues for a marked continuum between heritage institutions/practitioners, their nonheritage counterparts, and a hybrid semiheritage category, and proposes a matrix that situates institutions and individuals on perpendicular axes by their level of heritage. Falcone's account seems to remind us that however much Cartesianism has been criticized as a tool of domination by Foucault and others, the objective transparency of a Cartesian articulation remains an indispensable tool for social resistance (see for example: Foucault, 2006; also Heidegger, 1962 [1927]).

Perhaps the greatest strength of interpretive approaches, their sine qua non, is their humility, the recognition that truths are elusive. An example of such *lack* at the heart of knowledge is the wide gap that separates the experience of religious ritual, the lived temporality of the subject of the practice, the temporal detail in which each individual body/person comes to inhabit and perform the practice, and the scholarly emphasis on understanding religion as a system of symbols with definite meanings. As one of Winchester's Muslim respondents puts it, the prayer practice of salat does not "mean" that one is submitting to God, but it is the submission itself.

In his chapter, "Doing it" (Chapter 3), Winchester demonstrates the usefulness of an enactive approach, where the researcher strives after the embodied significance of religious practice by doing it himself (observance rather than observation) with exemplary ethnographic finesse. He participated extensively in the Muslim practice of salat, a ritual that entails definitively praying five times a day on set times, and in prolonged fasting twice a year according to the precepts of Eastern Orthodox Christianity. Such *doing*, Winchester shows helps one learn/live the magnitude of the effort, the vigilance over body, mind, or habit any of these practices or commitments entails. And especially for a new convert – the case that would most resemble the researcher's – the practice itself eventually congeals into faith. Or can always enact the event of faith, despite itself, as the researcher is reminded by one of his respondents Abe, in a "turnabout" as he calls it: "Such practices do not just express pre-existing creedal beliefs nor solely represent symbolic meanings; they also cultivate particular forms of sensory awareness, bodily comportment, practical know-how, and dispositions toward thought and action," things that "an exclusive focus on the symbolic–discursive registers" would miss.

The undermining of experience appears even more significant when we see in much religious practice, the priority of the body as a heuristic and an obstacle, yet also an aid, its transformation – its true conversion – as the objective and realized truth of faith. Analogical learning abounds, as we see, for example, in Winchester's exchange with a fasting Orthodox Christian couple on the metonymic relations between the attractions of gluttony, controlling the desire for food, and the temptations of passions where the "natural desire for God" has been disoriented. These experiences evoke and anticipate, as much as they echo, dynamic contradictions between passions and desire for God in the theological tradition of Orthodox Christianity.

Neosecularization or repaganization

These varied yet, by definition, limited expositions allow us to make a few general inferences on the contemporary legacies of the religious, pertinent to the sociological literature on the subject. First, whether we call it secularization (Berger, 1967) or neosecularization (Yamane, 1997; Casanova, 2007), it is surely true that a significant number of respondents mentioned in this volume exhibit incredulity toward the idea of a powerful, transcendental, masculine God. Their democratic ethos, rational minds, and moral compass simply find the notion unpersuasive. Whether it is the descendants that have inherited the trauma of the Holocaust (Jacobs), or those who make Buddhism their religion of choice (Falcone), or those that spiritualize nature and the environment (Gould), or in fact those pursuing a negative theology of sorts describing themselves as "nothing in particular" or "spiritual but not religious" (Stewart), many find the notion of the one God and his ostensibly sectarian demands and social consequences implausible, if not distasteful. As the homesteader Earnest remonstrates in frustration in Gould's imaginary potluck, "What does Jesus have to do with any of this?" This is a cosmopolitan, modern sensibility, representative of the inhabitants of a global multicultural village, inheritors of the Enlightenment whose primary faith lies in their own understanding, seemingly asserting along with Immanuel Kant (1997), "Have courage to use your own understanding!" They seem much more comfortable with the notion of an idealized moral (even divine) force, a spiritual presence inflected by beliefs based on their personal history, the elective affinity with a guardian deity or moral practice and such, depending on the person's cultural experiences and preferences. As Gould observes among Jews, nodding to the established research of Roof (1993, 2003) and Wuthnow (1998), there is "a rejection of biblical literalism and a coinciding greater acceptance, particularly among younger generations, of de-masculinized conceptualizations of God that are in keeping with the cultural innovations of the late twentieth century." Human life here, as MacIntyre evocatively observes, is the "unity of a narrative quest" where individual choice is increasingly obligatory (MacIntyre, 1981: p. 219).

This is surely a process of sublimation, as Freud (1961) prophesied, where the dark, secretive force of religion, its excessive demand, its grip on the soul of communities at large is replaced by a lighter, reasoned set of moral practices of one's choosing from a range of possibilities, one affiliation among several others. However devoted one may be to environmental values or their meditational practices, as compulsions they apply only to individuals, or at most to small groups. One may think of this process as secularization, a mitigation of the force of religion and its replacement by rationalized processes and institutions. Another way to think of these practices is repaganizaton, a return to the roots of religion (obviously a dialectical one) that Peter Gay (1995) for example already saw in the Enlightenment philosophers' insistence on the freedom of ideas. If the great monotheistic religions belonged to the era of empires, reflecting and legitimizing the sweeping powers of monarchs, the holds on the spirit simulating secular power, the multicultural global village seems well suited to the pagan gods.[3] With this profusion of cultures and subcultures, we seem to return to a time of small societies, which found their moral representations in pagan antiquity or the fraternal gods of animism. There, says Durkheim, the gods are not distant beings that crush the people with their superiority but "friends, relatives," they are "present in the things that inhabit his immediate surroundings and in part ... immanent in man himself ... not jealous and terrible," but expressions of "joyful confidence." This is so because these societies:

> ... are not Leviathans that overwhelm man with the enormity of their power and subject him to harsh discipline; he surrenders to them spontaneously and without resistance ... [W]hen he yields to its promptings, he does not think he is yielding to coercion but instead doing what his own nature tells him to do. (Durkheim, 1995 [1912], p. 226)

In the above description of Melanesian societies, Durkheim may easily have been talking about the "inner *bubba*" of one of Jacobs's respondents, "the total nurturing inner goddess type," or the theologies of compost, the "spiritual lessons of death and rebirth" that Gould's homesteaders invoke. This characterization of a freeing religion applies as easily to the "liminal nones" in Stewart's chapter, who switch between a religious affiliation or not, as they do to the ethnographer in Winchester's chapter who learns to be a Muslim one season, Orthodox Christian the next.

Nevertheless, the Judeo-Christian Islamic God continues to be an authoritative figure on the US religious landscape. This figure is yet keenly suspicious of the profuse attractions of paganism. For many Christians as well as Muslims and Jews, submission to God and the transcendental will of the *deus absconditus* is of a different class and must not be mixed with cultural interests; they insist their appreciation of nature and the environment, for example, is not its apotheosizing. Gould provides a dramatic representation of this difference and tension between "religion" and "spirituality" in her ethnography of silences. There is little patience here for any sort of hippie-paganism, or metaphorical associations between ecology and divinity. As Luke retorts to the notion of the Earth as a divine body, "There's the father, the son, and the Holy Spirit. That's it." Why "mess with that"? Likewise, for

Teresa, her gardening, however spiritual, must be completely distinguished from her religious identity, and she insists on a wall of separation between the two. "I'm a practicing Catholic! The garden has *nothing* to do with my religion" (Baugh, 2017, cited in Gould, Chapter 4). Any translation of the divine in the form of cultural and moral values would be similarly unthinkable to the orthodox Jews in the alumni gathering that Gould recounts or Winchester's companions performing salat five times a day, or the otherwise competing Shias and Sunnis whose theological and political differences are the subject of Hasnain's chapter.

To wit, this tension between cosmopolitan spiritualism and monotheistic orthodoxy seems like the modern variant of the age-old struggle between the Biblical religions and pagan cultures that Peter Berger, for example, illustrated in his classic *The Sacred Canopy* (Berger, 1967). For Berger, the Protestant Reformation was a return to the radical transcendence of God, lost in the charmed world of the Catholic with its mass, miracles, angels, the glorification of Mary, and the "immense network of intercession" uniting the person with the saints and to the dead (Berger, 1967: p. 117). Islam had made a similar critique of Christianity in the doctrine of *hullul* or incarnationism, the apostasy that somebody could stand beside God or intercede with him on one's behalf. The turn to spiritualism may be seen as once again a call for forces that are immanent, closer to people, their ideals of the self and their moral calling. Such transition is perhaps another re-enchantment, the cosmopolitan counterpart of charismatic Christianity which has taken the world by storm over the past few decades. Scholars have shown that the practices of spirit possession, speaking in tongues, and miraculous healing, which started with the Pentecostal faith to eventually spread to most Christian denominations (including Catholicism), are so popular because they respond to the deepest, often desperate, needs of people (Martin, 2002). This is particularly true for the global South, where a catastrophic modernity has failed its promise of security, health, and well-being, and the need for miracles is no less immediate than when Jesus of Nazareth walked the earth (Chestnut, 1997; Singh, 2017).

Religion and ideology

Another aspect of religion that this volume brings forth is the fungibility of religion and ideology, one substitutes for the other, stands for it, and has more or less the same social effects. If by "ideology," we understand a self-referential meaning system in the service of domination, we can already see the ideological significance of religion in the writings of Max Weber. Two somewhat paradoxical observations may be noted in Weber's comparative historical analysis of the soteriological religions that provided a rationalized system for understanding the world and the life beyond (see: Weber, 1948).

First, while the leaders of the religions, the ones who devise the theodicy, usually came from the elite, educated sections of the society, their permanent locus has been the "less favored strata;" it is people from the deprived classes who, given their tribulations, were most in need of redemption whether in this world or beyond. Second, however, in contrast, the religious system also served the purpose of legitimating good fortune. As Weber keenly observes, "The fortunate is seldom satisfied with the fact of being fortunate. Beyond this, he needs to know that he has a right to his good fortune. He wishes to be allowed the belief that the less fortunate also merely experiences his due" (Weber, 1948: p. 271). The rationale provided for suffering and its resolution thus also serves as a system of sacred legitimation of social status and inequities.

The confluence of religion and ideology (say, in its more secular moments) takes several different forms. Perhaps the purest example of this relationship is the national creed of American civil religion in the US, which mobilizes Christian themes to spiritually anchor the nation, in its history and its promise, in a higher criterion that draws at once on the bounty of Christian texts and people's faith (Bellah, 1967). Albeit supported by Biblical motifs such the exodus, promised land, messiah, and sacrifice, this religion – celebrated through national festivals such as Thanksgiving, Memorial Day, the birthdays of Washington and Lincoln, and by belief in God – is an inclusive faith oriented toward democratic ideals. Or that is at least so in its best proponents, such as Washington, Jefferson, and Lincoln. For, as we have seen in the political clout wielded by the Christian Right in the US since its alliance with the Republican Party in the 1980s, the US – notwithstanding a noble tradition of church-state separation – is hardly impervious to majoritarian religious domination, whether in the guise of civil religion or despite it (see, for example: Wilcox, 2018).

In the US, the ideological excess of religion is surely most poignant with regards to how God and Biblical statements have been championed for vicious, systematic, and never-ending attacks against LGBTQ people (Fetner, 2008). Religion has also been party to the scandalous treatment of African Americans and the Jewish people, with figments such as the curse of Canaan, Anglo-Israelism, the manifest destiny of the white people, and the justification of slavery as a punishment for sin and a sign of damnation (Fredrickson, 2015; Emerson and Smith, 2001). The criminalization of the racialized poor, its theological association with a state of being condemned, the continuous marking of groups of people as lazy or undeserving, to be followed by retribution in the name of God or nation which becomes the warrant for the exceptional violence of the US police state likewise show the vengeful side of religion (Bonilla-Silva, 2006; McNamee and Miller, 2009).

This aspect of religion is clearly evident in O'Brien's analysis of the lived contradiction of being queer and going to church, and in Lundskow's argument that the construction of the racial Other as an embodiment of Evil is constitutive of US nationalism. Thus, while civil religion may give a spiritual support to the national project, God and religious motifs are as commonly used for divine legitimation of hatred and resentment that preserves the ideological supremacy of the dominant group. These chapters, as much as human history, remind us that neither is foreign to religion, they are part of its Manichean soul, just like the two sides of man.

The diversity of American society, the trend-setting history of its democratic project, and its puritan as well as racial heritage make it a unique case for studying the religion-state relationship. Despite the commitment to a wall of separation, religion is persistent in its attempt to impose itself on the state. Hjelm's description of the manner in which the Church of Finland simultaneously asserts and obfuscates its status as the nation's primary faith, the "folk church" – a representative of the people's core heritage, values, and identity – illustrates another variant of this relationship (Chapter 6). It shows how the primacy of the dominant church is often maintained, in view of the secular character of the state, through silence and silencing, for example in the Finnish parliament; as if the subject were sacred, dangerous, as much a question of some apparently founding lack of a secular polity as of the politicians' profane electoral concerns. The Church itself must play deftly, presenting itself thickly as a stand-in for tradition – for the Christian heritage of the nation's "rhythm of ordinary days and celebration, work, and rest" – on its Finnish website, while putting up only a sparse front and pre-emptively declining any association with being the "state church" on the English version.

In India, the silence gives way to theatrical performances where rival religious groups stake their status claims in the public arena. In another reflection of majoritarian domination, it is the secular ethos itself which is challenged as a form of minority appeasement, indeed mocked as "pseudo-secularism" (Tejani, 2021). The challenge could not be more explicit as state ministers belonging to the ruling party don religious garbs, target minority places of worship, publicly flaunt their domination through Hindu symbols, while vouching for an ideology that reckons being Hindu as a necessary condition for authentic nationals (Jaffrelot, 2017). While Hinduism has been the default source of independent India's choice of linguistic identity (Hindi) and national symbols and imaginary (see: Pandey, 2012), this is a frontal assault against the state's secular potential that insists on "fixing" the founding act of the constitution itself (Sharma, 2020). Perhaps evident here is the daemonic force of the notion of the nation itself, a mystical community defined as much as a futuristic project as it congeals around an imagined, often tragic, past (Singh, 2017).

These ghosts of the past are equally intransigent and assertive in the case of China. Here, an otherwise radically future-oriented communist project shows its hopelessness in front of its obligation to the past, being tied to and dependent on the past. This is the compulsion of the past, as Wang shows, whether it is the attraction of power – for it is power that shines the brightest through the darkness of bygone times – or the lure, the spell of the past as fantasy, and hence its utility in captivating people, or literally holding them in captivity. The former appeals to their narcissism, the leader here being the narcissist-in-chief as Fromm (1964) has shown, the latter is their abandonment as objects of disgust, groups that must be expunged based on the command from the ego-ideal. The former belongs to the imaginary order, the latter its symbolic order counterpart. This fantasy of the past is a necessary supplement of the symbolic order, and albeit a myth it has a timelessness that outlasts any particular historical epoch.

Although the Chinese Communist Party is atheist, Wang shows that the ideological form of its governance is quite like religion. Here too there is a sacred, a holy form that serves as the founding pact of the society. This sacred is set apart from the profane and demands expressive performances including rituals of praise and loyalty. The sacred as the sovereign exception symbolizes the founding pact of the ideological state, while its anti-sacred counterpart is the *homo sacer*, the abominable reference of exclusion – the Party traitor, the landlords and such. Unlike Bellah's (1967) civil religion, a thin form of religion which the dominant community often wants to be stronger, here it is a strong ideology that imposes itself on a leery populace. In China, much like in India, the spell of the past now reflects increasingly in the form of the nation, even if occasionally disguised as a universalist working-class movement. Thus, whereas the cosmopolitan cultures of monotheistic Christianity seem to be slowly giving way to a profusion of religious choices and practices, a paganism of sorts (in which one may arguably include charismatic Christianity), in the previously pagan societies of China and India a unitary God is ascendant. This is a God who dwarfs all the deities of the past, consummates them; it warrants the greatest sacrifices, incessant paeans sung in its praise, and requires absolute faith and commitment. This God is the Nation.

Religion and identity

Another powerful way in which we find religion operative in these reports is as an identity around and in the name of which people can coalesce and define their interests, in fact define themselves. It helps define their self, tie them in communities in difference from other(s) and defend their apparent interests, quite often performatively. Hasnain's description of the Shias' attempts to define and re-define themselves in accordance with the dominant ideas and power of changing times explicates such performances of identity. This is inevitably a form of *méconnaissance*, as the community recognizes or presents itself based on pragmatic considerations, its aspirations, but also its founding traumas. The trauma is particularly potent for the Shia, a community bound in its memory and feelings of guilt and suffering for Hussain's martyrdom in the Battle of Karbala, and a history of theological and political suppression by the Caliphate ever since (Nasr, 2007). Thus, the contests over the processions on Muharram, their route and composition, are always as much about the consistency of an obligation to the past, a being-in-time of a community, as they are about tactical realpolitik and narrow sectarian and individual interests. A sociology of religion must not underestimate the command of this moral imaginary, this conscience of the collective. A command which is itself not without contradiction since Islam itself – and its dominant Sunni sect, in contrast with which the Shias have defined themselves – is under duress. As Syed Aga Hasan reminded his audience a century ago, the Shias as the yolk of Islam conceived as an egg could not survive if Islam itself were threatened.

The case of Judaism is perhaps even more poignant. Here an identity defined by a proud theological history as the source of the great monotheistic religions and glorious accomplishments in trade, finance, sciences, and the professions is burdened by a history of systematic persecution over several millennia, culminating in the disaster of the Holocaust (Wistrich, 2020). We can see these conflicts, inflected by and situated in personal and family histories in Jacobs's respondents. We see here survivors' feelings of guilt, the obligation to the heritage, and a somewhat rebellious resentment of this inherited pain, and hence a questioning of Jewish identity. This identity further withers away when people have several other identities based on lived experiences and affiliations of, say, gender, nation, or race with varying moral compulsions. The command of religion, of the past, however formidable, is one of several competing commands, and one is as if free to choose one's command.

The religions are surely conscious of this threat of the slow dissipation of their identity, and often assert their distinct status. Such assertion may be witnessed in the stubbornness with which some of Gould's respondents strive to maintain the distinction and primacy of their religious identity over other works. It is a practice in which social science itself is inculpated and frequently feels compelled to correct, as we see with Falcone's angst about the loss of Tibetan Buddhism's religious heritage as it is incessantly appropriated as but another Western cultural form. And yet we must remember the dimension of power in what comes shrouded in the sacred aura of "heritage," truth weathered by time. As Hasnain reminds us (confirming Weber), it is often but the elite that defines the interests of the group, and it happens to define them in its own image and in favor of its own status position.

The dimension of power in tradition or heritage is particularly evident in O'Brien's analysis of the odious manner in which Christian orthodoxy made the abnegation of particular sexual choices – characterized as sin and affliction – a condition for belonging to the Church. Indeed often, it is the excess itself, a utilitarian show of strictness as it were, which may be all that remains to distinguish heritage. This surely appears to be the case with Pope Francis's surprising decision invalidating gay marriage, "God can't bless sin;" giving the impression that "sin" was the only trademark distinguishing the Vatican.

Being strict is one way in which churches strive to keep religious identities meaningful (Schnabel and Bock, 2017). But perhaps much more important to church survival are the coalitions that denominations, if not whole religions have been able to make with the modern assertions of racial, ethnic, and national identity (Emerson and Smith, 2011). Religions have sought to connect (as always) with the power of the state, through the notion of the nation, and with racial supremacy and patriarchal domination. In adapting to the modern, traditional religion – in an expected show of survival instinct – has been quick to ride on the back of the ruling prejudices of the day, if not redefine itself to those terms. Religious identity is thus protean, adopting new forms, as we see for example in Lundskow's description of the unholy union of Christianity and white masculinity as American nationalism. A similar union is active in the anti-LGBTQ crusade of the Christian Right's coalition with the Republican Party (Fetner, 2008).

Obviously not all such unions are regressive, as we can witness in Gould's narrative of the environmental commitment of several religion communities, and also in O'Brien's report on preachers and churches that have championed a radically inclusive model of Christianity. Yet, it is the case that a lot of people fret about the moral overreach of institutionalized religions. Such moral overreach, as Stewart shows, is often the reason that an increasing number of people attempt to dissociate themselves from religious identity, even if they can't bring themselves to being described as "atheist." Thus, if it is insecurity, its dwindling influence, and fading identity that makes religion increasingly desperate to stick to its atavistic signs or attach itself to the latest social trends and prejudices, these choices may also be the greatest challenges to its survival. The religions of the world it would appear, like all modern subjects, have a choice to make.

Notes

[1] Durkheim is emphatic about human agency in controlling the gods, however fetishized they may appear. As he argues for the Jewish rituals, "When the Jew stirred the air at the Feast of the Tabernacles by shaking willow branches in a certain rhythm, it was to make the wind blow and the rain fall. The belief was that the rite produced the desired result automatically" (Durkheim, 1995, p. 33).

[2] On the dialectic of "hearing" in hermeneutics, see: Gadamer (1975), p. 458.

3   For a history of the ascendancy of power and masculinity in the Judeo-Christian God, see Pagels's fascinating study of the conflicting images of God in early Christianity (Pagels, 1976).

References

Alexander, M. (2010) *The New Jim Crow: Mass Incarceration in the Age of Colorblindness*, New York: The New Press.

Baugh, A. (2017) *God and the Green Divide: Religious Environmentalism in Black and White*, Oakland, CA: University of California Press.

BBC (2020) "George Floyd: What Happened in the Final Moments of His Life" BBC [online], Available from www.bbc.com/news/world-us-canada-52861726 [Accessed 27 March 2021].

Bellah, R.N. (1967) "Civil Religion in America," *Daedalus*, 96(1): 1–21.

Benjamin, W. (1996) "Critique of Violence" in M. Bullock and M.W. Jennings (eds) *Selected Writings, 1913–1926*, Cambridge, MA: Belknap Press.

Benveniste, E. (1973). *Indo-European Language and Society*, Coral Gables, FL: University of Miami Press.

Berger, P. (1967) *The Sacred Canopy*, Garden City, NY: Doubleday.

Bonilla-Silva, E. (2006) *Racism without Racists: Color-blind Racism and the Persistence of Racial Inequality in the United States*, Lanham, MD: Rowman & Littlefield Publishers.

Casanova, J. (2007) "Rethinking Secularization: A Global Comparative Perspective," in P. Beyer and L Beaman (eds) *Religion, Globalization and Culture*, Leiden: Brill, pp. 101–20.

Chesnut, R.A. (1997) *Born Again in Brazil: The Pentecostal Boom and the Pathogens of Poverty*, New Brunswick, NJ: Rutgers University Press.

Correll, J., Park, B., Judd, C.M., Wittenbrink, B., Sadler, M. S., and Keesee, T. (2007) "Across the Thin Blue Line: Police Officers and Racial Bias in the Decision to Shoot," *Journal of Personality and Social Psychology*, 92(6): 1006–23.

Durkheim, E. (1995 [1912]) *Elementary Forms of Religious Life*, translated and with an Introduction by K.E. Fields, New York: The Free Press.

Emerson, M.O., and Smith, C. (2001) *Divided by Faith: Evangelical Religion and the Problem of Race in America*, New York: Oxford University Press.

Fetner, T. (2008) *How the Religious Right Shaped Lesbian and Gay Activism*, Minneapolis: University of Minnesota Press.

Foucault, M. (2006) *The Hermeneutics of the Subject: Lectures at the Collège de France, 1981–1982*, New York: Picador.

Fredrickson, G.M. (2015) *Racism: A Short History*, Princeton: Princeton University Press.

Freitag, S.B. (1989) *Collective Action and Community: Public Arenas and the Emergence of Communalism in North India*, Berkeley: University of California Press.

Freud, S. (1939) *Moses and Monotheism*, translated by K. Jones, London: Hogarth Press and the Institute of Psychoanalysis.

Freud, S. (1961) *The Future of an Illusion*, edited and translated by J. Strachey, New York: W.W. Norton & Company.

Fromm, E. (1964) *The Heart of Man: Its Genius for Good and Evil*, New York: Harper and Row Publishers.

Gadamer, H.-G. (1975) *Truth and Method*, London: Continuum Publishing Group.

Gay, P. (1995) *The Enlightenment: The Rise of Modern Paganism, Vol. 1*, New York: W.W. Norton & Company.

Graham, B.A. (2020), " 'Swastikas and Nooses': Governor Slams 'Racism' of Michigan Lockdown Protest," *The Guardian* [online], Available from www.theguardian.com/us-news/2020/may/03/michigan-gretchen-whitmer-lockdown-protest-racism [Accessed 27 March, 2021].

Harper, A. (2021) "Capitol Attack Conjures American Legacy of Racial Violence," *ABC News* [online], Available from abcnews.go.com/Politics/capitol-attack-conjures-american-legacy-racial-violence/story?id=75331177 [Accessed 27 March 2021].

Hegel, G.W.F. (1998 [1807]) *Phenomenology of Spirit*, translated by A.V. Miller, Delhi: Motilal Banarsidass Publishers.

Heidegger, M. (1962 [1927]) *Being and Time*, translated by J. Macquarrie and E. Robinson, New York: Harper.

Jaffrelot, C. (2017) "India's Democracy at 70: Toward a Hindu State?" *Journal of Democracy*, 28(3): 52–63.

Kant, I. (1997 [1784]) "An Answer to the Question: What is Enlightenment," In M. Gregor (ed) *Practical Philosophy*, Cambridge: Cambridge University Press, pp. 11–22.

Kristeva, J. (1982) *Powers of Horror*, New York: Columbia University Press.

MacIntyre, A. (1981) *After Virtue*, Notre Dame, IN: University of Notre Dame Press.

Martin, D. (2002) *Pentecostalism: The World Their Parish*, Oxford: Blackwell Publishers.

McNamee, S.J., and Miller, R.K. (2009), *The Meritocracy Myth*, Lanham, MD: Rowman & Littlefield.

Merton, R.K. (1948) "The Self-fulfilling Prophecy," *The Antioch Review*, 8(2): 193–210.

Nasr, S.V.R. (2007) *The Shia Revival: How Conflicts within Islam will Shape the Future*, New York: Norton.

Pagels, E.H. (1976) "What Became of God the Mother? Conflicting Images of God in Early Christianity," *Signs: Journal of Women in Culture and Society*, 2(2), 293–303.

Pandey, G. (2012) *The Construction of Communalism in Colonial North India*, New Delhi: Oxford University Press.

Petro, A.M. (2015) *After the Wrath of God: AIDS, Sexuality, and American Religion*, New York: Oxford University Press.

Roof, W.C. (1993) *A Generation of Spiritual Seekers: The Spiritual Journeys of the Baby Boomers*, San Francisco: Harper Collins.

Roof, W.C. (2003) "Religion and Spirituality: Toward an Integrated Analysis," in M. Dillon (eds) *Handbook of the Sociology of Religion*, Cambridge: Cambridge University Press.

Rosensaft, M. (2001) "I Was Born in Bergen-Belsen," in A. Berger and N. Berger (eds) *Second Generation Voices: Reflections of Children of Holocaust Survivors*, Syracuse, NY: Syracuse University Press.

Schnabel, L., and Bock, S. (2017) "The Persistent and Exceptional Intensity of American Religion: A Response to Recent Research," *Sociological Science*, 4: 686–700.

Sharma, B. (2020) "One Year After Mass Protests, India's Muslims Still Live in Fear," in *Foreign Policy* [online], available at foreignpolicy.com/2020/12/18/one-year-mass-caa-protests-india-muslims-citizenship-amendment-act-modi/ [Accessed 27 March, 2021].

Singh, V. (2017) *Uprising of the Fools: Pilgrimage as Moral Protest in Contemporary India*, Stanford: Stanford University Press.

Singh, V., and Torkelson, J. (2020) "Caste, Race, and Abjection: An Essay on Sub-Humanity," *Humanity and Society*, 44(3): 243–67.

Tejani, S. (2021) *Indian Secularism: A Social and Intellectual History, 1890–1950*, Bloomington: Indiana University Press.

Weber, M. (1948) *From Max Weber: Essays in Sociology*, edited by H.H. Gerth and C. Wright Mills, London: Routledge.

Wilcox, C. (2018) *Onward Christian Soldiers? The Religious Right in American Politics*, New York: Routledge.

Wistrich, R.S. (2020) *Between Redemption & Perdition: Modern Antisemitism and Jewish Identity*, New York: Routledge.

Wuthnow, R. (1998) *After Heaven: Spirituality in America since the 1950s*, Berkeley: University of California Press.

Yamane, D. (1997) "Secularization on Trial: In Defense of a Neosecularization Paradigm," *Journal for the Scientific Study of Religion*, 36(1): 109–22.

Index

References to endnotes show both the page number and the note number (102n1).

www.ingramcontent.com/pod-product-compliance
Lightning Source LLC
Chambersburg PA
CBHW070613030426
42337CB00020B/3779